Public Policy and Higher Education

Amid changing economic and social contexts, radical changes have occurred in public higher education policies over the past three decades. *Public Policy and Higher Education* provides readers with new ways to analyze these complex state policies and offers the tools to examine how policies affect students' access and success in college. Rather than arguing for a single approach, the authors examine how policymakers and higher education administrators can work to inform and influence change within systems of higher education using research-based evidence along with consideration of political and historical values and beliefs.

Special Features:

- Case Studies—allow readers to examine strategies used by different types of colleges to improve access and retention.
- Reflective Exercises—encourage readers to discuss state and campus context for policy decisions and to think about the strategies used in a state or institution.
- Approachable Explanations—unpack complex public policies and financial strategies for readers who seek understanding of public policy in higher education.
- Research-Based Recommendations—explore how policymakers, higher education administrators, and faculty can work together to improve quality, diversity, and financial stewardship.

This textbook is an invaluable resource for graduate students, administrators, policymakers, and researchers who seek to learn more about the crucial contexts underlying policy decisions and college access.

Edward P. St. John is Algo D. Henderson Collegiate Professor of Higher Education at the University of Michigan.

Nathan Daun-Barnett is Assistant Professor of Educational Leadership and Policy at the University of Buffalo, State University of New York.

Karen M. Moronski-Chapman is a doctoral candidate in the Center for the Study of Higher and Postsecondary Education at the University of Michigan.

Core Concepts in Higher Education
Series Editors: Edward P. St. John and Marybeth Gasman

The History of U.S. Higher Education: Methods for Understanding the Past
Edited by Marybeth Gasman

Understanding Community Colleges
Edited by John S. Levin and Susan T. Kater

Public Policy and Higher Education: Reframing Strategies for Preparation, Access, and College Success
By Edward P. St. John, Nathan Daun-Barnett, and Karen M. Moronski-Chapman

Public Policy and Higher Education

Reframing Strategies for Preparation, Access, and College Success

Edward P. St. John, Nathan Daun-Barnett,
and Karen M. Moronski-Chapman

Routledge
Taylor & Francis Group

NEW YORK AND LONDON

First published 2013
by Routledge
711 Third Avenue, New York, NY 10017

Simultaneously published in the UK
by Routledge
2 Park Square, Milton Park, Abingdon, Oxon OX14 4RN

Routledge is an imprint of the Taylor & Francis Group, an informa business

© 2013 Taylor & Francis

Library of Congress Cataloging in Publication Data

St. John, Edward P., author.
  Public policy and higher education : reframing strategies for preparation, access, and college success / By: Edward P. St. John, Nathan Daun-Barnett, and Karen M. Moronski-Chapman.
    pages cm
  Includes bibliographical references and index.
  ISBN 978-0-415-89356-5 (hardback) — ISBN 978-0-415-89359-6 (pbk.) — ISBN 978-0-203-80540-4 (e-book) (print) 1. Education, Higher—United States. 2. Education, Higher—United States—States—Case studies. 3. Education and state—United States. I. Daun-Barnett, Nathan., author. II. Moronski-Chapman, Karen M., author. III. Title.
  LA227.4.S75 2013
  378.73—dc23

ISBN: 978-0-415-89356-5 (hbk)
ISBN: 978-0-415-89359-6 (pbk)
ISBN: 978-0-203-80540-4 (ebk)

Typeset in Minion
by Apex CoVantage, LLC

Printed and bound in the United States of America
by Edwards Brothers, Inc.

CONTENTS

LIST OF TABLES

LIST OF FIGURES

LIST OF TEXT BOXES

SERIES INTRODUCTION

I have the pleasure of serving, along with Edward P. St. John, as the coeditor of the Core Concepts in Higher Education Series, published by Routledge Press. With this series, we are aiming to generate core books that speak to the various themes and courses within the field of higher education. Ed and I have worked with a variety of leading authors in higher education to write seminal works that capture the salient issues and growth of our field. In addition, we have also contributed books to the series.

Public Policy in Higher Education: Reframing Strategies for Preparation, Access, and College Success, authored by Edward P. St. John, Nathan Daun-Barnett, and Karen M. Moronski, is the latest book in the Core Concepts series. St. John and colleagues have written a tremendous book that will become the go-to text for public policy classes and public policy scholars in the field of higher education. They have taken the confusing terrain of public policy and simplified it beautifully for students and professionals alike. This book is a foundational text.

In the book, the authors suggest that the combination of market approaches and educational accountability schemes implemented by many states, often in disjointed and contradictory ways, undermines states' achievement of their goals. They provide a rich and deeply contextualized overview of federal policy initiatives. As a historian, perhaps what I appreciate most about *Public Policy in Higher Education* is the context and development of the ideas presented in the book. The reader understands the history of each issue presented rather than seeing these issues in a vacuum.

One of the many strengths of the book is its bridging of K–12 and higher education policy. This is rarely done and, when it is, is typically not done well. In *Public Policy in Higher Education,* the authors link K–12 and higher education seamlessly for the reader, showing how the important issues connect and build on one another.

St. John and colleagues have written a reflective book that brings the work alive for the reader as he or she tries to make sense of the myriad state and federal policies shaping

American higher education. They examine the topic from the macro level to the campus level, helping the reader to understand the immediate and lasting impact of these policies.

Above all, St. John and colleagues root the text in an unwavering commitment to social justice.

Marybeth Gasman
Professor of Higher Education
University of Pennsylvania

PREFACE

Public Policy and Higher Education provides a metamethodology for developing and applying policy frameworks readers can use to examine policy options in higher education. We encourage readers to reflect on the assumptions they make when they analyze policy discourses within their state systems and at a national level and rethink how government strategies for expanding educational opportunity actually relate to student outcomes. We use the concept of *metaframeworks* as a way of viewing patterns of practice in government policy on higher education that are influenced by beliefs and historical trends. Policy frameworks function as archetypes or images of the government role. As a society, the United States is in the midst of a shift from the classic liberal democratic model that shaped expansion of access and equalization of postsecondary opportunity in the late 20th century to a market system informed by a more recent convergence of neoliberal and neoconservative ideologies that could undermine equity achieved in earlier decades. Often researchers and policymakers idealize images of the role of government in higher education policy, but such idealized images are seldom realized in practice (Hossler, Lund, Ramin-Gyurnek, Westfall, & Irish, 1997). Nonetheless, these frameworks merit attention and discussion as means of providing more explicit and conscious frames for examining alternative policy decisions in states and at the federal level.

In Part I, we examine how federal policy has become a powerful force during the past few decades in shaping and influencing the contexts of and incentives for state policy development and adaptation of K–12 and higher education. The federal government does not control educational systems, but federal policy has a substantial influence on policy development in states and institutions. We explain how federal policies create incentives that influence state and institutional policy decisions. We examine the arguments made about federal policy, the ways research was used to craft policy arguments, and the research that has evaluated the linkages between policy decisions and educational outcomes. Whereas research plays a role in federal policy development, it is not clear whether research findings are used to inform rational decisions or ideological beliefs held by policymakers who shape research and craft arguments for reform.

The chapters in Part I also review the range of federal and state mechanisms that influence higher education institutions. We argue that the frameworks developed in this volume can be applied to a range of substantive policy areas—and in fact provide a broad framework for thinking about the government role in the early chapters—but we leave it to readers to judge whether we have achieved this aim. Readers' examinations of the national trends in policies and outcomes along with summative reviews of research about how policy decisions link to subsequent outcomes provide the opportunity for readers to make their own judgments. Reading about and discussing policy rationales, strategies in relation to outcomes, and research that links policies and outcomes can build understanding about the alternative approaches to policy development at the federal, state, and institutional levels.

In the illustrative state cases in Part II, we encourage readers to think about how campus policy decisions are influenced by the frameworks that state governments have evolved as they respond to federal incentives and policies promoting the goal of expanding college opportunity. We argue that it is important to examine state educational outcomes in relation to the policies actually implemented within states and to use evidence from research on the linkages between policy decisions and relevant educational outcomes to test assumptions about those linkage structures. We do not assume there are simple solutions to the problems now confronting public systems of higher education. In fact, the case studies underscore the complexity of the problems facing states and the need for thoughtful, well-reasoned approaches to research informed policy creation.

The intent of the state case studies is to encourage readers to build their skills in analyzing the ways political values, beliefs, and traditions influence policy decisions and adaptations within state systems. The case studies consider some of the ways researchers and state officials have used research evidence about student outcomes related to preparation for, access to, and success in college as they craft and advocate for policy changes. We pose questions for readers about what they have observed about the relationships between policy decisions and outcomes to encourage reflection on and discussion about state policy frameworks.

As readers look across and compare cases, it will become evident that state policies on high school graduation, college admissions, and the financing of higher education have an influence on who attends college and whether there is equal opportunity to attend 4-year institutions within states. It is evident that it is extremely difficult to hold together political coalitions that can sustain comprehensive and cohesive policy frameworks that promote equal opportunity, even when there is a history of success within a state. Indeed, the state cases were selected because collectively they illustrate some of the ways state policy frameworks have been developed, adapted, and undermined over time. The cases can be used to inform discussion about policy, research, and strategy because of the following:

- Each of the state cases discusses the evolution of policy rationales, along with trends in policy decisions and outcomes related to preparation, enrollment, and degree completion. We encourage readers to use the evidence from the cases to test their own assumptions about the linkages between policies and outcomes.
- The cases examine strategies used by different types of colleges within states—especially 2- and 4-year public institutions—to improve access and retention. Since our ability to consider the role of institutional strategies was constrained

by the book's length, we encourage readers to think about the frameworks for institutional action created by state and federal policy frameworks.

- The cases provide information on recent policy developments and encourage researchers to think about how recent decisions may link to future outcomes. Policy issues change in states from year to year, so case studies of the type presented merely provide background for contemporary policy analysis.
- The consideration of how researchers and policymakers in different states have approached puzzling policy problems in the past can help new generations of analysts and advocates to think critically and analytically about the policy problems they confront in their own states.

There has been a decline in equal opportunity in the midst of the transition to universal access, a topic considered in Part III. The current market period has promoted uplift of high school education to prepare all students for college but, at the same time, it has limited financial access to public 4-year colleges. As federal and state policy analysts ponder strategies to promote degree completion, it is essential to include critical analysis of underlying inequalities. We raise questions for policy analysts, researchers, and activists to consider. As with preparation and access, the policy puzzle of retention is undoubtedly more complex than the simple notion of pulling policy levers, which pervades discussions of accountability in higher education.

Throughout this book, we call readers' attention to the ways policies link directly and indirectly to students' choices about preparation for, enrollment in, departure from, and completion of different types of colleges and universities. Whereas higher education research, along with research on the formation and the effects of policy, can be and has been used to inform policy decisions and educational practices, it is also important to recognize the limitations of research. Too frequently researchers and policymakers assume there are simple solutions to complex educational problems and social inequalities—mistakes we have made ourselves—in part because the logical models used in policy analysis and research oversimplify the complexity of education, governance, and student development.

Public Policy and Higher Education introduces the rationales used in recent decades to change higher education policy (Part I); places the current efforts to expand opportunity through improving preparation, access, and success into the policy context of states, developing new frameworks for examining higher education (Part II); and encourages reframing of policy for improving equal opportunity and other higher education outcomes (Part III). The book is written for administrators and policymakers in higher education, policy researchers, and graduate students who seek to learn more about the contexts of and theories and methods for policy decisions.

We made extensive use of nationally available data sources to develop and use a set of policy indicators for national and state educational policies. The indicators provide means for examining policy trends and outcomes nationally and for comparing state trends in state policies and outcomes to national trends. An appendix provides an overview of the data sources and methods for calculating indicators. We provide readers with the opportunity to compare states and think about how policies adopted relate to state outcomes. We also encourage critical thought about the ways policy frameworks migrate and develop as advocates for change wrestle with the realities of crafting new strategies.

With the page constraints on this book we could not include all of the analyses of indicators we had hoped to provide, so we also make available the Web page at the University of Michigan's National Center for Institutional Diversity (NCID) to provide supplemental information.[1] Each chapter concludes with reflective questions that encourage readers to think about the strategies used in a state or institution and to consider the relationships between policy implementation trends in educational outcomes. Some of these questions may reference figures accessible on the NCID Web page. The data we present in the state cases focus on public colleges and universities. Supplemental data on both nonprofit and for-profit independent colleges are available. Specifically, state-level trends in diversity and success of students enrolled in independent nonprofit and for-profit colleges is included on the NCID Web page. We encourage readers to consider additional information that is more up to date or expansive than could be included here. Such exploration will help readers develop their analytic skills and substantive knowledge.

In addition, we caution readers that any publication of trends and indicators is virtually out of date soon after publication, given the time it takes to calculate and publish this information. Our purpose in presenting trends in policy implementation and outcomes is to encourage readers to think about the problems they encounter and reframe their thinking about policy if and when outcomes are not as expected. Of course factors other than public policy influence outcomes in academic preparation, college access and diversity, and college success, but the relationships between policies and outcomes remain important considerations. Readers can usually search data sources on Web pages to get up-to-date trend data, but they also need to think about what the trends and relationships between policy and outcomes might actually mean and what their implications are. We hope this book has value beyond the immediate relevance of the trends reviewed because it encourages readers to think critically about frameworks, trends, evidence, research, and outcomes.

In an era of public accountability, much attention has been focused on holding schools, colleges, and students accountable. In fact, states and the federal government have made substantial investments in data systems intended for this purpose. Too little attention has been given to the responsibilities of legislators, governing boards, and administrators to make decisions that serve the public interest and the social good. To achieve these goals, it is important citizens have an understanding of the ways policies link to outcomes as well as an understanding of the social, cultural, and economic factors that shape and influence the intended outcomes. *Public Policy and Higher Education* encourages readers to think about these linkages, whether and how research indicators provide evidence about outcomes, and how indicators can be used in the process of holding public officials accountable for their decisions.

ACKNOWLEDGMENTS

This book combines three levels of analysis into new frameworks that readers can use to inform and reframe policy decisions in higher education: reviews of policy discourses; reviews of trends in policy and outcomes at the state and federal level; and reviews of research that examines links between policies and outcomes. We encourage researchers and policymakers to think through these multiple levels of policy data problems as they engage in their work. This book would not have been possible without funding from the Ford Foundation for Projects Promoting Equity in Urban and Higher Education at the University of Michigan's National Center for Institutional Diversity. The funding supported development of new policy indicators on racial inequality in higher education as well as extended and refined indicators of changes in policies and outcomes related to access that were developed and used in earlier research projects. Anna Chung, Daniela Pineda, Chiayu Chen, and Krystal Williams collaborated on the development of policy indicators. Phyllis Kreger Stillman provided editorial support throughout the project. We gratefully acknowledge all of this support. The views and interpretations in the book are the authors' and do not represent other organizations, groups, or individuals who provided support for this research.

1

INTRODUCTION

Over the past three decades, radical changes have occurred in public policies that alter the ways colleges are financed and students pay for college from those of a long, progressive tradition in U.S. higher education. A stratified market system of higher education has evolved in most states. The primary sorting criteria in this system are students' abilities and achievements defined by where they attended high school. States have adjusted their educational and school finance strategies by raising the standards for high school graduation, but these policies have not equalized opportunities to prepare for college.

The new high school graduation policies were advocated by reformers such as the National Governors Association (Conklin & Curran, 2005), the Gates Foundation (Hoffman, Vargas, Venezia, & Miller, 2007), and various other national groups (Commission on the Skills of the American Workforce, 2007; U.S. Department of Education, 2006). The new high school polices have been accompanied by market approaches in urban schools (i.e., charters, vouchers, and so forth) that create systems where students make choices of career fields and possible college majors as early as middle school (St. John, Masse, Lijana, & Bigelow, in press).

The market policies in higher education, institutionalized in the 1970s with federal need-based, portable grants, were developed based on arguments that free markets improve quality, increase innovation, and reduce costs (e.g., M. Friedman, 1962; Newman, 1971). We suggest in this text that the combination of market approaches and educational accountability schemes implemented by many states, often in disjointed and contradictory ways, undermine states' achievement of these goals.

While the federal government sets the directions for educational change through financial incentives, states maintain legal authority for public systems and are responsible for establishing policy frameworks—education and finance policies—that guide development of education systems and expand educational opportunities for their citizens. This disjunction between federal policy and state strategies is one of many problems facing educational reform in the 21st century. State policy frameworks are developed within belief and value systems about education and government held by politicians, analysts, and citizens. Even when public officials think through how various K–12 and

1

higher education policies interrelate, failure to adhere to these frameworks in annual budgeting can undermine their intent, especially as economic conditions and political ideologies change.

Many economists have studied market forces in higher education, but the shift in underlying policy frameworks has gone largely unstudied in economics or higher education. There have been strong rational arguments for market models of public finance in higher education since the middle 1960s (e.g., T. L. Freidman, 1962; Hansen & Weisbrod, 1969; Hearn & Andersen, 1995; Hossler, Lund, Ramin-Gyurnek, Westfall, & Irish, 1997); however, new ways of thinking have developed within states as they have adapted to new political ideologies and financial incentives, what we refer to as *state policy frameworks*, which have not been studied as such. Unfortunately, these frameworks are often disjointed and contain contradictory requirements, making it difficult for educators and students to achieve their aims. Policy frameworks are often aligned with political ideologies and beliefs that change over time, but sometimes a state can adhere to an old framework because of tradition long after it has lost functionality. Regardless of the type of framework states use, the interface between K–12 and higher education systems too often is not seamless and creates barriers for students and their families owing to financial and structural inequalities perpetuated within educational systems (St. John, Hu, & Fisher, 2011; St. John & Musoba, 2010). Yet it is possible to develop comprehensive and cohesive policy frameworks in states that expand opportunities for their citizens to find educational pathways that work.

Although individual policies are frequently studied and evaluated, the logic of frameworks that link policies within states is seldom reviewed, evaluated, revised, or redefined. Typically, new laws, standards, and funding schemes emerge in response to new federal initiatives with little collective discourse within states—or even at the federal level—about the implications for a state's K–16 system or the cohesiveness of pathways through educational systems. The federal Race to the Top competition provides a useful illustration of the challenges we face. In 2009, President Barack Obama signed into law the American Recovery and Reinvestment Act (ARRA) as a comprehensive strategy to address the recessionary challenges facing the United States. Part of this initiative was the creation of a $4.35 billion grant fund to incentivize states to adopt a set of neoliberal policy priorities including college and career readiness standards, expanded opportunities for school choice, data-informed decision making, and teacher accountability (U.S. Department of Education, 2010). The winners were the states that most successfully adopted the slate of policy preferences articulated by the Department of Education. There was no expectation that states develop an integrated statewide strategy tailored to the unique political climate of the state or the unique features of the respective education systems. Rather, states were evaluated on the degree to which they met the federal priorities; hundreds of millions of dollars were awarded to 12 states over the first two phases of the competition.

Further, the economic and social contexts within states are subject to frequent and sudden changes. For example, through most of the early 20th century, California's policy framework for high school preparation and college opportunity was unequaled (e.g., Kerr, 1963), but it has fallen from this lofty position in recent decades. In the current context of federal policy and global competition in the labor market, it is important for state and campus leaders to consider forces at work when planning and leading efforts to expand opportunity, the prevailing educational goal in nearly every state across the country.

FEDERAL AND STATE POLICY FRAMEWORKS

Whereas federal market strategies have overtly emphasized innovation, efficiency, and quality in recent decades, implementation of federal policies has fallen short of intent, since tax constraints and political attitudes shift before new policies are fully implemented. There is also great variability in the ways market-oriented policies have been implemented across and within state systems of higher education and local high school systems. Reform strategies originated by one state (e.g., Georgia's HOPE Scholarship or Indiana's Twenty-First Century Scholars) are adapted by other states, just as innovations by colleges (e.g., learning communities) are adapted by other campuses. A body of research has examined the patterns of diffusion of educational policy innovations across states and identified a number of factors related to adoption (Doyle, 2006; McLendon, Hearn, & Deaton, 2006), but very little of this work examines whether, or the extent to which, states adapt these strategies to the existing state context. Constraints on tax revenue and diversity in state frameworks (i.e., public attitudes and policy traditions) make it necessary to alter policies as models are adapted and altered through implementation. The variations in state markets should be of concern to educators, policymakers, and citizens within states because both the educational opportunities for citizens and constraints on strategy adoption by institutions are inexorably linked to and altered by state contexts.[1] Our core argument is that strategies for improving college access and reducing inequality must be adapted to state policy contexts because of the following:

- The shift from human capital to market theories as the underlying framework of education policy changes education in fundamental ways.
- High school graduation standards shape both patterns of high school dropout and the extent of college preparation but not necessarily the quality of preparation.
- State grant programs—merit- and need-based aid—influence student expectations about college choices during high school as well as the ability of low- and middle-income families to pay for different types of colleges within their states.
- Colleges craft financial aid packages to promote academic success within the constraints of federal and state student aid.
- Institutional strategies for improving academic success during college must be aligned with the preparation of students.

From Human Capital Theory to Market Models

During the last half of the 20th century, education policy was typically taught within a human capital framework. Human capital theory argued that both governments and individuals made decisions about education based on expected economic and human (individual and social) returns (Becker, 1964). The economic returns from education spending were seldom evaluated, but studies that did so raised doubts about prevailing policy (e.g., Hansen & Weisbrod, 1967). The federal government published reports recommending that states use manpower needs to guide decisions about which types of colleges and programs to build and support (Halstead, 1974). During the same period, international studies of higher education systems typically used human capital frameworks (e.g., Kerr, 1978). However, by the early 1970s market logic had begun to have a substantial influence on education policy.

The Newman Commission (1971), a study group for the U.S. Department of Health, Education, and Welfare (HEW), recommended portable grants as a means of equalizing opportunity and stimulating innovation, and soon a panel of economists made similar recommendations (Committee on Economic Development, 1973). Research by the National Commission on the Financing of Postsecondary Education (1973) confirmed that student aid had a more substantial influence on enrollment than direct institutional funding. These early studies influenced the general acceptance of market approaches to higher education funding at the federal level, a strategy that was rationalized in arguments about equal opportunity (Gladieux & Wolanin, 1976). The Pell grant program, introduced as Basic Educational Opportunity Grants (BEOGs) in 1972, adapted the human capital arguments to claim that portable, need-based aid could equalize educational access, and it is now the largest federally sponsored market-based policy for postsecondary opportunity.[2]

The grant-based system of need-based aid lasted for only a short period. In higher education, research showing that individuals benefit economically from education (e.g., Leslie & Brinkman, 1988) has been used to argue for loans rather than grants as the primary means of providing student aid (Bennett, 1986, 1987). Arguments for educational vouchers in K–12 education had been made in the 1960s (M. Freidman, 1962), but it took several decades for these arguments to take hold. Both public and private vouchers were tried in the 1990s, but research on their impact was ambiguous, as was the research on charter schools (e.g., Witte, 2000). In K–12 education, structural approaches to markets (e.g., charter schools to compete with public systems) became the dominant approach to introducing markets. Perhaps one of the critical markets influencing K–12 opportunity is the real estate market. Parents who can afford to do so vote with their feet and choose to live in communities with high-performing schools. These patterns accelerated in the second half of the 20th century, particularly in response to desegregation efforts.

When economists assess and evaluate market policies in higher education, they frequently assume that equal opportunity exists in K–12 education (Lleras, 2004); if this assumption were not made, it would be extremely difficult for them to estimate the impact of market-based reforms in college aid, even when randomized experiments were used. Yet, economists have also uncovered some of the problems with the application of market theory in education. Early econometric studies of the impact of Pell grants found that constraints on academic preparation in high school limited college choices for new enrollees in community colleges and proprietary schools (Manksi & Wise, 1983). Analyses of the impact of costs, even causal analyses, are biased in ways that cannot easily be corrected without considering differentials in prior preparation. Instead of considering market barriers, much of the education research community blames schools and students for failures.

There have been only a few actual experiments studying vouchers and other market mechanisms. Findings indicate that these models have not reduced inequalities in access to quality education. Research using experiments with random assignment has shown repeatedly that state and local attempts to equalize educational opportunities have mostly failed: school quality and access to the best schools remain unequal, even when there are modest gains in parents' perceived satisfaction (Metcalf & Paul, 2006; Witte, 1998, 2000). Thus the association between state policies and inequality in education markets merits closer study, not because we should do away with markets but rather so we can find better ways to reduce inequalities given the prevalence of market mechanisms in education.

Markets are not only part of the problem with inequality, they can also be part of the solution if the appropriate mechanisms—and necessary funding—are put into place to promote greater fairness.

States infrequently consider the role of their market-oriented policies in contributing to or undermining equal opportunity in education; indeed, the linkages between market forces and fairness are poorly understood in state governments. For nearly a century, K–12 education was compulsory and appropriately considered a basic right; higher education was generally available and heavily subsidized by the public. The general subsidies to public universities in the first half of the 20th century mostly benefited middle- and upper-income families, who had greater access (Hansen & Weisbord, 1969). Contemporary market models evolved as a result of shifts in political ideologies and funding constraints without strong empirical evidence to support new policies and without effective evaluation strategies to assess the impact of the policies. Yet, there was brief period of relative equality across racial/ethnic groups in the opportunity to enroll in college, as historic inequalities in college access were largely remedied by federal court decisions calling for desegregation, and the implementation of Pell grants in the 1970s (St. John, 2003).[3] Despite that brief period of success in terms of access, there has never been equality across racial/ethnic groups in rates of degree attainment.

By the late 1980s, the federal government had shifted its focus from equalizing opportunity in preparation and college opportunity to emphasizing improvement in educational outcomes and equal treatment for all students (Finn, 1990), a strategy that continues in No Child Left Behind. During the same period, the federal government shifted aid strategies from emphasizing need-based grants to relying primarily on loans (Hearn & Holdsworth, 2004). Although the American Recovery and Reinvestment Act of 2009 (ARRA) included new federal spending on education, most of it is short-term stimulus funding rather than a long-term reinvestment used to reward states that adopted the range of federal policy priorities for education. Subsequent budget deals have gutted much of the new investment in education that had been included in the stimulus. Thus it is up to the states to figure out how to equalize educational preparation under the new market conditions. Most states have constitutions that emphasize equal opportunity, yet they have failed to adapt their new market approaches to increase fairness, so greater inequalities have emerged.

The Eroding Dream

When Martin Luther King Jr. originally made his "I Have a Dream" speech in 1963, the federal courts were actively considering cases on school desegregation. The federal government was nearing the starting point of programs promoting equal educational opportunity in K–12 and higher education, the Elementary and Secondary Education Act of 1965 (ESEA) and the Higher Education Act of 1965 (HEA). At the time, states were responsible for funding both K–12 and higher education, and there had been some court cases requiring states to equalize funding for higher education. ESEA Title I provided supplemental funding for compensatory education for low-income students, and HEA Title IV funded national need-based grant and loan programs. These policies set the United States on a trajectory toward improving equity in education, at least for a brief period.[4]

There are two principles of educational opportunity that most citizens of the United States would agree are important for all: access to a quality K–12 education, what we call the *implied promise of fairness* in education for all, and *equal opportunity* to achieve a college education.[5] States have an obligation to provide a basic education to all, a commitment that is necessary because of the requirement for mandatory schooling. If the implied promise is broken for some students because of the failure of the state to provide an adequate basic education, then these early inequalities require attention and adjustment by public colleges and universities if higher education is to play its role in promoting equal education opportunity. In other words, to the extent that colleges are public institutions, they are an extension of their states and have the obligation to promote fairness.[6]

In addition, it is incumbent on government to balance *the promise* of fair opportunity to prepare and *equal opportunity* to enroll in higher education, once given such preparation, with a distribution of tax dollars through means that ensure cross-generational uplift.[7] Failure to provide taxpayer support would lead to a highly elite system of education with little opportunity for uplift across generations.

The ways governments choose to structure and finance education change over time. In the mid-1900s, public education was subsidized by states, but access was unequal. After first tackling the problem of segregation in K–12 education after *Brown v. Board of Education* (1954), the federal government focused on expanding opportunity for K–12 education and equalizing opportunity to enroll in higher education, providing supplemental programs and funding through the ESEA and the HEA. Both conditions—the promise of quality K–12 schools and equal opportunity for higher education—were largely achieved for a brief period in the 1970s (St. John, 2003). Compensatory education, delivered through the ESEA, created some fairness in preparing for higher education; federal student aid programs based on need equalized opportunities for college enrollment. The helping hand of the federal government aided fairness in K–12 education and equality in college access in the 1960s and 1970s, but the underlying framework of federal education policy shifted to a quasi–market model that did not have this same emphasis on equalizing opportunity, a change in policy that we consider in Part I.

The election of President Ronald Reagan ushered in a new era in education policy. Although Reagan was aligned with a neoconservative antitax, antientitlement philosophy (Drury, 1997), his presidency has been widely recognized as the turning point in educational policy in the shift to neoliberalism (e.g., Harvey, 2005). Careful study of presidential speeches (Posselt, 2009) shows that the roots of these "new" visions were established earlier: first by President Nixon, who promoted markets with the introduction of Pell grants; and then by President Carter, who tried to cut the costs of government aid and shifted Pell from a low-income program to one giving all students access to grants and loans by removing the income cap—a change that had an almost immediate impact on the expansion of inequality. So although the neoliberal era ushered in by Reagan may have accelerated the change in trajectory, the underlying ideas were already established in the policy and ideologies of the Democratic and Republican presidents who preceded him.

The ideological shifts in American culture and politics are important to the study of higher education policy because of their influence on public finance, government regulation, and curriculum. *Neoliberalism* is appropriately characterized as valuing freedom of choice over equal rights (Harvey, 2005), whereas *neoconservatism* is antientitlement and antitax (Drury, 1997). In contrast, liberalism values equal opportunity, which predisposes proponents toward need-based aid and other programs that equalize opportunity for education, health care, and so forth. The national trajectory shifted from a sustained period of movement toward liberal social programs from the Depression through the 1970s to the neoliberal period that emerged full scale in the 1980s. Neoconservative arguments about great books and the humanities (e.g., Bloom, 1987) had received substantial attention and added to the critique of higher education (Drury, 1997). Much as *A Nation at Risk* (U.S. Department of Education, 1983) critiqued liberal education reforms and started a trajectory toward central control of curriculum and standards (Ravitch, 2010), the critiques of education levied by Secretary of Education William Bennett and his leadership team, suggesting that universities raise tuition to increase revenues for loans (Bennett, 1986, 1987; Carnes, 1987; Finn, 1988a, 1988b), were made during a period when federal aid was shifting from an emphasis on need-based Pell grants to student loans (Hearn & Holdsworth, 2004; St. John, 1994a, 2003). Since the early 1980s there has been a troubling reliance on the market model, with inadequate federal investment in need-based grants and an overemphasis on loans for low- and middle-income students. In this volume, we explore how the global transition—the internationalization of labor and international competition among universities (St. John, in press)—coincide with a new set of conditions in higher education and encourage readers to reflect on the course of public policy in higher education.

We summarize the ideological shifts in political ideologies and their manifestations in Table 1.1. We conclude that during the global period there has been a break in the implicit social contract framed by human capital theory, which guided higher education finance for nearly a half century (Rawls, 1971) from the end of the Great Depression through the end of the Cold War. Rather than being perceived as an investment with returns to society in the form of educated workers who pay back society in taxes on income gains and through economic gains in science, spending on higher education has been aligned with narrower rationales related to the advancement and commercialization of science (Slaughter & Rhoades, 2004; Powers & St. John, in press; Priest & St. John, 2006). In this new age, it has been much more difficult for advocates of equal opportunity to build support for need-based student aid as a means of equalizing higher education opportunity.

Table 1.1 Changes in Political Ideologies Influencing Higher Education

Period	Political Ideologies	Values	Higher Education
Progressive century	Conservative	• Economic development • Low taxes	• Classical education • Science & technology, discovery promoting economic growth
	Liberal	• Social progress • Cross-generation uplift	• Education for justice and social good • Equal opportunity
Global period	Neoconservative	• Antisocial programs • Reduce taxes	• STEM pipeline • Merit aid • Corporatization of science
	Neoliberal	• Markets & efficiency • Universal human rights	• Fill gaps in STEM pipeline • Equalize preparation requirements

States' Responses to the Federal Market Model

In Part I we examine the general pattern of how states have responded to the market model of federal student aid, the policy trends raising educational standards for graduation, and the privatization of public colleges that have corresponded with unequal representation and a growing racial and economic gap in completion rates in 4-year colleges. However, the correspondence between the emergence of market policies based on federal loans and expanding privatization of public colleges after 1980 are not the sole cause of increased inequality, because states are the primary source of support for higher education; but this federal market creates the policy context in which states and institutions adapt their financial policies. A few states have been exceptions to the general pattern of growing inequality, illustrating the potential for comprehensive strategies to deliver on the promise of equal opportunity. The roles of state policies on student financial aid and high school reform both merit attention when considering issues related to equal opportunity.

The shift in who pays the cost of attending a public college from taxpayers to students and their families contributed to inequalities in preparation, access, and college success in most states. In many cases, this shift is the consequence of market-oriented policies that are either poorly structured or fail to address longer-term implications. For example, only a few states have a history of linking funding for state need-based grants to tuition charges. Under the best of circumstances, these awards lose their purchasing power simply because tuition and fees rise while the award remains the same. Unfortunately, there has been a tendency to cut all higher education budgets at the same time, which simultaneously leads to increased tuition and decreased grants—meaning that the shifting burden of cost to parents and students is accelerated. The correspondence between trends in two indicators during the 1990s and early 2000s (St. John, 2006; St. John, Williams, & Moronski, 2010), the fall college continuation rate for spring high school graduates and the ratio of public tuition and the average state funding for need-based grants,[8] confirms a relationship between state efforts to maintain grant aid and the rate of initial enrollment. During most of the period, the link was tight: when the percentage of costs covered by students increased, continuation rates declined, and vice versa. The tight link between these two indicators broke down in the late 2000s, a development that appears to be related to the impact of high school reforms. Despite increasing costs for students and parents, continuation rates increased.

Changes in state requirements for high school graduation also influence both overall opportunity and whether there is equity across income and racial/ethnic groups in access to different types of opportunities. During the past two decades, all states adopted new math standards, as advocated by the National Council of Teachers of Mathematics (NCTM) (2000), most raised graduation requirements for math and other subjects, and some implemented exit exams for graduation (Daun-Barnett & St. John, 2012; St. John, 2006). These policies are important relative to higher education because

- a period of decline in high school graduation rates usually follows implementation of higher graduation standards (a pattern for which there is evidence, as reviewed in Chapter 4);
- the extent and speed of recovery in graduation rates after implementation of new graduation requirements is dependent on the supply of teachers prepared

to teach the advanced subjects required and the attention paid to the organizational and cultural aspects of school change (a topic that should be further studied); and

- the ability of colleges to craft bridge programs and academic support apparatus builds upon prior preparation of students (a topic of increasing interest to policy researchers).

Along with raising standards, charter schools were implemented across the United States, bringing a new type of K–12 market to public education. At the outset of the charter movement, these new quasipublic schools were exempted from state requirements,[9] but increasingly states apply the same graduation requirements and testing to both public and quasipublic schools. Federal policy now promotes charter schools and other small schools as an alternative to public schools, creating parallel systems within most urban school districts. A few well-funded charters have gained public attention, but overall charters do no better at graduating students or improving test scores than public schools (Eckes & Rapp, 2006, 2007; Ravitch, 2010).

Charter and public schools now face similar challenges in urban areas. Both types of schools compete for teachers and students and struggle to upgrade curriculum, although charters may have an advantage because they can attract money from foundations and other sources to develop new curriculums, while public schools have a uniform curriculum. However, the problems that underlie implementation of the new standards involve more than selecting and implementing a curriculum or hiring teachers. The methods used to teach advanced math and other subjects are not engaging to all students and, whereas high failure rates were acceptable in the past, increased graduation requirements force schools to increase achievement.

The Critical Importance of Sustained, Comprehensive Strategies

Reducing inequality in preparation, access, and college success is a complicated process for states. State policies on school and college funding originally developed prior to and independent of the early federal efforts to reduce inequality through student financial aid (Title IV of the HEA) and compensatory education (Title I of the ESEA) in 1965. They also developed independent of one another, which, during periods of declining state revenues, has the effect of pitting one system in competition with the other for scarce resources. Over the decades, as the focus of federal policy shifted to a market model, some states accelerated privatization (i.e., shifting the costs of college from taxpayers to students and their families). By the 2000s, the federal market model in higher education emphasized loans, and the federal emphasis in K–12 education introduced quasipublic schools that competed with public schools under different constraints and incentives.[10]

In the 21st century policy context, state education and finance policy decisions should recognize the consequences of each policy on the competing public, private, and proprietary systems of higher education and the public, quasipublic, and private systems that compete in K–12 education.[11] Typically state policies on higher education, high schools, and public finance are not well coordinated. This disjointed policy environment was further undermined by efforts to improve accountability as a mandate for retaining federal student aid—a systematic approach that forces reporting schemes, alignment of curriculums, and tests. An unfortunate reality that goes largely unnoticed is that international benchmarks rating U.S. education were lower in the 2000s (U.S. Department of

Education, 2006) than in 1983 when *A Nation at Risk* was published (U.S. Department of Education, 2003). Three decades of accountability schemes implemented within market environments have influenced education in unintended ways: the quality of public schools and the percentage of students graduating from high school declined, as did college degree completion (Bowen, Chingos, & McPherson, 2009).

In these conditions, states are left to create coordinated approaches that combine academic and financial strategies in coherent ways to *make sure market and accountability strategies work as intended.* But do they? Unfortunately, they usually don't. We conclude that a comprehensive, coherent approach that coordinates diverse strategies in ways that allow schools and colleges to compete for students is the most workable approach in the policy context of the early 21st century. We reach these conclusions based on recent research (e.g., St. John, Hu, & Fisher 2011; St. John & Musoba, 2010) coupled with the analysis of state models in Part II.

States selected for case studies represent models worth careful study. However, this is a convenience sample in the sense that we worked with policymakers in many of these states on analyses reported in the case studies. Only the Michigan and California cases were developed independent of collaboration with state officials; they were chosen because they include distinct features and policy priorities that merit attention in other states. California provides an example of the low-tuition, high-grant model; Minnesota provides an example of the high-tuition, high-grant model; Florida provides radically divergent models reflecting the evolution of comprehensive, coordinated policies (Chapters 9 and 10); and Michigan provides an example of high tuition and low grants that in many ways embodies the neoliberal ideology (Chapter 11). North Carolina provides a case that runs counter to recent trends: increased public investment in colleges and their students in spite of the difficult economic conditions of the early 2000s (Chapter 12). In combination, these cases provide a view of a diverse range of state strategies, allowing comparisons of different approaches. As part of each case, we consider how different types of institutions have adapted as state policies changed in the late 1990s and early 2000s, the time period studied. We provide evidence that will help readers assess how well campus and state strategies work along three dimensions: improving quality (academic outcomes), maintaining diversity, and reducing achievement gaps (a measure of equity within systems), while also meeting demand at a fair cost for taxpayers and families who pay full costs. It has been extremely difficult for states to maintain integrated models and a workable approach, given the economic volatility in states combined with shifts in federal policies and funding.

There was evidence in several state cases of policymakers using research as feedback to modify, adapt, and refine government policy and campus strategies. In some states, research played a role in shaping and sustaining strategy: California has been a subject of study for decades (Hansen & Weisbrod, 1967, 1969; Smelser & Almond, 1974), Minnesota became a national model in the 1980s (Hearn & Anderson, 1985, 1995; Hearn & Longanecker, 1983), and Indiana has more recently emerged as a model (St. John, Hu, & Weber, 2000, 2001; St. John & Musoba, 2010). Florida is a compelling alternative model, even though it has not been as widely studied. However, all of the states are susceptible to the vagaries of the tenuous national and global economies.

The fact is campuses and states are challenged by new conditions that require alternative strategies for developing P–16 education policy. In Part III we discuss ways in which policymakers, campus administrators, and faculty can work together to improve quality, diversity, and financial stewardship. For the past few decades, government agencies have been responding to taxpayer concerns about the costs of the public sector of the economy. At the same time, public, private, and proprietary colleges continue to be dedicated to raising and spending money (H. R. Bowen, 1983; Hossler, 2004).

POLITICAL SHIFTS AND POLICY ANALYSIS

As the evolution of policies and policy rationales outlined above illustrates, most policymakers and researchers treat their beliefs about the goals of public policy as though they were true, seldom subjecting them to research evidence and open debate. However, there are vastly differing political views on the role of education, the value of providing access to it, whether the government should be responsible for funding education, and, if so, how to go about it. Part II uses case studies to focus on the political aspects of policy decisions in states as an integral part of state policy frameworks. Below we introduce our approach to discussing political views or frames of policy decisions. We consider the role of both political ideologies and analytic approaches, two key components of framing and rationalizing policy decisions.

Political Shifts

The classic liberal and conservative arguments are placed in a historical perspective and used to describe the current ideological clash about education and educational finance and the postprogressive stance used in the book. Our aim is to provide the facts in ways that are open to interpretation without taking a stance on how strategies will link to outcomes. Instead, we examine assumptions about the benefits of markets and recognize the importance of improving quality and economic productivity as well as equity. Although economic theories of human capital and markets had a substantial influence on education policy in the 20th century, these arguments were not the basis for early public investments in education.

Placing Recent Trends in Their Historical Contexts

Much of the current debate about education policy is framed within a clash between conservative and liberal values. For example, many conservatives believe that markets provide opportunities for innovation and improve excellence for all (e.g., Finn, Manno, & Vanourek, 2000), while many liberals argue that the role of government should be to equalize opportunity (e.g., Oakes, 1985), the ideology that shaped the ESEA and the HEA in the 1960s and 1970s. When these frames are used, the debates about educational systems, funding, and policies are often formed as either/or dialectics. Although we agree that there are radically different values among those on the political right and left, we also recognize the need to elevate political discourse above ideological clashes. It may help to take a step back and consider contemporary education policy in a historical context.

The history of education as typically portrayed is framed within the values of the Enlightenment. It is important to recognize that the emergence of the modern nation state, and later our democratic form of national government, grew out of the accumulated wealth of nations and the shift in theological logic about human rights (Fogel, 2000; Polyani, 2001; Taylor, 2007). The creation of schools and colleges in the early colonies set the trajectory of education in the United States before public education as we now know it emerged (Reese, 2005; Thelin, 2004a). Higher education institutions were founded as the nation moved westward during the colonial period and afterward. Most states and territories had high schools, academies, and colleges of various types, often with little distinction among them (Thelin, 2004a). Professional education in business and medicine took place in private proprietary schools, as public and private colleges focused mostly on the liberal arts. Most colleges were aligned with faith traditions and their presidents were usually members of the clergy.

Faith traditions were central to curriculum in early American schools and colleges during the colonial period and the nation's first century (Somerville, 2009; Taylor, 2007). The faith-based orientation of colleges began to change in the late 1800s, but progress toward this secular notion of education and liberal arts occurred gradually after the creation of public education (Reese, 2005). Although some states had created public universities before the Civil War, the Land Grant Act of 1865 set up a framework for all states to create public universities (Jencks & Riesman, 1968; Kerr, 1963).

A general state policy framework, or ethos, emerged that public universities should be accessible to all who qualified. Recently, in a historical discussion of the public role in higher education appended to *Crossing the Finish Line* (Bowen, Chingos, & McPherson, 2009, p. 240), Eugene Tobin argued:

> America's public flagship universities were created to meet the social and economic development of the states that chartered them, to serve as the great equalizer and preserver of an open, upwardly mobile society to provide "an uncommon education for the common man." Any resident, regardless of socioeconomic status, who fulfilled a standard set of academic requirements, would, in theory, be admitted to one of the state's public higher education institutions. In principle, the flagship university of the late 19th and early 20th century was an institution that served everybody, but in an era when few people completed high school (and many who did pursued non-college proprietary curriculum), the notion of the "people's university" was more of a symbol than a reality.

This description of early American public universities captures the ideology of social *and* economic development, the core values of the progressive trajectory in American education during the century ending in the 1980s (St. John & Parsons, 2004), after which the core value became economic rather than social development. The Wisconsin Idea[12] and the growth in the belief that the boundaries of the University of Wisconsin were the boundaries of the state embodied this progressive expectation for higher education at the turn of the 20th century (Wisconsin Higher Education Business Roundtable, n.d.).

Public high school systems developed after public universities. The public school movement, a process that converted Protestant schools into public schools, began in earnest in the 1880s (Reese, 2005). High schools were slow to develop, and when they became generally available they followed a comprehensive pattern, providing vocational, liberal arts, and college preparatory education. The evolution of the comprehensive high school was largely a consequence of two developments through the early part of the 20th century. First, by 1918, every state in the nation had passed laws both curtailing child labor and providing compulsory education, with states responsible for providing that education (Cook, 1912; Deutsch, 1917; Resnick & Resnick, 1985). Second, historians of the comprehensive high school (Hammack, 2004; Krug, 1964; Wraga, 1994) typically trace its origins back to the Cardinal Principles of Secondary Education (Commission on the Reorganization of Secondary Education, 1918), because it delineated very clearly a new vision for a broader, more accessible, and practical/vocational curriculum for the masses. The Catholic schools, which resisted the Protestant-centric curriculum of early "public" schools, developed college preparatory high schools (Gleason, 1995). The current struggles to transform public high schools into college preparatory schools involves changing deeply embedded cultures, not only of schools but also of the working-class communities in which many are situated.

These efforts come in a new historical period. The emergence of the global period is every bit as world changing as the early period of nation building. After the end of the Cold War, corporations rapidly internationalized, creating a radically different context for public policy (T. L. Friedman, 2005; Stiglitz, 2002). In higher education, the movement toward market systems and loans is global although not universal (Henry, Lingard, Rizvi, & Taylor, 2001).

Clashing Political Ideologies

The new global ideology is neoliberal, valuing individual rights over the social good (Harvey, 2005), which is why markets are valued so consistently across the political spectrum. In the progressive period in U.S. education, from the end of the Civil War to the end of the Cold War, conservatives argued for education as an instrument for economic development, while liberals argued for social class uplift (St. John & Parsons, 2004). The older economic arguments about human capital supported both social and economic views of investing in education. The new market period is different, not only because of the focus on individual economic returns but also because of the interpretation of rights and freedom to choose that underlie the newer market strategies. For more than three decades, arguments about individual choice and economic development have prevailed in debates about education rather than arguments based on the common good and equal educational opportunity.

It has been a complicated period for the old liberal goal of social uplift of more people into the middle class, for which education was seen as the vehicle. Attempts to expand funding for public education and student aid have often not been successful at the federal level, whether national debt was growing, as in the 1980s and 2000s, or shrinking, as it did in the 1990s. The challenge has been how to merge the philosophies of markets and individual freedoms with attempts to expand the middle class. It is possible that new economic arguments about the workforce (Commission on the Skills of the American Workforce, 2007), markets, and educational opportunity will merge into a new progressive rationale for reinvestment in education. There is some evidence of this, especially in southern states. The Obama administration has been arguing for reinvestment in education and substantially increased funding for education in the American Recovery and Reinvestment Act of 2009. Billions of dollars have been distributed to states for higher education and to fund innovations in urban and rural high school education. Yet questions remain about whether the reinvestment in education can be sustained, given growing government debt in the United States.

Postprogressive Stance

We take a postprogressive stance in this book.[13] We recognize that inequality within nations and in access to education have grown during this period of globalization, and financial and environmental conditions make it difficult to sustain investments designed to reduce inequality in education. Environmental decline is also a serious global problem.

The neoliberal emphasis on individual rights, which favors consumption and the concentration of wealth, makes it difficult for any government to sustain commitments to equal education or environmental improvement.

In the postprogressive period, we argue, improvement in quality and equity can be achieved through state policy priorities, but it is first necessary to discern how individual policies relate to outcomes and then to refine policies as part of an iterative process of change. If we assume that any specific set of policies will result in equalizing opportunities, we will miss the opportunity to craft new strategies that may work better. In short, we advocate thorough, systematic experimentation in education policy, where the states are laboratories and the education research community provides scientific evidence to influence the reformulation of integrated policy strategies. The case studies presented in Part II illustrate that a combination of policies will work in different ways over time in different settings depending on circumstances. Those who value equal opportunity in higher education and study financial aid tend to argue for need-based student aid (Bowen et al., 2009; McPherson & Schapiro, 1991, 1998; St. John, 2003). However, it is also possible to craft merit grants to provide an equalizing force, even though substantial sums of money from these grants go to upper-income families, as the Florida case illustrates.

We encourage readers to step back from the debates about specific strategies and focus on how combinations of strategies already in place within states are working. It is difficult to hold together a political coalition to support a policy approach, but there are ways to do it. For example, Indiana increased its investment in need-based aid in the 1990s and 2000s but included merit features in the grant program, an approach that had the support of conservatives in the state (Indiana Case: Part II). The state provided a higher basic grant to students with honors and college preparatory diplomas than to students with regular diplomas. From an old liberal vantage, the compromise was troubling because it penalized students who were tracked out of these courses, generally including higher numbers of low-income, underrepresented students. Yet the strategy also provided incentives for students to take advantage of advanced preparatory courses, which all high schools were required to offer.

We encourage readers to ponder the problem of building and holding together a consensus, consider evidence about the relationships between policies and outcomes, and reach informed judgments about political positions and policy arguments. We recognize and encourage advocacy within education systems, but we also encourage openness about strategies and outcomes. The evidence from state cases in Part II illustrates that states adopt very different strategies for the improvement of education and for higher education finance, in part as a result of the political histories of their states. Further, to maximize the impact of funding and education resources, universities must craft strategies with knowledge of the ways state policy actually works rather than what worked in a campus in another state with a different policy context.

Policy Analysis and Interpretation

This book seeks to bring the ideological debates about human rights and economic development into full view of policymakers, analysts, and researchers who examine policy issues in higher education in the United States. The role of ideology is vitally important in efforts to understanding inequality and the privatization of colleges; moreover, most of the policy literature in this field is largely silent about the role of recent changes in political ideology.[14] In undertaking this task, we take a postprogressive stance that recognizes the fact that the global trajectory complicates policy analysis in education (St. John, 2009a). The "post" aspect of our stance is based on our understanding of the lack of a shared social contract in the global period, while the "progressive" orientation represents the value we place on educational uplift and social progress. We do not assume readers share these values but instead encourage reflection on values and strategies. Although the tools of policy analysis are still extremely useful, the contexts for interpreting policy studies and political actions are different than they were when progressive values of social *and* economic development prevailed. We use the term *the progressive century* to refer to the sustained period from the post–Civil War period and the creation of land-grant universities through the end of the Cold War, during which public investment in higher education was thought to be linked to social progress and economic development.

Policy Analysis

There are many methods of policy analysis, but we focus on how the analysis of problems and cases through two traditions, economic and political, can inform government and institutional decisions in the postmodern period. Both traditions influenced the frameworks developed in this volume.

Human capital theory provided a general framework for cost-benefit and policy analysis in education. Using the logic of human capital,[15] it is possible to estimate the economic value of spending on different types of programs (Levin & McEwan, 2000). This logic turns the analysis of policy options into a set of choices that are rationally analyzed and discussed. This method can include consideration of constraints, incentives, direct and indirect effects, and so forth, all necessary components of crafting both government and institutional policy decisions. This type of research is rare in policy research on higher education (e.g., Paulsen, 2001a, 2001b; St. John & Masten, 1990) because it relies on a form of grand economic theory that is seldom used in higher education studies.

Another tradition used in business education and policy analysis involves case studies.[16] Commonly held assumptions and frames in a field of study can be used to analyze cases and project decisions. Bolman and Deal (1991/1996) illustrate the value of trying out different framing assumptions in analyzing cases and policies. We extend this approach by proposing new frames that have emerged from practices in case study states. Frames provide ways of noting what assumptions are taken for granted in planning and budgeting. Yet as conditions change in states and institutions, it is necessary for policy and strategy to change to keep pace.

Critical-Empirical Approach

The critical-empirical approach to policy analysis involves deconstructing claims or assumptions, examining evidence in relation to those claims, and reconstructing understanding (St. John, 2003, 2007, 2009a). When it is applied to the analysis of policy decisions in states and institutions, this approach can facilitate discourse among analysts and advocates holding different ideologies if there is a willingness to suspend arguments and discuss trends, evidence, and research. With open exchange it is possible to build new coalitions, a process that has worked well in discussions among Republican and Democrat policy analysts in Indiana with regard to school finance issues (Theobald, 2003), early education research (St. John, Loescher, & Bardzell, 2003), and higher education finance (St. John, 2003).[17]

Our approach to policy analysis and research involves examining multiple and often competing hypotheses about and rationales for policy decisions, replacing the single-hypothesis approach to policy research and analysis. Research is frequently used to build rationales for reform (St. John & Parsons, 2004); the expectation is that critical-empirical research will discern and test competing claims about a problem and use evidence to rethink and refine the rationales developed to formulate and implement policy.

CONCLUSION

Critical analysis of policy rationales and related evidence is used as the review method in the analytic chapters in this book. In Part I, we provide a broad view of the impact of the ideological shift on policy in higher education (Chapter 2), present our approach to the book (Chapter 3), and examine multiple rationales related to preparation (Chapter 4), access (Chapter 5), and academic success (Chapter 6). These chapters reviews rationales for policy changes, examine trends in federal policy and related outcomes, and review studies that focused on testing hypotheses. They were constructed to enable readers to make their own judgments about policies and outcomes in these three areas. Part II presents case studies of states that have developed policies related to rationales for reforming higher education. These chapters encourage readers to ponder the strengths and limitations of the approaches used in each state and how they might inform strategies in other states. The states were chosen because of the range of ideologies and policies evident and because of access to information based on our past experiences as researchers. In Part III we focus on how administrators and researchers can work to inform education reform within states and institutions of higher education. Chapter 13 raises questions about the framing assumptions in use in policy decisions and research. Chapter 14 turns to the problems of the social good and how to promote uplift in a period of constrained taxpayer support for colleges and their students.

Rather than arguing for a single approach or "best practice," we examine the ways in which policymakers, administrators, and professors have endeavored to inform and influence change within existing systems of higher education and how they have advocated for changes in educational systems. Our purpose is to inform judgment and practice rather than to argue for any particular policy or set of policies. In the long run, informed judgment by experts and policymakers is needed to shape the trajectory of higher education in states and to guide institutions through these troubling times.

The first reflective exercise (Text Box 1.1) encourages readers to examine and discuss state and campus context for policy decisions and provides discussion questions for comparing state and institutional contexts. Readers can develop their own cases as they work through the book, using the reflective questions to guide case research. The discussion questions encourage readers to think about the implications of the content in the chapter and related texts to inform their understanding of the role of public policy in higher education.

Text Box 1.1 Questions on Policy Contexts in States and Campuses

1. How do K–12 and higher education, along with financial policies, vary across states?

2. How well aligned are states' policies in K–16 education with federal policies on preparation, access, and college success?

3. How do you think alignment between K–12 and higher education policies varies across states?

4. What are the issues facing your state and campus with respect to:

   a. Preparation (examples: outreach to schools and students, marketing and information dissemination, admissions standards)

   b. Access/Enrollment (examples: student aid, bridge programs, partnerships with high schools)

   c. Academic Success (examples: academic support, options for students who want to change majors, continuity of student aid packages, state funding of degree completion)

5. How have policies on these issues been framed in the past?

   a. Are the policies coherent and linked in logical ways?

   b. Has a guiding philosophy or strategic plan been used to develop these policies or did they just evolve?

6. How has research been used to inform the creation or reformulation of policies in your state?

Part I

The National Policy Discourse

2

POLITICAL IDEOLOGIES AND POLICY MATTERS

The federal government began to focus explicitly on college preparation, access, and degree completion only in the last half century, but federal involvement in higher education has a much longer history. Financial aid developed as a primary feature of federal higher education policy as part of President Lyndon Johnson's Great Society programs, but there were earlier federal roles in funding institutions, litigation about the public interest, and research funding. As an introduction to the problems for higher education created by shifts in political ideologies, we examine how political ideologies have influenced changes in federal policy over the past two centuries in institutional funding, court decisions and resulting regulation, funding for research, and federal financial aid.[1]

FEDERAL PROGRAMS FUNDING INSTITUTIONS

The role of the federal government in providing direct funding for colleges and universities is more limited than its role in funding research or student aid, but it has been going on longer. The Northwest Ordinance in 1787 provided land for education purposes as the nation expanded westward. Vincennes University in Indiana, for example, was founded as Jefferson Academy in 1801 as one of many institutions growing out of that early legislation. West Point, founded in 1802 as a college for military and engineering education, was the first federal institution of higher education (Thelin, 2010). The Morrill Land Grant Acts of 1862 and 1890 also provided land to establish universities for education in engineering and the mechanical arts. The second Morrill Act provided funding only under the condition that state institutions were either desegregated or that the state provided separate but equal alternatives—thus initiating the funding for public historically Black colleges and universities (HBCUs). Today Howard University and other HBCUs receive federal support through Title III of the Higher Education Act (HEA).[2] In spite of this long history of federal policies and programs, institutional funding remains a tertiary role behind student aid and research funding (Finn, 1978; St. John & Wooden, 2006). Our discussion of federal funding for institutions examines this situation from the stances of historically situated ideologies and constituencies and provides a brief case history of the Developing Hispanic Institutions Program (Title V of the HEA as amended).

Evolution of Political Ideologies

There were three periods of grand ideologies in the United States: (1) from the founding and westward expansion of the country through the Civil War, (2) the progressive century following the building of cross-country railroads and the land grant universities, and (3) the global transition (St. John, in press). Competing ideologies during each of these periods shaped and influenced the ways the federal government created, sustained, and ended programs that provide direct funding for institutions of higher education.

In the founding period of the democracy, land was the nation's greatest resource, so providing land was a reasonable way to go about subsidizing the start-up of colleges and universities that promoted social expansion (e.g., Northwest Ordinance) and supported economic development (e.g., Land Grant Acts). In early American history there were tensions between Federalists, who believed in a strong national government, and Anti-Federalists, who advocated for states' rights. The Northwest Ordinance was a form of compromise with an emphasis on local action that supported states' rights. The Land Grant Act of 1862, which carried forward this tradition, was enacted during the Civil War, a time when it benefited the northern and western states.

The second Land Grant Act, of 1890, introduced a new form of compromise that enabled more southern and border states to take advantage of the land grant option. This piece of legislation, passed before *Plessy v. Ferguson,* provided a legal rationale for separate but equal. Even northern states like Maryland and West Virginia founded historically Black colleges under the act. The mechanisms for compromise between states' rights and federal interests had a major influence on the construction of federal policies affecting higher education during the founding and expansion periods.

The progressive century was a period of sustained federal support for the economic development of states and the nation, along with social uplift of groups. Both of these intents were evident in the Land Grant Acts and the strategies used by the colleges and extension services to promote the development of agriculture and homemaking. Once the compromise had been made to allow for segregated colleges, there were pockets of the country that resisted the progressive features of these institutions. Further, the idea that supporting higher education had both social and economic benefits was part of the ethos establishing teachers' colleges in the late 19th and early 20th centuries as well as the expansion of state institutions before and after World War II.

There was a shift in the debates about civil rights after World War II. During the early 20th century the Democratic Party had a large southern conservative contingent that opposed desegregation as a strategy for social progress and uplift, creating problems for President Franklin Roosevelt as he attempt to develop policies to move out of the Great Depression (T. L. Freidman, 2005). The Republican Party had strong northern and western progressive contingents with values centered in the traditions of Theodore Roosevelt and Abraham Lincoln (Newton, 2006). The Supreme Court's *Brown v. Board of Education* decision (1954) was followed by a period of further reconfiguration of political interests in K–12 and higher education. Even after the *Brown* decision, both K–12 and higher education in the South remained segregated (Williams, 1997).

The civil rights movement, especially President Johnson's leadership, which led to the passing of the Civil Rights Act of 1964, led to a re-sorting of the political parties. In this context of shifting political values and interests, the arguments for federal institutional funding took shape and led to Title III of the Higher Education Act of 1965, comprising the largest federal institutional aid programs of the late 20th century. The neoconservative views of Presidents Richard Nixon, Jimmy Carter, and Ronald Reagan furthered this realignment as a new set of political arguments emerged in presidential speeches and policies on higher education (Posselt, 2009). For example, Nixon introduced a privatized approach to public health care, Jimmy Carter argued for using zero-based budgeting as means of reducing government costs,[3] and Reagan furthered arguments for increasing the role of the private sector in government.

There was strong lobbying for direct federal support for colleges as part of the political upheaval that led to Johnson's Great Society programs. Interest groups representing historically Black colleges thought to be out of the educational mainstream, small liberal arts colleges threatened by the rapid growth of public universities, and community colleges expanding to meet the enrollment challenge created by the baby boom generation, which was then reaching college age, were among the most vocal advocates for direct federal funding (Jacobs & Tingley, 1977). Congress responded to these three interest groups by creating the Developing Institutions Program under Title III of the Higher Education Act. The initial premise of the law was that these institutions required federal support to enter the mainstream. However, by the early 1970s it became evident that institutions did not cease having financial need after the grants ran out, so an advanced program was created in the HEA Reauthorization of 1972. The major difference among the institutions funded in the basic and advanced programs in the 1970s was their size, length of time in the program, and level of funding (Weathersby, Jacobs, Jackson, St. John, & Tyler, 1977).

There had also been arguments for general institutional funding for colleges and universities that served low-income students (Gladieux & Wolanin, 1976), but the research conducted on this option indicated that institutional aid was not as effective in promoting access as student aid (Weathersby et al., 1977). Student aid became the primary means of federal support for higher education, which was well funded through the 1970s (see also Chapter 3).

During the administrations of Jimmy Carter and Ronald Reagan there were shifts in the underlying philosophy of government (Posselt, 2009). Both the Carter and Reagan presidencies argued for limited government and expanded individual rights. Under Jimmy Carter, there was a great emphasis on zero-based budgeting as a means of constraining federal expenditures (St. John, 1994a). Carter also responded to demands for higher education tax credits by raising income eligibility for federal aid programs in the Middle Income Student Assistance Act of 1978. Reagan continued these initiatives, reducing funding for several aid programs, eliminating Social Security Survivor Benefits (once the largest federal program), and emphasizing loans as the primary form of student aid, issues further discussed in the chapters that follow.

The critical point, from the perspective of shifting political ideologies, is that the earlier emphasis on equal rights had given way to newer demands for support for all students. President Bill Clinton continued down this path with support of tax credits for higher education and perpetual underfunding of Pell grants (St. John, 1994a, 2003). The ideological shift toward neoliberalism had not only altered the trajectory toward equal opportunity but also set the United States on the course toward higher costs and higher student debt.

Institutional aid programs, however, survived this period of policy reconstruction. Political constituencies for land grants, Title III, and the Fund for Improvement of Postsecondary Education (FIPSE) have all been able to successfully advocate for continuation of these programs through strong national political constituencies. In fact, one major new institutional aid program was created during this period of ideological shift: the Hispanic Service Institutions Program funded under Title V of the HEA.

Research Rationalizing Federal Funding
for Minority-Serving Institutions

HEA Title V essentially grew out of the Title III Program, which had previously funded the early Hispanic-serving colleges, like Pan American University and New Mexico Highland University, but there was no comparable set-aside for these programs, as there was for HBCUs. Further, since a set-aside could be subject to litigation, it was thought best to create a new program rather than provide a set-aside under the older Title III program (Pineda, 2009). In response to extreme challenges in expanding access for Hispanic students, the 1998 amendments to HEA established Title V as a separate program for Hispanic-serving institutions (HSIs). For FY2005, Title V funded 194 awards and grants through an appropriation of $94.9 million and the same amount was appropriated for FY2006, during which 163 grants were expected to be awarded (Mercer, 2008, p. 1).

In many respects the creation of Title V runs counter to current political ideologies. But trends in preparation (Chapter 4), access (Chapter 5), and degree completion (Chapter 6) reveal that the Hispanic population is growing across the United States and has been dramatically underserved, which makes it possible to craft a rationale for continued funding.

To inform the debate of Title V, Daniela Pineda undertook a study of HSIs funded through Title V to examine the impact of degrees produced using "differences of differences" (DID) analysis (Pineda, 2009), a new method for investigating the impact of institutional funding of academic success, finding that sustained institutional funding had an impact on the number of bachelor's and associate's degrees produced. Pineda's research adds new information to the debate about the efficacy of institutional funding versus student financial aid.

In the current policy context, it is evident that the market model of high tuition is problematic, especially given the emphasis on loans. The old question of institutional versus student aid should be revisited, with an emphasis on finding methods for restoring balance in access to higher education across income and racial groups.

THE COURTS

The federal courts have had a substantial influence on the evolution of higher education institutions throughout their history. The evolving ideological beliefs about the public good have had an influence on the appointment of Supreme Court justices and other federal judges and the decisions made in federal courts. Judicial activism that changes interpretations of the Constitution have been influenced by conservative and liberal Supreme Court justices and federal judges over time as they have responded to political pressures and prior case law, interpreted by their own beliefs. Below we briefly discuss major Supreme Court decisions shaping higher education access policies and provide an overview of the role research has played in desegregation litigation.

Political Ideologies and the Courts

The Supreme Court played a major role in the emergence of American private colleges and corporate form in the Dartmouth College Case of 1819. In recognizing the corporate form of the university, the Supreme Court confirmed the independence of the university from the state. The Dartmouth University home page (http://www.dartmouht.edu/home/about/history.html) includes the following statement about the case:

> The Supreme Court decision in the famous "Dartmouth College Case" of 1819, argued by Daniel Webster (Dartmouth Class of 1801), is considered to be one of the most important and formative documents in United States Constitutional history, strengthening the contract clause of the Constitution and thereby paving the way for all American private institutions to conduct their affairs in accordance with their charters without interference from the state.

This interpretation of the decision illustrates the clash between federal economic interests and states' rights during the early American period. The creation of the contract clause, along with the ability of universities and other entities to form corporations, helped create both the nonprofit and for-profit corporate sectors in U.S. colleges founded across the United States as part of westward expansion (Thelin, 2010). They were free to succeed or fail independent of the states in which they were found.

Perhaps the most complicated area of litigation from the early period through the progressive century was the evolution of litigation on segregation of public facilities after the Civil War. The Land Grant Act of 1890 had set precedence for separate colleges for Blacks and Whites prior to the Supreme Court's decision in *Plessy v. Ferguson* in 1896. This interpretation of protection clauses under the Fourteenth Amendment was an early form of judicial activism. Although the Fourteenth Amendment established equal rights as an illustration of the transition to a socially progressive nation state, the southern states and northern border states were not ready to integrate colleges or their K–12 education systems. It was difficult to maintain equal rights for education within the segregated systems that ensued.

This ill-conceived interpretation of the Fourteenth Amendment was only partially corrected through the *Brown v. Board of Education* decision in 1954 by the Warren Court (Newton, 2006). The litigation by the Legal Defense Fund (LDF) of the National Association for the Advancement of Colored People (NAACP) had pushed states to expand resources in order to assure equal education opportunities in a separate system. For example, the 1938 *Gaines v. Canada* decision required the state of Missouri to provide a law school for Blacks or admit them into White schools. A law school for Blacks was then created on the Lincoln University campus in Jefferson City, the capitol of the state, in an old beauty supply store. The NAACP was prepared to challenge this as separate but not equal when Gaines disappeared under suspicious circumstances in Chicago, after which the NAACP abandoned the case (http://en.wikipedia.org/wiki/University_of_Missouri). The *Brown* decision, however, created a new precedent, indicating that separate was not equal. Chief Justice Earl Warren narrowly constructed the decision so that it applied only to K–12 education, not higher education. It was not until the *Adams v. Richardson* decision in 1973 that higher education was included in the desegregation actions of the U.S. Department of Education. It took further litigation through *Adams v. Califano* (1977) in the Washington, D.C. District Court for the federal courts to force the federal government to require southern and border states to develop plans for desegregating public higher education systems along with equal support for the development of HBCUs and White institutions.

This line of litigation is illustrative of social progressive values during what we have referred to as the American progressive century. The *Plessy* decision, like the 1890 Land Grant Act, privileged states' rights over national interests in social and economic progress. This established the southern states as bastions of racism for the first half of the 20th century. It took military intervention after World War II to begin the process of breaking down these institutionalized forms of racism, which ran counter to the Constitution's Fourteenth Amendment, thus providing the legal basis for overturning *Plessy*.

Although it is appropriate to view the stream of litigation about segregation by the LDF as pursuing equal rights established in the Fourteenth Amendment and part of the socially progressive century in the United States, the subsequent decision by the Supreme Court in *United States v. Fordice* in 1992 stressed the role of individual rights consistent with neoliberalism. The Supreme Court accepted the argument by Mississippi that the freedom to choose a college was an acceptable interpretation of the role of equal rights in desegregation (Williams, 1997). The result of this decision has been a greater emphasis on the desegregation of historically Black colleges as a condition for providing greater financial support for these institutions. States like North Carolina had approved plans that supported both desegregation of state systems and the development of HBCUs before the *Fordice* decision. The more recent litigation and settlements in middle southern states (i.e., Alabama, Mississippi, and Louisiana) after *Fordice* used the newer, narrower interpretation of the law.

In a related strand of higher education litigation, policymakers have used affirmative action as a method for desegregating historically predominantly White institutions (PWIs). The landmark litigation in this area continues to be the Supreme Court's ruling in *Regents of the University of California v. Bakke* (1978), which struck down the use of racial quotas but not race or factors related to race in decisions about admissions. In its most recent decisions on affirmative action—*Gratz v. Bollinger* (2003) and *Grutter v. Bollinger* (2003)—the Supreme Court has upheld the use of affirmative action, citing broad criteria, but it has not allowed quotas based on race (Orfield, Marin, Flores, & Garces, 2007). The Bush administration adopted a narrow interpretation of the decisions, using the precedent to litigate against law schools and colleges that used innovative approaches to admissions and student aid. More recently, however, the U.S. Department of Justice (2011) issued guidance to achieve diversity. The new regulations provide a more expansive interpretation of the case, which encourages innovative approaches to selection that promote diversity, consistent with the research on student learning cited in the original decision.

Clearly there have been major shifts in dominant ideologies over time in the United States, from a tension between early federalism and debates over states' rights, to a tension in the values placed on economic development versus social uplift, and finally to the current period of valuing individual rights and economic development of social equity and uplift. Not only have decisions of the Supreme Court on topics in higher education evolved with these ideological shifts, but the court decisions are subject to various interpretations based on the perspectives of the justices, litigants, and practitioners interpreting the laws. Legal matters play a very substantial role in policy on and the governance of higher education.

Challenge: Desegregation of Public Higher Education

The federal courts consider findings from research during the litigation process and opposing parties provide supporting research directly related to their legal arguments. Researchers in higher education have played a role in the evolution of court-ordered remedies in higher education. For illustrative purposes we consider how research was framed before and after the *Fordice* decision, which reshaped the federal role in the desegregation of HBCUs.

The Department of Justice did not actively pursue desegregation of state systems until after the 1997 Washington, D.C., Federal Court decision, which required states to develop desegregation plans (Williams, 1988). Several states had approved plans under the initial round of decisions, but a few states resisted final settlement (e.g., North Carolina developed a systemwide plan desegregating public colleges, whereas Mississippi, Alabama, and Louisiana did not comply until after *Fordice*). The overall goal of the early planning was to desegregate predominantly White colleges and equalize funding for HBCUs.

While many researchers were engaged in the research on the problems, two states stand out as having had a substantial role during this early period. Larry L. Leslie (1977; Leslie & Brinkman, 1988) was the Department of Justice's primary expert on equalizing funding. An expert on both institutional and student aid, Leslie provided reviews of state funding formulas and guidance to the courts on equitable funding for institutions. Clifford Conrad was the leading expert on academic programs influencing student choice of institution. His work examined topics related to program duplication and the movement of programs and departments across campuses (Conrad & Shrode, 1990; Conrad & Weertz, 2004). Conrad and Leslie's scholarship had a substantial influence on early remedies, and they continued to work with the Department of Justice after the *Fordice* decision; however, the basis for federal court decisions shifted in major ways, especially with respect to student choice (Williams, 1997).

After Fordice

The *Fordice* decision shifted the agenda of the federal courts from the desegregation of predominantly White institutions to recognition of the central role of student choice. In Mississippi the issue of student choice had been the focal point in the *Fordice* case; based on the final decision, admissions criteria became a major issue in upholding the decision for White campuses, while funding programs to expand White enrollment became the primary legal issue in approval of plans for HBCUs (St. John, 1998).

Walter Allen has long been an important scholar in advocacy for HBCUs. His scholarship on education choices by African Americans (e.g. Allen, Epps, & Haniff, 1991) was uncontested in litigation. In addition, Conrad and Leslie developed an Alabama desegregation plan for the Department of Justice (Conrad & Leslie, 1994), but the Court focused on student choice (i.e., what would influence Whites to enroll) in deciding on programs to fund at HBCUs (Conrad, Brier, & Braxton, 1997; St. John & Hossler, 1998). With funding from the University of Alabama, a forensic research firm conducted surveys on White high school students, providing evidence to the Court (Hossler, St. John, Foley, Ramin-Gyurnek, & Smail, 1995; Hossler, 1997). This research used a critical-empirical approach to demonstrate how different remedies were linked to student outcomes, using enrollment, choice of major, and persistence as measures of student choice (St. John & Hossler, 1998).

Although litigation of desegregation is no longer a major legal issue, the development of HBCUs has continued to be an important policy matter. In addition to being a front line of access for African Americans (e.g., Brown, Butler, & Donahoo, 2004), HBCUs continue to play an important role in preparing future generation of scholars (Felder, 2012).

FEDERAL RESEARCH FUNDING

Although there was a history of federal funding of agricultural research as part of the land grant programs, federal research funding really took off in the United States during and after the war effort in World War II (Kerr, 1963; Thelin, 2010). Initially, funding for research was largely limited to elite universities but was eventually extended to a large number of universities. The growth in federal funding for research has had a substantial influence on the strategies universities used to compete in the late 20th century, as more government agencies and industries became involved in funding of research projects (Slaughter & Leslie, 1997; Slaughter & Rhoades, 2004). In the 21st century, it is appropriate to consider the roles of both government and corporate funding because of the growing importance of entrepreneurialism among faculty in major research universities. In the funding of research, relationships are established between university researchers and representatives of federal agencies, nonprofit foundations, and corporations. States also provide some research funding but generally do not serve in the intermediate role of managing federal research funding.

Political Ideologies and Federal Research Funding

Initially the federal government provided funding for projects thought to be in the federal interest, from advancing the agricultural and industrial revolutions of the late 20th century through competitive positioning during the global economy in the current period. Historians have pointed to the role of land grant universities in bringing a utilitarian emphasis to scientific research (Veysey, 1965). Whereas some historians question the overall impact of the early land grant colleges compared with traditional colleges and universities (e.g., Thelin, 2010), there is little doubt that the shift toward science, postgraduate/doctoral education, and university research occurred in a way that included both land grant and traditional universities (e.g., University of California and Harvard). The fact is that the introduction of science and research were part of the economic development of the 20th century, building on foundations laid in the progressive movement in higher education of the late 19th century.

Shelia Slaughter's critical analyses of the ways universities have responded to competition for government and corporate funding for research are interesting. Her early research pointed to the congressional testimony of research university presidents as an indicator of the push toward valuing economic development over social uplift (Slaughter, 1991) and the ways universities stunted the growth of majors in education and other middle-class fields as means of building capacity in science (Slaughter, 1993). Her scholarship on academic capitalism has shown how the research alliance between universities, businesses, and governments has become a form of academic capitalism (Slaughter & Leslie, 1997) and the ways these developments impact academic governance and the operation of universities (Slaughter & Rhoades, 2004).[4] Her work illustrates that positioning for research funding has become a more crucial factor shaping early 21st-century research universities than the competition for students.

The distinction between competition for research and for students is crucial in building a 21st-century perspective of university finance. Most models of university finance are concerned with the distribution of the general fund (the combination of tuition and state revenue) and how these funds are distributed within universities (Priest, Becker, Hossler, & St. John, 2002; Priest & St. John, 2006). As discussed previously, the concept of enrollment management providing a balanced portfolio of students is now frequently described as a matter of providing revenue for the operations of individual academic units (Hossler, 2006). These financial constraints make it difficult for many colleges and universities to meet full student financial need (McPherson & Shapiro, 1998; St. John, 2003). The enrollment management challenges in elite research universities are further complicated by the prepositioning for Science, Technology, Engineering, and Math (STEM) research funding, which deemphasizes teacher education and other middle-class fields (e.g., Slaughter, 1993). Competitive positioning has serious implications for both the financial management of universities and the framing of the STEM pipeline.

During the late 20th century there was substantial growth in research funding, especially for health and science research (St. John & Wooden, 2006). In the early 21st century a global pattern of government support for the development of university-business partnerships has emerged as a means of promoting economic development (Powers & St. John, in press). There has been a shift within universities from an emphasis on scientific and engineering discoveries and the general good (i.e., economic development supporting social uplift and process) to creating patents and new businesses. Often when corporations fund scientific research, the result is patented products for the corporations. Government funding often results in university patents and new business spinoffs. Thus universities with inventors on their faculties are in a position to share the economic benefits of new discoveries as part of the new economy. These newer patterns undermine older concepts of the public benefits of scientific progress and favor the concentration of wealth among the economic elite.

The other complicated artifact of the prepositioning of nations, economies, and research universities for competition for research funding and the economic benefits of scientific discovery is the hegemony of the logic of the STEM pipeline on the educational system as a whole. As is evident in the discussion of academic preparation (Chapter 4), the preparation standards for undergraduate math and science education are now requirements for high school graduation in many states. This complicates the transition from high school to college. The new standards are not high enough for STEM majors in elite universities (although they are sufficient to enter many other colleges and universities and most disciplines) (St. John, Masse, Lijana, & Bigelow, in press). At the same time, about half of the projected occupational positions over the next decade do not require the level of math preparation now required in high schools (Bureau of Labor Statistics, 2011).[5] Thus, while STEM pipeline arguments dominate education policy and relate to the competitive positioning of universities for science education and research, these arguments are not necessarily well aligned with labor market demand or the preparation requirements of the great majority of undergraduate programs in community colleges and 4-year institutions with professional and vocational programs to train students for high-demand professions (e.g., culinary professionals, nurses, health care technicians, elementary school teachers, etc.).

Responding to Federal Research Priorities

The research priorities for universities are substantially influenced by the federal funding agenda, especially in science and technology. The federal agenda is increasingly related to economic development and war efforts in the Middle East—priorities that influence the placement of funding.

Trends in Federal Research Funding

Trends in federal research funding clearly show a concentration on science and technology and on applied research over basic research—themes consistent with arguments about global competitiveness.

The emphasis on science and technology is evident in the breakdown of federal research funding by agency (Figure 2.1). The most substantial portion of research funding is allocated annually by the Defense Department, which had a growing share of research funding during the petroleum wars in the Middle East (Afghanistan and Iraq), reaching nearly $81 billion in 2006. Most defense research heavily emphasizes technology and engineering. Health and Human Services and the National Institutes of Health, agencies with a focus on medical research, funded more than $40 billion of research annually in the 2000s. The National Science Foundation and the Department of Energy had lower amounts. Authorization for research funding by the Department of Education and other agencies combined accounted for a substantially smaller total than the agencies reported in this trend analysis. These trends reflect the emphasis on STEM fields within federal policy, consistent with the ideologies of the global period.

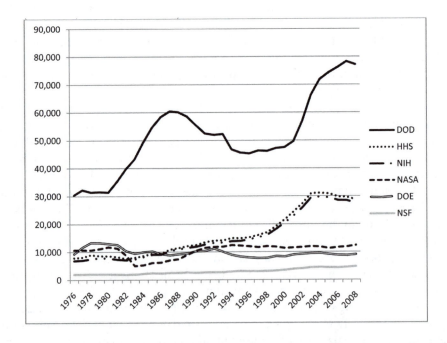

Figure 2.1 Trends in Federal Research & Development by Agency, 1976–2008 (in Millions of 2007 Constant Dollars)

Source: Imputed from American Association for the Advancement of Science (2009). Programs: Science and Policy. Retrieved from http://www.aaas.org/spp/rd/guihist.htm

In addition, basic research has increased over time but did not grow as fast as funding for applied research in recent decades (Figure 2.2). The emphasis on applied research illustrates the commercialization of research, consistent with federal legislation. Much of this shift is a result of the 1980 Bayh-Dole Act, which effectively gave universities the ability to move their ideas from research to commercial application and has led to an increased emphasis on patents and college-business partnerships.

Development of University Partnerships

The expansion of corporate-university-government partnerships is an outgrowth of the federal government's emphasis on applied research in science and technology. In fact, the global movement toward university-business partnerships has been accelerated by federal investments. To illustrate the consequences of these developments, we critically examine a few of the essays in a recent volume by international authors examining these trends, *Higher Education, Commercialization, and University-Business Relationships in Comparative Context* (Powers & St. John, in press). The analyses in this book focus on challenges to the aim of promoting social justice within the global period.[6]

The movement toward university-business partnerships tends to delimit them as emphasizing a distinct mission—entrepreneurialism—rather than examining how the influence of corporatization cuts across university missions. For example, in addition to arguing that entrepreneurialism is a third mission along with teaching and research, Etzkowitz (in press) recognizes the problem of higher education reinforcing class division in society through "meritocratic access to professions" (p. 8), but he does not dwell on the ways corporate sponsorship reinforces the redistribution of wealth, a serious problem for developed nations in the global economy (T. L. Friedman, 2005). This oversight is

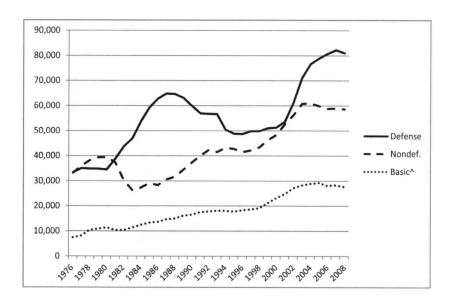

Figure 2.2 Trends in Federal Research & Development, Defense, Nondefense, and Basic, 1976–2008 (in Millions of 2007 Constant Dollars)

Source: Imputed from American Association for the Advancement of Science (2009). Programs: Science and Policy. Retrieved from http://www.aaas.org/spp/rd/guihist.htm

problematic because it releases universities from their historic responsibility to promote the social good. Such views simply do not recognize the implications of the decline in the social service mission for equality within developed countries or the role of corporate links in reinforcing the redistribution of social class. This limitation seems pervasive within this group of papers: they tend to focus on the movement toward the corporatization of universities without addressing the broader social consequences. However, the authors do address important social issues within this movement.

For example, Clements and Powers (in press) examined the reasons U.S. institutions have not embraced a broad set of social obligations, the *Nine Points,*[7] as part of the movement toward corporatization. Their quantitative analyses revealed, "Specifically, those institutions with more financial and personnel resources and those institutions that commercialized their technologies more successfully were more inclined to sign the *Nine Points* document than those institutions with less resources and less success with commercialization" (p. 78). Further, the qualitative analyses found that "institutions that aspired to increase royalty revenues were among those less likely to endorse the *Nine Points.* As such, it appears that ethical practice may be a casualty for them" (p. 86). Clements and Powers conclude that "universities with smaller and less influential technology transfer programs, a weaker resource base, and fewer patenting collaborations with others were less likely to sign" (p. 85). This recognizes the failure of most universities to embrace the older social good arguments central to the service missions of higher education in the United States.

This is problematic because only the wealthy universities with a well-developed focus on technology transfer can afford to take the moral high ground. The economically challenged universities were protective of institutional interests with respect to potential revenue. This pattern suggests that the financial pressures of an extended period of economic stress will likely result in the protection of institutional interests over public interests, a potential problem exacerbated by the privatization of public universities now under way in the United States (Priest & St. John, 2006; also see Part II of this volume).

Consequences of Changing the Elite Model

In the older model of academic elitism, the quality of research output was a major factor in rating a university. In the new model, the generation of business partnerships has become a major outcome of university funding relationships, with new corporate forms being created to generate profits for universities. Julie Lydon and Robert Morgan (in press) examined the difficulties of broadening access within European universities: "We argue that one of the key components and objectives of the Bologna Process, devising a system allowing easy mobility of students by virtual automatic transfer between institutions, is unlikely to be realized easily. For this to occur, degree programs must be easily readable and comparable. Therein lies the difficulty" (p. 167). In spite of governing policies that seek to expand access, the actual functional mechanisms within universities make such transitions difficult and slow.

The traditions of European universities undermine opening them up to authentic exchange. Lydon and Morgan (in press) also discuss the argument that the Humboldt conception of the university is not consistent with the new structure. Nevertheless the process of encouraging the exchange of credits and degrees continues, especially in participating institutions that form "clusters of trust" (p. 171). These clusters of trust are built on and extend the human networks of scientists that fuel the knowledge economy.

The European process creates opportunities for exchanges among the willing, broadening the base communities that promote corporate-university collaboration in the sciences.

Corporate-University-Government as a Metamechanism for Social Inequality

The more serious problem, which is difficult to see and discuss within the movement, is one of the consequences of the movement toward the corporatization of academe. The realignment of business, universities, and government strategies in pursuit of economic advantage in the global economy has reversed the implied social contract of prior decades evident in the post–World War II period in the United States, Europe, and Japan.

Stepping back from the arguments about economic strategy and social egalitarianism within the movement toward the corporatization of higher education in the 21st century, we must view the larger problems facing academe to provide an appropriate perspective on the problem. An alternative way to think about the current context is to contrast two periods: the progressive period of higher education within nation states, roughly from the emergence of western democracies to the late 20th century, and the global period, with its emphasis on corporatization, starting in the late 20th century (Table 2.1). This transition explains the transformational changes in teaching, research, and service occurring within major universities in the United States and internationally.

The shift to a global period emphasizing the corporatization of higher education has taken form in teaching (e.g., electronics courses) as well as in research and service. While corporate-university partnerships have become the dominant form of service, we ask service to whom and for what purpose? In the older national frame, there was a broader concept of the social good. In the new period, there is diminished taxpayer support for colleges and their students, suggesting that private economic benefits outweigh whatever good might accrue to society. Undergraduate education, the core function

Table 2.1 Comparison of the National Progressive and Global Corporate Periods for University Missions

Period	Teaching	Research	Service
National progressive	Teacher/professor interaction Movement toward greater access and gender/racial equality Government subsidies to institutions (low tuition) and students (grants/scholarships)	Faculty research for advancement of knowledge Economic development from gains in technology and productivity Government funds research programs in public interest	Faculty and extension services support social and economic projects New knowledge contributes to social as well as economic progress
Global corporatization	Use technology to extend pedagogies Universal access through class stratification Shift to high tuition and high loans as means of reducing taxpayer costs per student	Faculty collaborate with corporations on research in science and technology Universities focus on profits from patents and spin-offs Governments invest in corporate-university research partnerships	Corporate-university partnerships become new strategy for economic development (University research partnerships that promote social justice and equal opportunity)

of universities, languishes as government and corporate investments in research foster economic development through the advancement of scientific knowledge. However, universities and corporations are largely motivated by a pursuit of money: alternative revenue sources for universities and profits for corporations.

These developments add a troubling dimension to the internal economic motives of and financial mechanisms within universities. In 1980, slightly before the emergence of the global economy as we now know it, Howard Bowen (1980) developed the revenue theory of costs: in pursuit of their missions, universities raise all the money they can and spend all they raise. With the alteration of missions in the global period—especially the shift in emphasis from service to entrepreneurialism—we are left to wonder about the underlying motives of universities and their subunits (schools, colleges, and corporations) as they continue to pursue the goal of raising all the money they can. Institutions that are able will seek additional revenue streams that may distract from their undergraduate missions. Research on the problem points to the conclusion that money from these alternate revenue sources generally is not reinvested in the academic side of the university enterprises or at least not in subsidizing the costs of educating students (Hearn, 2008; Slaughter & Rhoades, 2004).[8] There is a danger that the new emphasis on university-corporate relations, especially the development of new hybrid forms of quasiuniversity organizations, will substantially alter the historic core mission of universities.

CONCLUSIONS

Public policy has a very substantial influence on the practices of administrators and faculty members in colleges and universities. There is a plethora of ways federal policy on health care, science and technology, environmental safety, and other matters influence academic life. This chapter has explored only a few topics as a means of illustrating the importance of policy. In our discussion, we have considered the ways political ideologies have changed the interpretation of laws and practice.

One of our arguments throughout this volume is that there have been major changes over time in the dominant public ideologies that shape and influence higher education through the policy process. We focus on how the new ideologies of accountability, privatization, and markets converge to influence the strategies that states, universities, and colleges use to encourage preparation, promote access through enrollment management, and encourage retention. In contrast, this chapter has stepped back to examine how some of the grand changes in policy from the founding period to the Civil War, during the progressive period after the Civil War, and into the recent global transition and neoliberal period have changed from promoting the common good to promoting economic development. In our discussion of the federal role in funding institutions, supporting research, and interpreting the Constitution and laws of the nation, we have introduced the use of ideologies as a way of exploring challenging issues in higher education as a field of study. The questions in Text Box 2.1 invite readers to explore these issues.

Text Box 2.1 Questions About Policy Matters

1. How have arguments about—and rationales for—the federal role in funding educational institutions changed over time?

2. What challenges related to the public funding of universities merit more attention by researchers and policymakers? Why?

3. How does the competitive positioning of universities for research funding influence teaching and student life in your institution?

4. What policy issues related to the federal role in research are of interest or concern to you?

5. How have legal interpretations of the public interest in higher education changed over time as reflected in critical decisions by the Supreme Court?

6. What issues have yet to be litigated but should be considered within higher education institutions?

7. How have rationales been framed to support policy decisions and what are the political orientations of those rationales?

8. How can or should research be brought to bear on these policy questions?

9. What is the relationship between matters that concern faculty, students, and administrators and the types of cases that rise to consideration by the Supreme Court?

3

POLICY FRAMES AND MARKET FORCES

Public policy decisions are made through political processes involving social interactions and the use of rationalizations and research. After World War II, systems approaches developed in global defense efforts were adapted to education and social programs (Schultz, 1968), leading up to and including the Elementary and Secondary Education Act (ESEA) and the Higher Education Act (HEA) as part of President Johnson's Great Society programs. Yet throughout most of the last half of the 20th century, political and social scientists argued that political process involving social interaction—and lobbying by vested interest groups—prevailed over the espoused rationality of the policy process (Lindblom, 1959; A. Wildavsky, 1979). This tension has also been evident in analyses of higher education policy, where sociopolitical process provides a better explanation for the evolution of HEA student aid programs than does the theory of rational research-based decisions (Hearn, 1993, 2001a, 2001b). In recent decades, a sociopolitical process that involves the misuse of statistics in support of a policy agenda is common in education, as it is in other areas of public policy.

To build a personal understanding of policy processes in higher education, we encourage readers to recognize the roles of argumentation and coalition building as sociopolitical processes in constructing rationales for policy change. Rationales are historically situated within policy discourses, as is the use of research to make political arguments. Of course research that evaluates the effects of policies or that projects future conditions can inform policy decisions, but people in government bodies use this research to develop rationales for creating and funding programs using political ideologies as their guide for selectively interpreting research. Thus there is a great deal of "fibbing with numbers"—what has been called "proofiness"—within the construction of rationales for policy and public funding in all areas of policy discourse (Strogatz, 2010, p. 8). Like science and defense policy, education policy has been misinformed by research that sets out to prove a point of view (Seife, 2010). To complicate matters, policy research is frequently conducted under contract with federal agencies. As a consequence, researchers frequently develop statistical analyses aligned with programmatic agendas of those funding agencies, often using the scientific paradigm of hypothesis testing, adapted to mean "proving the case," as the method for their work. Discerning the role of evidence—and the extent of proofiness as contrasted to authentic, objective research—in rationale building requires critical analysis of claims in relation to the quality of research used in support of those claims.[1]

This chapter introduces the metaframework we used for examining policy processes in higher education. We consider the role of policy frames as the logic structures used in political processes to rationalize advocacy for specific policy decisions, along with the framework guiding our studies of the impact of public policy. We also discuss how we use reviews of research on the effects of policy decisions—recent econometric and policy studies along with our own research—to examine federal policy rationales in Part I and to interpret policy outcomes in the state cases in Part II.

We use a three-level approach to presenting and analyzing policy in higher education: policy frames as an approach to the review of claims made in the policy discourse; the analytic frames used to examine the impact of policies; and the uses of evidence relative to links between policies and outcomes and as a basis of information for reconstruction of policy. We adapt this approach in the chapters in Parts I and II and encourage readers to use this approach as a way of framing policy decisions and analyzing practice problems within colleges as they to adapt to new conditions.

LEVEL 1: POLICY FRAMES

We use the concept of *policy frames* to characterize the frameworks of laws, budgets, and regulations that governments use to control and finance higher education. In the social progressive era—from the 19th century through the late 20th century—liberal and conservative policymakers generally supported investing in higher education to promote economic development and social progress. The new era of globalization has ushered in new market mechanisms that shift a larger share of the burden of funding higher education from taxpayers to students and their families, a process characterized as privatization (Priest & St. John, 2006). Privatization of public higher education in the United States has been accompanied by increasing economic inequalities in college access. But this is not a universal pattern; some states have used purposeful action to remedy economic inequalities. It is important to understand the role that framing and frameworks play in crafting public policy and government budgets and how they can remedy or exacerbate economic inequalities.

Public Policy and Higher Education uses the concept of policy frames as a mechanism for examining the rationalizations and logics states and the federal governments adapt in crafting policies to encourage and finance higher education preparation, access, and retention in the market period. The sociopolitical processes of policy decisions involve lobbying by interest groups, construction of rationales for policy decisions by executive branch administrators and legislators, and implementation of policies through annual budgeting. The creation and continuation of programs for student aid and other policies affecting higher education are only part of the policy cycle; the annual budget process also plays a crucial role. For example, historically the authorized maximum for the Pell grant awards has been substantially higher than what is possible given the actual annual funding of Pell grants (Advisory Committee on Student Financial Assistance, 2010; St. John, 1994a, 2003). By disconnecting the policy from appropriations, policymakers have been able to avoid making difficult decisions about how best to shift budgetary priorities for Pell as the proportion of eligible students increases.

The prior history of political action within states and the institutional policy context also play a substantial role in the construction of new programs and annual budgets. Privatization, market forces, and student choice are all now integral parts of national, state, and campus policy decisions. It is important to recognize the major shifts in policy that have taken place nationally in recent decades. As economies and societies changed to adapt to globalization, the contexts for policy decisions changed. We suggest that the rationales policymakers develop are informed first by the sociopolitical context and then by the solutions they perceive to be at their disposal. The role of political rationales in shaping policy research and political decisions and the specific logics that combine into crafting specific policy decisions in government and higher education have also changed. The U.S. federal government transitioned to a social progressive model of control, finance, and regulation of higher education in the late 20th and early 21st centuries. State governments have proceeded with adaptations to the new market conditions and the neoliberal ideologies of markets and individual rights at varying speeds, adjusting for state histories and political context. These conditions create new contexts for the development of academic and financial strategies within colleges and universities—and they make it more difficult for policymakers to fit prior rationales, like the classical liberal notions of equity, into their formulation of policy preferences.

Historical Trajectories and Public Policy

Modern universities were formed during the nation-building period of world history, from the emergence of the Enlightenment era in the 1700s through the emergence of the global period in the late 20th century. Globalization changes the basic patterns of financial policies affecting higher education and is changing decision-making processes.

The economic development of nations in western Europe in the 18th century created a new wealth and a middle class that sought educational opportunity and human rights (Polyani, 2001; Taylor, 2007). The migration to the New World was an example of the ability of populations to fund their own migration to North America, especially to New England. These migrations were based not only on the pursuit of religious freedom but also on the growing recognition of the rights of individuals. Colonial education was founded during this period, beginning with Harvard in 1636. The American and French Revolutions carried forward the concepts of human rights to self-government, realized first in the United States and then more slowly in western Europe.

After the Civil War, the federal and state governments began to develop their modern roles in higher education, which took shape with the creation of land grant colleges. Challenged by this competition from new universities, the older traditional public and private colleges and universities began the shift toward secularization (Marsden, 1994; Thelin, 2004a). Curriculums changed rapidly in the late 19th century, from faith traditions to science and Enlightenment thought.[2]

From the late 1860s through the late 1970s, public higher education was conceived of as a public good. This became a sustained period of social and economic progress, broken into periods of growth and economic stress. Most states maintained low tuition in their public colleges and universities throughout the 20th century. Student aid was created after World War II to make institutions more accessible, first for veterans through the GI Bill and eventually with generally available aid as part of the National Defense Education Act (NDEA) and HEA student aid programs. The early student aid programs provided subsidies to low-income students so that they could pay their living costs and modest tuition charges. Throughout this century of progress, government and citizens emphasized both economic and social progress, and both of these pervasive rationales benefited higher education (St. John & Parsons, 2004). These programs were sustainable largely because a relatively small proportion of the population attended college and tuition levels remained low—two conditions that have changed considerably.

The neoliberal turn of the 1980s, led by Margret Thatcher in England and Ronald Reagan in the United States, shifted the value base for policy to economic development and individual rights (Harvey, 2005). Emphasizing individual rights led to reductions in tax rates and a shift in the emphasis from low-cost public higher education to higher-cost privatized higher education. The burden of paying for college in the United States shifted over the next three decades from taxpayers to students: college tuition rose as tax subsidies to public colleges declined as a percentage of education fees, and the emphasis of federal student aid shifted from highly subsidized need-based grants to generally available loans (Hearn & Holdsworth, 2004; Priest & St. John, 2006; St. John, 2003). By the 21st century, the use of tuition and loans as a means of expanding higher education had become part of the agenda of the World Bank (Stiglitz, 2002). But neoliberalism was not limited to changes in public funding of higher education. Corporations globalized as production shifted from the United States and western Europe to China and India (Harvey, 2005), and the great U.S. universities entered a new period of global competition (B. Wildavsky, 2010).

We recognize these recent and major shifts in our reviews of the policy literatures on preparation, access, academic success, and other policy matters in Chapters 4–6. It would be a mistake to review literature and policy decisions from different historical periods without recognizing the major changes in the trajectories of social and education policy. For example, it is difficult to compare the role of government after the Civil War, when states were building land grant universities, to the period after World War II, when universities were adjusting to federal investment in research and the enrollment of veterans—the context for the Truman Commission on Higher Education (Thelin, 2004b). During both periods the country was recovering from war and investing in public higher education, but the conditions of the nation were very different. However, both of these periods—the late 1860s and late 1940s—were within the same major historical trajectory of nation building, a historical period that differs from the current period of globalization in some crucial ways.

There has been a shift from emphasizing the social good to valuing individual rights in the construction of education and social policy. After more than a century of gradual progress toward greater social mobility and equality in educational access, the new emphasis on individual rights has resulted in greater inequalities in educational access and attainment. Growth of inequality within nations corresponds with engagement in the global economy (Freidman, 2005), but is not caused by it. Looking at the western democracies, there is great variation across nations in the extent of public investment in students (St. John, Kim, & Yang, in press). Markets and privatization are not the ultimate causes of inequality in college access, but they have evolved simultaneously.

Political Ideologies in the Global Period

Individuals within democratic societies hold different beliefs about the role of government, but the collective political will is influenced by the media and global trends. Beliefs about the role of government, as with beliefs about religion and God, are not easily subjected to empirical tests. In pluralist democratic societies, differences in beliefs should not merely be tolerated but should be embraced as a source of insight and understanding.

Consider the emergence of the American democracy after the Revolutionary War. Thirteen colonies with differing religious beliefs came up with a constitutional form of government that not only ensured individual rights but also provided means of working through conflicting values in the formation of policy at the national level while states retained some rights (Taylor, 2007). Most public and private universities remained faith-centric for nearly a century after the Revolution, unimpaired by national policy in the fledgling nation. In the century leading up to the Civil War, faith differences across the colonies faded as regional differences in states' rights and slavery took center stage in national debates.

During the century of progress after the Civil War, the United States developed railroads connecting the nation and public colleges across the states as economic and social development became comingled values. By the early 20th century, there were differences between and within political parties about the means of progress and public investment. Government policies promoting economic development were the priority of conservatives, while investment in education emerged as a priority for social progressives from the late 19th through the early 20th centuries (Reese, 2005). During the Great Depression, the federal government and states invested in social welfare programs as means of expanding opportunity. Although there were differences across states in access to education, K–16 education was well established before World War II. Most citizens had an opportunity to enroll in K–8 schools, high schools were generally available, and public and private colleges were located in most states, although there were racial, gender, and financial barriers to access.

The Supreme Court's *Brown v. Board of Education* decision in 1954 shifted attention to desegregation and led to a new wave of education and social policies promoting equal opportunity. The Great Society programs further extended the nation's commitment to equal opportunity. The Pell grant program was originally proposed by President Richard M. Nixon's administration—the most conservative president between World War II and the election of Ronald Reagan—a shift that fit conservative ideology because it reframed federal priorities from funding institutions to providing portable aid to the neediest students. In fact, throughout the century of progress, there was a general consensus that government had a role in both social and economic progress, with political conservatives emphasizing economic strategies and liberals emphasizing social programs and policies. Indeed, efforts were made to desegregate public school systems across the nation and public universities in southern states, but recent evidence indicates that racial inequality persists, and racial disparities at college graduation have widened rather than contracted in recent decades, as we will illustrate in this volume. Among the changes in public policies evident in the new global period, the conservative argument has shifted from constraining investment in socially progressive programs to a claim that education and social programs were too costly for taxpayers and had gone too far.

The new ideologies in education were ushered in under Ronald Reagan's presidency. His first secretary of education, Terrell Bell, developed a ban on socially progressive education innovations through the national study group that produced *A Nation at Risk* (Ravitch, 2010). William Bennett, President Reagan's second secretary of education, argued that colleges were greedy and had raised tuition to obtain more funding to increase revenue by maximizing student aid, which would rise along with tuition (Bennett, 1987); this was part of his rationale for shifting from grant aid to loans. Bennett's arguments ultimately provided rationales for cutting funding for education. During this period of transition, liberals in Congress focused on maintaining funding. Indeed, Pell grants were actually renamed after Senator Claiborne Pell, from the original name Basic Educational Opportunity Grants (BEOGs), as part of this defensive posture taken by Congress.

Federal student financial aid programs continued to change, especially with the lifting of the income cap as part of the Middle Income Student Assistance Act of 1978. This shift in eligibility not only increased the costs of the programs (St. John & Byce, 1982) but also introduced the concept of universal benefits from federal education programs. The liberal position also shifted after 1980, from advocating for investment in education and social programs to using market mechanisms for promoting educational opportunity. In this new context of privatizing higher education, President Clinton pushed through tax credits for middle-income families and promoted new loan programs, including new loan forgiveness schemes for students who went into teaching or other forms of public service. Al Gore ran for president in 2002 with a platform of extending tax credits for higher education, while George W. Bush argued for extending funding for Pell grants. The traditional liberal and conservative positions on public funding for higher education had become blurred. President Obama shifted to claiming a "progressive" position. He pushed for doubling the Pell grant maximum as part of the health care legislation, but it remained unlikely that the new maximum would be met in the annual budget, given the large deficits and the growing number of eligible students applying for federal aid.

The shift to market models of public finance coupled with new standards for high schools without funding for implementation of these standards have institutionalized inequalities in K–12 education that render equality of opportunity in postsecondary education only a dream in many states. But some states have made substantial progress toward equality, even in the face of these new market conditions. Specifically, the ways states adapt their education policies to the new market conditions have an impact on growth and decline in inequalities within state systems, just as they do in fostering improvement or decline in academic outcomes.

Uncovering Rationales Used in the Policy Process

The concept of policy rationales provides a way of viewing arguments used to develop policy. In discussing policy rationales in Part II, we illuminate the relationship between education policies adopted and both achievement- and equity-based outcomes. This approach provides a window on both neoliberal concerns about education quality as integral to individual rights and social progressive concerns about equal opportunity as a social good. It is important to recognize that policy rationales are metaframeworks developed and used by the power elite in policymaking and funding policy research. As new rationales become pervasive in the discourse, they become part of the logic used by advocates for and critics of specific policies. For example, the overarching rationale for improving high school preparation as the major strategy for broadening college access and academic success in college has become so pervasive that it is now largely unquestioned. In the process, the emphasis on preparation in high school deflects attention from concerns for the growing cost of college and the role that colleges and universities need to assume to help students succeed in postsecondary education. In Chapters 4–6 we break down the components of this rationale—preparation, access, and success—and compare them to the preceding rationales of comprehensive universal high schools and need-based student aid as means of equalizing postsecondary opportunity. In Part II, we explore how the new and old rationales have played out in the global period within states.

More specifically, we define *policy rationales* as arguments developed through political agendas that use research to advocate for reform. Over the past three decades, rationales for reform have been carefully crafted by coalitions of government officials and the educational research completed by for-profit and nonprofit corporations that provide contract research for governments. Initially, many of the studies used to rationalize the new education and public financial policies were flawed methodologically (Becker, 2004; Heller, 2004a). Many of these studies had a low quality standard and used proofiness as integral to the construction of text. In contrast, in recent years the methodologies of this advocacy research have improved (e.g., Bloom, Thompson, & Unterman, 2010), but the intent of using research to build rationales for reform has not changed. The emphasis on new uniform standards for high school graduation and the use of market forces—two contradictory policies with respect to innovation[3]—continues, based on advocacy research but unfettered by critiques of it.

Researchers engaged in rationale building with the support of government and foundations design studies to prove hypotheses rather than to step back from the discourse and examine the actual effects of policies. The current wave of experiments uses random assignment of students to treatment or nontreatment schools, a method recently used in studies of small schools in New York (e.g., Bloom, Thompson, & Unterman, 2010). With supplemental funding from foundations, it is possible that schools will have better achievement outcomes; but when new policies are implemented based on these results, it is likely the reforms will not have the same effect without supplemental funding (Ravitch, 2010). The same is true for the range of initiatives supported by many foundations—the cost of innovation makes the scalability of new strategies impractical in many cases. The phenomenon of using research to build rationales merits attention. Reviewing evidence from the research, as a means of testing whether political rationales hold up, helps place the roles of rationales into realistic perspectives.

We use multiple methods to examine the ways research has been and continues to be used to build policy rationales. First, we look at the policy and research literature in tandem to illustrate research findings and how they are used in policy. We adapt the approach to the analysis of reasoning and evidence based on in the critical analytic works of Jurgen Habermas in his research on communicative action (Habermas, 1984, 1987, 1990). His method involved discerning claims, examining evidence related to a claim, and reconstructing the claim based on consideration of a broader range of evidence and theory. This approach has been used previously to illustrate how rationales are constructed in policy (St. John, 1994b, 2003, 2006) and is used again in Part I to illustrate how rationales about policy have evolved in the literatures on preparation, access, and college success as central processes in the academic pipeline, along with other policy matters affecting higher education.

Second, we review evidence on the policies implemented in relation to key educational outcomes. The correspondence between policies and trends is interpreted relative to the linking structures in the analytic frames used in this book, as explained below. Over the past three decades, the senior author has worked with foundations and federal agencies to build frameworks that illustrate links between policies and outcomes independent of ideological arguments about policies per se. The intention of this body of work has not been to advocate any particular course of policy but rather to build an understanding of the ways policies link to outcomes, both intended and unintended. This approach uses a critical-empirical method to test alternative propositions, not only one's own hypotheses but also alternative hypotheses proposed by others (St. John, 2007, 2009a, 2009b), which removes some of the bias implicit in using scientific methods such as experiments to prove hypotheses. The very act of setting out to prove one's own point of view creates a bias that is extremely difficult to overcome.

By developing analytic frameworks that identify linking structures that are tested in different bodies of research, it is possible to step back from the specific links espoused within a particular paper or research report written at a specific point in time and interpret it relative to the literature and multiple rationales used within the policy discourses. This approach is central to our reviews in Part I and Part II. In Part I, we use the method to establish the general pattern of linkages between political policies and outcomes. The cases in Part II illustrate both the general patterns and the ways individual states combine policies to overcome any unintended consequences that may arise. In other words, the cases illustrate how policies based on an ideology—such as beliefs about the inherent value of a specific policy like merit aid—can be combined with other policies to overcome some of the negative aspects of the policy (e.g., differentiating thresholds of merit awards). For example, the Florida Bright Futures program uses a comprehensive state framework to mitigate inequalities related to the implementation of merit grants.

Third, we examine research that tests links between policies and outcomes. The senior author has conducted numerous studies using state policy indicators, the primary data source used for this book, including prior reports and publications with this book's co-authors. The state indicators were originally developed through a grant from the Lumina Foundation for Education (St. John, Chung, Musoba, Simmons, Wooden, & Mendez, 2004) and have been adapted and updated in numerous subsequent studies. During the past few years, with support from the Ford Foundation, the indicators have been extended to include data on racial disparities in high school graduation and college completion. The indicators data, including the trend tables and figures presented in this book, are currently maintained and generally available through the National Center for Institutional Diversity (http://www.ncid.umich.edu/). In addition to the trend analyses, the trends have been referenced in empirical studies of links between policies and outcomes from recent research (e.g., St. John, 2009a; St. John & Musoba, 2010). We include new analyses on the impact of state policies on high school and college graduation rates for students from diverse ethnic groups as appendices in this book. Finally, we carefully review research by economists concerned about these same issues as an additional source of evidence on links between policies and outcome explained below. The review of empirical studies of linking structures provides more confirmatory evidence of cause-effect than is possible from review of either the policy discourse (Level 1) or of trends in policies and outcomes (Level 2).

LEVEL 2: EXAMINING TRENDS IN POLICY INDICATORS

We use two interrelated analytic frameworks to construct ways of viewing how policies link to outcomes in K–16 education. The first approach—referred to here as the *pathways to college framework* (PCF)—focuses on the ways public finance and education policies link to educational attainment. We use the term *academic capital formation* (ACF) to refer to the social processes that enable prospective first-generation college students to learn about college, navigate through college, and give back to society as they realize the inner social and psychological gains of educational attainment (St. John, Hu, & Fisher, 2011). We use the individual-level PCF, developed originally as the balanced access model (St. John, 2002, 2003), as a basis for discussing the meaning and impact of policy as well as to provide a logical basis for linking policy to intermediate outcomes for individuals. We use the logic structure of the PCF in building understanding of proofiness as a misuse of research in policy rationales and for the review of research in Chapters 4–6. Specifically we use our analytic framework to link state and federal education and finance policies—the shaping forces within state education markets—to student outcomes. This framework has guided empirical studies of state indicators (St. John, 2006; St. John & Musoba, 2010). We describe the state indicators used in this study in the Appendix.

Pathways-to-College Framework

Sociological, economic, and education theories have been widely used for research on college enrollment and attainment in higher education. The frameworks derived from these theories focus on students' education choices. In theory, individual students have the freedom to make education choices in higher education, a factor that is essentially embedded in every decision about subsidies for students and institutions, academic requirements, and support services. But in the reality of education choice, there are economic and social constraints on students' college choices and persistence that are difficult to control for within statistical models that test theory. In contrast, policy decisions about K–12 education have been somewhat simpler to analyze and predict because enrollment is compulsory until age 16 or 18 in most states. But families also exercise choices about where to live within cities of whether to move from one community to another, which influences the choice of K–12 schools. Further, when school districts have charters or other choice schemes, educational choices are more explicit and evident for families. So choice often plays a role in K–12 education as well as in higher education.

In recent decades a series of federal studies used simplistic theories to explain educational attainment, largely overlooking the role of finance and social capital (e.g., Adelman, 1999; Berkner & Chavez, 1997; Choy, 2002a, 2002b). The balanced access model was first developed in collaboration with the Advisory Committee on Student Financial Assistance (2002; Fitzgerald, 2004; St. John, 2002); it identified the roles of academic preparation, encouragement services, access, and college success as well as how policies were linked to these outcomes. It was recognized that the balanced access model overlooked the role of social and academic capital, but it was the best available logic structure at the time (St. John, 2003, 2006; St. John & Musoba, 2010). The following linkages are considered in the policy research and trends reviewed in Chapters 4–6 and are summarized in Figure 3.1:

- *Guarantees of student aid to support costs of attending encourage student preparation* (linkage 1). Indiana's Twenty-First Century Scholars was the first state-level program to provide this guarantee for low-income students who took a pledge to prepare. Other states have since adopted this program feature as part of state grant programs, but follow-through on states' commitments remains a crucial issue, even in Indiana (see Chapter 10).

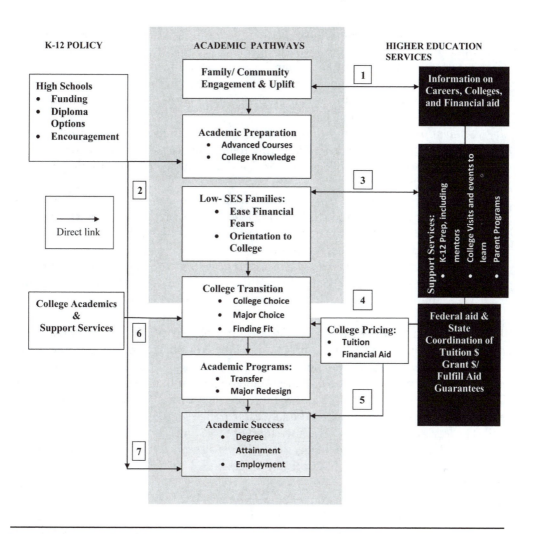

K-12 POLICY

ACADEMIC PATHWAYS

HIGHER EDUCATION SERVICES

High Schools
• Funding
• Diploma Options
• Encouragement

Family/ Community Engagement & Uplift [1]

Information on Careers, Colleges, and Financial aid

[2]

→ Direct link

Academic Preparation
• Advanced Courses
• College Knowledge

[3]

Low- SES Families:
• Ease Financial Fears
• Orientation to College

Support Services:
K-12 Prep, including mentors • College Visits and events to learn • Parent Programs

College Academics & Support Services

[6]

College Transition
• College Choice
• Major Choice
• Finding Fit

[4]

College Pricing:
• Tuition
• Financial Aid

Federal aid & State Coordination of Tuition $ Grant $/ Fulfill Aid Guarantees

Academic Programs:
• Transfer
• Major Redesign

[5]

[7]

Academic Success
• Degree Attainment
• Employment

Figure 3.1 Academic Pathways Theory of Change

- *High school graduation requirements linked to preparation in high school, as measured by high school courses completed* (linkage 2). Many federal policy studies have examined the correlation between high school courses and college outcomes. Using a proofiness tactic, many policy reports assumed that increasing requirements would improve college outcomes. Researchers tested this proposition to debunk this assumption. Research evidence relative to this linkage is reviewed in Chapter 4.

- *Postsecondary encouragement programs that include guaranteed student aid for low-income students influence preparation, especially courses completed* (linkage 3). These linkages were first studied for Indiana's Twenty-first Century Scholars Program and were part of the recommendations of the Advisory Committee on Student Financial Assistance and other groups. A similar assumption of linkages was made by advocates of merit aid who argued that these programs would influence academic preparation. Evidence about the effects on encouragement without aid guarantees is sparse and not reviewed.

- *Student financial aid and college prices link to college enrollment* (linkage 4). This linkage was central to the social progressive arguments used in the early advocacy for federal student aid programs, overlooked in research that focused on the role of academic preparation, and reconsidered in the balanced access model by the Advisory Committee on Student Financial Assistance (2010). Research evidence is reviewed in Chapter 5.
- *Student financial aid and college prices link to persistence and degree attainment* (linkage 5). Federal aid has a direct link to persistence as do other factors, including institutional and college support services (linkage 6). Research evidence is reviewed in Chapter 6.
- *High school graduation requirements link to college transitions* (linkage 6) along with college support and student aid. The review of research on patterns of enrollment in Chapter 5 considers the possibility that high school policies have an influence on trends in degree attainment.
- *High school graduation requirements and college support link to college success* (link 7). The logic that high school policies influence college success has not been tested. We examine related research and retention and persistence in Chapter 6.

The reviews of the federal policy development in Chapters 4–6 examine how policies—programs, funding, and so forth—link to outcomes routinely considered in the policy discourse. We seek to raise awareness of the ways policies and the discourse on policies, including the competing rationales for specific policies, influence education outcomes. Theoretically this type of analysis and critique provides a means of holding state officials accountable for their actions. Trend analyses of policies and outcomes at the national and state levels are the most easily understood of these links (Level 2). Review of empirical studies that consider these linkages (Level 3) is also important and should be more seriously considered in the policy decision process.

State Policy Frameworks

Education remains the responsibility of states and to a lesser extent local communities, in the United States. A federal role in need-based aid developed in the late 20th century, first through the legal process of promoting desegregation after the Supreme Court's 1954 *Brown* decision and later with the National Defense Education Act (1958) and the Great Society education programs (1965). However, the federal role in the desegregation of higher education did not begin in earnest until after the Supreme's Court's *Adams v. Califano* decision in 1977 and after the creation of the federal student aid program, including the voucher-like Pell grant program (as BEOGs) in 1972. Before the publication of *A Nation at Risk* (ANAR; U.S. Department of Education, 1983), the federal role was largely to provide supplementary support for special programs and services in K–12 education and student aid in higher education. After ANAR, the federal government systematically began to develop a strong regulatory focus, using standards, testing, and accountability as means of imposing federal policy initiatives on states. Although No Child Left Behind solidified the federal regulatory role in 2001 for K–12 education, the regulatory arm of federal policy has not been pervasive in higher education.[4] Both the financial and regulatory roles of the federal government are designed to influence state policies on education.

The framework for examining state and federal policy (Figure 3.2) recognizes the federal role in promoting attainment through educational programs, regulation, and financial aid. On the one hand, federal policy can be viewed as having a direct effect on outcomes—an approach historically used in econometric studies of Pell grant funding (Hansen, 1983; Kane, 1995). On the other, federal policy is consistent across states, while state policies vary. Therefore it is possible to discern the effects of state policies in models that compare states with federal policy and programs treated as constants. As background, we explain the three levels of this policy model and the ways we use it in *Public Policy and Higher Education*.

The Educational Attainment Pipeline

Federal policy in education increasingly focuses on expanding the educational attainment of the population. In demographic or trend-based studies of attainment using state data, it is important to consider variables related to the following:

- *Demographic Context*. At a minimum, data on the ethnic composition of the state's population and the extent of wealth, poverty, and education are required as controls for studies of policy. In statistical models, we developed indicators for the state-level equivalent of variables for family income and parents' education, which are frequently used in studies of college access that utilize individual-level data.
- *Academic Preparation*. In national studies of enrollment in 4-year colleges, it is desirable to consider the specific courses students take in high school. In most states, high school graduates are qualified for enrollment in a 2-year college if they have received a high school diploma. The indicators track high school graduation rates and college continuation rates—enrollment in 2-year *and* 4-year

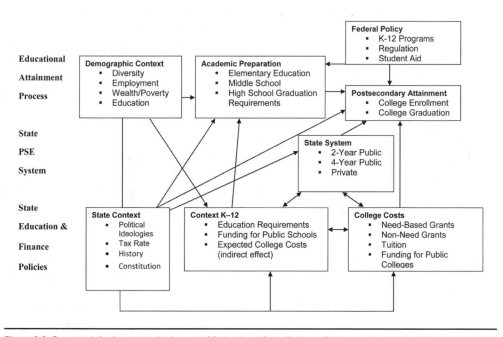

Figure 3.2 Framework for Assessing the Impact of Federal and State Policy on Postsecondary Attainment
Source: Adapted from St. John, Chung, Musoba, Simmons, Wooden, & Mendez, 2004.

colleges. State standards for high school graduation provide an indicator of the level of preparation of high school graduates.[5]

- *Postsecondary Attainment.* We consider indicators of the impact of public finance on college attainment: (1) Enrollment rates for high school graduates; (2) college graduation rates within 7 years by first-time students enrolling in 4-year colleges; and (3) degree completion rates after 7 years for first-time students in 2-year colleges. In the case studies, these variables are broken down for public, private, and proprietary colleges within states.

Levels of Policy

The logic of this framework informs the presentation of trend data in Parts I and II and is used for our fixed effects studies of the impact of state policy (e.g., St. John, 2006). Our discussion and analyses focus on two levels of policy:

- *Federal Policies.* We examine national trends in educational outcomes in relation to federal policy in Chapters 4–6.
- *State Policies (Part II).* State control and funding of higher education (see state system box in Figure 3.2) along with student aid supporting students who enroll in public and private college (see state policies level of Figure 3.2) are examined. The case studies provide trend analyses of state policies, which are examined in relation to attainment outcomes.

The Role of State Education and Finance Policy

State education policies, including graduation requirements, link directly to high school graduation rates and achievement test scores (we focus on average state SAT scores). In the cases in Part II, we examine how combinations of policies evolved in states during the 1990s and 2000s (Level 1 analysis). We also examine trends in high school graduation, college enrollment, and degree attainment in relation to these policies (Level 2 analysis), providing an information base about the ways in which policies affect outcomes within states.

Historically, the content of education was a matter of local control, although state and federal influence on content requirements in K–12 have increased substantially over time. The financing of higher education remains the primary means that states can use to promote degree attainment, and K–12 funding levels continue to influence high school completion rates. The statistical models, described below as part of the Level 3 analysis, provide further evidence of the empirical basis for the links between policies and attainment outcomes.

Using Analytical Models for Interpretive Purposes

There is weak link between quality research and policy rationale building that undermines the public good in education. Not only are research findings adapted to build arguments for policies, but, during this new period of regulation and markets in education (contradictory policy mechanisms), both high-quality and faulty research has been conducted in support of policy rationales.[6] Given the relationships between researchers, advocates, and policymakers, it can be difficult to untangle the purpose or meaning of a particular research study or to detect when numbers are used for proofiness.

The critical-empirical approach to research and literature reviews (St. John, 2007, 2009b) provides a means of taking an objective stance relative to one's own position on policy. While policy researchers, advocates, and policymakers take positions that promote particular strategies, they should also maintain openness as to whether the policies they favor or alternative policies actually work better. The critical-empirical approach involves discerning competing claims about a policy, examining evidence related to the claims, and reconstructing understanding based on the evidence. When people with different political values enter into a process of considering evidence openly, it can result in new policy decisions (e.g., Theobald, 2003; St. John, 2009a; St. John & Musoba, 2010). The analyses of federal policy (Part I) and state case studies (Part II) are presented using this approach: reviews are used to discern claims and policies (Level 1 analysis); trends are presented to provide a prima facie case of policy links (Level 2 analysis); and prior research is reviewed to discern confirmatory evidence related to cause (Level 3 analysis).

The process of reconstructing understanding is left to readers who—as students, professors, policymakers, and policy advocates—can reflect on their own positions, based on evidence. Given the changing nature of education policy in the global period, even the most ardent advocates should periodically reflect on their positions (e.g., Ravitch, 2010). In this book, we focus on the underlying shift from a socially progressive education system to a market system that values individual rights over equal opportunity. In Part III we encourage readers to ponder ways of bringing reform into a better balance between academic and equity goals as aims that have mutually enhancing synergies.

LEVEL 3: RESEARCH BASE

Trends in policies and outcomes may reveal coincidental occurrences not causally connected as well as real covariance that has an underlying cause; for policymakers it can be difficult to distinguish between the two. Whereas political advocacy is integral to the policy process in democratic societies, the process is undermined by arguments that rely on false statistics or proofiness. To guard against this, it is crucial that (1) there should be a logical link between the policy and the outcome being advocated, (2) trends support the logic of the policy advocated, and (3) if new programs are proposed, quality research is conducted to test the efficacy of the policy. Defining a reasonable quality standard in research is not a simple matter, but policymakers and reformers should be prepared to contend with this issue in advocating for major reforms.

As will become evident to readers in the reviews of policy in Chapters 4–6, policy advocates have frequently relied on faulty rationales and poor-quality evidence to support their claims. When one believes passionately in an issue, it is easy to grab whatever evidence there is that supports one's position and use it to make an argument. In our view, the risks of making mistakes—using poor evidence to build faulty cases—are greater than the risks of losing a political argument. When we use faulty evidence to argue for a case, the case is accepted and becomes policy; unfortunately the policy based on faulty evidence may turn out to have the reverse of the effect intended or may have serious unintended consequences. Under those conditions, researchers bear some moral responsibility for the people hurt through these policies. One of the reasons Diane Ravitch's *The Death and Life of the Great American School System* (2010) stands out as exemplary in the policy literature on education is that she reflects on evidence over time and sometimes changes her position on the strategies she had previously advocated as a senior policy-maker in education. It is important to be as open to evidence that may contradict our positions as to evidence that supports them. Contrary evidence should be valued because it can help policymakers rethink their positions and reconstruct policies that work better for the public good, economic and social.

Types of Research Informing Policy Rationales

To inform readers about related policy research, we review recent research that meets reasonable quality standards. Our review is not exhaustive but it is comprehensive. We seek to provide broad evidence about policy links that merit consideration by readers rather than relying only on our own research. The remaining chapters in Part I on preparation, access, and degree attainment include three types of review evidence:

- Reviews of studies using individual data that examined links between policies and outcomes consistent with the ACF model (Figure 3.1) and the balanced access model. We include reviews of some of the reports that stimulated the Advisory Committee on Student Financial Assistance (2010) review of studies, which used multivariate methods.
- Reviews of studies that use financial indicators to examine links between education and finance policies on preparation, access, and degree attainment (studies using fixed effects regressions).
- Recent studies of preparation, access, and completion meeting contemporary causal standards (e.g., experiments and quasiexperimental designs including hierarchical linear modeling, regression discontinuity, hazard modeling, and regressions with instrumental variables [IV]).

In theory, a multivariate study that includes appropriate control variables provides a way of discerning when a policy (e.g., grant aid) is associated with an outcome (e.g., college enrollment). Yet recent debates about the quality of research have focused on limitations of multivariate methods, including problems with omitted variables and heterogeneity (Becker, 2004; Heller, 2004). Since researchers find these problems difficult to address fully, especially omitted variable bias, given the limitations of extant databases, it is important that the limitations be recognized when the findings are interpreted for policy studies. Our review method recognizes the major problems in the discussion without casting blame on researchers. Our intent is to inform the interpretations of research constructed within policy advocacy. Our reviews consider studies of preparation (test scores, courses completed, and graduation rates as intermediate outcomes), access to 2- and 4-year colleges (as thresholds of access related to preparation and affordability), and persistence/degree attainment.

The indicators were developed to examine how state education policies influence preparation, access, and degree attainment. The initial study examined the impact of state grants on enrollment rates using fixed effects regression analyses to control for state differences (St. John et al., 2004). The use of state indicators has been extended to examine other policies and outcomes related to access, preparation, and degree attainment (including the analyses in the Appendix). In addition, a few researchers have used the state indicators in fixed effects studies (e.g., St. John, 2006) and multilevel models (e.g., Daun-Barnett, 2008b). These studies provide a body of research that overcomes some of the omitted variable problems associated with the earlier multivariate studies of student outcomes.

Finally, economists affiliated with the National Bureau of Economic Research (NBER), education foundations, and other organizations have produced research studies that address some of the problems with causal inference. This includes difference in differences as a method of comparing states to examine the effects of state merit aid programs (e.g., Dynarski, 2002), regression discontinuity studies on the impact of guaranteed student aid awards (DesJardins & McCall, 2009), and experiments with high school reform (e.g., Bloom et al., 2010). Although this newly emerging body of research overcomes many of the causal inference problems associated with other types of policy research, the studies frequently have limited generalizability. In addition, the experiments are highly costly and difficult to replicate through policy mandates.

Structured Reviews

As the third level analysis in Chapters 4 through 6 we provide a systematic review of exemplars of all three types of studies to document the empirical relationships between policies and outcome (the linkage structures in Figures 2.1 and 2.2) and to illustrate how research can inform policy advocacy. We review selected studies of all three types related to academic preparation (Chapter 4), access (Chapter 5), and persistence/degree attainment (Chapter 6).

Academic Preparation

The academic preparation rationale for college access used the correlation between completing advanced high school courses and college enrollment as a basis for arguing for high standards as a means of promoting college access and completion. Much of this debate omitted links between state education policies and preparation, so it was easy to use the findings to advocate for policies that could have unintended effects. Our review method corrects for this omission using a two-step process.

First, we conducted a review of studies using individual databases with information on courses completed, achievement, and graduation. As a first step, we considered the roles of SES (linkage 1), state education policies (linkage 2), and student aid using a straightforward format. We reviewed individual research reports and articles using this format before completing the summative reviews in Chapters 3–6. We compared studies to build an understanding of the linking structure to policy outcomes, along with the limitations of research that should be considered before using findings to advocate for specific policies. Our discussion of implications looks across studies and considers whether the research is consistent with trends, providing a way of illustrating the role of research in constructing policy rationales. This method provides a way of illustrating responsible ways of discussing research findings in the advocacy process.

College Access

There has been extensive research and reviews on the effects of student aid on college enrollment (e.g., Leslie & Brinkman, 1988; Heller, 1997), but these studies did not have an influence on the decision to reduce funding for student aid in the 1990s (e.g. Advisory Committee on Student Financial Assistance, 2002). In contrast, there has been only very limited research on the links between high school graduation requirements and college enrollment. Policy advocates used research that showed correlations between high school courses and college outcomes as a basis for arguing for raising graduation requirements for all students within states (e.g., Conklin & Curran, 2005); at the time, there was only limited research that examined the unintended consequences of changes in graduation requirements. For example, Manset and Washburn (2000) found the implementation of mandatory exit exams had caused many special education students to complete high school without diplomas. We review examples of research used in advocacy for new requirements and studies of the consequences of both financial and educational policies for enrollment in 2- and 4-year colleges.

This review examines evidence of empirical linkages between policy changes and degree attainment rates. Much of the discourse on attainment has focused on student preparation, but the impact of ability to pay for college has largely been overlooked until recently, with the publication of the U.S. Department of Education's *A Test of Leadership: Changing the Future of U.S. Higher Education,* a 2006 report that considers both preparation and financial access. An emphasis on funding students has proved difficult to maintain, given the federal budget deficits, so the state role in financial aid takes on more importance. The literature review and the case studies provide further evidence to inform advocacy for a balanced approach.

Degree Attainment

Most of the federal research has focused on degree attainment in higher education. The policy arguments about preparation, financial aid, and support services have all been made, but until recently degree attainment was not a major policy issue. The publication of Bowen, Chingos, and McPherson's *Crossing the Finish Line: Completing College at America's Public Universities* (2009) has raised awareness of the role of finances in the policy discourse. These analyses consider not only academic preparation and financial aid but also interventions within higher education. It is an opportune time for higher education policymakers and advocates to consider more balanced approaches to advocacy for reforms influencing college success. The analyses in this volume add to the newly emerging body of work that links public policies to degree attainment for diverse groups.

BALANCING RATIONALITY AND ADVOCACY

The United States led the global rush to market models in K–12 and higher education at the same time as new conservatives were pushing an accountability-driven approach to reform in K–12 education that limited innovation,[7] arguing that K–12 policy should focus on outcomes rather than equalizing input (Finn, 1990) and the waste in higher education (Bennett, 1987). These arguments for control and regulation through accountability and reducing costs prevailed, limiting the role of the market forces put into motion by charter schools in K–12 education and the privatization of public higher education.

Given the political constraints on tax increases, it is unlikely the United States will return to a social progressive period in which taxpayers support higher education, a pattern still evident in some European countries. Instead, the potential economies of the market model, at least for taxpayers, need to be weighed against the inequalities of the dysfunctional model that has evolved. Under these conditions, how can higher education adapt and find better ways to emphasize equity once again? Since we don't assume progressive change, we end up raising questions for readers to ponder and discuss rather than arguing for any particular policy solution.

To help readers prepare for reading this book, we raise some questions for reflection and discussion (Text Box 3.1). To some extent, we all view policy through our personal experience. To encourage open discussion of the problems facing higher education in the United States, we encourage readers to reflect on how their own education experiences relate to their views on education and finance policies. It is important to have an understanding of one's own views and those of others if you hope to have open and critical conversations about education policy and the ways researchers can work with policymakers to inform and transform policy.

Text Box 3.1 Questions on Policy Frames and Market Forces

1. How has the privatization of public higher education (i.e., increased emphasis on tuition and loans as means of paying for higher education) affected you?

2. Did you have opportunities to prepare academically for college? Did your high school have advanced placement courses? Did you have an opportunity to take the most advanced course in your school?

3. How does your own experience influence your views about education and public finance policies?

4. What are your opinions about tax rates? Should taxes for your social group be increased to support higher education for all students? Is it better to borrow and pay for college than to pay taxes?

5. Which of your views on educational opportunity do you believe to be true regardless of research evidence?

6. Do you have more favorable views of research findings if findings support your opinions than if they do not?

7. How do you respond to research that contradicts your own personal beliefs and assumptions?

4

COLLEGE PREPARATION

Higher education and public high schools evolved independently in the United States without strong alignment between the two systems (Reese, 2005; Thelin, 2004). This chapter examines the shift in political arguments about pathways between high school and college within state systems of education. We apply our three-level analytic method to illuminate the challenge by (1) reviewing the emergence of the college preparation rationale as an outgrowth of the standards movement, the reactions to the standards movement among K–12 policy researchers, and the emergence of standards-oriented research in the field of higher education; (2) examining trends in higher education policies and outcomes during the decades of high school reform; and (3) reviewing the literature on high school preparation in relation to policies and trends.

THE POLICY DISCOURSE ON COLLEGE PREPARATION

Most researchers and policymakers who follow higher education as a field are not well versed on the policy discourse or educational reform as it applies to high schools. Instead, the problem of P–16 education is more typically treated as a recent problem. Given that the discourses on college preparation are now inexorably intertwined with the topic of college preparation, it is important to step back and consider how this came about. Since federal policy in education started to shift after World War II, it is important to start with the focus on desegregation and educational innovation in the postwar period before jumping into the standards movement and subsequent developments. The post–World War II period, with its rapid expansion of educational opportunity, set the stage not only for the high school reform movement but also for the change from social progressivism to the neoliberal global period.

The Misalignment of K–12 and Higher Education

In 1899, John Dewey addressed the challenge of creating a unified K–16 system of education, illustrating that the problem was far more complex than simply aligning the high school curriculum with college admissions standards (Orrill, 2001). He first articulated the different origins and subsequent trajectories of elementary education and college education and then demonstrated the complexity and variety of institutional structures that grew as a result—including grammar schools, academies, high schools, technical/ vocational schools, and normal schools—making the call for unity difficult to attain in practice. Efforts were made throughout the 20th century to increase the alignment of these two systems, but with marginal success.

In 1870, the University of Michigan began to accredit high schools that offered a curriculum consistent with the admissions expectations of the institution. The North Central Association of Colleges and Secondary Schools, following the recommendations of the Committee on College Entrance Requirements, expanded upon the Michigan model by establishing standards for high school certification and college admission among all members of the association (Conley, 1995).

In 1892, the National Education Association (NEA) commissioned the formation of the Committee of Ten, to be led by Charles Eliot, president of Harvard College, to examine the articulation of the programs of study in high school with the admissions requirements in college (National Education Association, 1894). Eliot and others in the New England states were concerned about the uniformity of the high school curriculum relative to admissions requirements but were disinclined to abandon their current model, admissions testing. Instead of following the accreditation model, the Association of Colleges and Secondary Schools of the Middle Atlantic States suggested the creation of a joint board of examiners, and the College Entrance Examination Board (CEEB) was formed (Lazerson, 2001). The CEEB created a series of college entrance examinations in the common subjects and allowed institutions to decide which tests they would require for admission and what test scores were necessary on those exams. Both accreditation and admissions testing remain part of the P–16 alignment puzzle but did not substantially alter the relationship between the two systems.

The creation of the comprehensive high school as envisioned by James Conant (1959) was at least in part an attempt to address the tension between increasing demands for college preparation and rising calls to address the vocational training of students. The creation of the advanced placement (AP) curriculum was an attempt to more closely align the senior year of high school with the first year of college. In 1951, educators at Harvard, Yale, and Princeton met with their preparatory school colleagues at Philips Exeter, Phillips Andover, and Lawrenceville to rethink the transition from high school to college (Blackmer, Bragdon, Bundy, & Harbison, 1952). They developed a 7-year plan, creating a series of examination-based courses that would allow the best and brightest to avoid duplication of courses in high school and college; thus the AP program was born.

Post–World War II

The United States underwent an unparalleled economic boom after World War II. It became the world's biggest source of manufactured products, not only because of the expansion of production in this country during the war but also because of the devastation of manufacturing capacity in Europe and Asia. The Marshall Plan rebuilt European nations after the war, while the Colombo Plan facilitated economic development in Asia as the colonial period came to an end. Education and manufacturing were part of the reform efforts internationally after World War II. In the United States, the GI Bill sent many returning veterans into the nation's colleges (Thelin, 2004); there was also a new emphasis on innovation in science and math education and the beginnings of a push for desegregation (Reese, 2005).

Desegregation of the armed services occurred during the war, and many African American veterans came home with the expectation of greater social progress with respect to racial equity. During the early 20th century, the National Association for the Advancement of Colored People (NAACP) had litigated against separate but equal more than a dozen times before the historic Supreme Court decisions in *Brown v. Board I* (1954) and *Brown II* (1955). One strategy involved cases that caused great expense in higher education for southern and border states. For example, the Supreme Court's 1938 decision in *Gaines v. Canada* resulted in the founding of a law school on the campus of Lincoln University in Jefferson City, after a qualified Black student had been denied admission to the University in Missouri in Columbia, about 20 miles to the north. Another strategy involved litigation regarding unequal schools, leading to the Supreme Court's *Brown v. Board I* (1954) decision, which set the nation on the path toward the desegregation of K–12 education. However, this decision was narrowly framed to apply only to K–12 education (Newton, 2006); college desegregation did not begin in earnest until after the Court forced the federal government to become more involved.

K–12 desegregation began after the 1954 *Brown* decision, starting with the legislated de jure segregation in the southern and border states followed by de facto segregation in other states. James Coleman (1965) identified the problem of White flight from great American cities, a highly controversial finding at the time. By the early 1970s, northern school districts began to experiment with new market strategies enabling school choice in school desegregation, especially magnet or theme schools (Alvis & Willie, 1987; Willie, 1976), an approach that was widely adopted in urban schools across the United States. The first magnet schools were in Boston, Massachusetts, a state actively engaged in innovation in education during the period (Katz, 2001). Thus innovation became one of the strategies used in early efforts to make integration an attractive alternative to White flight.

Educational innovation was stimulated by the space race, especially science and math education. After the Russians launched Sputnik, the first satellite, Congress passed the *National Defense Education Act* of 1958, which became a major source of funding for innovation in elementary and secondary math education. Although many of the math programs tested during the period either faded away or were absorbed into math textbooks, the student aid programs—the National Defense Education Loans—became the first generally available federal aid program and still remain, albeit in an altered form.

The Elementary and Secondary Education Act of 1965 (ESEA) was passed during this period of innovation in education. The major program in the ESEA was Title I, which provided funding for compensatory education for schools with low-income students to accelerate learning in reading and math (Wong, 2003). By design, Title I served as a means of uplifting students with educational barriers resulting from attending racially and economically segregated schools, but supplemental educational support was usually given to any student with learning difficulties. Title I originally had only modest regulatory requirements, and it also became a source of innovation among schools.

The Higher Education Act of 1965 (HEA) also promoted equal opportunity. Title IV of the HEA became the umbrella for existing financial aid programs (e.g., National Defense Education Programs became National Direct Student Loans) and launched the means-tested Equal Opportunity Grants (EOGs), the first generally available federal grant programs, as well as funding for guaranteed loans. EOGs were apportioned to institutions based upon the number of low-income students they served. As part of a reauthorization of the HEA in 1972, the federal government created Basic Educational Opportunity Grants (eventually renamed Pell grants) as the first portable federal grant program.[1] In addition, Title III, the largest federal program for institutional aid (funding institutions rather than students), funded the development of Historically Black Colleges and Universities (HBCUs), community colleges, and liberal arts colleges as well as innovative higher education programs (St. John, 1981). More recently, tribal colleges and Hispanic Serving Institutions (HSIs) have been added to the list of institutional aid programs under Title III. Within 10 years of the education acts, by 1975, college enrollment rates were nearly equal across racial and ethnic groups (St. John, 2003). The end of this period in education came about as a result of strong critiques of educational innovations, a concern that eventually led to the standards movement (Ravitch, 2010).

The Emergence of the Standards Movement

The publication of *A Nation at Risk* (ANAR) (U.S. Department of Education, 1983) is appropriately viewed as a reactionary move away from the progress in educational access and innovation. At the time of the report, the nation was highly ranked internationally and deeply engaged in making up for the early history of unequal education. It was less than 30 years after the *Brown v. Board of Education* decision but only 5 years after *Adams v. Califano* in 1977. At this point, there was only a limited history of college desegregation in the South, which began in earnest after 1975. The argument for shifting federal programs from targeting on improving opportunity for underrepresented groups to be support for all (i.e., ANAR) came at a time when a new, more equitable pattern was not yet firmly established but progress had been made.

Ronald Reagan ran for president in 1980, arguing that social and educational programs had gone too far and needed to be constrained; a reactionary stance compared with the socially progressive periods during the presidencies of Kennedy, Johnson, and Nixon.[2] Reagan's platform included the elimination of the U.S. Departments of Education and Energy, which had been created by President Jimmy Carter.[3] Reagan's first secretary of education, Terell Bell, had the task of salvaging a role for the Department of Education. As a former commissioner of education in the Department of Health, Education and Welfare (HEW),[4] Bell had been an advocate of creating a Department of Education. To save the fledgling department, Bell used the theme of national leadership to promote a new federal role that did not involve major new programs or funding.

ANAR provided a critique of educational programs, especially new and innovative programs that steered away from traditional content areas, and advocated for higher standards, specifically in high schools (Ravitch, 2010). Until that point, the nation's public high schools had been expected to serve multiple roles (Reese, 2005), and college had been for a select few. It was possible to secure professional jobs in business with just a high school education until, after the return of the GIs, more emphasis was placed on college education. Advocacy for the alignment of the high school curriculum with college admissions expectations, a policy laid out in ANAR (Daun-Barnett, 2008b), was a radical change. ANAR rapidly became a rationale for shifting the intent of high schools from serving as comprehensive, local institutions with a curriculum defined by local school boards to becoming part of a national system of college preparatory high schools.

There was a problem with high school graduation rates before ANAR was published. In 1969–1970, the high school graduation rate had been 78.7% but had incrementally dropped to 71.8% in 1979–1980 (National Center for Education Statistics, 2009). It is possible that the emphasis on innovative approaches to education had influenced this decline. Had the study group that created ANAR focused on graduation rates as the problem, they might have advocated for different priorities. In any case, the idea of raising requirements without recognizing the substantial financial investment required to provide the upgrade was irresponsible and not consistent with the historic federal role in education. Expanding the college preparatory curriculum has been embraced by states largely as a revenue-neutral education reform strategy, which has likely undermined the effort. Recalibrating schools in this way requires new personnel, extensive retraining, and a support mechanism that assists students and parents through the transition from high school to college. There was no mention of the added investment in ANAR, and states that have adopted the standards have not increased their investment commensurate with the increased cost. Since 1965, the federal government had provided funding for improvement in educational opportunity, particularly through Title I, but the resources were not sufficient to fund this sort of transformation. The problem was that the Reagan administration did not conceive of education as a federal responsibility, so any argument for new programs with new funding was unlikely to be heard.

Encouraged by the federal government after the publication of ANAR in 1983, states began adopting policies that developed standards for all K–12 education, aligned content and testing with standards, and raised graduation requirement for high schools in most states. Before examining the role of political ideologies in the crafting of this report and how new ideologies evolved that changed the education system, it is important to consider the condition of the system at the time. In 1980, the United States had the highest proportion of adults with a college education and was near the top in terms of high school graduation rates among the member nations of the Organisation for Economic Cooperation and Development (OECD). Although the structures of educational systems varied across states, the U.S. system included

- comprehensive high schools that provided general, college preparatory, and vocational tracks;
- community or junior colleges and vocational schools that provided both programs for the first 2 years of college that could transfer to 4-year colleges and technical programs that trained students for the trades;
- extensive systems of public 4-year colleges along with public research universities;
- independent private colleges and universities that provided a parallel system of education; and
- for-profit colleges providing degree programs and technical certification in the trades.

Whereas the higher education system has continued to develop along the structural patterns noted above, there have been substantial changes in high schools over the past three decades, moving toward tighter alignment of high school graduation requirements with admissions standards at 4-year colleges. At the same time, the charter school movement has expanded as part of the larger school choice movement and the influence of NCLB (U.S. Department of Education, 2010); voucher programs have been tested in large public school districts with mixed success (Carnoy, 2001); and small schools, themed schools, and small schools within schools have emerged in response to growing pressures for secondary school reform (Lee & Ready, 2007). This change in trajectory in the United States not only has implications for higher education policy but has become integral to it as many higher education planning groups focused on high school graduation requirements as a central issue during the early 21st century (e.g., Conklin & Curran, 2005; Hoffman, Vargas, Venezia, & Miller, 2007; Kazis, Vargas, & Hoffman, 2004).

A new ideology of education reform followed ANAR. Chester Finn Jr., assistant secretary of education for the Office of Educational Research and Improvement (OERI), argued that the historical focus on equity in funding and inputs was beyond the scope of federal responsibility; instead, public policy in education should focus on student outcomes like test scores (Finn, 1990). Over time, the alignment of curriculum and testing became the standard practice and was reinforced as a matter of national policy by both Bill Clinton's Goals 2000: Educate America Act and George W. Bush's NCLB Act.

Text Box 4.1 Characteristics of Integrated System of 9–14 Education Considered Part of Consensus on 9–14 Reform

Secondary/postsecondary share responsibility

- K–12 and postsecondary standards, assessment, and expectations for student academic effort are aligned to first-year college-level academic expectations at the broad-access higher education institutions, thus reducing the need for remediation.

- K–12 and postsecondary share responsibility for successful student transitions between levels of education, including transitions for the most vulnerable youth.

Multiple pathways to a postsecondary credential

- K–12 and postsecondary work together to provide well-defined curricular pathways to a postsecondary credential for all students. The number need not be large, but one or two pathways are insufficient to meet the diverse backgrounds and learning styles of the nation's young people.

- Most students—not a select few—have opportunities to accelerate their education and to undertake college credit-level work while in high school.

Seamless accountability, finance, and governance systems:

- A state's accountability system follows students across sectors through linked data collection systems, and states can hold high schools and postsecondary institutions accountable for improving their course- and degree-completion rates.

- A single state education finance system distributes funds, especially from kindergarten through college, and creates incentive for an integrated system. Collaborative or joint governance structure plan, set goals, and monitor results across all the education systems.

Source: Hoffman, Vargas, Venezia, & Miller, 2007, pp. 2–3

The movement toward accountability is no longer a problem just for K–12 education but is widely advocated for higher education as well. By the end of the 2000s, foundations and government agencies were pushing for a new consensus for accountability, including content alignment from the 9th through the 14th grade. For example, the Gates Foundation sponsored the publication of *Minding the Gap* (Hoffman et al., 2007) and a national conference on the topic.[5] Jobs for the Future was an outgrowth of this work; their strategy for an integrated approach to achieving equality in education is illustrated in Text Box 4.1 and referenced in the remainder of this section. This approach to high school and community college education could easily transform accountability schemes into an approach for regulating K–12 and postsecondary education (higher education, community colleges, and other types of postsecondary institutions).

Constructive Critiques of the K–12 Standards Movement

The K–12 accountability movement has been widely criticized, in part because it does not solve underlying problems of inequality. Oakes (2003, 2005), for example, has consistently documented the inequities inherent in the tracking of students within high schools, especially after school desegregation, because the experiences of students across those tracks vary dramatically. There has also been evidence of higher rates of failure in early grades and referral to special education for minorities and other low-income students in elementary schools (Manset, St. John, Hu, & Gordon, 2002; St. John, Manset-Williamson, Chung, & Michael. 2005). Imposing an accountability system with an emphasis on testing has not remedied these systemic inequalities.

Although an integrated system for grades 9 through 14 (Text Box 4.1) does not provide an explicit remedy for this systemic bias, it does include language about multiple "pathways" through high school and college. In one sense, the language of pathways potentially transforms the meaning of tracks; however, the possibility of de facto tracking remains. For example, Anthony Carnevale (2007) noted the tracking problem in high schools, in which about one third of the students were being prepared for college, one third for careers, and one third for dropping out. He argues for standards that improve opportunity: "The path of least resistance for reform is the current trajectory from high school up the education pipeline toward postsecondary education" (p. 21). Yet many question whether tighter alignment of high school and community college education will overcome the embedded pattern of tracking or replace it with a system that extends the years of education and the opportunities for dropping out. In fact, several states have raised the general graduation requirements to the preparation standards of a 4-year college (e.g., see the Indiana and Michigan cases in this book).

Another critique has focused on the excessive testing within the K–12 system of accountability, especially for high school seniors. Kirst et al. (1998, 1999, 2001) argue that misalignment has resulted in a complicated array of tests, each serving a different purpose, with the result being an increased emphasis on preparation for end-of-course exams, mandatory exit exams, college admissions tests, and college-level placement tests. This line of critique, based on Stanford's Bridge Project, argues for a tighter alignment of the graduation requirements for high school with admissions standards for 4-year colleges—a topic examined in multiple states (Kirst & Venezia, 2004). The coalition supporting the 9–14 system took the step of emphasizing high school–college alignment but did so within a framework that included accountability within both K–12 *and* postsecondary education.

The argument for innovation in high school reform has adapted to the new narrative about college preparation. Chubb and Moe (1991) argued that market competition would introduce innovation into education reform; this was perceived as novel at the time, providing an alternative to accountability as a means of reform. The argument was used by advocates of vouchers (e.g., Peterson, Howell, Wolf, & Campbell, 2003). What these advocates have failed to recognize is that education, even with school choice, is an imperfect market that requires some correction from public policymakers. Qualitative studies of the public and private schools engaged in competitive markets have revealed that public and private schools resisted voucher students and thus reproduced the channeling of students to specific schools (Ridenour & St. John, 2003; St. John & Ridenour, 2000). Further innovations in public schools intending to develop competitive niches have been undermined by school accountability schemes that mandated curriculum for routine tests (St. John & Ridenour, 2001).

Discourses can adapt to absorb critiques. The process can be characterized as cooptation or compromise, but underlying issues about accountability often go unaddressed in the process. The major issue lingering is, will alignment increase (through better academic preparation) or decrease (partly because of decreased high school graduation rates) access to college?[6] This question can only be partially addressed by examining the relationship between trends in standards and graduation rates, the step we take below, because the nature of standards can change. There is a big risk in promoting systemic change through accountability without giving sufficient emphasis to innovation, an implicit partner of reform during the period of equity. These issues matter in higher education as the accountability debates move forward into a new decade and policymakers increasingly recognize rapidly growing costs and less than stellar outcomes in terms of measured student learning and degree completion rates.

Research Promoting Higher Standards for Graduation

The federal government initiated a series of studies that focused on rigor of curriculum as an explanation for the access gap in higher education. After a period of relatively equal college enrollment rates for minority and majority students in the 1970s, a gap opened in the early 1980s for African Americans and Hispanics compared with Whites. In 1986, a study of the causes of the gap was commissioned at Pelavin Associates, a private firm with a policy research contract for the Office of Planning, Budget, and Evaluation (OPBE).[7] Previously, access research had focused on student aid and considered academic preparation as a control variable (e.g., Jackson, 1978; Manski & Wise, 1983). The final report reinforced a well-established correlation between math courses completed and college access (Pelavin & Kane, 1988, 1990)—in particular the correlation between completing algebra I in junior high school and college enrollment.[8] At the time, none of the states required algebra I for graduation, so it was a finding that had no immediate implications for policy. It did, however, provide ammunition for a growing neoliberal contingent except for people building a rationale for the accountability movement.

The Pelavin report was followed by numerous federal reports that focused on high school math courses as the primary predictor variable for college enrollment (several of which are discussed below). The Office of Educational Research and Improvement picked up on the theme in Adelman's toolkit (Adelman, 1999), a report that emphasized the importance of academic preparation in bachelor's degree attainment. The National Center for Educational Statistics (NCES) also funded several studies that reached a similar conclusion (e.g., Berkner & Chavez, 1997; Choy, 2002a) with respect to college enrollment and student persistence. Berkner and Chavez's report (1997) went so far as to claim that all racial differences in college access were explained by completing the right high school courses and taking the steps necessary to attend college (completing admissions exams and applying to college by the spring of the student's senior year).[9]

There were serious problems with the logic of the models, especially given that many colleges do not require either admissions tests or advanced application. There were also many difficulties with using measures of curricular quality as an explanation for the gap in college enrollment: (1) there had been equity in enrollment across racial but not income groups in the 1970s (St. John, 1994, 2002, 2003); (2) the reports did not consider the role of student aid, the focus of many prior federal studies of access because aid was the federal government's primary role in higher education; and (3) the reports made serious statistical errors that were not acknowledged.[10]

It is important to admit to the problems when flawed statistical results are used in policy advocacy. The NCES and OERI reports were extensively used in policy reports; for example, many of the chapter authors in *Minding the Gap* (Hoffman et al., 2007) referenced these reports in building the case for more rigorous courses for high school graduation. Further, many states adopted a requirement for algebra I for high school graduation, a topic considered further below. More recently, the final report of the Spellings Commission on the Future of Higher Education (2006) referenced no fewer than 10 of these statistical reports issued by the U.S. Department of Education.

Certainly rigorous high school math courses should be required for students who plan to enroll in 4-year colleges. Screening some students out of courses with higher standards could seem prejudicial, as suggested in critiques of tracking. Yet if all students are expected to go on to 4-year colleges, then such requirements would be reasonable for high school graduation. However, if such requirements are implemented, attention should be paid to equalizing opportunities for students to gain access to and complete these courses (i.e., making them available in all high schools). Given the complex history of racial segregation, tracking, the differentiation of high schools in urban areas (with only a few in most cities having a history of college prep curricula), and the decline in the high school graduation rate after 1970, an alternative to current accountability schemes (i.e., aligned standards, curriculum, and tests) should have been considered at state and federal levels. Instead, the federal government threatened to withdraw funding if states did not comply with unfunded accountability requirements. Accountability (i.e., mandated testing) was required to receive federal funding in NCLB, but sufficient funding was not provided to implement higher standards. Similar patterns are evident in some of the state cases in the volume.

Financial Incentives and Preparation

Three new lines of argument evolved in the 1990s relative to the role of financial aid in promoting access to higher education: the historic federal role and policy research on student aid recognized links between preparation, financial aid, and college enrollment (Jackson, 1978; Manski & Wise, 1983); some researchers documented a correlation between merit aid and student achievement and argued that merit aid would influence improved academic preparation (Bishop, 2002, 2004); and programs that guaranteed student aid for low-income high school students were associated with improved preparation and higher enrollment rates for low-income students (Evenbeck, Seabrook,

St. John, & Murphy, 2004; St. John, Hu, & Fisher, 2011). Guarantees of financial aid in middle or early high school have the potential to influence academic preparation by easing concerns about costs among low-income families provided that the signals are clear and the criteria for eligibility are simple (Daun-Barnett, 2011).

There are major differences between merit- and need-based financial aid with respect to who receives the aid (Heller, 2004b; Heller & Marin, 2002). Merit aid is disproportionally awarded to high- and middle-income students who have modest or no financial need, while need-based aid is targeted to students from low-income families who may not otherwise be able to afford college. Dynarski (2000) found that the merit-based Georgia HOPE scholarship had a positive effect of increasing participation in higher education by approximately 7%, but it also increased the participation gap between Black and White students. In an ideal system colleges would limit considerations of merit to the admissions process and award institutional aid based upon demonstrated need rather than merit (McPherson & Schapiro, 1998). Competition for high-ability students by colleges and the aims of states to retain high-achieving students are among the rationales for merit aid.

Whereas the role of student aid is normally considered part of enrollment research, its potential impact on preparation is a distinct issue that happens earlier in the education pipeline. A student would have to know about aid awards by at least 10th grade for the aid to have an impact on preparation. The financial aid guarantees in Twenty-First Century Scholars, the Washington State Achievers, and the Kalamazoo Promise, for example, have this type of award feature and have a documented positive effect (DesJardins & McCall, 2009; St. John, Hu, & Fisher, 2011).

The role of student financial aid in academic preparation remains a contested issue. The education policy literature of the 1990s drew an artificial distinction between preparation and student aid, leaving student aid out of the analyses on enrollment. In this book, we take a more balanced approach, considering the role of finances throughout the educational pipeline. Both the availability of student aid and the expectation that students and their families can afford the cost of college can have an effect on the decisions students make about their high school curriculum and the effort they give to their coursework, but to date these relationships have not been confirmed through empirical evidence.

A Troubling Discourse

The policy discourse is troubling, not only because of the misuse of research in the proofiness rationales of policy advocacy, but also because the barriers for preparation have not been fully addressed. Underlying the debate is a huge assumption that has largely gone unexamined: all students have to be more highly prepared than in the past in order to enroll in college.

In the 1960s and 1970s, the United States had a highly successful system of education that provided multiple pathways through high school and into college. The new graduation standards advocated by the National Governor's Association (Conklin & Curran, 2005) aligned high school completion with admission to a 4-year college—a standard that prioritizes the 4-year path at the expense of others. One of the pathways in the old system was from high school to employment, possibly with some additional postsecondary education in some of the trades. The technical education provided by community colleges and proprietary schools often led to employment, with many students not continuing on to a 4-year college. The jobs that low-income students could get after a technical education did not always pay sufficiently to cover the debt necessary if low-income students wanted to attain a 4-year degree, especially in proprietary schools (Grubb, 1996a, 1996b). In fact, there was an embedded incentive in the old system to drop out when a threshold for employment was met. These barriers to attainment merited attention, but having a technical pathway was not necessarily a problem.

Policy advocacy to improve high school preparation is intertwined with advocacy for science, technology, engineering, and mathematics (STEM) education. An underlying assumption is that to be competitive in the international labor market and to participate in a 21st-century knowledge economy, the American workforce must have a stronger educational foundation in science and math (e.g., Commission on the Skills of the American Workforce, 2007), a claim that is reminiscent of the post-Sputnik era. There are also renewed calls for more innovation in STEM education (National Governors Association, 2007). If we look back to the 1960s, the period of growth in high school graduation rates, high school graduates benefited from math innovations funded by NDEA. In the middle 1970s when college enrollment rates were nearly equal across racial groups,[11] there was a substantial emphasis on innovation in both higher education and K–12 education.

The decline in high school graduation rates in the 1970s could have been an early warning sign of a problem, but the accountability approach that emerged—raising graduation requirements and using alignment of tests and content—stymied innovation, a clear intent of *A Nation at Risk*. Although the movement toward more rigorous standards for high school graduation may be appropriate, it should not occur at the expense of curricular innovation. The alignment of curriculum and testing reduces the freedom of teachers to adapt and change and to develop a curriculum that actually accelerates learning, which leads to students going to college underprepared (St. John, Masse, Lijana, & Bigelow, in review).

A further complication is that the economic rationale for pushing preparation and college for all has weakened, at least temporarily. The decades of encouragement for more students to prepare for and enroll in college has had an apparent impact on enrollment rates, which increased considerably after 1980. But the links between college degrees and employment after college weakened since the economic recession of 2008, partly a consequence of an anemic labor market (Marksjarvis, 2010).

The argument that improving high school preparation was the best means of improving access to postsecondary education took hold in the discourse on higher education without critical thought about the quality or meaning of the research cited. The statistical problems with the finding that high school math courses are correlated with college enrollment were largely overlooked by advocates for altering graduation requirements. The use of the correlation as part of reports advocating for changes in high school graduation requirements illustrates a form of proofiness that misuses statistical research to promote political agendas. We have reached a point in time when it is possible to discern the relationship between policies and their outcomes. High school preparation is likely to remain a crucial issue in public policy over the next few decades, as states adjust policies to enable more students to prepare for and complete college.

CHANGES IN GRADUATION POLICY AND EDUCATIONAL OUTCOMES

An examination of trends in state policies and related outcomes provides a way of viewing the relationship between the trends in policies and achievement outcomes (see Table 3.1).

First, we examine trends in policies affecting the academic curriculum of high schools in relation to the policy discourse on academic preparation for college above. This provides insight into the ways state policymakers in K–12 and higher education responded to policy research and advocacy reports. Next we examine trends in related outcomes—test scores and high school graduation rates—the intermediate achievement outcomes directly related to these policies. Changes in access occur as a consequence of changes in preparation (i.e., courses completed, achievement, and graduation), other policies (including student aid), and other factors, including economic conditions in states.

Changes in Graduation Policy

State policymakers responded to arguments about education reform in the 1990s and 2000s, as illustrated in the trends in Table 4.1. One of the early targets of education reform was the content of the academic curriculum. In 1990, only seven states had established math content standards consistent with those articulated by the National Council of Teachers of Mathematics (NCTM); by 2000, all 50 states had adopted those standards. None of the states required algebra I for high school graduation in 1990, the point at which the algebra findings were widely distributed (e.g., Pelavin & Kane, 1990). The number of states with this requirement increased steadily and reached 26, more than half, by 2010. This illustrates the impact that the correlation between 8th-grade math and college enrollment, the central finding of the Pelavin and Kane report, seems to have had on K–12 policy.

The number of states requiring at least one math course for graduation also increased. Most states (33) required only one or two courses for high school graduation in 1990, and only 11 required three or more. By 2010, the number had reversed: 31 states required three or more courses while 13 required only one or two. Only six states retained local control over curriculum. Some or all districts within local control states required one or more math courses, and the number of math courses required at the local level in these states may have increased. The overall pattern of change toward more math requirements reflects the emphasis on math education and STEM fields in the policy discourse. Yet since the new graduation standards often require more English, science, language, and other advanced subjects, the influence of advocacy for improving the STEM pipeline has not been the only force for change.

Standards for other content areas, including English, were also implemented during the period. In math, most states have standards consistent with recommendations of the National Council of Teachers of Math (NCTM). In contrast, literacy and English standards vary more substantially across states, where debates about phonic versus critical literacy are still being waged. Therefore the meaning of math standards is more constant across states than are standards for English or other subjects, which are more likely to be influenced by local and state politics.

It is important to recognize that, while this period might be characterized as one of constraining the high school curriculum, the policies adopted since 1980 exhibit efforts both to constrain the curriculum as well as to differentiate it. In addition to the standardization of course content, other policies related to high school graduation requirements also changed during this 20-year period: the number of states with honors diplomas rose from 15 in 1990 to a high of 22 in 2005 but dropped to 14 in 2010; the number of states requiring exams to graduate increased from 15 to 28; and the proportion of high schools offering advanced placement (AP) courses increased substantially (from 45% in 1990 to 67% in 2010).

Table 4.1 State K–12 Policy Indicators for Selected Years, 1990–2010

	1990	1995	2000	2005	2010
Policy-related variables					
State established content standards in math	7	46	50	50	50
Requires 3 or more math courses for graduation	11	12	21	28	31
Requires 1 or 2 math courses for graduation	33	31	24	17	13
Requires at least algebra I or above	0	2	12	22	26
High school curriculum is locally controlled	6	7	5	5	6
Offers an honors diploma	15	17	19	22	14
Exam required for high school diploma*	–	12	14	19	28
Percentage of schools participating in AP*§	45%	51%	58%	62%	67%
Percentage of students taking SAT∞	42%*	41%	44%	49%	
9th-grade cohort size (millions)	3.2	3.32	3.79	3.96	
Outcomes of Interest					
SAT verbal mean	500	504	505	508	
SAT math mean	501	506	514	520	
SAT combined	1001	1010	1019	1028	
Graduation Rate**	73.6	71.8	71.7	74.7	

Source: Promoting Equity in Higher Education Project, National Center for Institutional Diversity (NCID). University of Michigan, Ann Arbor.

*Based on numbers reported in 1991.

§Reflects the median percentage for AP and the median dollars per FTE for K–12 expenditures.

†Dollars reported are unadjusted.

∞These numbers reflect the national figures reported by Educational Testing Service.

**National Center for Education Statistics (2009). Table 103, High school graduates, by sex and control of school: Selected years, 1869–1870 through 2018–2019. Digest of Education Statistics. Retrieved November 12, 2010, from http://nces. ed.gov/programs/digest/d09/

The availability of AP courses in high schools also has variable meaning across states. A few states pay for of the cost of taking the AP exam,[12] but most do not. Further, access to AP courses in high school is subject to tracking and other sorting mechanisms, as is access to an honor diploma. Nevertheless the wide adoption of AP courses illustrates that a college-related curriculum has become more widely available, consistent with advocates of 9–14 education (see Text Box 4.1).

Outcomes Related to Graduation Requirements

The outcomes related to standards and other graduation requirements are achievement on tests and high school graduation rates. In Table 4.1 we use SAT scores as illustrative. The individual and state average scores for other standardized tests tend to vary with the SAT, the admissions test used by most top-tier universities. These relationships hold even after controlling for the proportion of state residents who take the SAT—a necessary adjustment given that SAT takers in ACT states tend to score higher because only top students considering schools out of state take the test.

The correspondence between implementation of new policies and test scores seems clear. As more math policies were implemented, SAT math scores rose. In addition, the percentage of students taking the SAT increased, which does not normally correspond

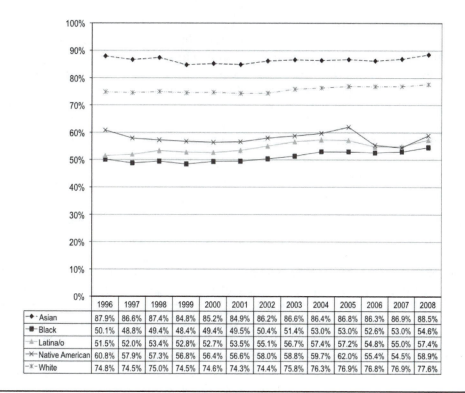

	1996	1997	1998	1999	2000	2001	2002	2003	2004	2005	2006	2007	2008
Asian	87.9%	86.6%	87.4%	84.8%	85.2%	84.9%	86.2%	86.6%	86.4%	86.8%	86.3%	86.9%	88.5%
Black	50.1%	48.8%	49.4%	48.4%	49.4%	49.5%	50.4%	51.4%	53.0%	53.0%	52.6%	53.0%	54.6%
Latina/o	51.5%	52.0%	53.4%	52.8%	52.7%	53.5%	55.1%	56.7%	57.4%	57.2%	54.8%	55.0%	57.4%
Native American	60.8%	57.9%	57.3%	56.8%	56.4%	56.6%	58.0%	58.8%	59.7%	62.0%	55.4%	54.5%	58.9%
White	74.8%	74.5%	75.0%	74.5%	74.6%	74.3%	74.4%	75.8%	76.3%	76.9%	76.8%	76.9%	77.6%

Figure 4.1 U.S. Public High School Graduation Rates for 9th-Grade Cohorts by Race/Ethnicity

Source: Data from NCES Common Core of Data © 2011 Projects Promoting Equity in Urban and Higher Education, NCID at the University of Michigan.

with increased scores.[13] However, there could be confounding factors such as the increased availability of AP courses, so we need a better standard of proof of relationship. There was no relationship between English/literacy standards, also adopted in all states, and test scores in English, which increased only modestly over time. If AP is the explanation, one would expect the verbal score to increase at the same or a similar rate as the one in math. Of course standards can vary along with the content of English courses, which may be a confounding factor that makes this comparison inappropriate.

Graduation rates continued to decline from 1990 to 2000, but they rose between 2004 and 2008 (National Center for Education Statistics, 2009). The reasons for the decline and rise in rates are not readily apparent, nor are the reasons why the reform policies only modestly narrowed the gap across races. It is possible, for example, that the initial policy adoption of more rigorous requirements led to the decline, and the adaptation of school systems to the new reforms allowed the entire system to adjust, leading to stronger outcomes. A closer examination of state variation across states (Part II) can help inform this process. Below we briefly consider the links between policies and these outcomes.

Many of the K–12 reform policies in recent decades have been rationalized as means of closing the opportunity gap for underrepresented minorities compared to majority students (an issue discussed above). NCLB required that states report their outcomes disaggregated by race/ethnicity precisely for this reason. Yet when trends in high graduation rates are examined by racial/ethnic group (Figure 4.1), there has been only a slight narrowing of the gap. Graduation rates for Whites improved slightly between 1996 and 2008, rising from 74.8% of entering freshmen to 77.8%, a 3 percentage point gain. In contrast, the graduation rate for Latinos/as rose from 51.5% to 57.4% from 1996 to 2008, a 5.9 percentage point gain. African Americans improved their graduation rate by 4.5 percentage points over the 12 years, from 50.1% to 54.6%. Most of the improvement for Whites, Latinos/as, and African Americans occurred in the 2000s, which is the time period of the most substantial changes in graduation requirements. So there is some reason to conclude that the new policies have worked. Yet the overall gains remain small and the gaps loom large.

Interpreting Trends

There appears to be a relationship between math achievement and policies promoting math, a logical and reasonable outcome; however, caution should be used in interpreting these trends. A number of other factors, including population migration and state demography, can influence outcomes. It is also possible that other policies at the state or federal levels, not accounted for in the tables above, have influenced these outcomes. In addition to examining the correspondence between policies and trends in outcomes, it is important to look at research that examines the links between policy decisions for high schools and related outcomes. We summarize research on the relationship between requirements for graduation and related outcomes below. The research findings merit consideration in policy deliberations about high school reform and college admissions, but there are many remaining questions about the ways education policies are linked to outcomes related to academic preparation, college access, and college success.

THE RESEARCH BASE ON ACADEMIC PREPARATION

States have adopted a wide array of policies intended to influence student outcomes in high school, and, in many cases, those policies have been rationalized to better prepare students for college. This section summarizes research examining the effects of policy on student achievement and high school completion. Substantial advances have been made in recent years by education researchers and economists studying the factors influencing student achievement and high school completion. Therefore we provide a summative review to help readers sort through the research evidence. We first summarize research using state indicators, including new analyses for this book, and second summarize key studies using other sources of data, including the large-scale federal longitudinal studies.

Research Using State Indicators

One analytic strategy for evaluating the influence of policies on educational outcomes is to examine state-year panel data that include indicators for state demographic characteristics, educational outcomes, and educational policies. The key to drawing inferences from these sorts of analyses is to employ fixed effects regression techniques or alternative quasiexperimental approaches that can account for differences between states and changes that occur over time. We know that comparisons of states on educational measures are difficult because states are unique and complex places with different histories, structures, ideologies, and political preferences. Comparisons between states are naturally limited because analyses cannot control for all unique state characteristics. Fixed effects models, however, allow the examination of *within* state differences over time, recognizing that many characteristics of states remain constant. The empirical strategy, then, is to examine the relationship between the outcomes of interest and the adoption of particular policies while fixing the effects of states and adding controls for characteristics that may change.

In earlier work conducted by the senior author and colleagues, indicators were developed and analyzed to examine the relationship between key state policies intended to influence high school preparation for college and two important outcomes pertaining to college access—SAT math scores and high school graduation rates. In that work, St. John (2006) explores the impact of state requirements in math courses, adoption of NCTM content standards, mandatory exit exams, the presence of an honors diploma alternative, average K–12 expenditures per student, and the proportion of high schools offering AP courses in the state on aggregated student outcomes. The study found, after controlling for poverty, race, and state population, that between 1991 and 2000, state education policies were related to both SAT math scores and high school graduation rates. Yet the upturn in graduation did not occur until the 2000s, so it is possible that an analysis of more recent trends would have a different finding.

In its review of the research on exit exams, *Incentives and Test-Based Accountability in Education,* the National Research Council (2011) concluded that exit exams for high school students did not improve achievement and actually reduced high school graduation rates. Given these results, we conclude that policymakers should reconsider the use of high school exit exams. Other incentive-based testing strategies had mostly mixed results. The Research Council provided guidance on the design of research that could further test the effects of incentive-based testing schemes at the state and local levels.

Adding the requirement to complete three or four math courses was positively related to average SAT math scores (controlling for the proportion of the high school cohort that took the SAT) but negatively related to high school graduation rates. It may be that the policy raises the bar higher than some students are able to achieve, which increases the dropout rate, but those who are able to fulfill the requirement are better prepared for college and more competitive in the admissions process. Adoption of state content standards in accordance with the NCTM guidelines and the expansion of AP offerings exhibited the same relationships, which should not be surprising given that state reform strategies typically address both course requirements and content standards concurrently. Mandatory exit exams did not affect SAT math scores, but it appears that graduation rates grew subsequent to the adoption of the policy. K–12 funding was not related to SAT scores but was positively related to high school graduation rates.

In a more recent study, Daun-Barnett and St. John (2012) updated the analyses through 2008 and considered the level of rigor expected in math (as approximated by whether states identify which courses to take, including algebra I, geometry, and algebra II). The findings were similar, though with several important differences. Where K–12 funding was significant relative to high school completion through the year 2000, it was also positively related to SAT math scores when more recent data were included. The relationship between mandatory exit exams and high school graduation rates is reversed in the most recent analysis, suggesting that the test may be a barrier to high school completion. The difference may be a consequence of the amount of time it takes to fully implement a policy, which is commonly phased in gradually. Finally, requiring specific courses in math does not appear to affect either SAT math scores or high school graduation rates.

Recent Studies of High School Graduation

We examine research published in three areas: statistical analysis reports published by the U.S. Department of Education, research published as part of the National Bureau of Economic Research (NBER) working paper series, and peer-reviewed articles in top journals in education, including *Educational Evaluation and Policy Analysis,* the *American Educational Research Journal,* and *Educational Policy.* This summative review is not exhaustive but is representative of the broader literature in this area. We draw upon these sources to examine the various approaches to establishing and examining the linkages of state policies to student outcomes.

Course Requirements and Student Course Taking

The first important linkage between course requirement policies and student success is established through student course-taking patterns. NCES has examined this relationship in several reports. Statistical analysis reports issued by NCES, including those discussed earlier in the chapter, serve as a useful barometer for trends in student outcomes over time, but they are less robust in terms of assessing the impacts of policies on those outcomes. Horn and Nuñez (2000) found that first-generation students are more likely to be from low-income families, less likely to complete algebra I in 8th grade, less likely to take advanced math in high school, and less likely to attend college even if they completed a college preparatory curriculum. Two reports on course taking in math and science (Dalton, Ingels, Downing, & Bozick, 2007; Planty, Provasnik, & Daniel, 2007) concluded that students in 2004 were completing more courses in both math and science than high school graduates from 1982 but that gaps by race and ethnicity remained and that high school students were completing more demanding courses. In 1982, just over 10% reported taking calculus or precalculus; that number increased to 33% in 2004. These reports suggest that requiring more of students in high school has resulted in more students who are well prepared. These reports, however, do not discuss the declining graduation rates over the same time periods. Planty and colleagues (2007) considered course taking among dropouts in 2004 and concluded that they progress at a slower rate than traditional graduates, but the authors did not address the changing graduation rates. A 2008 report links course taking to achievement and finds that students improve in math from 10th to 12th grade by one third of a standard deviation, which represents a shift from basic to intermediate concepts; they approximate that 4% of students reach an advanced level of proficiency by the end of high school (Bozick & Ingels, 2008).

More recent analytic reports by NCES avoid some of the incendiary claims heavily criticized in the earlier reports. They are appropriately cautious about the generalizability of their findings, but they continue to omit important factors related to course taking and achievement that should be considered or at least acknowledged. Two examples are illustrative. Schools vary in terms of their curricular offerings; therefore some students will not be able to complete a particular sequence because it is not available to them. Similarly, whereas the studies acknowledge motivation as a possible factor, they do not acknowledge that some sequences will not allow students to make additional progress, meaning that they have gone as far as they can go in high school—a finding illustrating the cumulative nature of the early years of schooling and the consequences for later success. Thus it continues to be necessary to view college preparation as a P–16 issue and not just an issue for high schools.

Education researchers have examined the relationship between established policies and student course-taking patterns utilizing more sophisticated quasiexperimental techniques, and their findings are instructive but limited in similar ways. Clune and White (1992) found that in high-requirement states, students completed more courses in the core academic subjects and higher levels of coursework in math and science. Their study was limited to four purposefully selected states and did not consider trends in high school completion or transcript patterns for noncompleters, a potential source of bias, because a higher bar may prevent more students from completing high school and may thus lead to an overestimation of the increases in course taking. Allensworth and colleagues (2009) focused their attention on the requirement policies of the CPS and found that although more students took entry-level courses (English I and algebra I), failure rates in those courses increased and test scores remained unchanged. The implication here is that prior preparation is an important factor, but in order to substantially improve these outcomes, more must be done to improve student learning in the earlier grades. Allensworth's study addresses school-level selection bias, which is common in these sorts of studies. However, even at the district level, it is unclear how well the Chicago findings will generalize well to rural or suburban settings or to other states.

In addition, economists have not examined course-taking patterns as an outcome of state, district, or school policies; instead, they consider course taking or strength of curriculum as a control in studies of student achievement, examined in the next section. Overall, despite the fact that course taking is the critical link between graduation requirement policies, student achievement, and college readiness, the research in this area is not fully developed; therefore the NCES reports, which are largely descriptive in nature, may fill an important void in the policy discourse. This has ultimately led to the adoption of these policies with limited empirical support for their impact. If anything, the work by Allensworth is suggestive that the policy has limited if any impact, particularly in urban districts.

Student Achievement

Despite the voluminous literature examining student achievement, NCES has published relatively few reports on the topic. Such reports typically rely on comparisons utilizing National Assessment of Educational Progress (NAEP) data, including summary trend analyses in the annual *Digest of Education Statistics* (National Center for Education Statistics, 2010; Rampey, Dion, & Donahue, 2009). Trend analyses of NAEP suggest that mean test scores declined or remained flat in both math and reading across the age cohorts from 1990 to 2004. The 2008 results suggest a modest increase, but the difference is not significant. The only group for whom there appear to be consistent gains comprises 9-year-olds, where gains in both reading and math have been slow but consistent since 1990. These reports also suggest that some progress has been made in terms of narrowing gaps by race. Both Black and Hispanic students have posted larger increases over time than White students across all three age cohorts.

Another source of trend data on student achievement is the series of longitudinal studies conducted by NCES. A 2006 report tracks changes in 10th-grade test scores in math and reading across three time periods—1980, 1990, and 2002. In reading, there were no detectable differences in the aggregate from 1980 to 2002, but there were differences by racial/ethnic groups. Both African American and Hispanic students were less likely to demonstrate the highest level of proficiency in reading in 2002 than in 1990. In math, test score trends indicate significant positive growth from 1980 to 2002, but most of that gain occurred between 1980 and 1990 (Cahalan et al., 2006); the gains from 1990 to 2002 are significant but the effect size is small, suggesting that not much progress had been made when many of these state policies were taking effect.

Course-Taking and Student Achievement

Educational researchers have frequently considered the relationship between high school graduation requirements in the core academic subjects and student achievement as measured by test scores, particularly in math; generally the findings are mixed. Chaney, Burgdorf, and Atash (1997) conclude, in their analysis of NAEP data and the 1990 high school transcript study, that most students were not affected by the policy because they were already taking more courses than were required, but that for marginal students there might be an effect. Lee, Croninger, and Smith (1997) tested the constrained curriculum hypothesis and found that when schools narrow curricular options in math, students' math scores rise. They also concluded that adopting this policy at the school level does not increase achievement gaps by socioeconomic status. Lee and colleagues pay particular attention to the structure of the school and utilize multilevel modeling techniques, but their findings may not generalize well to the state policy context, in part because they do not account for the potential selection bias associated with schools' ability to choose the curriculum they offer based on the students they serve. Teitelbaum (2003) found that when schools adopt higher requirements in math and science, the number of courses they complete increases, but there is no apparent effect on levels of achievement. Like Lee and colleagues, Teitelbaum focuses on school policy and is therefore limited in similar ways; but in this case, his findings contradict the earlier work.

School Choice and Student Achievement

School choice has been an issue of great public policy debate for decades. Educators, policymakers, and researchers have considered a range of strategies, including public choice alternatives, charters (public and private), and vouchers. Education researchers and economists have spent a great deal of time examining the influences and implications of choice strategies, and their conclusions are mixed. Generally, education researchers approach these questions from a sociological perspective concerned with the potential for exacerbating existing inequities through the use of market forces in education. Economists, on the other hand, embrace market-based solutions to entrenched education problems. Some economists argue that choice benefits students by providing a range of opportunities and introducing competition and, if the market works as it should, it should drive down the unit cost of education. For example, Hoxby (2002) argues that the key linkage between school choice and student achievement is school productivity and that choice forces schools to respond to market forces and to become more productive in the process. These different orientations to the problem lead to slightly different questions and conclusions regarding the effects of school choice strategies. NCES has not entered into this policy conversation largely because their sources of data are not designed to address variations on school choice.

One version of public school choice is the magnet school model employed across many urban districts in the United States. In districts that adopt a magnet model, high schools or communities within schools are identified with a particular curricular focus. Students are then given the opportunity to apply to a range of schools in the district with programs aligned with their academic and career interests. Generally, this model assumes that 8th-grade students (and their parents) are sufficiently aware of their options and know what careers they would like to pursue. The concern among critics is that magnets effectively redistribute students by schools and that schools serve as ability tracks, leaving some schools to serve the least prepared students. Archibald (2004) conducted a study of district magnet policies combined with public data from the common core of data (CCD) and found that among urban school districts with five or more high schools, magnet schools were not related to differences in student achievement or school attendance. His findings suggest that magnets do not provide the benefits advocates might suggest.

Bifulco, Cobb, and Bell (2009) conducted a study of interdistrict school choice in Connecticut and reached much more optimistic conclusions. Their study of data from Connecticut's central cities suggests that magnet schools lead to less racially and economically segregated school settings for students and have a positive effect on math and reading achievement. Cullen, Jacob, and Levitt (2006) examined data from school choice efforts including magnets and career academies in Chicago and found that although students who choose to attend a school other than the one assigned by the district exhibit higher achievement and greater probability for high school completion, those differences are attributed to selection, meaning that they differ on unobserved characteristics like motivation. Their study illustrates one of the reasons why Hoxby (2004) suggests that economists are well suited to address questions related to education reform—econometrics provide a variety of analytic tools to deal with studies of nonrandom samples, where problems of selection are particularly common.

Teacher Quality and Student Achievement

In recent years, schools of education have come under fire from policymakers concerned that teachers are not adequately prepared to educate future generations. As a consequence, recent policy dialogues have debated the merits of evaluating teacher performance relative to student achievement. Clotfelter, Ladd, and Vigdor (2007) found, in a study of North Carolina teachers, that the quality of teacher training made a difference in terms of student achievement. In particular, their findings suggest that years of experience are positively related to student test scores and that state licensure, board certification, teacher test scores, and subject certification were all positively related to student achievement. Clotfelter and colleagues also found that teachers from very highly competitive undergraduate institutions were more likely to have students who achieved better.

In a study of teacher qualifications in New York City, researchers found that the gap in teacher qualifications has narrowed since 2000 (Boyd, Lankford, Loeb, Rockoff, & Wyckoff, 2008). Consistent with prior work, they noted that less prepared teachers were disproportionately found in the highest-need schools in 2000. Since then, the proportion of teachers with fewer than 3 years of experience, who are uncertified, or who attended the least selective undergraduate institutions have decreased in low-poverty schools and their teachers' test scores have risen. The authors suggest the narrowing gaps are a result of the hiring of new teachers, particularly by replacing temporarily licensed teachers with participants in the Teaching Fellows program and Teach for America.

High School Completion

A potential concern for policymakers is whether increasing course requirements will limit students' chances for completing high school. The research on this question has been mixed. Most studies of graduation requirement policies focus on the relationship between course taking and student achievement. Hoffer (1997) found, in his analysis of the National Education Longitudinal Study (NELS) 1988 data, that higher course requirements in math had no discernible effect on high school dropout behavior or student achievement. Teitelbaum (2003), in a literature review, concluded that prior research had found no relationship between course requirements and high school completion. More recent research examining the relationship between these state-level policies and aggregated state outcomes demonstrates that high-requirement states have lower high school graduation rates on average than low-requirement states (St. John, 2004). The differences may reflect changing patterns over time. The state policy context regarding course requirements was much less rigid in the late 1980s and early 1990s than it was near the turn of the 21st century.

Policymakers frequently debate the merits of social promotion—the practice of promoting students to the next grade before they have demonstrated their capability to master coursework at the current level. Jacob and Lefgren (2007) examined the effects of grade retention in Chicago public schools (CPS). In 1996, CPS eliminated the practice of social promotion and began assessing students at 3rd, 6th, and 8th grade to ensure proficiency. Jacob and Lefgren found that the effects of grade retention differed by age. Students held back in 6th grade demonstrated no differences in terms of completion rates, but older students who were held back a year were less likely to finish high school. The implication is that educators need to address deficiencies earlier, not only because of the cumulative nature of content but also because younger students are less likely to be affected.

Mandatory exit exams have been adopted by a number of states to hold schools and districts accountable for student outcomes. Carnoy and Loeb (2002) analyzed state data for the National Assessment of Educational Progress (NAEP) and found that in high accountability states, test scores were higher on average and there was no effect on high school completion. Papay, Murnane, and Willett (2008) focused their attention on the effects of high stakes testing in urban settings in Massachusetts and found that implementation of the Massachusetts Comprehensive Assessment System (MCAS) reduced a student's probability of finishing high school on time by 8 percentage points. A similar trend was evident when students failed the 8th-grade assessment. Their findings do not generalize to rural or suburban communities, suggesting that high-stakes testing may have a disproportionate impact on students from urban schools—many of whom are low-income underrepresented minorities.

High schools have been a target for reform for many years, and policymakers are insistent that policy levers can improve high school outcomes. Of course as the review of literature above demonstrates, there are trade-offs to any policy decision, and it has been difficult to tease apart the relative effects of multiple policies or to weigh effectively the costs and benefits of each alternative. Course-taking policies may increase the number of courses completed in the core subjects, but the possibility exists that fewer students will be able to complete high school. Charter schools may demonstrate improved student achievement in some cases, but the selection processes vary and the cost of scaling these interventions are costly at a time when state and local budgets are shrinking. Exit exams feed into our fixation on accountability and may help to shine a light on the disparities in educational outcomes by race and income, and, as some suggest, there may be benefits to students in terms of increased test scores, but the impact of these tests for high school graduation rates remains an unanswered question. Past research has demonstrated that retaining students at grade level may reduce the chances that students will finish high school, but more recent evidence suggests that this may depend on how early in their schooling they are held back.

The picture is even murkier when you consider that policies are never adopted in isolation. Every state has a unique combination of policies intended to influence student outcomes in high school, and those policy preferences interact differently within the state's unique social and political context. Equally, districts are often free to exercise discretion on a number of these fronts. For example, CPS might eliminate the practice of social promotion, but other districts continue to use the practice within the same state. Or New York City might embrace alternative paths to teacher training that are not employed in the more moderate size cities upstate. The differences may help us explain contradictory findings like the differences between the state-level analyses of test scores and high school completion conducted by Carnoy and Loeb (2002) and the district-level analysis in a single urban community as presented by Papay et al.(2008). The context matters both because we are discussing different students and different policy combinations.

CONCLUSIONS

When researchers and policymakers discuss issues related to the role of graduation requirements and choice schemes in outcomes, it is important to distinguish between (a) policy rationale building to make arguments for new public policies and (b) research using sound logic and methods that assess the links between policies and student outcomes. After three decades of reforms based on spurious use of correlations between family background variables, high school course completion, and college enrollment rates, it is time for a new generation of research that actually assesses how policies are linked to student outcomes. The purpose of such research should be to inform the refinement of educational policies and school reforms.

In this chapter, we first presented a review of the policy discourse, including the uses of research in rationale building, trends in policies in relation to outcomes, and a review of recent research examining the links between policies and outcomes. The topic of college preparation had not been a major issue in earlier periods, when access was relatively elite, or even in the movement toward mass access after World War II through the GI Bill and the enrollment of the baby boom generation (the children of World War II veterans). However, as federal support for grants declined, a gap opened in enrollment rates for majority and underrepresented minority students (URMs). Policy analysts working under contract for the U.S. Department of Education focused on differences in access to advanced math (algebra I, geometry, and algebra II) as an explanation for the gap. A subsequent wave of policy reports focused on this correlation, and new policy rationales were developed that argued for improving high school preparation as a means of narrowing the gap in college enrollment. Thus college preparation became central to the policy discourse on higher education as most state higher education agencies became advocates for raising standards.

Second, we reviewed trends in policy changes and related high school outcomes indicating an evolving pattern. In the 1990s, states implemented new math standards and raised requirements, and the number of students taking that SAT rose, as did their average scores on the math portion of the test. High school graduation rates declined slightly in the late 1990s but have improved in the early 21st century. There has also been a slight narrowing of the gap in high school graduation rates between URM groups and majority students, although these gaps remain substantial. With the improved standards and math requirements and the rise in graduation rates, it appears that more students are entering college academically prepared, at least if readiness is measured by completion of courses, standards for courses, and test scores. There is still a substantial need for improvement in graduation rates, especially given that K–12 education is arguably a right of citizenship (Moses & Cobb, 2001; Perry, Moses, Wynne, Delpit, & Cortes, 2010). Improving the quality of math and other college preparatory education to provide more students with meaningful opportunities to realize this right is a challenge for educators and policymakers.

Third, we found that the research evidence on the effects of new policies on achievement and high school graduation is mixed; but when the research is placed in a proper chronology, there does seem to be some improvement in outcomes that is directly linked to educational policies in the 2000s. However, the gaps in opportunity to graduate from high school remain substantial for African Americans and Latinos/as compared with Whites. We suggest a few questions about policy formulation and research for researchers and policymakers (Text Box 4.2). Although equity may have been one of the espoused rationalizations for the policies considered above, it may not have been a central concern in the actual formulation or adoption of those policies.

Text Box 4.2 Questions About Academic Preparation

About Policy

- How could policymakers make better use of research in their deliberations, given the ambiguities of the research?

- How can researchers be more effective addressing and answering policy-relevant questions and conveying their findings to the policy community?

- How have old liberal, conservative, neoconservative, and new progressive political rationales informed policies on academic preparation?

- Given their imperatives for election and reelection, should legislators be concerned about the links between implemented policies and outcomes, or should they emphasize policies advocated by their political constituents?

- How should policy analysts working in state and federal agencies or conducting studies for these agencies respond to political pressures to present research that supports the political positions?

- How might policy change to reflect a genuine commitment to achieving racial/ethnic equity across academic preparation?

About Research

- Why is it important to look at the role of policies in place within states when considering the relationships between high school courses completed and achievement outcomes and high school graduation?

- What roles do family income and financial aid play in students' decisions to complete high school or to take rigorous courses in high school?

- What types of interventions are likely to overcome barriers created by differences in parents' experience with college and the ways students learn about barriers to college and pathways through college?

- Does research on the effects of educational requirements and school-choice schemes explain the trends in test scores and graduation rates?

- What topics related to academic preparation merit further research?

- How might our questions differ if we researchers wish to make equity a central part of the policy dialogue?

5

ACCESS TO HIGHER EDUCATION

Access to higher education is in its fourth stage of evolution in the United States: (1) from the colonial period through the Civil War college access was limited, although there were proposals for a new generation of public colleges; (2) between the Civil War and World War II, the nation's systems of public and private nonprofit colleges developed, but there was still limited access; (3) from World War II through the 1980s was a period of mass access owing to the return of veterans, followed by the enrollment of their children (Trow, 1974); and (4) the current period, which is characterized by movement toward universal access (Altbach, 2010). This period of transition to universal access—when all adults are encouraged to attain some type of postsecondary education—coincides with U.S. engagement in the global economy and growing inequality in wealth and educational attainment (Freidman, 2005). In the earlier period of mass higher education, the discourse on access focused on structural solutions to meeting demand, like master planning and formula funding in states (e.g., Halstead, 1974), while federal policy focused on student financial aid (e.g., National Commission on the Financing of Postsecondary Education, 1973). The shift to market systems of higher education in the United States and other developed countries has altered public finance (Slaughter & Leslie, 1997), including the use of accountability mechanisms and trade-offs of state appropriations for increased institutional autonomy.

The emphasis on improving academic preparation (Chapter 4) is appropriately understood as an artifact of this period of transition to universal access. Viewed from this vantage point, the underlying logic for the rationale might be viewed as follows: If college is desirable for all students, then all high school students should be educated to an acceptable college preparatory standard.[1] Yet, the problems created by expanding access are more complicated than simply improving preparation. Altbach (2010) argues, "As access expands, inequalities within the higher education system also grow, conditions for study for many students deteriorate" (p. ix).[2] The linkages between access, public finance strategies, and inequalities are well established in the comparative literature on public finance (e.g., Friedman, 2005).

This chapter examines the financial aspects of the discourse surrounding college participation, whereas the new policy environment for quality of education and retention are considered in the next chapter. We start with an examination of how the discourse on access and the public financing of higher education shifted during the transition from the structural period of mass access to a period of globalization and the push for universal access. Next, we consider how racial representation in higher education—the proportion of students by race/ethnicity compared with their proportion in the population—changed during the transition to universal access, focusing on the roles of college choices and enrollment management. We also provide a review of the research literature to explore how changes in policy—both finance policies related to tuition and student aid and preparation policies—are associated with college enrollment rates and choice of institution type.

POLICY DISCOURSE ON COLLEGE ACCESS

From the 1950s through the 1980s the policy literature on college finance and access was situated within the dialectic between rational/structural models that established and used systemic approaches to framing policies, while many critics argued that politics prevailed over rational analytics (Hearn, 1993, 2001; Parsons, 2004). The transition to universal access, a change situated in globalization and the privatization of higher education (Priest & St. John, 2006; Slaughter & Leslie, 1997), has altered the political and systemic aspects of public finance and access to higher education. Thus, while the debates about college preparation have dominated the policy discourse on access in Washington, D.C., there were fundamental shifts in the public financing of higher education in states and at the federal level.

Building a Mass System of Higher Education
A structural systematic approach was used to develop mass systems of education in the United States after World War II. Access to higher education before World War II was appropriately characterized as "elite," with a relatively small percentage of the population attending college. After World War II, massive numbers of veterans returned and enjoyed the benefits of the GI Bill, which sent large number of adults to college and changed the in loco parentis aspect of campus life across the nation (Thelin, 2004b). The federal investment in the GI Bill substantially benefited the U.S. economy during the economic boom following World War II (Bound & Turner, 2002). Also following World War II, the federal government adopted a systematic approach to the development of new social programs. During World War II, the United States used the Program-Planning-Budgeting System (PPBS) as part of the strategy for international cooperation among the allies; this systematic approach migrated into federal and state policy at war's end (Shultz, 1968). At the federal level, the Higher Education Act and many of the other Great Society programs were developed using systems methods. Over time, these methods changed, but they continued to be used until strategic planning came into higher education policy in the early 1980s (St. John, 1994a).[3] Below we recount the use of systems approaches at the state and federal levels.

States Developed Mass Public Systems of Higher Education
The 1960s and 1970s brought a period of mass expansion to higher education. In a very real sense, two generations gained access in rapid succession as the baby boomers (i.e., the children of the World War II generation) followed the GIs to college. During the 1970s, college enrollment rates expanded only modestly, but state systems were expanded

rapidly to accommodate the growing population (e.g., Balderston, 1974; Weathersby & Balderston, 1972).

States used rational models to plan for the systematic development of higher education in the 1960s and 1970s, and the federal government encouraged master planning in states (e.g., Halstead, 1974), a systematic process modeled after political agreements in California. The Higher Education Act (HEA) actually funded states to develop coordinating commissions and statewide plans for higher education as part of Title XII of the 1972 reauthorization of the HEA (Gladieux & Wolanin, 1976), but states had pushed toward systematic approaches long before federal encouragement.

Most states had developed public systems of higher education by the late 1960s (Lee & Bowen, 1971, 1975). Many states followed the California model, with its research universities, state colleges and universities, and community colleges. The comprehensive colleges were composed of upgraded normal schools (i.e., teachers' colleges), nursing schools, and technical colleges that expanded to offer comprehensive programs across the curriculum. In some states like New York, all 4-year and 2-year colleges were included in the same system, often with one or more "flagship" research universities. Frequently community colleges were formed from older, often locally developed junior and vocational colleges. Many states took on a larger share of funding the development of community colleges.

State systems were built to accommodate an expanding population of college-age students. Budget funding formulas were the cornerstone of rational state planning. There was an extensive literature on methods of developing state formulas, especially in the 1990s, as states began to reduce spending (e.g., Brodie, 1996; Burke, 1994; Layzell & McKeown, 1992; McKeown, 1996). Indeed, as the shift to market systems occurred in the 1990s, many state budget officers resisted, arguing for the retention of rational models. But as researchers began to study the costs and benefits of higher education as an area of investment, market forces and arguments about taxpayer savings were already taking hold (e.g., Hansen & Weisbrod, 1967). The Carnegie Commission (1973) argued for raising the percentage paid by students and families to 20% of education costs. The clash between market forces and rational funding models was well under way in the 1980s.

The federal government strongly encouraged states to develop grant programs in the 1970s. The State Student Incentive Grant Program was set up to provide matching federal funding for need-based grants in states (Gladieux & Wolanin, 1976), although funding was never sufficient to encourage states to invest at the level needed to accommodate rising tuition charges (St. John, 1994a). Institutional lobbyists argued for retaining subsidies to colleges rather than state investment in need-based aid when tax revenues were not adequate. Therefore, in most states, market models emerged as an artifact of politics, supporting the hypothesis that social process dominated over rationality in constructing higher education policy (e.g., Hearn, 1993; Wildavsky, 1969, 1979). This early federal push to adopt the market model was adopted in a few states, including Minnesota (Chapter 7), but most states followed the structural approach to funding through the 1980s.

Federal Program Planning and the Great Society

President Lyndon B. Johnson used PPBS as a systematic framework for promoting his Great Society Programs in Education (St. John, 1994a, 2003). Major programs were introduced with strong economic rationales. Federal student aid programs became the primary mechanism for supporting access for low-income students, a rationale accepted based on arguments of economists and social progressives. Most of the programs authorized in the HEA—Educational Opportunity Grants, College Work Study, and National Direct Loans—were campus based in the sense that the federal government provided grants to institutions based on proposals that these campuses would provide funding for low-income students following federal need-analysis requirements. The 1965 HEA authorized the Guaranteed Student Loan Program, which combined programs in states with a federally administered program, was the first national program with portable student aid (i.e., students could apply directly and take funds to their colleges); the earlier loan program (National Direct Student Loans) had funded campus-based lending.

In the 1972 amendments, the Basic Educational Opportunity Grants (BEOGS, now Pell) were introduced as a major new program (Gladieux & Wolanin, 1976) by President Nixon based on arguments by economists and were part of the Senate version of the reauthorization bill. Meanwhile the House proposed a major new institutional grant program under Title I. The compromise required formation of the National Commission on the Financing of Postsecondary Education to study likely benefits of institutional versus student funding. The final report provided estimates of the benefits of the two approaches, including higher enrollments from funding of student grants rather than institutions (National Commission on the Financing of Postsecondary Education, 1973). The findings were disputed (e.g., Dresch, 1975), but subsequent studies confirmed higher enrollment with increased investment in student need-based grants that were portable (St. John, 2003; Weathersby, Jackson, Jacobs, St. John, & Tingley, 1977). Gaps in enrollment rates for minority students compared with majority students nearly disappeared during this period (St. John, 2003).

In 1978, President Jimmy Carter responded to pressures from the political right to give tax credits for higher education by promoting expansion of student financial aid to middle-income students. The Middle Income Student Assistance Act of 1972 reauthorized Title IV of the HEA but removed income caps for Pell grants and guaranteed student loans. The provisions for Pell had promoted choice of college as well as basic access for low-income students. Once income caps were removed, middle-income students could receive funding through Pell, especially when they attended expensive colleges and universities. Also, colleges and universities redirected funding from Supplemental Educational Opportunity Grants from low-income students to middle-income students (St. John & Byce, 1982). At the time, institutions had substantial discretion for the distribution of SEOG aid among students with financial need, so this form of federal aid was shifted to middle-income students at many institutions. Thus, by the early 1980s, institutional preferences had begun to influence a shift in the use of federal dollars as an artifact of the discretion built into these programs. As a result, after a period of equal enrollment opportunity for Whites, Blacks, and Hispanics in the 1970s, a gap in enrollment opportunity reopened (St. John, 1994a, 2003, 2006).

In the late 1980s, during President Reagan's second term, the administration began a line of inquiry that further undermined the federal role in the privatization of public college in the high-tuition high-loan market-based system that had developed. Secretary of Education William Bennett (1986, 1987) and Assistant Secretary Chester Finn Jr. (1988a, 1988b) developed arguments that colleges were wasteful and were raising prices to increase their revenue from Pell grants, arguments not supported by research during the period (e.g., McPherson & Shapiro, 1991). During the late 1980s, funding for Pell declined as these arguments caught the attention of the press (St. John, 1994a). There was also an increased emphasis on federal and private loans as a means of funding college students (Fossey & Bateman, 1998; Hearn & Holdsworth, 2004).

From Structural Models to Market Models

After World War II, the United States followed a systems approach to developing higher education. The structural aspects of the state strategies included formation of state planning boards, master planning to build new campuses and programs, and formula funding of institutions. This provided a structural approach to responding to demand, but college enrollment rates remained stagnant in the late 1960s and 1970s even though colleges expanded to meet the demands of the burgeoning baby boomer population. States, however, had not yet initiated large-scale efforts to prepare all students for college (Oakes, 1985); that level of preparation was reserved for those students tracked to attend 4-year colleges and universities.

The federal government used a structural systems approach for student aid (designing, funding, and evaluating effects of major programs), which was initially made available through institutional grants to colleges and college awards to students. Federal loans were portable—if qualified students could take out federal loans—which is consistent with a market model for funding higher education. In the 1970s, the federal government expanded market systems of student aid that allowed students to apply directly to the federal government for grants (Pell) and loans. However, by the 1980s colleges had begun to leverage student aid, directing grants to students who would boost prestige at the same time the federal government redirected Pell grants to middle-income families without fully funding maximum awards (McPherson & Shapiro, 1991, 1998). The federal market system had been undermined even before the nation entered the transition to global markets in the 1990s.

Imperfect Markets in the Global Period

Currently, federal policy on access is framed as a national imperative in response to international competition. President Barack Obama set the goal of having 60% of the population complete college degrees as a response to the declining U.S. ranking in college access (de Nies, 2010). In his 2011 State of the Union speech, Obama evoked Sputnik as an image to stimulate a deeper American resolve to improve competitiveness in education (Obama, 2009), much as in 1958, when this image had stimulated passage of the National Defense Education Act. President Obama's voice is one of many calling for action on education reforms to expand preparation for and access to college (see Chapter 4), yet the problems remain. There has been a large disconnect between rhetoric about access and funding mechanisms that ensure opportunity.

Despite what appear to be potentially debilitating headwinds for many students and families considering college, enrollment rates have continued to increase in recent decades, during a period when the size of the college-age population was in decline (after the baby boom students had passed through their college years). Whereas enrollment rates were relatively flat in the 1970s, a period when total enrollment increased substantially, overall participation rates started rising in the early 1980s and have continued to rise. Providing at least initial access may not be as serious a challenge as retention (see Chapter 6) but as Hoxby (2004) cautions, the choice of college may be more important than whether or not students attend. Similarly, conversations regarding the equitable distribution of opportunities for low-income, first-generation, and underrepresented minority students have shifted to considering the quality of the institutions attended (Bowen & Bok, 1998; Bowen, Chingos, & McPherson, 2009). In recent decades many nations have passed by the United States in terms of the proportion of adults with a college education; the United States is now ranked 12th, with 40% of adults having a postsecondary degree (Organisation for Economic Co-operation and Development, 2010). Gaps are even greater when we consider high-demand careers in the science, technology, engineering, and mathematics (STEM) professions—e.g., the United States ranked 27th in terms of the production of engineers.

It is important to consider the meaning of access in relation to public funding. College prices have risen substantially since the 1980s, especially in 4-year colleges. If tuition charges rise substantially faster than student aid, access to more expensive colleges becomes more limited for low- and lower-middle-income students, which has been the case in the United States (Advisory Committee on Student Financial Assistance, 2010), an issue of choice that has real implications for long-term labor market outcomes. Below we examine how the discourse on public funding has changed in states and at the federal level as imperfect market-based systems developed.

State Funding and Higher Education Markets

The older, structural model of state funding relied on per student subsidies to public colleges to hold tuition down, something like the contemporary public school model. In contrast, during the transition to the global economy, states have shifted to relying more substantially on tuition as a substitute for tax dollars for public higher education (or privatization), which accounts for the substantial increases in tuition charges over the past decade and has been no more clearly evident than in states like New York, where the public system is a state agency and tuition is appropriated by the legislature. During periods of declining tax revenues, student tuitions have risen and the legislature has kept all or a significant portion of those tuition increases to offset losses in other revenue streams. To illustrate how the market model emerged in most states, we compare the old and the newer market models.

The old model of funding higher education emphasized subsidies to institutions and low tuition, an approach that had a high cost for state taxpayers per student enrolled. Access was also limited in this model because a specific number of slots were funded each year and enrollment targets were set by funding. The funding level really was thought to be the lever of providing access, especially access to many 4-year institutions that held down enrollment and did better with revenue per student. It was anticipated that enrollment would decline in the 1980s (National Center for Education Statistics, 1980); as enrollment trends illustrate, this did not happen.

Many analysts had predicted private colleges would close and public colleges would contract and merge in the 1980s after the peak of the baby boom generation passed through higher education (e.g., National Center for Education Statistics, 1970; Breneman, Finn, & Nelson, 1978). States tried to plan rationally for the expected decline, and several states decided to constrain or cap funding. For example, when Minnesota put a funding cap in place in 1977, the state university system responded by capping enrollment and maintaining education revenue per student, while state colleges let enrollment rise to meet the unexpected demand and lost revenue per student because of the cap on state funding (St. John, 1991a).

Minnesota provides one of the most interesting examples of efforts to adapt state funding strategies to the emergence of market conditions (as discussed in Chapter 6).

James Hearn and David Longanecker (1985) wrote a compelling paper on the strategy developed to balance average costs, funding, and state grants. They argued that students and their families should pay 33% of costs and need-based state grants should be used to equalize enrollment opportunities. Minnesota eventually adopted this idealized version of the market model—with a balanced emphasis on funding of colleges, families paying their share of costs, and need-based aid for students who could not afford to attend—and held to it for a sustained period (Hearn & Anderson, 1995). However, most states found it difficult to follow this version of a market model (Hossler, Lund, Ramin-Gyurnek, Westfall, & Irish, 1997), and even Minnesota found it difficult to sustain over time.

During the mid-1990s, state systems were constrained by declining state budgets and growing public priorities in healthcare, corrections, and K–12 education. Many states "retrenched," effectively decreasing funding for higher education due to limited state revenues (St. John, 1994b). There was tremendous resistance to raising taxes in the 1980s and the 1990s (St. John, 1994a) and a simultaneous shift of the burden of paying for college from taxpayers to students. States with revenue shortfalls routinely cut funding for public higher education because it was one of the few discretionary items in state budgets. As a consequence, an increasing proportion of the cost was passed on to students and their families (St. John, 2003).

Still another shift in public funding started in the 1990s and continued into the 2000s: funding for state need-based student financial aid did not rise at rates sufficient to keep pace with tuition (see Figure 5.1), while funding for non-need (mostly merit) grants

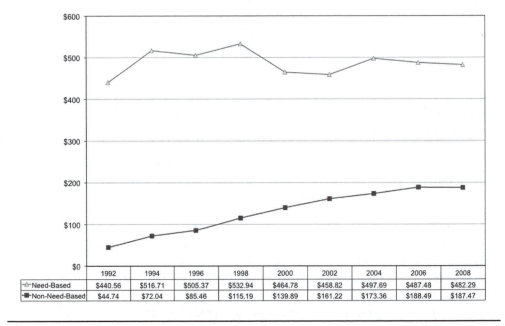

	1992	1994	1996	1998	2000	2002	2004	2006	2008
Need-Based	$440.56	$516.71	$505.37	$532.94	$464.78	$458.82	$497.69	$487.48	$482.29
Non-Need-Based	$44.74	$72.04	$85.46	$115.19	$139.89	$161.22	$173.36	$188.49	$187.47

Figure 5.1 Trends in Average State Need-Based and Non-Need-Based Undergraduate Grants per FTE, 1992–2008 (in 2008 Dollars)

Source: Data from National Association of State Student Grant & Aid Programs © 2011 Projects Promoting Equity in Urban and Higher Education, NCID at the University of Michigan.

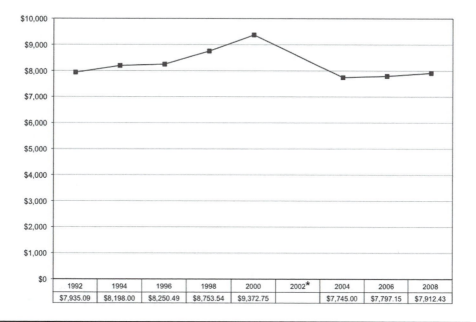

	1992	1994	1996	1998	2000	2002*	2004	2006	2008
	$7,935.09	$8,198.00	$8,250.49	$8,753.54	$9,372.75		$7,745.00	$7,797.15	$7,912.43

Figure 5.2 Trends in Average Annual Amount of State and Local Appropriations per FTE for the Public Higher Education System (in 2008 Dollars)

Source: Data from NCES Integrated Postsecondary Education Data System © 2011 Projects Promoting Equity in Urban and Higher Education, NCID at the University of Michigan.

*This data is missing in the Integrated Postsecondary Education Data System (IPEDS).

increased in many states. Advocates of need-based aid (Heller & Marin, 2002, 2004) were critical of this shift, suggesting that policymakers were abandoning the essential purpose of equalizing postsecondary opportunity through financial aid programs. Researchers found that the new merit programs improved enrollment within states, but there were inequalities among beneficiaries in terms of institutional choice (Dynarski, 2002; St. John et al., 2004). Thus there began to be substantial differences in the patterns of access across states, as illustrated by the state cases in Part II.

The average state appropriations per full-time-equivalent (FTE) student to institutions were slightly more than $9,200 in both 1992 and 2008, although there was variation in this rate over time (Figure 5.2). In the 1990s there was pattern of increase in state funding per FTE student, peaking in 2000 and followed by a period of decline. Further, since the percentage of students enrolling in 2-year colleges increased during the 2000s, some of the decline in average funding could be attributable to the increased share of the total number of students attending less costly 2-year colleges. Arguments about growth in spending by institutions as a factor pushing up costs still have relevance.

The weighted average tuition charge in public colleges in the United States (Figure 5.3) is the average amount of tuition charged a full-time student, weighted by the FTE enrollment by campus within states. This measure of tuition increased substantially between 2000 and 2008, a period when state funding of institutions per FTE was declining (compare trend lines in Figures 5.2 and 5.3). Since this measure of average tuition is adjusted for the increase in enrollment at less expensive 2-year colleges, it is lower than the average amount charged and lower than increases in charges in public

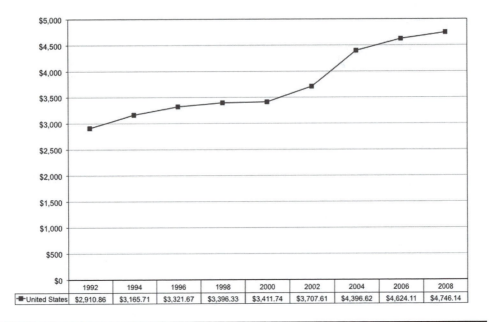

	1992	1994	1996	1998	2000	2002	2004	2006	2008
United States	$2,910.86	$3,165.71	$3,321.67	$3,396.33	$3,411.74	$3,707.61	$4,396.62	$4,624.11	$4,746.14

Figure 5.3 Trends in the Average Amount of Undergraduate In-State Tuition and Fees per FTE in Public Higher Education System in the United States, 1992–2008 (in 2008 Dollars)

Source: Data from NCES Integrated Postsecondary Education Data System © 2011 Projects Promoting Equity in Urban and Higher Education, NCID at the University of Michigan.

colleges but higher than the average in 2-year colleges. It represents the average amount paid by the average student in public institutions, which increased substantially in the early 2000s.

Trends in the ratio of average in-state tuition charges to average state grant funding per FTE provides an indicator of how well states are supporting low- and middle-income students with financial need (Figure 5.4). There was a decade (1998–2008) of steady decline in this ratio, indicating that students and their families were paying a rising percentage of college costs in a period in which tuition was rising. Since there was also a gap in Pell grants compared with the average cost of attending a public 4-year college (Figure 5.5), the affordability of public 4-year colleges substantially declined in the early 21st century. These changes in state policy influenced the development of an imperfect market model, with high costs for families and limited need-based grant aid. The new model reintroduced inequalities in enrollment opportunities after a brief period of near equal opportunity, especially in 4-year colleges. Some leading economists recognized the need for an increase in need-based grant aid for the United States to maintain global competitiveness (e.g., Fogel, 2000; Friedman, 2005), but policymakers adapted without regard for these classic liberal rationales, instead developing arguments for the new strategies of promoting access (i.e., loans). Researchers who examine policy processes have used terms like *logics* (Bastedo, 2009) and *rationales* (Moses, 2010; St. John & Parsons, 2004) to dissect new arguments. In reality, excuses were made for the new conditions as politics prevailed, imperfect markets developed in states, and new inequalities emerged.

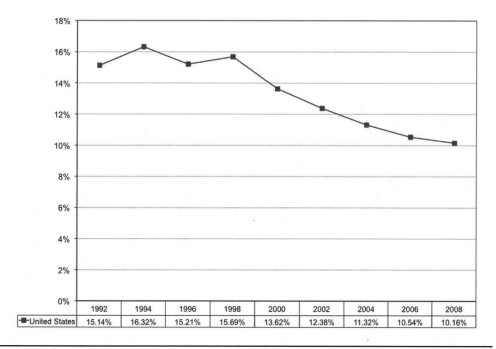

Figure 5.4 Trends in the Average per FTE Funding of Need-Based Grants as a Percent of the Average Public College Tuition Charge for Full-Time Students

Source: Data from NCES Integrated Postsecondary Education Data System and National Association of State Student Grant & Aid Programs © 2011 Projects Promoting Equity in Urban and Higher Education, NCID at the University of Michigan.

Federal Contributions to Market Imperfections

Economists originally argued for portable need-based grants as a reasonable means of federal support for equalizing access to higher education (Committee on Economic Development, 1973; McPherson, 1978; National Commission on the Financing of Postsecondary Education, 1973); they assumed a rationality of human capital investment, which placed an emphasis on need-based grants. The cost of college represented a substantial portion of a low-income family's budget, which made the cost greater than the disposable income; low-income students could no longer afford college even though there were known long-range economic benefits. Between 1973 and 1980, Pell grants were the cornerstone of the market model, effectively increasing the purchasing power of qualified students who did not have the means to pay for college. In 1978, MISAA opened the door to federal grants for middle-income students. Arguments about institutional waste and raising prices to maximize revenue from grants (Carnes, 1987; Finn, 1988a, 1988b) also created doubts about the federal role in a market model of higher education. Trends in the Pell grant reveal a dramatic problem (Figure 5.5).

The maximum Pell grant was nearly equal to the average cost of attendance (COA) at a public 4-year college (i.e., tuition plus living costs) in 1975 and 1980. There was a half-cost provision in the original Pell program, which meant that Pell would pay only 50% of the cost of attending. But even this grant meant that students in the lowest income groups—those with no expected family contribution—would generally be able to pay for a 4-year college if they qualified academically through state grants, institutional

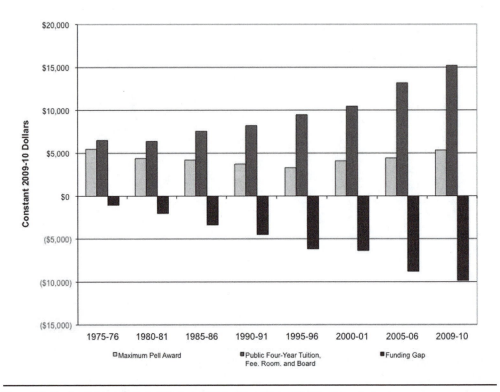

Figure 5.5 The Gap Between the Actual Maximum Pell Award and University Attendance Costs

Source: Data from College Board: Trends in College Pricing 2010, Table 5a: Trends in Student Aid 2010, Table 8 © 2011 Projects Promoting Equity in Urban and Higher Education, NCID at the University of Michigan.

grants, and other scholarships. However, the gap between the Pell maximum and the average public tuition charge grew steadily after 1980. In 2005, the gap between the maximum grant and the COA was about $8,000, and it grew to about $10,000 by 2010. State grants, institutional grants, and other scholarships still fill some of this gap for the typical low-income student, but a substantial portion is made up by work and borrowing, placing the burden on students. Middle-income students also face serious challenges in paying for college: their grant awards are lower than those for low-income students because their parents are expected to pay more, and they also face substantial work and loan burdens after federal, state, and institutional grant aid (Advisory Committee on Student Financial Assistance, 2010).

Since federal and private loans make up a substantial portion of the gap, students must manage their debt and work more hours as they navigate college. Many college students are part of the working-class economy, working in the service industry in low-income jobs as they progress through college. Loans, unlike grants, are not an equalizing force in the United States for low-income students, because a large debt burden can deter college attendance altogether or impact lifestyle choices after college (i.e., ability to buy cars and homes), and there are no guarantees that a student's degree will pay high enough dividends in the labor market to counteract this debt.

Much of our public policy focuses on equalizing opportunity across socioeconomic strata, but we are equally concerned with disparities by race and ethnicity. As discussed earlier, much of the litigation up to and including the *Brown v. Board of Education* decision focused on overcoming inequalities for African American students. The same was true for the Great Society programs of the 1960s, in large part because African Americans constituted the largest minority group in the United States. Today, the civil rights conversation has shifted to include the inequalities experienced by Hispanic students and families. The Latina/o population has grown at the fastest rate of any subgroup in the United States for the past several decades. According to the U.S. Census Bureau (2011), in 1970 Hispanics accounted for 4.7% of the total U.S. population in 1970, 12.5% by 2000, and more than 15% in 2010; projections estimate that Hispanics will account for nearly one quarter of the population in 2050. Today slightly fewer than 67% of Hispanic high school graduates attend college (compared with 71% of White students), but the numbers are misleading. Approximately 70% of Hispanic youth between the ages of 18 and 24 not currently enrolled in school have earned a high school diploma or equivalent, compared with more than 92% of White students (Heckman & LaFontaine, 2007). Of those that go on to college, a disproportionate number attend community colleges and, as a result, only 18% of Hispanic high school completers earn a bachelor's degree (compared with 38% of White students) (Pew Hispanic Center, 2004).

Inequality and the Market Model

A complicating factor for many Hispanic youth is their immigration status. In 2004, an estimated 11 million people were undocumented in the United States (Urban Institute, 2004), and as many as 1.8 million of those were under the age of 18 (Pew Hispanic Center, 2006). More than 80% of these undocumented immigrants come from Mexico and Latin America (Urban Institute, 2004). In 1996, Congress passed the Illegal Immigration Reform and Immigrant Responsibility Act, which prohibited undocumented students from being considered for in-state tuition if any U.S. national did not qualify for the same benefit (i.e., the in-state tuition charge). Since 2001, members of Congress have proposed the Development, Relief, and Education for Alien Minors (DREAM) Act to repeal the provision of the 1996 act applying to the children of undocumented immigrants (Feder, 2010). Cost is a critical barrier for many Hispanic youth, and the added burden of paying out-of-state tuition prevents many from even considering college as an option. The DREAM Act would give states the option to decide residency for the purposes of higher education. It would also provide minors under age 16 provisional legal status if they had been in the United States for at least 5 years and met several other conditions (Morse & Birnbach, 2010). If they completed 2 years of college or military service, they could become eligible for permanent resident status. Advocates have fought for the bill for more than 10 years, but the DREAM Act has not passed, largely because it is embroiled in a much larger and more contentious immigration debate. In-state tuition is not the only barrier for Hispanic students, but it is a high-profile public policy issue with the potential of providing opportunities to a growing number of Hispanic high school graduates.

The model of public finance of higher education envisioned by the economists whose research influenced policy in the 1960s and early 1970s was realized only briefly in the late 1970s. College access grew in spite of the imperfect market. The level of debt middle- and low-income students must assume to enroll in 4-year colleges with limited institutional aid dollars has the effect of limiting social mobility because of the long-term commitment to loan repayment. As students make choices about college, they seldom have a good understanding of the consequences of their choices. The message that student aid is available has been widely transmitted, but the complexity of managing debt is not sufficiently communicated to students and families preparing for the college years.

Access, College Choice, and Diversity

Federal and state funding and financial aid policies have a direct influence on students, but these effects are mitigated through the roles that institutions play in marketing and student financial aid. Most campuses coordinate marketing, admissions and student aid under the rubric of enrollment management. The enrollment management literature was largely developed for 4-year colleges (e.g. Hossler, 1984, 1987; Hossler et al., 1990), although the methods have been widely adapted across sectors of higher education. Further, a substantial portion of college students are adults, especially in community colleges, proprietary schools, and comprehensive colleges, all of which use marketing strategies to reach potential students. Adult students typically take evening and weekend classes or online programs. Earning a college degree has become a lengthy process for many of these students, who often take courses periodically and on a part-time basis. In addition, a growing number of professionals in the workforce must continue to take content courses to keep current in their professions and trades.

It is necessary to consider enrollment across all age groups to develop a complete picture of racial representation in higher education. Our analyses in this section use representation ratios: the percent of FTE students of a racial or ethnic group divided by the percentage of the group in the population (see Appendix). We first examine trends for enrollment in any institution and then consider racial representation in different types of institutions.

Access

Access and diversity are two interrelated issues: access, as the percentage of college-age students who enroll (or alternatively as the percentage of high school graduates who enroll), and diversity, the percentage of underrepresented minority students, especially important in 4-year institutions (Bowman & St. John, in press). If opportunity for low-income students to enroll in 4-year colleges is limited for financial reasons, public and private 4-year colleges will have greater difficulty enrolling URM students because of the correlation between income and race/ethnicity. The emphasis on improving the preparation of high school graduates (Chapter 4) undermines historical arguments about preparation as the primary cause for the lack of diversity in 4-year colleges.

The opportunity to enroll in a college of some type is increasingly available. As noted above, overall participation rates have risen for both traditional-age and nontraditional students alike (National Center for Education Statistics, 2010). As early as 1992, 75% of all high school graduates enrolled in college at some point (National Center for Education Statistics, 2004). But the marketing and aid strategies used by elite institutions along with the screening functions of their admissions processes limit access (Steinberg, 2002). Some 4-year colleges are still open to any students who want to enroll—formerly known as "open door" colleges—but state funding now limits this policy even in many community colleges (Zimmer Hendrick, Hightower, & Gregory, 2006). Community colleges in California and Florida, for example, have been forced to limit enrollment, either choosing among students or limiting access to courses (Education Commission of the States, 2000). Many of these essentially open-access 2-year institutions also offer some programs (e.g., nursing) that are selective in their admissions (American Association of

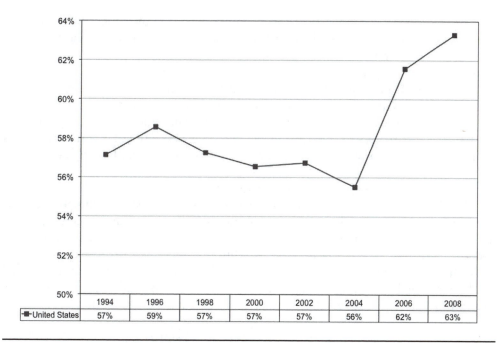

	1994	1996	1998	2000	2002	2004	2006	2008
United States	57%	59%	57%	57%	57%	56%	62%	63%

Figure 5.6 Trends in U.S. College Continuation Rate (Ratio of High School Graduates to First-Time Freshmen)

Source: Data from Postsecondary Education Opportunity © 2011 Projects Promoting Equity in Urban and Higher Education, NCID at the University of Michigan.

Colleges of Nursing, 2010). Even some propriety institutions have adopted selective criteria, although many still remain open to any student willing to enroll and pay the price, often through excessive borrowing.

Trends in college continuation rates—a measure from Tom Mortensen's *Postsecondary Education Opportunity*—provide an indicator of the rate of enrollment of high school graduates for the subsequent fall term (Figure 5.6). This measure is the ratio of the number of first-time fall enrollments divided by the number of high school graduates the prior spring. Whereas the enrollment rate hovered around 56% from 1994 to 2004, it rose to 62% in 2006 and 63% in 2008. This suggests a substantial recent increase in enrollment. Trends in enrollment indicate that most of the gain was in public 2-year and private for-profit colleges. Nevertheless, these trends suggest that improvements in high school graduation requirements could have contributed to the rise in continuation rates, a topic discussed in Chapter 4.

As is the case with the general access indicators, under- and overrepresentation of racial groups within different types of colleges must be carefully interpreted. It is important to consider patterns of representation to discern where barriers exist and whether underrepresentation is a matter of choice or constraint. The research on this question has been limited, but the differences in college preparation across groups (see Chapter 4) demonstrate that substantial numbers of potential students are not prepared to attend 4-year colleges after high school and therefore face constrained college choices.

Interpreting the meaning of enrollment ratios of this type is complex and requires an understanding of the roles of two different markets for higher education: institutions typically considered in the college choice and enrollment management literature (i.e., public and private 4-year colleges); and institutions typically open to most students regardless of preparation, including adults involved in training programs (i.e., public 2-year colleges and for-profit colleges). The college participation rates at any institution have become less of an issue for all groups except Hispanics, but it is important to consider what types of institutions students actually have access to, where potential students can make it through institutional screening and acquire funding sufficient to pay enrollment costs. Our analyses of trends confirm what others have suggested—in many ways the really important issues of equity are questions of college choice (Hoxby, 2004).

Diversity and College Choice

If their ability to pay, as measured by unmet need (expected family and student contribution after grants) is too high, students committed to going to college are confronted by difficult choices about whether to start in a 2-year college or to take on a substantial work and loan burden to pay for a 4-year college.[4] Thus the ability of 4-year colleges to attract URM students from low- and middle-income families is limited by the current financial conditions of higher education—a problem that also confronts the majority of students from groups that have historically been overrepresented in elite institutions.

The Front Line of Access: Public 2-Year Colleges

The recent literature on college access advocates for universal access to the first 2 years of college, with an emphasis on the alignment of grades 9 through 14 (e.g., Hoffman, Vargas, Venezia, & Miller, 2007). In most states, public 2-year colleges remain affordable and frequently provide opportunities for dual enrollment in college-level courses during the last 2 years of high school. Community colleges provide a low-cost alternative for states and students. Although there continue to be problems with the rates of degree completion in 2-year colleges, it is evident they are highly accessible (Figure 5.7). The challenge for community colleges continues to be one of capacity. As pressure increases to educate more students and state budgets fail to keep pace with rising costs, community colleges are asked to serve more students with great need while using limited resources.

Again, a transformation in patterns of access is evident. Black students were underrepresented in public 2-year colleges in 1992 (0.88 ratio) but overrepresented at the end of the decade (1.11 ratio). In contrast, Whites were modestly underrepresented in 1992 (0.96 ratio) and substantially underrepresented by 2008 (0.85 ratio). Hispanics had been overrepresented in community colleges during the 1980s but were slightly underrepresented in the 1990s. In addition to the complex legal issues related to Hispanic immigration and college access, there were changes in the census that increased the count of Mexican immigrants in 2000, so that the population base for the ratio grew.

Both American Indians and Asian Americans were consistently overrepresented. Native American enrollments in college have increased steadily since the early 1980s, roughly in line with their proportion in the population (National Center for Education Statistics, 2008). For Native Americans in many regions across the United States, tribal colleges provide the front line of access. More than 10% of the Native American population attending college are enrolled in the 35 tribal colleges (American Indian Higher Education Consortium, 2007). Asian Americans enroll at most types of institutions at higher rates than other groups, illustrating the emphasis placed on education in many Asian cultures. However, there are underrepresented Asian populations, like Hmong

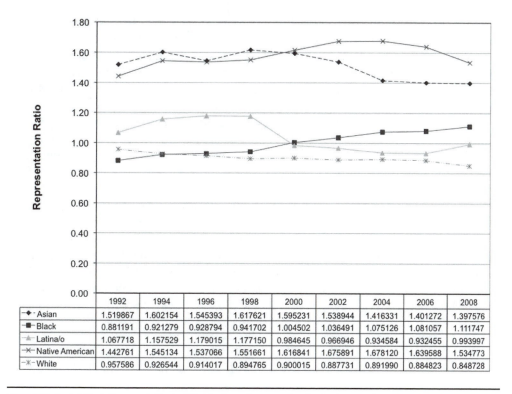

	1992	1994	1996	1998	2000	2002	2004	2006	2008
Asian	1.519867	1.602154	1.545393	1.617621	1.595231	1.538944	1.416331	1.401272	1.397576
Black	0.881191	0.921279	0.928794	0.941702	1.004502	1.036491	1.075126	1.081057	1.111747
Latina/o	1.067718	1.157529	1.179015	1.177150	0.984645	0.966946	0.934584	0.932455	0.993997
Native American	1.442761	1.545134	1.537066	1.551661	1.616841	1.675891	1.678120	1.639588	1.534773
White	0.957586	0.926544	0.914017	0.894765	0.900015	0.887731	0.891990	0.884823	0.848728

Figure 5.7 Racial/Ethnic Representation in All Public 2-year Postsecondary Institutions as a Proportion of the U.S. Population.
Source: Data from NCES Integrated Postsecondary Education Data System and U.S. Census Bureau © 2011 Projects Promoting Equity in Urban and Higher Education, NCID at the University of Michigan.

Americans, who are difficult to identify, given the limitations of existing sources of data (Lee & St. John, forthcoming).

Academics, Finances, and Diversity in Public 4-Year Colleges

Public 4-year colleges are highly diversified in their admissions standards and ability to subsidize high-achieving students with substantial financial need. A subset of public universities are highly selective—including the University of California, University of Michigan, University of Virginia, and University of North Carolina—and function in many respects like elite private colleges in their admission processes. Many more public 4-year colleges and universities, on the other hand, have more modest admissions thresholds, admit most students who meet those standards, and provide only modest student financial aid. The Advisory Committee on Student Financial Assistance (2010) has carefully analyzed trends in enrollment rates broken down by income and preparation. They conclude that many low- and middle-income students who qualify academically for enrollment in a 4-year college have constrained opportunity because of the large work/loan burden (i.e., costs of attending after expected parental contributions and grant aid) (Advisory Committee on Student Financial Assistance, 2010). From the literature summarized below, it is safe to assume that (1) there are both academic and financial barriers to public 4-year colleges and (2) low- and middle-income students are more sensitive to price than their higher-income peers.

Trends in racial representation in public 4-year colleges indicate that gaps were narrowing during the early 21st century but that substantial inequality remains (Figure 5.8). Consistent with the trends above, Asian Americans and Native Americans are well represented, but there are diversity challenges even for these groups. In 1992, African Americans were substantially underrepresented in public 4-year colleges (0.75 ratio) but were only moderately underrepresented in 2008 (0.90 ratio). During the same period, Whites maintained a representation ratio approximately equal to that of their percentage of the U.S. population (between 1.0 and 0.98). The challenges for diversity are largely at the most elite public institutions, where the battles over affirmative action are now being waged (Moses, 2001, 2002, 2006). The group most substantially underrepresented is Hispanics (ratio between 0.58 and 0.60).

Given there are many low-income students who qualify for but do not have the opportunity to enroll in 4-year colleges (Advisory Committee on Student Financial Assistance, 2010; St. John, 2006), there are reasons for concern about inequalities that result from an imperfect market. It is possible to have financial mechanisms that function fairly across ethnic and income groups, controlling for preparation (McPherson & Shapiro, 1991, 1998). What is needed is more careful study of patterns of fairness and discrimination across the states, which is, at least in part, the reason we wrote Part II with cases that focus on states.

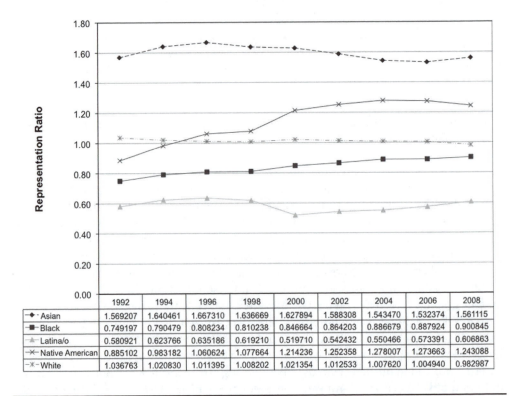

	1992	1994	1996	1998	2000	2002	2004	2006	2008
Asian	1.569207	1.640461	1.667310	1.636669	1.627894	1.588308	1.543470	1.532374	1.561115
Black	0.749197	0.790479	0.808234	0.810238	0.846664	0.864203	0.886679	0.887924	0.900845
Latina/o	0.580921	0.623766	0.635186	0.619210	0.519710	0.542432	0.550466	0.573391	0.606863
Native American	0.885102	0.983182	1.060624	1.077664	1.214236	1.252358	1.278007	1.273663	1.243088
White	1.036763	1.020830	1.011395	1.008202	1.021354	1.012533	1.007620	1.004940	0.982987

Figure 5.8 Racial/Ethnic Representation in All Public 4-Year Postsecondary Institutions as a Proportion of the U.S. Population

Source: Data from NCES Integrated Postsecondary Education Data System and U.S. Census Bureau © 2011 Projects Promoting Equity in Urban and Higher Education, NCID at the University of Michigan.

Making Sense of Access and Diversity

The United States and many other nations are pushing to expand access to higher education as a means of improving their competitive positions in the global economy. But many questions linger about inequalities in access (e.g., Altbach, 2010; Freidman, 2005). This examination of trends in the United States revealed (1) an expansion of access, meaning that a greater proportion of the total population was attending colleges and universities, and (2) persistent participation gaps by race in 4-year colleges, both public and private. The overall pattern shows increasing equality in access for African Americans but not for Hispanics; however, access has many meanings. Economic and academic factors have sorted more minorities into 2-year programs in public and proprietary colleges. There are some hopeful signs, such as the gains in access for minorities in public 4-year colleges in the present century, but persistent disparities remain, particularly with respect to disciplinary choices and participation in highly selective institutions, where the economic benefits are greatest.

POLICY RESEARCH ON ACCESS

Policymakers have invested considerable time and energy in trying to increase the proportion of adults with a postsecondary education. The current administration has set the goal of having the most educated workforce across the globe (Obama, 2010). It may be argued that the policies initiated to improve access are informed by research, but it is less common for researchers to evaluate those policy strategies to assess whether they work as intended. Below we summarize research on whether students choose to enroll in college (enrollment), and if so, what types of institutions they choose to attend (choice). We consider the strengths and limitations of three approaches of recent research (since 2000), with an emphasis on how the findings help to explain trends in access and college. The review covers recent literature in four areas:

- *Enrollment studies* (using the state indicators), including state-level studies using fixed effects models and hierarchical models examining enrollment using both state indicators and individual-level student data.
- *National Center for Education Statistics (NCES) reports* examining trends in enrollment patterns across different groups of students (mostly descriptive studies).
- *Educational research* examining social attainment, institutional structures on college enrollment and choice (most don't consider the role of student aid).
- *Economic studies* that examine the effects of financial aid and tuition on student enrollment choice (but often don't account for the students' situated contexts).

Studies Using State Policy Indicators

The state indicators used throughout Parts I and II were developed originally for analyses of the impact of state grants on enrollment (St. John et al., 2004; St. John, Chung, Musoba, & Simmons, 2006), but they have also been used to examine the impact of state grants on enrollment rates in different types of colleges in state-level studies (St. John, Chung, Musoba, & Chung, 2006), for two-level modeling of the impact of state grant aid on enrollment and college choice with national longitudinal data (St. John, Chung, Musoba, & Chung 2006; St. John, Chung, Musoba, & Simmons 2006), and with applicants for the Gates Millennium Scholars (GMS) program (St. John, Hu, & Fisher, 2011). The combination of studies illustrates that state indicators of policies and outcomes provide a data resource for research and that there is substantial variation across states policies, making it possible to assess the impact of different policies on student aid and tuition.

State-Level Studies

State-level studies treat individual states as the unit of analysis. Fixed-effect analyses control for differences beyond variables in the model attributable to states. A team of researchers conducted three studies using the same base model. The analysis included variables on population demographics (percent poverty and percent minority groups), size of the population, tax rates, and per student expenditures on K–12 education, along with variables related to need-based and non-need-based aid.

- *The impact of state grants and tuition on state enrollment rates.* The initial study using the state indicators focused on the effects of state funding per student for both need-based and non-need (mostly merit) grants on college enrollment rates (St. John, Chung, Musoba, & Simmons, 2006). It should be noted that the analyses to date have examined students who enrolled from 1992 to 2000 and therefore are not applicable to the more recent trends. The work found that both need- and non-need-based aid was positively associated with enrollment rates, although the effect was substantially greater for need-based aid. Tuition rates in states were not significantly associated with enrollment rates, controlling for other factors. The percent of students in public 2-year and private colleges (variables included in this analysis only) was positively associated with total enrollment rates within states.[5]
- *The impact of state grants and tuition on enrollment rates in different types of colleges (i.e., the distribution of students within state systems).* Using the same model, the study team examined the impact of tax rates, average public tuition charges, state funding for need-based grants, and state funding for non-need (mostly merit) grants on enrollment rates for public 2-year, public 4-year, private, and proprietary colleges (St. John, Musoba, Chung, & Chung, 2006). These analyses found that high state tax rates were positively associated with enrollment rates in public 4-year colleges and negatively associated with enrollment in proprietary institutions; state funding for non-need grants was positively associated with enrollment rates in public 4-year colleges within states; and higher public tuition was negatively associated with the percentages of students enrolled in private nonprofit colleges and public 2-year colleges.
- *The impact of high school graduation requirements on enrollment rates.* While the new state graduation requirements were positively associated with SAT scores and negatively associated with high school graduation rates, these requirements were not significantly associated with college enrollment rates within states (St. John & Musoba, 2006). Further, state funding per student in K–12 education was positively associated with high school graduation rates.

Two-Level Models Using State Indicators

Using hierarchical modeling, it is possible to examine both state- and student-level variables associated with college enrollment. Two studies have used this approach.

First, St. John and colleagues used state indicators with the National Longitudinal Study of the 1992 high school graduating class to examine the impact of state grants and tuition on enrollment (St. John, Chung, Musoba, & Simmons, 2006). Controlling for individual variables related to student background and achievement, both tuition charges and need-based grants were positively associated with enrollment. These findings further reinforce arguments about high tuition and high grants as an economical strategy for states seeking to improve enrollment rates of traditional college-age students. Additional analyses used the same model to compare enrollment in 2- and 4-year colleges to nonenrollment and found that average in-state tuition was negatively associated with rates of enrollment in 2-year colleges and positively associated with enrollment in 4-year colleges. State funding per student for need-based grants was positively associated with enrollment in 2-year but not 4-year colleges. By 1992, most states' need-based grant programs were sufficient to promote access to 2-year but not 4-year colleges. Non-need grants were not statistically significant predictors. Further analyses broke down students by income groups and found that need-based grants had positive associations with overall enrollment and enrollment in 2-year colleges by low-income students; need-based grants were positively associated with enrollment by middle-income students and their enrollment in 2-year colleges.[6]

Second, this approach was used in a study of the impact of state grants and tuition charges on college choices by applicants to the GMS program (St. John, Hu, & Fisher, 2011). This sample of 2000, 2001, and 2002 applicants included over 3,000 students who had applied for the GMS award; slightly more than half had received the award. At the individual level, the analyses controlled for background and prior achievement. Among this group of high-achieving, low-income, underrepresented minority students, the analyses found that state funding for need-based grants was positively associated with enrollment in selective and low-selective colleges compared with colleges with midrange selectivity; state funding for need-based grants per student had a substantial positive association with enrollment in selective colleges but not low-selective colleges as compared with mid-selective colleges.

National Center for Education Statistics Studies (Mostly Descriptive)
The NCES reports on access in the late 1990s were subjected to extensive review, pointing to misuse of multivariate statistics (e.g., Becker, 2004; Heller, 2004). The recent NCES reports are largely descriptive, with a series of tables and charts relating student background characteristics and school factors to a range of measurable outcomes like enrollment and institution type. The reports on enrollment patterns issued by NCES contractors are now judicious in their claims as they examine trends among important subgroups of students. Peter and Horn (2005) examined changing patterns in educational outcomes by gender and found that girls have closed the gap with boys in terms of academic preparation for college and women have surpassed men in terms of college enrollment rates. Horn, Cataldi, and Sikora (2005) looked specifically at the group of students who delayed entry into college and found that those students were less likely to achieve success in postsecondary education relative to their peers who attended college directly out of high school. The authors also recognized the limitations of their analysis and acknowledged the potential sources of bias, including the endogeneity of delayed entry to the interpretation of their findings. Similarly, Chen and Carroll (2005) considered the pathways to postsecondary education for first-generation college students and found that these students tend to be less prepared for college-level work and less likely to attend college. Both Horn and colleagues and Chen acknowledged some of the

limitations in their analyses but did not address the potentially important influences of college cost on delayed entry and college enrollment among first-generation students.

Education Research on the Effects of Preparation

The quality of the academic preparation students receive in high school is a primary concern for school leaders and researchers alike. Without an effective academic foundation, students are unlikely to succeed in college. A study of the 21st Century Scholars program in Indiana (St. John, Musoba, Simmons, & Chung, 2004) found that participation in the program, which addressed both academic preparation and financial access for low-income students, was positively related to both aspirations to attend college and decisions to enroll. Researchers in Chicago (Allensworth, Nomi, Montgomery, & Lee, 2009) found that establishing a college preparatory curriculum for all students attending school in a high-need district did not lead to greater college participation rates—a finding that, while limited to a particular high-need urban context, runs counter to conventional wisdom that policies to promote stronger academic preparation will improve college access.

Another method of preparing students for college is to provide them with better information. Bell, Rowan-Kenyon, and Perna (2009), in a series of state case studies, found that students in states with merit aid programs, like Georgia's HOPE or Florida's Bright Futures, were more likely to be informed about the college choice process and prepared to navigate it. The same was true for students who reported participating in outreach programs like Upward Bound and AVID. The critical linkage between the policy and enrollment appears to be whether students have access to the information they need to be prepared for college. Perna and Titus (2005) found that parent involvement as a proxy for social capital is positively related to students' choosing to attend either a 2- or 4-year institution, although this study did not consider whether policy efforts enhance the role of parents or influence whether students will be prepared to choose a college.

Testing is an important policy lever utilized today as part of accountability programs in states to assess the degree to which students are prepared for college by their schools and teachers. Perna and Thomas (2009) found that both students and school administrators perceived mandatory exit exams as a barrier to college access. Their analysis did not consider whether the presence of the policy actually affected students' decisions to attend college, but it suggests that the policy has an effect on shaping the context within which students live and attend school. Deil-Amen and Tavis (2010) found, in a phenomenological investigation of students' experiences, that low ACT scores had a negative effect on students' postsecondary plans and aspirations. Their investigation also confirmed that students are underinformed about the admissions process and the relative importance of test scores. These findings are particularly important, since a number of states now provide the ACT for 100% of their high school students, the assumption being that more students are likely to consider college if they have completed the necessary steps.

Economic Research on State Subsidies and Tuition Policy

States invest a substantial amount of public money in postsecondary education, with the largest portion allocated as direct appropriations to public colleges and universities. In prior work, Heller's summary of earlier research (1999) concluded that tuition had a stronger effect on students' enrollment decisions than any of the subsidies. More recent work does not examine this relationship, which may be a limitation, given the pace at which tuition charges have risen over the past decade. Black and Sufi (2002) found that low-income African American students were more likely to attend college than other low-SES groups throughout the 1970s and 1980s. During the 1990s, however, African American students were less likely to attend college across all SES groups; the authors suggest that price may have been an important contributing factor. Flores (2010) conducted a study of the impact of state DREAM Act policies and found that foreign-born noncitizen residents were more likely to enroll in college after states allowed in-state tuition for those students. This is a fairly recent development in a number of states, but enrollment changes are consistent with basic economic theory of students' responses to price.

The Washington, D.C. Tuition Assistance Grant (TAG) was created to bridge the gap between in-state and out-of-state tuition for residents of the district to attend public colleges and universities in surrounding states. Kane (2004) examined the impact of the program and found that when it was launched, enrollment of D.C. students in out-of-state colleges doubled and the proportion of D.C. students attending college grew by 15%. In most cases, tuition reciprocity agreements would not be viewed as mechanisms to increase college enrollment as much as college choice, but given the limited availability of low-cost alternatives in the capital district, the TAG program does seem to operate that way.

Economic Research on Need-Based Aid

The primary mechanism for the federal government and states to reduce the financial barrier to college in market-based systems has been the provision of aid to eligible students. The federal Pell grant program is the largest need-based aid program in the country, accounting for more than $32 billion in aid to students in 2010 (U.S. Department of Education, 2011b). Ruben (2011) utilized regression discontinuity with expected family contribution (EFC) as the cut score to compare whether Pell-eligible students at the cut point were more likely to attend college than students from families with similar income levels without Pell eligibility. The findings show that there is no difference between these two groups of students in terms of on-time college enrollment. The analysis does not consider delayed entrance, so it is possible that eligibility will result in increased attendance among those who choose not to enroll directly in college. Evidence from a state grant program is more promising. Kane (2003) examined the impact of the CalGrant program in California and found that it increased college attendance rates by 3% to 4% and affected students' choice of institution within the state.

Economic Research on Merit-Based Aid

No fewer than 15 states have elected to support student aid programs designed to reward high school academic success (Doyle, 2010). The largest and longest-established of these programs is Georgia's HOPE scholarship, which guarantees full tuition and fees to a public college or university in the state for any student who completes high school with at least a 3.0 GPA. Dynarski (2002) examined seven of these programs and found that on average, college participation rates improved by 5% to 7% in adopting states. In Georgia, she found that gaps between African American and White students grew in terms of college attendance, but the same patterns were not identified in other states—a finding she concludes is related to the academic standards imposed by the state of Georgia. Ness and Tucker (2008) explored the impact of eligibility for the Tennessee Merit Aid program on students' plans to attend college. Their findings suggest that low-income and African

American students were more likely to report that eligibility influenced their decision to plan for college. The authors suggest that even if the distribution of aid is inefficient, it may have a larger positive effect because it both eliminates the cost for students and increases their aspirations and plans for attendance. One of the more contentious policy debates in financial aid revolves around whether and to what extent merit aid programs have replaced and should replace need-based programs as a matter of state policy. Doyle (2010) found that, over time, need-based programs changed incrementally and there was no evidence to suggest that merit programs had a negative impact on the growth of need-based aid.

Economic Research on College Choice

Hoxby (2004) points out that whereas access has been a public policy priority for many years, the real question today is college choice. Although the choice of institution is a critical part of the process for students, it has not been a focus of attention for NCES. With the exception of the Digest of Education Statistics, which reports enrollment trends by sector, only one statistical analysis report has addressed the issue of institutional choice. Lee and Carroll (2001) examined undergraduate enrollments by sticker price—an important difference by sector and institution—and found that among students attending a high-tuition college or university, choice of public or private institution was influenced by reputation, financial aid, faculty, and job placement. Those choosing less expensive colleges indicated that being close to home, low tuition, peer attendance, and the option to live at home were all important. The lack of attention paid to institutional choice by NCES may be a function of two factors. First, the lack of appropriate data makes this a difficult question to explore. In particular, the lack of data on college cost or measures of the student search process in the NCES studies makes it difficult to address these questions. Second, college attendance has been a much more important policy priority than the type of institution attended. Recent works (Bowen et al., 2009; Roderick, Nagaoka, Coca, & Moeller, 2008) have begun to illustrate why institutional choice should be an important policy priority.

Policies intended to influence both academic preparation and ability to pay for college have important implications for choice of institution among students, but the linkages between the policies and outcomes have been less frequently examined. For example, Ceja (2006) looks at the role of information in the choice process among Chicana/Chicano students. His findings illustrate the important role of information among this important subset of students, but he does not examine the state and institutional policy efforts to improve the accessibility of relevant information even though the policies researchers consider in the context of college choice operate at the federal, state, and institutional levels.

Economic Research on Federal Policy

The Pell grant is the largest federal grant program, but it is more commonly thought of as a tool to improve college access than choice of institution. Federal loan programs have grown increasingly prominent as a strategy to improve postsecondary outcomes. Kim (2008) found, in an analysis of different aid packages, that receipt of grants or a combination of grants and loans had a positive impact on whether students attended their first-choice institution. However, there were differences by race, suggesting that benefits accrued to White and Asian students but not African American or Latino/a students. Kim's analysis does not specify the source of the aid, so it is possible that students are reporting loans from state or private sources as well as federal; but given the relative size of the federal programs, the findings are suggestive.

There are several federal initiatives targeted to the middle class that have been linked to students' choice of institution. Ma (2003) found that Education Savings Plans (529 accounts) are linked to household savings, which has an indirect effect on choice of institution. Her findings suggest that 529 accounts do not appear to replace individual savings and that the incentives may benefit middle- and upper-income families to a greater extent than lower-income families. Long (2004) examined the impact of federal tax credits on higher education and concluded that there was no effect on whether students enroll in college; however, Long also reports that federal tax credits are related to increasing prices at community colleges. Research on the influences of federal policies on choice of institution is not yet fully developed, perhaps as a consequence of shifting policy priorities. To this point, more emphasis has been placed on college attendance; therefore the empirical work focuses more on the decision to attend college rather than on which institution a student chooses to attend.

Economic Research on State Finance Policies

Research on the relationship between state policy and students' choice of institution focuses on public subsidies and tuition policies. State appropriations are related to tuition setting at public colleges and universities. Tuition policy, in turn, influences choice in relation to the costs of attending alternative institutions—including community colleges and private institutions (both nonprofit and for profit). Perna and Titus (2004) found that increased public investment in higher education reduced the likelihood that students would choose to attend an out-of-state college. They also found that as community college tuition falls, students are more likely to attend this type of institution. Rizzo and Ehrenberg (2004) examined the relationship between in-state and out-of-state tuition rates and enrollment patterns at public flagship institutions and found that as Pell awards increased, so did in-state tuition rates at the flagships. At the same time, flagship institutions did not appear to use nonresident students as revenue generators but rather as a source of enhanced quality and prestige. Shin and Milton (2006) found that after controlling for competitive tuition levels and the state wage premium, tuition prices do not have an effect on 4-year college enrollment; however, they also note that as private tuitions rise, attendance at public institutions increases.

Institutional Policies Affecting Net Price

A number of researchers have examined the impact of institutional strategies designed to influence student choice. DesJardins, Ahlburg, and McCall (2006) found that at a single institution, the fit between students' expectations for financial aid and the actual package awarded was an important factor influencing whether or not students chose to attend the institution; when the aid package was less than a student expected, the odds that he or she would attend the institution dropped. Avery and Hoxby (2003) found that among high-achieving students applying to a selective institution, more generous aid packages increased the chances that a student would attend the institution—a finding consistent with traditional rational theories of college choice. However, they also found that students responded more favorably than expected to increases in loans and the amount of grants rather than the proportion of cost covered by the grants. The study makes some assumptions about aid awards from institutions students chose not to attend and it does not adequately account for nonmonetary factors that might influence a student's decision in a rational way, but the findings suggest that students, even high-achieving students, are not always rational in the college choices they make.

Two studies examined the institutional policy among elite private institutions to replace loans with grants for all admitted low-income students. Researchers at Harvard found that, subsequent to the establishment of the policy, more low-income students enrolled in the college, but that this was largely a function of an increased pool of low-income applicants (Avery et al., 2006) because of changes in the way students were recruited from nonfeeder high schools. Linsenmeier, Rosen, and Rouse (2002) were more modest in their findings, suggesting that another institution's program had no significant effect overall among low-income students but did have an effect in terms of enrolling more low-income African American students. This study exploits the natural experiment resulting from the immediate adoption of the program, but it does not account for the potential influence of the program as a marketing tool—a strength of the Harvard program.

State appropriations, financial aid programs, tuition policies, tax incentives, and institutional aid have been considered in economic research. This literature has effectively isolated the potential effects of these policies. Unfortunately it is difficult to ascertain from these studies the degree to which other state efforts influence the same decisions; after all, these policies are not crafted in a policy vacuum. A new financial aid program may play an important role, given the state context, but it is likely to interact with other policy initiatives. Indiana is instructive. The 21st Century Scholars program is primarily a guarantee of tuition for low-income students who take a pledge to prepare for and apply to college. However, in addition to the financial assistance, Indiana adopted a rigorous academic curriculum to prepare students for college-level work. It is likely that *both* of these efforts play an important role, but it is difficult to assess their relative importance.

Research on Access

There has been extensive research on college access during the past decade. The consensus is that both academic preparation and financial aid matter in college access. The basic model of high tuition and high need-based grant aid has the greatest potential of equalizing the opportunity for qualified low-, middle-, and high-income students to enroll in high-quality colleges. There are some risks with this approach, which are evident from the research by economists using indicators: (1) when tuition increases faster than grants or if grants awards are reduced, the equalizing potential of aid declines; (2) efforts to improve academic preparation for underrepresented students can improve college access if they can afford to pay for college; and (3) merit-based aid also expands enrollment opportunities, especially in selective 4-year colleges, but merit aid also increases inequalities. States and the federal government are faced with difficult choices about how they craft strategies to promote access and equalize opportunity for students to enroll in 4-year colleges.

CONCLUSIONS: COLLEGE ACCESS, CHOICE, AND DIVERSITY IN THE 21ST CENTURY

As a conclusion we step back from the policy debates, trends, and research to review findings across the three topics, compare findings, and raise questions for the next generation of policy and research on access.

Key Findings

1. The policy discourse of higher education access combined structural and market arguments after World War II:

   a. Most states followed a pattern of providing funding per student for public colleges (a structural model), only partially adopting student aid as a tool in funding access in the past three decades, during which tuition rose as a consequence of the decline in state subsidies to colleges.
   b. The federal government introduced student aid after World War II through the GI Bill and the Great Society programs and, after a brief period of successfully improving equity in the 1970s, with the implementation of Pell grants, has failed to fund Pell grants at a level that would equalize opportunities for equally prepared students to enroll in 4-year colleges.
   c. With a few exceptions—such as a coordination of state policies in Minnesota (Chapter 8) and the HEA reauthorization of 1972, which the created Pell grants—research has had only modest influence on the course of public policy on public finance of higher education and its links to college access.

2. Trends in participation, as measured by the representation of racial/ethnic groups in higher education, reveal:

   a. Access to 2-year degrees and other certificate programs in community colleges and proprietary schools has shifted toward overrepresentation of minority students.
   b. Opportunities to enroll in public and nonprofit 4-year colleges remain inequitable, although there was modest narrowing of the gap for African Americans compared with Whites and increased underrepresentation of Hispanics.

3. The review of the literature on college access reveals four strands of research—NCES descriptive studies, educational research, economic studies, and indicators research—which yield inconsistent patterns of evidence:

   a. After a period of methodologically problematic studies in the 1990s, NCES has provided descriptive studies of college access in the 21st century, but these studies provide little new insight into access challenges.
   b. With few exceptions, education research on access has focused on the role of academic preparation and, as a consequence, has added only modestly to the debates on college access.
   c. Economic research has isolated variables related to specific public policies to examine the impact of student aid (merit and need-based grants) and tuition, confirming research from prior decades that these policies influence enrollment.
   d. The analyses of access and college enrollment using state indicators found that K–12 policies are not significantly associated with college enrollment rates but that state finance policies—tuition and both need-based and non-need (mostly merit) aid—had an influence on enrollment and college choice.

Cross-Level Analysis

The linkages between policy research and policy decisions are weak, with only modest evidence that research is used to inform policy decisions, in contrast to using research as a tool to build policy rationales (e. g., Chapter 3). In the field of higher education, some researchers in the late 20th century focused their studies on the impact of financial aid on college access. Heller (1997) provided an excellent summary of prior research, illustrating consistent findings that student grants had a substantial impact on college enrollment, especially for low-income students. In this century, there has been very little research by higher education researchers on the role and effects of tuition and student aid on college enrollment. Economists have begun to fill this void. Economists pioneered research on student aid and price response in the 1960s. The early research by economists had a substantial influence on the development of the federal student aid programs, but it is not yet certain if the current generation of economic research will have an influence.

Analyses of policy decisions at the state and federal level reveal attempts to summarize research on finance to influence policy. The most successful effort by higher education scholars to influence state funding was in Minnesota, after Jim Hearn and David Longanecker (1985)—a professor at the University of Minnesota and an administrator for a state coordinating agency, respectively—wrote a compelling essay on state funding strategies, influencing the state to adopt a coordinated approach to state finance. On the other hand, Hearn (1993) also argued, in another essay, that research had very little impact on federal policy, a pattern evident in this chapter. The review of the history of the policy discourse on higher education is generally confirmatory of Hearn's argument that the social process has dominated over rationality in higher education policy.[7]

In our examination of trends in student outcomes in relation to research evidence on the impact of public finance policies, we find that (a) trends in access to 4-year colleges during this century demonstrate that federal student aid and patterns of inequality in access correspond and (b) research on federal and state student aid consistently finds that low-income students are most substantially influenced by student aid and tuition whether or not they have taken steps to prepare to enroll in 4-year colleges. The research and trends correspond reasonably well. The relatively low costs of attending community colleges compared with 4-year colleges explains how access (as measured by rates of enrollment and racial representation) can increase while at the same time access to more expensive 4-year colleges remains unequal. Thus the conclusion that politics prevail over rationality is further confirmed. For questions, see Text Box 5.1.

Text Box 5.1 Questions About Public Policy and College Access

1. Is access still a challenge in the United States? Is access to 2-year colleges nearly universal? What about 4-year colleges?

2. Should higher education policymakers and/or researchers be concerned about college affordability?

3. Are federal Pell grants sufficient to ensure access to 2-year colleges? Is the assurance that all students will have access to 2-year colleges sufficient as a policy goal?

4. Does it matter if students amass substantial debt from enrollment in 2-year colleges? What is an acceptable level of debt, and does this differ depending upon the student? Is it fair that on average, low- and middle-income students must borrow more to enroll in 4-year colleges than their peers with more financial resources? Does the prospect of debt deter enrollment?

5. How can states and institutions ensure affordability to public 4-year colleges?

6. Should states consider measures of student engagement and/or academic achievement as part of their accountability systems along with degree completion rates?

7. What are the risks and benefits of merit and need-based grants as strategies for ensuring financial access to 4-year colleges?

8. Based on the research, what federal policies are likely to equalize opportunity for enrollment in 4-year colleges for equally prepared students regardless of income?

9. What role do research and politics play in the development of new programs?

10. How can research be more effectively integrated into the policymaking process?

11. How do annual budget decisions by states and the federal government undermine attempts to ensure financial access for low-income students?

12. What are some of the important, unanswered research questions related to the role of policy in college access?

6

COLLEGE SUCCESS AND DEGREE COMPLETION

The increased global competition for educated workers (Chapter 4), the rising costs of attending public and private colleges (Chapter 5), and the emphasis on public accountability have converged to create a focus on improving degree attainment in the early 2000s. A few publications have called attention to troubling retention rates and possible remedies (e.g., Bowen, Chingos, & McPherson, 2009; Carey, 2008; St. John & Musoba, 2010). The long tradition of research on retention and persistence in higher education suggests a potential for using studies of interventions to inform the dissemination of innovations and their adaptive redesign. Yet government responses to budget constraints in 2011 have created new challenges for federal, state, and institutional efforts to promote persistence in higher education.[1] Government constraints on higher education only increase the need for innovation; further advances in research and intervention are needed. This chapter describes how state and federal policy, funding, and programs link to persistence and degree completion; examines trends in degree completion by diverse groups using indicators of retention; and reviews research linking policy to retention, persistence, and degree completion. We use the term *retention* for continuation at the original campus and *persistence* as the process of educational attainment inclusive of transfer.[2]

STATE AND FEDERAL POLICIES LINKED TO RETENTION

Although retention has long been a subject of study in the field of higher education, state and federal policies that focus on persistence and improving degree attainment are relatively recent, underfunded, and understudied. Given the seriousness of financial challenges for students, institutions, and states in the early 21st century, greater attention to the links between policy and persistence is needed. To further the conceptualization of these linkages, we review recent developments in policy on retention at the state and federal levels, scholarly research on persistence and retention, and the potential for further convergence between research, policy, and innovation. State and federal policymakers focus greater attention on degree completion, based upon the assumption that college-educated workers are more employable, earn a higher wage, are more civically engaged, and will contribute more to the tax base. Collectively, a more educated populace is thought to be more innovative, more entrepreneurial, and more attractive to globally competitive knowledge-producing employers, thus attracting jobs and growing the economy. Institutions, on the other hand, care as much about retention as they do about degree completion. Colleges and universities are often judged by the number of students they graduate, so they seek to retain students even if the better course of action for the individual is to transfer to another institution.

Federal and state policy designed to improve completion rates and, by extension, grow the human capital of the state or the nation operates indirectly by first influencing the practices of colleges and universities, which will affect the likelihood that students will remain enrolled in college and earn their degrees. Financial aid programs appear to be an exception, given that many of these programs fund students directly; but there is also variability in the aid provided by institutions. By virtue of their expectations for higher education, policymakers are likely to care more about student persistence to degree completion than institutional retention in a specific campus, but most efforts to improve completion rates use the same institutional measures of degree completion at the first institution attended within 150% of the time anticipated for the degree.

State Policy on Persistence and Degree Attainment

During the era of master planning and per student funding of higher education, degree completion was usually treated as a production issue related to workforce development (e.g., Halstead, 1974). There were a few exceptions to the general pattern. For example, the state of New York provides Bundy Aid for higher education—subsidies for independent colleges based upon the number of degrees granted and the level of the degrees conferred (Cuomo & Megna, 2011), and Minnesota had a full-year funding formula that was adjusted for fall to spring departure (Berg & Hoenack, 1987). Some researchers recognized that improved retention could mean additional revenue for colleges, recommending enrollment management strategies (e.g., Bean, 1990; Hossler, Bean, & Associates, 1990), but the old structural model of funding gave way to the privatization of public colleges (Chapter 5) before institutions had a chance to use follow-through on this strategy (Patton, Morelon, Whitehead, & Hossler, 2006).

During the global transition, states reduced funding for public colleges as a response to declining tax revenues, undermining the old logic for improving retention and persistence (Chapter 5). For example, from 2009 to 2011, state support declined by an average of 2.1%, with five states experiencing real declines of more than 15% (Palmer, 2011). We examine three developments in state policy on retention and persistence: development of state accountability and data systems, performance funding as a specialized form of accountability, and new stresses on state budgets.

Accountability and Data Systems

Most states had developed multiple state systems by the late 1960s and several states (e.g., Illinois, New York, California) had well-established coordination boards (Glenny, 1971, 1973). As part of the 1972 reauthorization of the Higher Education Act, the federal government provided funds for state planning under section 1202. To receive the funding, states had to form 1202 planning commissions and all states responded to these incentives (Glenny, Bowen, Meisinger, Morgan, Purves, & Schmidtlein, 1975). Whereas colleges and universities had been required to provide annual reports on students, finances, and other topics to the federal government since 1965,[3] most states did not have systematic methods of reporting. As part of planning, states were encouraged to develop state accountability and reporting systems. Some states developed supplementary surveys to complete the summary forms provided to the federal government, and a few (e.g., Indiana, Texas, Florida) developed student record data systems. In theory, the state coordinating agencies were designed to provide coordinated state budgets for higher education and a systematic way of reporting information, as a parallel to the federal system. After federal funding for the 1202 commissions ceased, most states continued some form of coordination.

During the global transition, the federal government has taken new approaches to encouraging states to develop accountability systems in higher education. In the 1990s, early in the global transition, state support of higher education declined and federal encouragement for state coordination assumed a new form. The Clinton administration encouraged states to develop systems of reporting to the public on retention outcomes, but there was resistance, and these early efforts failed (St. John, 1994a). However, efforts have continued. Recently the federal government invested in the development of centralized student data systems in most states, with the intention of creating comprehensive P–16 data systems integrating K–12 and higher education data into one seamless system (Institute of Education Sciences, 2011).

Accountability

There has been a strong push for improving accountability systems, with encouragement by scholars, national associations, and the federal government (Heller, 2001; Lombardi & Capaldi, 1996; Zumeta, 2001). Most recently, the George W. Bush administration, under the leadership of Secretary of Education Margaret Spellings, issued a report advocating greater accountability in *A Test of Leadership* (U.S. Department of Education, 2006). The accountability movement has a strong emphasis on improving retention through the use of performance funding and other mechanisms. By the start of this century, however, problems with the traditional assumptions about public funding, which underlie these schemes, became readily apparent; consequently progress has been slow (St. John, Kline, & Asker, 2001). If states reward colleges with high retention rates, then state funding favors elite colleges and undermines access. It is better to reward value added—to fund increases in persistence over the probable rates of entering students—if the aim is to improve the number of degrees attained. Although research can be used to inform such policy adaptations, such models of public funding are more complex than typical state budgeting. Funding per degree, in contrast, could undermine quality because institutions might respond to that incentive by making it easier to earn the degree.

Data reporting and accountability are set up to help state agencies meet challenges within state higher education systems. The major challenges for the coordinating agencies during the global transition have been coordination with K–12 education to align curriculum content and assessment (Chapter 4); tax revenue shortfalls affecting appropriations to higher education, resulting in higher tuition and lower student aid (Chapter 5); coordination of course and degree articulation to ensure easy transfer between 2-year and 4-year colleges within states (Townsend, 2001); and coordinated development of public and private systems of higher education to meet expanded demand (Zumeta, 2001, 2004). All of these coordination mechanisms could have an influence on opportunities for students to enroll and persist to the earning of a degree, but there has not been adequate research on this policy linkage. These strategies for rationalized development of coordinated systems are also more difficult to maintain in periods of financial stress and privatization of public 4-year colleges, in large part because those required to collaborate toward alignment are in fact competing for scarce resources.

The long history of institutional autonomy, particularly among public 4-year institutions, has undermined efforts to coordinate higher education (Schmidtlein & Berdahl, 2005). With increasing budget challenges, more flagship public universities are pushing for greater autonomy and independence from their states (Gonzalez, 2011). New York State, for example, is considering providing public universities with the discretion to set differential tuition rates, to expedite capital expenditure programs through institutional foundations, and to enter into public/private partnerships (New York State Senate, 2011). Given the budget challenges in higher education, it is increasingly likely that many of the leading public universities will gain greater freedom from state policy.

However, as the enrollment patterns illustrated (Chapter 5), 2-year colleges face different challenges and conditions. They have low tuition rates and are a low-cost college alternative (Voorhees, 2001). In 2010, community college tuition and fees averaged $2,713 across the country, compared with in-state tuition rates at public universities of more than $7,600 (Baum & Ma, 2011). Two-year colleges are subject to financial constraints because of their low tuition rates and challenges in state support. To the extent that states take actions that increase tuition or reduce services in community colleges, retention and degree completion rates within state 2-year college systems may decline; because of competition, community colleges may also become more selective in terms of the students they serve. The links between state funding and student retention are further discussed below.

State Data Systems

The push to create student record data systems has been a centerpiece of the federal reform efforts in this century. As mentioned earlier, attempting to coordinate reporting across states has been a federal priority for more than 50 years, but recently those efforts have intensified. In 2002, Title II of the Educational Technical Assistance Act created the State Longitudinal Data System Grant Program "to aid state education agencies in developing and implementing longitudinal data systems" (Institute of Education Sciences, 2011). Since 2005, the program has provided funding to nearly every state in the country and has provided renewal grants to as many as half. The Data Quality Campaign (DQC) established a collaborative partnership with the Bill & Melinda Gates Foundation and a range of state and national education organizations in 2005, which has served to advocate for stronger data systems overall and a source of political support to develop stronger P-20 data systems at the state level. In its work, DQC has identified 17 separate sources of support from three federal departments to fund portions of the larger data system (Data Quality Campaign, 2011).

The challenge state policymakers face as they develop these data strategies is twofold. First, institutional autonomy is valued among the higher education community, and it is reluctant to open the door to stronger measures of accountability. This is a challenge in the public sector but is particularly strong in private higher education. Today, even among the states with the strongest, most coordinated data systems, private higher education is seldom involved and most states do not have the mechanisms in place to compel the participation of private institutions. In 2006, a total of 39 states had postsecondary data tracking systems (AACRAO, 2004) but only 8 included private not-for-profit institutions.

By 2011, most states had created or were in the process of developing postsecondary data systems, but no progress has been made in including private higher education.

Second and perhaps more problematic, state policymakers are seeking to create these data systems without plans for how they will be utilized. Given that a number of states have attempted to tie funding to measures of performance (discussed below), institutions are suspicious of policymakers' motives in developing student record data systems. The politics of accountability aside, gathering and reporting data is an expensive proposition for any institution. Today, most colleges and universities employ full-time staff dedicated to federal and state reporting requirements. To maintain eligibility for federal Title IV financial aid, colleges and universities are required to respond to nine comprehensive surveys for the Integrated Postsecondary Education Data System (IPEDS) on issues pertaining to institutional characteristics, enrollment, pricing, financial aid, degree completion, graduation rates, financing, and staffing. State reporting requirements can be similarly onerous and, as state budgets shrink, fewer resources are available to use the data in meaningful ways. The DQC has noted that despite the great progress that has been made in terms of developing the systems, states have not made much progress in terms of utilizing the data (Data Quality Campaign, 2011).

State Performance Funding, Budgeting, and Reporting

Burke (2005) notes that during the 1990s, state coordinating bodies entered into arrangements with states, trading greater accountability for increased institutional autonomy. These bargains indicated a shift away from accountability based on inputs into the system to the outcomes that result from postsecondary education. The basic theory is straightforward: (1) when institutions are accountable for a set of outcomes, they will develop appropriate strategies to address those outcomes in an effort to capture as much funding as possible, and (2) states can use the power of appropriations to hold institutions accountable for poor performance and reward positive performance. As currently crafted, these policies tend to treat all institutions as essentially the same, failing to recognize that they serve different purposes and should be accountable for different outcomes. States have adopted essentially three different performance-based incentive programs that operate in different ways.

In practice, performance funding ties some portion of state funding directly to performance on key indicators. When those objectives are met, institutions receive predetermined levels of additional support. Performance budgeting focuses on the development, implementation, and presentation of institutional budgets and leaves distributional decisions to the discretion of internal systems or coordinating agencies. It is assumed that by making institutional data publicly available and open to scrutiny, institutions will improve on designated indicators. Nearly a third of states or state systems have adopted the least flexible performance funding approach (the proportion of state appropriations tied to performance ranges from 1% to 5% or 6%) (Burke, 2005); more than half have adopted performance reporting requirements. The vast majority of states indicate retention and degree completion as a required indicator. Of 29 states with performance reporting, 24 include indicators of completion and retention, and 10 of 11 performance funding states do the same.

During the 1990s and into the early part of the 21st century, state policy focused on increasing access to higher education. Whereas state policymakers are concerned about degree attainment, they are also interested in greater efficiency in higher education (McLendon, Hearn, & Deaton, 2006). Efficiency from a policymaker's perspective amounts to serving more students with fewer state resources. States face pressures to fund K–12 education, healthcare, and corrections. When revenues decline, higher education has been the easiest for states to cut because the deficiencies can be made up by students through tuition and fees; conversely, postsecondary education has generally received the largest gains when state revenues were strong (Delaney & Doyle, 2007). It is much less clear today whether, in the global period, the balance wheel will restore funding to higher education to the degree it has in the past.

Performance approaches to accountability have been difficult to implement and enforce. The important question to answer is whether performance-based accountability schemes have had an effect on outcomes. Burke (2005) found that states perceived the programs as being only marginally beneficial and in many cases reported that there was no impact; however, research indicates that the use of performance programs does appear to influence institutional performance on degree completion and/or research productivity (Shin, 2010). One problem is that states use a laundry list of performance indicators (an average of 40) rather than targeting critical issues (Burke, 2005).

Financial Stress and Degree Attainment

Each state has evolved its own strategies for aligning high schools, community colleges, and 4-year colleges as well as the use of state student aid to mitigate the cost of attendance for low- and moderate-income and/or high-achieving students. As states adjust their unique strategies of coordination and finance, their decisions influence retention and degree completion as well as enrollment. Although we are able to review general, national trends in retention from nationally reported data, trend analyses do not explicitly capture the linkages between strategies and student outcomes in the 50 states. The case studies in Part II provide more evidence to consider relative to linkages between state policies and student outcomes within the national market systems of higher education.

Federal Programs Focusing on Persistence

Since the early 1970s, federal student financial aid programs have focused on access, choice, and persistence (Gladieux & Wolanin, 1976), although access and choice tended to have a more explicit focus on federal policy than degree completion. Historically, an extensive body of research linked student aid to persistence in higher education (Leslie & Brinkman, 1988), and there is evidence that changes in student aid have influenced changes in persistence rates over time (St. John, 1989, 1990). Although the direct effects of financial aid are historically important matters for national policy, the 2008 reauthorization of the 4-(P. L. 110–315) placed a more direct emphasis on retention. Whereas the major federal student aid programs were reviewed previously (Chapter 5), we now refocus on the relationship between federal financial aid policy and student retention subsequent to the reauthorization of HEA, along with the ways these policies have been undermined by the financial crisis.

Long-Standing Programs

A few federal programs have historically had an emphasis on retention. The TRIO programs, funded under Title IV of the Higher Education Act, began in 1964 with the Upward Bound Program (U.S. Department of Education, 2011c). Over 45 years, the TRIO programs have been expanded to include Talent Search and two extensions of the Upward Bound Program (Math and Science and Veteran's Upward Bound)—all of which focus on pre-college outreach and preparation—along with the postsecondary Student Support Services (SSS) and the McNair Scholars programs designed to identify and support low-income, first-generation, and underrepresented minority students as they earn their baccalaureate degrees and transition to graduate level education (Office of Postsecondary Education, 2011). The Educational Opportunity Centers (EOC) provide outreach, support, and financial literacy services targeting adult learners returning to college. In 1998, the federal GEAR UP program was added to the family of precollege outreach efforts under the Higher Education Act (Alderete, 2006).

Although these programs have a long history, comparatively little work has been done to evaluate them. Mathematica conducted an evaluation in the late 1990s of the Upward Bound Program with mixed findings. Overall, modest gains were found in course taking, high school completion, and college enrollment, and these gains were slightly larger for African American and Hispanic students (U.S. Department of Education, 1999). The final report of the longitudinal evaluation concluded that the program had no effect on overall college enrollment rates, financial aid applications, or bachelor's degree completion, but that more students completed vocational or certificate programs and that Upward Bound programs were more effective for lower-aspiring students and those entering the program with lower levels of academic preparation (Seftor, Mamun, & Schirm, 2009). A similar, smaller-scale evaluation of Talent Search found that the program appeared to have stronger positive impacts on students' financial aid application and college enrollment behaviors, though their findings were tempered by the fact that the study was not randomized (unlike the Upward Bound evaluation) (Constantine, Seftor, Martin, Silva, & Myers, 2006).

Similar evaluations have been conducted of the postsecondary TRIO programs. Student Support Services was found to have a positive effect on college GPA, course credits earned, and retention rates, and these findings were stronger in the first year when levels of service were higher (Chaney, 2010). The evaluation also points out that effect sizes depend upon the level of service received, suggesting a potential selection bias assuming those that receive more services choose to do so for different reasons. Neither the McNair Scholars program nor that of the EOC has been evaluated nationally.

Recently the federal government has expanded its efforts to serve underrepresented populations at the nation's Historically Black Colleges and Universities. Under Title III of the Higher Education Act, the U.S. Department of Education is sponsoring the Predominantly Black Institutions formula grant program to improve outreach to low-income and first-generation students served at institutions with more than 40% African American enrollment (Office of Postsecondary Education, 2011). In most cases, it is too early to tell whether these postsecondary initiatives are likely to influence student outcomes, but it is clear that greater attention is being paid to postsecondary success today than in years past.

Higher education faces a serious challenge because current federal programs supporting persistence are at risk of being dismantled. The federal government just recently cut funding for the Leveraging Educational Assistance Partnership Program (LEAP), which provides a federal match to states who offer need-based scholarship programs (Section 407, HEA of 2008) (Inside Higher Education, 2011). The LEAP and other need-based programs have a well-documented impact on retention and persistence (Rong & St. John, 2011; St. John, 2006). It is uncertain what the impact of cutting federal LEAP funding will be on state funding for need-based grants, but once the incentive of the federal match is eliminated, it is likely states will look to cut their funding for these programs as well. As part of LEAP, states fund two-thirds of the costs and the federal government funds one-third, but federal funding has always been limited. All states developed state grants programs after this program was created in 1972, but it was never funded at a level that incentivized states to meet full financial need, and only a few states have attempted to provide need-based aid at this level (see Chapter 5 and state cases).

A Major New Program Dismantled

The attempt to bring the health care bill in as budget-neutral has had a seriously problematic impact on federal programs to support retention. A new federal program, Grants for Access and Persistence (GAP), had been authorized in the Higher Education Act of 2008. This new state partnership program was modeled after Indiana's Twenty-First Century Scholars program and authorized funding for states to develop new partnerships for student financial aid that supported access and persistence. The structure of the program required notifying low-income students of eligibility, and providing last-dollar grants equaling tuition after other state and federal grants, and support services for retention at degree granting institutions. As part of the law, states were required to indicate a "nonbinding estimate" of the award level under the program (HEA 2008, 122 STAT. p. 3221), unlike the Twenty-First Century Scholars program, which provided a guarantee that the state award would cover estimated need as part of the program design (Lumina Foundation, 2009). GAP-eligible students would receive an award through all years of eligibility to encourage degree attainment. The Secretary of Education was authorized to fund pilot programs under the Access and Persistence Grants Program. A pilot program was established with matching funds from foundations and other sources (Oliver, 2009).

Federal funding for GAP has been eliminated,[4] which creates serious problems in some states that had initiatives planned as pilots for this program. A few states received grants to begin to develop new partnerships through this initiative. In addition, although the award commitments to students under GAP were nonbinding, the information that grants would meet needs encouraged students to apply and enroll in partner institutions; the cut in funding could affect such students, given the start-up process under way in some states. Thankfully the bottoming out of the federal share of this innovative new program has not completely killed the concept; for example, the Gates Foundation has created a fund for this purpose.[5] This program is an illustration of an effort to improve persistence and completion informed by research and rationalized in neoliberal terms but reflecting core classic liberal values.

Federal Monitoring of Access and Persistence

The Higher Education Opportunity Act of 2008 reauthorized the Advisory Committee on Student Financial Assistance (ACSFA) through 2014 and directed it to continue to monitor net prices and their effects. It also required annual reports analyzing the adequacy of need-based grant aid for postsecondary enrollment and the graduation rates of low- and moderate-income students. In 2010, the Advisory Committee released *The Rising Price of Inequality,* documenting increases over time in net prices. The continuation of these efforts in the near future will, if nothing else, at least provide documentation of the financial challenges facing students as they seek to persist in higher education.

Beyond documenting the gaps between college costs and the level of need-based financial aid for low- and moderate-income students (e.g., ACSFA, 2010), the Advisory

Committee faces a serious challenge in documenting the impact of student aid on persistence. Although a few researchers have adapted retention models to examine the direct effects of federal financial aid on persistence (see review below), the impact of federal programs on persistence and degree completion is a topic that merits future study.

Persistence Research

There is a long tradition of theory-based research on retention and persistence in higher education. Retention studies focus on whether students persist in their original institution, while *persistence* refers to students' success across the system of higher education, including transfer. Retention is captured in most state and federal studies that consider degree completion, but it is limited because retention research considers only students who stay in their institution of origin. The federal government now requires colleges and universities to report on 6-year degree completion rates as a measure of retention without considering transfer. Understandably, research on retention and persistence often uses similar theories, which complicates efforts to review and use research to inform policy.

Retention Theory and Research

Early studies of retention within institutions used student data and multivariate methods (e.g., Astin, 1975). Retention theory and research have mainly focused on persistence between the first and second year of college. The two major theories of persistence focus on academic and social factors related to retention (i.e., Bean, 1980, 1983; Tinto, 1975, 1982), with most research examining academic engagement and integration, the topics for which there is the most substantial confirmatory research (Braxton, 2000; Pascarella & Terenzini, 2005). Student financial aid has not been as consistently studied, but theory reconstruction in this area has focused on costs or ability to pay (e.g., Cabrera, Nora, & Castañeda, 1992, 1993). A recent study adapting the integration model to the High School and Beyond database, which tracks retention to completion within campus of origin, found a positive association between funding for state grants and retention in a 4-year college (Rong & St. John, 2011).

Further refinement of persistence theory is necessary to consider the impact of campus interventions on student retention. A systematic review found that while many interventions in student and academic services (e.g., learning communities) have been rationalized based on retention research, few studies actually evaluated these programs using generally accepted methods (Braxton, McKinney, & Reynolds, 2006; Patton, Morelon, Whitehead, & Hossler, 2006). Quality research on student outcomes can be achieved through the adaptation of persistence models developed for institutions (e.g., St. John, 1992; Musoba, 2006; Hossler, Gross, & Ziskin, 2009). Further progress in this type of logical and model reconstruction can inform future efforts to improve degree attainment in institutions and state systems.

Persistence Research

Most federal and state data systems can be used to examine persistence inclusive of transfer, an important outcome if improved degree attainment is the aim of public policy. Persistence to degree is logically aligned with social theory on attainment and economic theory on human capital. Early models used national data systems to examine the impact of student aid on persistence, adapting social and economic theories and Tinto's theory of social integration as factors in persistence (e.g., St. John, 1989; St. John, Kirshstein, &

Noell, 1991).[6] This framework has been used to compare the impact of student aid on retention during different historical periods using multiple longitudinal cohorts (St. John, 1999) and has been adapted to the study of within-year persistence and appropriate ways of examining whether students can afford to pay for continuous enrollment (e.g., St. John, Oescher, & Andrieu, 1992). This framework has been further adapted to integrate the roles of predisposition about costs and financial aid as means of showing the direct and indirect effects of student aid (e.g., St. John, Paulsen, & Starkey, 1996; St. John, Cabrera, Nora, & Asker, 2000).

State data systems have also been adapted in studies of persistence, but the capacity to consider integration theories is limited because these variables are not routinely collected. The adapted social, economic, and higher education theories have been used with state data systems to examine the impact of state grants on retention within state systems (Hu & St. John, 2000; St. John, 1999; St. John, Hu, & Weber, 2000). There have also been recent efforts to use state student record databases to assess educational challenges at the campus level and to evaluate interventions designed to improve retention (Hossler, Gross, & Ziskin, 2009; St. John & Musoba, 2010). This area of research has potential for informing states and campuses about strategies for improving retention, transfer, and persistence to degree—issues that will be of increasing importance in the decades ahead.

Improving Retention, Persistence, and Degree Completion

Retention, persistence, and degree completion have become important considerations in public policy. Yet while government policymakers mention retention when they formulate policy, the changes in public finance of higher education in the past two decades have undermined this outcome because of rising net costs for students with financial need. Research on student aid and persistence can be used and has been used to advocate for funding of student aid programs; it can also help institutions adjust to the new conditions.

Colleges and universities face difficult choices about how to use pricing strategies—the combination of tuition and student aid—to attract college students who will be able to pay for 4 years of college and to persist beyond the 4th year when necessary for completion. In particular, campuses are faced with difficult choices about how to invest available funds to generate revenues and to maintain financial health (Hossler, 2006). The economic conditions that have undermined state and federal funding of higher education and student aid programs may well have lasting effects, increasing the importance of research that informs strategy and adaptation. Once major cuts are made to these programs, it is hard to restore funding. Policymakers and researchers face new challenges in creating and evaluating programs and funding strategies that improve rates of college success in a period of financial constraints.

TRENDS IN DEGREE ATTAINMENT

Graduation rates have been reported by postsecondary institutions to IPEDS since 2002. Overall graduation rates—degrees attained in institutions of origin within 150% of the time to degree[7]—remained relatively stable, but there were substantial and slightly increasing gaps between Whites and Asians and underrepresented minorities (Figure 6.1). While the overall rate of change in completion rates was modest, there was a slight decline in graduation rates for all groups after 2006.

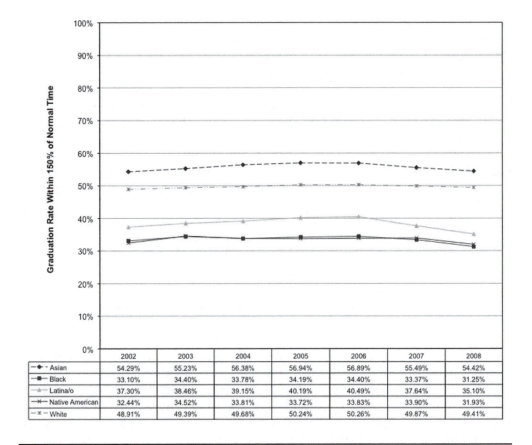

Figure 6.1 Trends in Graduation Rates in All Postsecondary Institutions

Source: Data from NCES Integrated Postsecondary Education Data System © 2011 Projects Promoting Equity in Urban and Higher Education, NCID at the University of Michigan.

	2002	2003	2004	2005	2006	2007	2008
Asian	54.29%	55.23%	56.38%	56.94%	56.89%	55.49%	54.42%
Black	33.10%	34.40%	33.78%	34.19%	34.40%	33.37%	31.25%
Latina/o	37.30%	38.46%	39.15%	40.19%	40.49%	37.64%	35.10%
Native American	32.44%	34.52%	33.81%	33.72%	33.83%	33.90%	31.93%
White	48.91%	49.39%	49.68%	50.24%	50.26%	49.87%	49.41%

The decline after 2006 could be related to the worsening economic conditions for students: increased tuition, failure of government grants to keep up with price increases, a growing student debt burden, and a worsening labor market. Discovering the reasons for this shift would make interesting research questions for policy researchers or dissertation students. It is difficult to untangle how trends in federal policy relate to degree completion rates. Institutions usually package student aid on top of federal and student grants. In addition, campuses design and implement academic programs and support services to encourage degree completion.

Public 2-Year Colleges

The national graduation rates for public 2-year colleges are exceedingly low (Figure 6.2). Whites graduated at the highest rate in 2002 (27%) and at the second highest rate (24%) in 2008. The graduation rate for Asians grew slightly during the period (rising from 25% to 26%). In contrast, the graduation rates for African Americans and Latinos/as declined at a higher rate than for other groups (to 14% for African Americans in 2006 and 16% for Latinos/as). Native Americans graduated at about 20% across the 4 years.

The trend to decreasing opportunity to complete degrees and the widening of the opportunity gap is actually more apparent in community colleges than in other sectors.

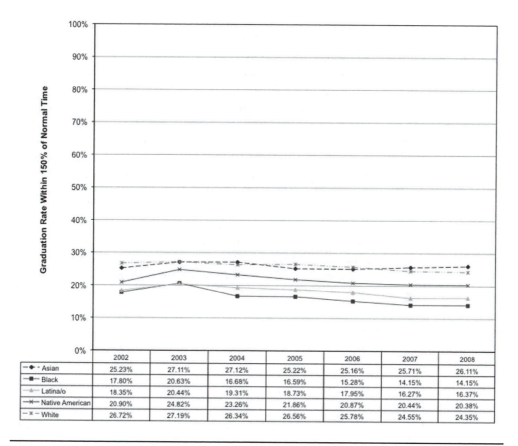

Figure 6.2 Trends in Graduation Rates in All Public 2-Year Postsecondary Institutions

Source: Data from NCES Integrated Postsecondary Education Data System © 2011 Projects Promoting Equity in Urban and Higher Education, NCID at the University of Michigan.

Whereas financial conditions could explain the growing gap in completion—especially since community colleges typically have fewer institutional resources to dedicate to student aid than public 4-year colleges—the more troubling aspect of the growing differential in degree completion rates is that African Americans are enrolling in public 2-year colleges in increasing numbers (Chapter 5). Further, given the reforms in K–12 preparation (Chapter 4), it is doubtful that declines in preparation explain the widening gap.

Public 4-Year Colleges

In contrast to public 2-year colleges, there has been a pattern of gradual improvement in degree completion rates within public 4-year institutions (Figure 6.3); all groups had higher completions rates in 2008 than in 2002 in spite of the troubling conditions of public funding for higher education in the United States. Further research is needed to discern the extent to which institutional investments in student aid, academic programs, and support services contributed to the gains. Such research can help inform public policy and institutional strategy in the decade ahead if college completion continues to be an issue of concern for policymakers in states and at the federal level.

Even with gains in completion rates overall, the gaps widened for underrepresented minority (URM) students compared with Whites and Asians. Once again the reasons for the widening opportunity gap are troubling and merit scrutiny. There are three plausible explanations for how academic preparation may be a contributing factor. First, it is possible that the college preparation curriculum would have gotten worse for URM students who qualified for and could attend public 4-year colleges than for White and Asians. This seems unlikely given recent state and federal efforts to improve the high school curriculum, but it is not beyond the realm of possibility given Kozol's (2005) recent findings of weaknesses in urban education in the United States. Second, it is possible that student aspirations have changed and, as a result, more underprepared students are attending college. This is plausible given that we have shifted from mass to near universal access to college. But if that is the case, we suspect that trends will recover after the system adapts to the new expectations. Third, it is possible that institutions are less effective in serving the needs of less prepared students than in years past. On its face, it seems implausible, but evidence suggests that remediation, for example, has not been a successful institutional strategy to address underpreparation. It is also the case that as institutions seek prestige and attract higher-profile students academically, they will

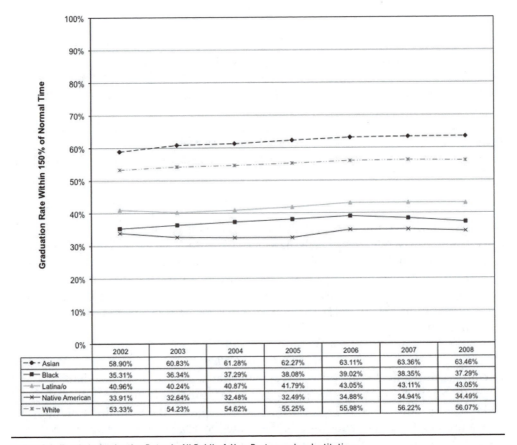

	2002	2003	2004	2005	2006	2007	2008
Asian	58.90%	60.83%	61.28%	62.27%	63.11%	63.36%	63.46%
Black	35.31%	36.34%	37.29%	38.08%	39.02%	38.35%	37.29%
Latina/o	40.96%	40.24%	40.87%	41.79%	43.05%	43.11%	43.05%
Native American	33.91%	32.64%	32.48%	32.49%	34.88%	34.94%	34.49%
White	53.33%	54.23%	54.62%	55.25%	55.98%	56.22%	56.07%

Figure 6.3 Trends in Graduation Rates in All Public 4-Year Postsecondary Institutions

Source: Data from NCES Integrated Postsecondary Education Data System © 2011 Projects Promoting Equity in Urban and Higher Education, NCID at the University of Michigan.

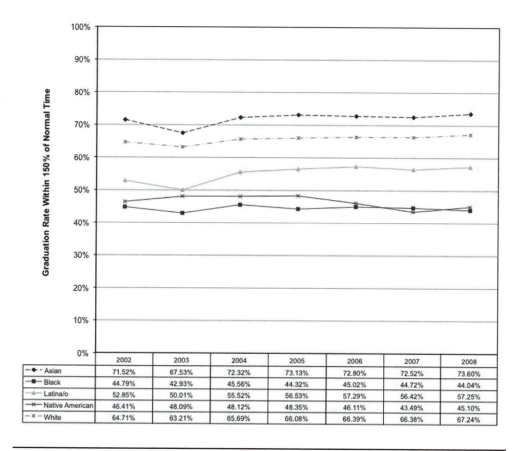

Figure 6.4 Trends in Graduation Rates in All Private Nonprofit Postsecondary Institutions

Source: Data from NCES Integrated Postsecondary Education Data System © 2011 Projects Promoting Equity in Urban and Higher Education, NCID at the University of Michigan.

change their structures to eliminate those services designed to help students who are less prepared; such has been the case at the University at Buffalo. Further, if researchers and policymakers think that lack of campus support contributed to the decline, it is necessary to consider whether support services got worse during the decade. Of the possible explanations, the growth in unmet need after grants and resulting growth in loans for undergraduates remains a strong possibility, given the differences in incomes of URM student and majority students.

A challenge for policymakers and researchers who are concerned about degree completion in public 4-year colleges is to differentiate between cross-sectional evidence about completion for any single cohort and trends in cohorts over time. No doubt the differentials in preparation and support influence differences in the success rates for any single cohort, but variability in those same academic, financial, and student supports over time must be considered to discern reasons for differences in trends for cohorts of URM and majority students. Further, it is crucial to recognize gains in outcomes—the overall trend toward improvement—along with the differentials in making judgments about future policy changes and intervention strategies.

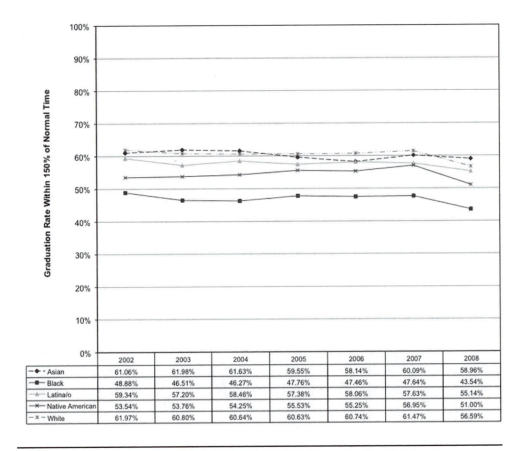

	2002	2003	2004	2005	2006	2007	2008
Asian	61.06%	61.98%	61.63%	59.55%	58.14%	60.09%	58.96%
Black	48.88%	46.51%	46.27%	47.76%	47.46%	47.64%	43.54%
Latina/o	59.34%	57.20%	58.46%	57.38%	58.06%	57.63%	55.14%
Native American	53.54%	53.76%	54.25%	55.53%	55.25%	56.95%	51.00%
White	61.97%	60.80%	60.64%	60.63%	60.74%	61.47%	56.59%

Figure 6.5 Trends in Graduation Rates in All Private For-Profit Postsecondary Institutions

Source: Data from NCES Integrated Postsecondary Education Data System © 2011 Projects Promoting Equity in Urban and Higher Education, NCID at the University of Michigan.

Private 4-Year Colleges

Of the postsecondary sectors in the United States, the not-for-profit private and independent colleges have the best overall completion rates (Figure 6.4). In 2008, more than two thirds of Whites (67%) and Asians (73%) from the 2002 entering cohort had graduated, as had more than half of the Latinos/as (57%). In contrast, the completion rates for African Americans and Native Americans were below 50% (44% and 45%, respectively) and did not improve during the decade.

The private nonprofit colleges, like the other groups, face major challenges with respect to gaps in opportunities to complete degrees. Although private universities have narrowed the enrollment gap for URM groups (see Chapter 5), they have a widening gap in degree completion. These issues merit the attention of institutional researchers and leaders in private colleges.[8]

For-Profit Colleges

Compared with public colleges, the 6-year completion rates at for-profit colleges are high for all students except African Americans, consistently higher than 50% for Whites,

Asian, Latinos/as, and Native Americans (Figure 6.5). Interpreting the meaning of the high rates of completion in for-profit colleges compared with public 2-year colleges is a complex matter. Proprietary colleges are criticized because of larger dropout rates and high levels of student debt (Baum & Steele, 2010), yet overall they are moderately successful (i.e., they have higher completion rates than 2-year colleges). The clock-hour programs in proprietary schools allow students to engage far more frequently while they are enrolled and to complete their degrees or certifications more quickly than community colleges. Given the comparative data on retention, researchers and policymakers should investigate the reasons for success and consider the ways in which these successful methods can be adapted for public 2-year systems, with their extremely low completion rates.

Proprietary schools are not, however, without problems. The completion rate for African Americans hovered around 48% from 2002 until 2007 but dropped to 44% in 2008 (Figure 6.5). This is a cause for concern, especially given the overrepresentation of African Americans in this sector. As is evident from the review of research below, degree completion in proprietary education is not a widely investigated subject.[9]

RESEARCH LINKING POLICY AND OUTCOMES

In recent years, federal policy priorities have shifted from an emphasis on access to college to a focus on degree completion. The Obama administration proposed replacing the College Access Challenge Grant initiative with a more comprehensive and generous College Access and Completion Fund (Moltz, 2009). In 2011, the U.S. Department of Education published the College Completion Toolkit to give states guidance on promising strategies to improve performance (U.S. Department of Education, 2011a). Among their preferred policy strategies were performance funding, P–16 curricular alignment, simplified transfer articulation, and data-driven decision making.

Since 2000, the National Center for Education Statistics (NCES) has published 10 statistical analysis reports examining trends in student persistence and degree completion. These reports draw on two primary sources of data—IPEDS and the Beginning Postsecondary Studies (BPS). IPEDS provides annual census data of all colleges and universities receiving federal resources and can be used to track enrollments, degree completions, and graduation rates over time. The longitudinal BPS study began following its third cohort of beginning postsecondary students in 2006 and is a representative source of data allowing researchers to follow students' pathways through college, including student persistence, transfer behavior, and degree completion.

The NCES reports paint a consistent picture of persistence and completion trends and the factors known to be associated with student outcomes. Among the entering class of 1995–1996, most students who enrolled at 4-year institutions remained in school (only 18% had left) (Berkner, Horn, & Clune, 2000). At 2-year colleges, the attrition rate after 3 years was nearly 40%. The NCES report focused on comparisons of the for-profit sector with community colleges and other less-than-4-year not-for-profit institutions; they found that degree attainment rates were generally better among the for-profit institutions. No attempt was made to consider how enrollments differ across those institutions. A follow-up survey with the same cohort of students found that better-prepared students were more likely to attend 4-year institutions and persist to degree and that both institutional type and delayed entry were predictors of student success in college (Berkner, He, Cataldi, & Knepper, 2003).

These results are consistent with Horn and Kojaku's (2001) findings that the strength of the high school curriculum was a strong predictor of persistence and transfer behavior among beginning postsecondary students. Adelman's (2006) follow-up to the Toolbox study reinforced this notion that the strength of the high school curriculum is the strongest determinant of bachelor's degree attainment. Wei and Horn (2002) examined differences between Pell-eligible and noneligible students; they observe that Pell students exhibited a greater number of risk factors for failing to persist in college. Chen (2007) examined a series of linkages between concerns about the cost of college and student persistence among part-time-enrolled students, finding that nearly two thirds of part-time students worked to address financial concerns and that these students were less likely to persist and complete degrees.

Institutional characteristics have been an important consideration in a number of the recent NCES reports. Horn and Peter (2003) examined institutional aid practices and found that high-achieving high school students received more generous institutional award packages at less selective institutions. These findings do not address specifically whether institutional aid affects student persistence or completion but raise an important question relative to the selection of students: if less selective institutions are attempting to compete for high-achieving students, fewer slots will be available for middle-achieving students, who will be pushed to community colleges or the for-profit sector. Peter and Forrest Cataldi (2005) examined the pathways and destinations of students who chose to attend multiple institutions; they found that community college enrollees, traditional-age students, and dependent students were more likely to attend multiple institutions, and this pattern was problematic for students who began at 4-year institutions. It is not possible to draw causal inferences from these analyses but the findings are not surprising. Analyses focusing specifically on community college students revealed that these 2-year institutions were more likely to retain and graduate students who were either committed to earning a credential or to transferring to a 4-year college than other students (Horn, Nevill, & Griffith, 2006).

Collectively, the NCES reports paint a picture of the potential challenges thought to influence students' pathways through college and to a degree, but they are limited. These are descriptive reports intended to illustrate relationships but not designed to test causal patterns. Because they choose to target reports to particular issues or challenges, many of these reports are not designed to weigh the relative influence of different factors. Typically, these reports also follow a series of outcomes for a subset of students or they focus on a particular institutional type, which is a useful descriptive tool but requires that other analytic strategies be employed to conduct more rigorous evaluative studies. In the sections that follow, we focus on two separate outcomes—student persistence and degree completion. Generally speaking, the former is of particular interest to educational researchers, whereas the latter is a focus of economists, typically in relation to labor market outcomes.

Financial Aid Policy

There are two sets of policies researchers have considered in relation to the likelihood of students persisting in college—financial aid and placement in college remediation programs. The linkage between financial aid and persistence has been contested for many years. Tinto's early work on student persistence suggested that the effect of financial aid was relevant in students' decisions to attend college and their choice of institution, but that it did not have a direct effect on students' persistence within an institution (Tinto, 1993); however, it may affect persistence indirectly in terms of full-time status. Work study may have a positive effect, particularly as a strategy to engage students in the institutional community.

Dynarski (1999) examined the effects of eliminating the Social Security death benefit for higher education and found that students who lost a parent were more likely to attend college and persist to degree when the program was available. Bettinger (2004) examined the relationship between receipt of the Pell and persistence among students attending institutions in Ohio. Using regression discontinuity analytic techniques, Bettinger found that students receiving Pell were more likely to persist than similar non-Pell-eligible students. Turner and Bound (2003) analyzed the historical impact of the GI Bill on postsecondary outcomes for military servicemen, revealing that the GI Bill had a positive impact on college attendance and degree completion for White men and African American men outside of the southern states. The aggregate effect, however, was a widening gap between Black and White college enrollees post–World War II.

Titus conducted two separate studies of the effects of financial policies on college degree completion—the first examining longitudinal data from BPS and the second utilizing state-year panel data—with consistent findings. In the first study, Titus found that neither tuition nor state appropriations were related to degree completion but that need-based aid was positively related (Titus, 2006). In his fixed effects analysis of aggregated state data (Titus, 2010), similar results were found: tuition, appropriations, and merit aid programs were all unrelated to the proportion of degrees completed in a state, but need-based aid was positively related to degree completion. Ishitani (2006) came to a different conclusion regarding the effects of financial aid in analyzing data from the National Education Longitudinal Study (NELS) on the pathways of first-generation students and those whose parents had not finished a college degree. He found that both grant aid and work-study programs were negatively related to student persistence, particularly in the first 2 years—a finding that contradicts the limited contribution Tinto suggests may be present. Ishitani uses event history analyses and addresses the critical dimension of time but does not account for probable sources of selection bias. It is likely that aid-eligible students are less likely to persist by virtue of other characteristics, such as level of preparation or engagement in the social and academic fabric of the institution. More recently, Chen and St. John (2011) utilized the Beginning Postsecondary Study (BPS) and state indicator data to examine the effects of state financial aid policies on student persistence. Their findings suggest that state need-based aid programs are positively related to student persistence.

Financial aid policy is more frequently considered at both the state and federal levels, but institutions play an important role in financial aid as well. DesJardins and McCall (2010) conducted a series of simulations to assess the relative effects of a range of institutional aid policies. Overall, financial aid increases the chances a student will complete their degree. Frontloading aid by providing more generous packages during the first 2 years may influence dropout in the second 2 years, when loans increase in lieu of grants. Loan replacement policies, like those adopted at Princeton University and others, appear to reduce the probability of stopping out. Institutional policies represent an important area for future research on the effects of aid on student persistence and completion.

Academic Remediation

A substantial body of research in recent years has considered the impact of remedial education on students' chances for success in college. Remediation has been a contentious policy issue. The larger policy question is whether or not to fund remedial course work, particularly at 4-year institutions, but the primary concern is whether these courses improve students' chances for success, including persistence. On this question the research is mixed.

Bettinger and Long (2005) examined patterns of remediation for college students in Ohio and concluded that math remediation has a positive effect on persistence, but there was no effect for English remediation. Attewell, Lavin, Domina, and Levey (2006) used national data to examine the effectiveness of remedial education and concluded that remediation in reading had a clear negative impact on degree completion, remediation in math exhibited a weak negative association, and writing was not related to 4-year degree completion. Bahr (2007) considered the question of remedial effectiveness, examining data from the community college system in California and finding no differences between remedial and nonremedial students in terms of degree completion.

More recent studies of remedial effectiveness attempt to address and minimize potential sources of selection bias. Martorell and McFarlin (2007) used a regression discontinuity design to address the potential sources of selection bias, and their findings in Texas were mixed. They found that math remediation had a positive effect on grade in a first math course, but it was not related to persistence or degree completion. Calcagno and Long (2008) paid particular attention to the fact that a proportion of students do not comply with their remedial placement; these researchers' findings in Florida suggest a positive effect on persistence and total credits earned but no effect on degree completion. The bottom line, based upon existing research, is that the effects of remediation are modest when observed and may have less impact on longer-term outcomes like degree completion than on intermediate outcomes of achievement and persistence.

Overall, these findings suggest that although academic preparation is an important consideration, the likelihood that remedial students will persist to degree completion is not substantially improved, even controlling for potential sources of selection bias. These analyses speak much less specifically about the importance of price, appropriations, and merit aid on the college cost side.

CONCLUSIONS

Persistence and degree completion are becoming increasingly important policy matters. This is more complex for policymakers and researchers interested in policy outcomes than either preparation or access. The problem is that institutional practices, along with state and federal policies, have effects on persistence. But the direct effects of policy are difficult to evaluate because of the impact of campus practices in academic programs and student support as well as student aid packaging at the campus level. It will be very difficult for the federal government to construct accountability policies that actually encourage gains in attainment and reductions in disparities in degree completions rates.

The severe financial conditions of higher education, including the large debt burden of undergraduate students, is likely to have a substantial influence on future rates of degree attainment in the United States regardless of whether or not new accountability policies are implemented. For example, at the same time states like Minnesota and Indiana were implementing performance funding that rewards degree completion, they were reducing funding for need-based aid (see cases in Part II). In these states, it is highly likely that state policies will have contradictory impacts. The problem is that in this two-barrel approach to public policy, institutions are being held accountable for negative outcomes likely caused by state austerity. In these conditions, the wealthier universities with more funds for student aid and specialized programs are more likely to benefit from performance funds than 2-year colleges that are financially strapped by declining state support and increased demand for their services. Given the uncertainties about the future of persistence research in support of campus, state, and federal policies on retention, we encourage readers to ponder the practical problems related to making progress on this vital policy topic (Text Box 6.1).

Text Box 6.1 Questions About Policy, Persistence, and Research

1. How well does persistence research document and measure the effects of campus interventions designed to improvement persistence?
2. What are the strengths with research on the impact of student aid on persistence?
3. How do state policies on public funding of colleges and students impact degree completion rates?
4. How can institutions document the impact of changes in state funding on degree completion rates of their students, and is it politically feasible to conduct and report such research?
5. How does the traditional liberal political ideology relate to public decisions about funding of institutions and students?
6. How does the neoliberal political ideology relate to public decisions about funding for institutions and students?
7. How can state policies best be crafted to support improvement of degree completion in public colleges and universities?
8. How should state policies on retention and completion be evaluated? And by whom?
9. Given the complexities of state involvement in funding of public colleges and universities, how can the federal government design retention policies with high odds of improving degree completion?
10. How important are funding for public colleges and/or for student financial aid to the prospect of improving degree completion rates in the public sector?
11. How should private non-profit colleges craft their arguments for state funding of student financial aid?
12. How should private for-profit colleges engage in debates about persistence, given the public distrust often exhibited about their impact and the debt of their students (graduates and drop outs)?

Part II
Case Studies

7

THE OLD LIBERAL MODEL

The California Case

In the social progressive period after World War II, California became a national and international model for planning and financing higher education. The legacy of the California Master Plan for higher education is well known among scholars of higher education globally. The 1960 plan for the three-segment system—a state system of community colleges providing local access for all, state universities as comprehensive colleges for mass higher education serving the top third of all high school graduates, and research universities as the engine of economic development, accepting only the top 12.5%—became a model for planning in other states and nations. The agreement between President Clark Kerr of the University of California and Chancellor Glenn Dumke of California State Colleges resulted in a coordinated approach to the growth of the systems and provided a framework for the state to become a national leader in access to and quality of public higher education (Smelser & Almond, 1974; Kerr, 1963). This is a frequently told story of systemic educational transformation through political cooperation. But the landscape has changed, radically, as portrayed in a 2009 press release: "The state's financial crisis is battering its world-renowned system of higher education, reducing college opportunities for residents and threatening California's economic recovery" (Chea, 2009, p. 1). In November 2011 the California crisis became national news when students protesting tuition increases at the University of California–Davis (UC Davis) were pepper-sprayed by campus police. A call for the resignation of the chancellor followed (L.A. Now, 2011).

This chapter untangles issues related to the causes and consequences of the decline in college access in California, comparing the state case to general trends in U.S. higher education. First we revisit California's legacy of equity in higher education, before examining recent trends in K–12 policy and public finance in relation to trends in access and racial/ethnic representation in the state system of higher education. It is too early to predict how the current crisis will be resolved: whether California will survive this political storm as it has others without major changes in the state system or if a new pattern of financial and systemic restructuring will emerge.

CALIFORNIA'S LEGACY OF EXCELLENCE AND EQUITY

Its master plan set California on a trajectory to greatness in its higher education system. The differentiated system was not only a model for other states and nations, but California also had the best college enrollment rate in the nation and more top-rated research universities than any other state. Staying the course was often difficult, since the system resisted change in the face of new challenges—an approach that eventually resulted in erosion in access, largely as the consequence of an acute financial crisis.

The California Master Plan

The University of California, one of the original land grant colleges, rapidly gained distinction (Marsden, 1994; Thelin, 2004b) and was the first university where direct delegation of authority over academic matters was given to the faculty (McConnell & Mortimer, 1970; Fitzgibbons, 1968). As in many other states, higher education evolved largely based on community advocacy and competition among college campuses. By the 1940s the University of California had developed a multicampus system. Teacher normal schools (e.g., Chico State College) were combined with technical colleges (e.g., Pomona), and comprehensive colleges (Los Angeles) were formed into a state college system in the first half of the 20th century; community colleges also emerged, usually in partnership with school districts.

With the return of World War II veterans to California campuses after passage of the GI Bill, all of the campuses began to grow, especially the state colleges and universities. There was tension among the systems but plenty of opportunity to grow, given the rapid growth of the state population, provided that politics was not allowed to prevail over rationality. Indeed, the plan has been heralded as a triumph of planning over chaos (Kerr, 1963; Smelser & Almond, 1974). The master plan guided development of three multicampus systems: the University of California, California State Colleges and Universities, and California Community Colleges.

Within this scheme, state colleges and universities had greater opportunity to grow in size, while the campuses of the University of California had the opportunity to concentrate on research excellence. UC Berkeley became the icon of the research university (Kerr, 1963), and UC Davis, San Diego, and Irvine also became leading research universities, often counted among the nation's top institutions. At the same time, California state colleges and universities and California community colleges also became models for the development of state education systems (Lee & Bowen, 1971, 1975). As part of the plan, California maintained a commitment to low tuition and high grant aid in spite of serious financial challenges.

Weathering Political Storms

Soon after the master plan was initiated, the Free Speech Movement (FSM) came to the University of California (Cohen & Zelnik, 2002) with immediate effects. In his run for governor in 1968, Ronald Reagan campaigned against the protesters and the image of liberal intellectuals. Early in his first term, he turned his attention to the UC budgets (Evens, 1970) and implemented the first education fees. At the same time, students lobbied within campuses to use funding for student-oriented programs, including peer advising and other programs to engage students (St. John, 1973). As at many universities, the institutions within the UC system weathered the storm of student protest by adapting and finding new ways to involve students (McGrath, 1970; St. John & Regan, 1973). A new center was established at Berkeley that focused initially on governance, with an eye to UC becoming a national model (e.g., Glenny, 1973; Glenny, Bowen, Meisinger, Morgan, Purves, & Schmidtline, 1975; McConnell & Mortimer, 1970).

After being pushed out of the presidency of the UC system by Governor Reagan, Clark Kerr went on to head the Carnegie Commission on Higher Education, providing a new phase of leadership to the nation (Carnegie Commission on Higher Education, 1973). He continued to provide national leadership in higher education in the United States and nationally through study groups (e.g., Carnegie Council on Policy Studies in Higher Education, 1980; Kerr, 1978) and public commentary for the next two decades (Kerr, 1991, 1994, 2002). Kerr was not alone in leaving a leadership role in California higher education to go on to make national policy recommendations: Pat Callan, former commissioner of the California Postsecondary Education Commission (CPEC), has provided leadership in higher education finance (e.g., Callan, 2002; Callan & Finney, 1997), and former commissioners of California's student aid system have led national and international studies (e.g., Kipp, Price, & Wholford, 2002; Marmaduke, 1988). Because of the visibility of the California system, along with its adherence to a distinctive model of governance and finance, leaders in the system have frequently been viewed as national leaders in higher education.

Constraints of Tax Revenue

Since the passage of Proposition 13 in 1978, California has capped property taxes, which has severely constrained tax revenues. As one *LA Times* reporter (O'Leary, 2009, p. 1) put it: "Before Prop 13, in the 1950s and '60s, California was a liberal showcase. Governors Earl Warren and Pat Brown responded to the population growth of the postwar boom with a massive program of public infrastructure—the nation's finest public college system, the freeway system and the state aqueduct that carries water from the well-watered north to the parched south."

Attempts by liberal leaders to get around the provisions of Proposition 13 have largely failed (O'Leary, 2009, p. 1): "Beholden to a tax-averse electorate, the state's liberals and moderates have attempted to live with Proposition 13 while continuing to provide the state services Californians expect—freeways, higher education, prisons, assistance to needy families and, very important, essential funding to local government and school districts that vanished after the antitax measure passed."

Proposition 13 was not the only voter-passed ballot initiative constraining taxpayer support. An even tighter constraint on tax rates was imposed the following year. Proposition 4, known as the Gann Amendment, limited most state and local government expenditures from tax sources: "The Gann limit, as it is often called, was not exceeded [i.e., limits on tax increases] until the 1986–87 fiscal year when $1.1 billion was refunded to taxpayers" (Institute of Governmental Studies, 2011, p. 1).[1] In addition, in 1988 California voters amended the State Constitution in Proposition 98 to establish "a minimum annual funding level for K–14 schools (K–12 schools and community colleges). Proposition 98–related funding constitutes over 70 percent of total K–12 funding and about two-thirds of total community college funding" (Legislative Analyst's Office, 2005).[2] After Proposition 13 restricted increases in property taxes for schools, Proposition 98 ensured that other state revenues would be redirected to K–14 education, thus limiting tax revenues for colleges and other state functions. These later provisions provided a modest protection for funding for public schools and community colleges but did not accommodate future enrollment growth; subsequently, therefore, it was possible to cut funding per student to public schools as the school-age population grew. Further, the 4-year institutions did not even have this minimal protection in a severely constrained tax environment.

In combination, these constraints have handcuffed the state's efforts to fund higher education consistent with the master plan. There was substantial redirection of state tax revenues to local schools in subsequent years, but the antitax contingent has imposed several constraints on the state's ability to raise new taxes, causing a retracing in state financing of higher education along with other public enterprises in the state (St. John, 1994b). Indeed, it has long been evident in California that it would be necessary to re-structure the system of higher education finance in order to meet expected demand for access. Rather than engaging in a comprehensive restructuring of access to higher educa-tion, state leaders sought short-term fixes.

In California there was a sustained pattern of resistance to market-based remedies to the financial constraints on growth. In the late 1980s, after an update to the master plan called for dozens of new universities that the state could not afford, St. John undertook a study for the California Postsecondary Education Commission (CPEC) that focused on state strategies for financial access. It was apparent at the time that the market model adopted by Minnesota could be adapted to address the access challenge in California (St. John, 1991a). Analyses conducted originally for CPEC demonstrated how increases in tuition and student aid could be used to expand universities in response to anticipated demand (St. John, 1994a). The problem in California, as in other states at the time, was that the historic commitment to low tuition represented an important issue among lib-erals that could not be overcome in the budgeting process. Other states adjusted incre-mentally to high tuition—and a few of these states (e.g., Minnesota, next chapter)—have made substantial investments in need-based student aid when it was desperately needed. But California stuck to its goal of providing mass higher education with low tuition and state grants for high-achieving low-income students who attended the state's private col-leges. As we discuss in the final section of this chapter, the state was finally forced to raise tuition dramatically and the reverberations are still being felt.

A Renewed Focus on Access

During the 1990s and 2000s, higher education access was a major topic among research-ers and policymakers in California as the state engaged in debates about the renewal of the master plan. Much of the debate has focused on expanding access and equalizing opportunity, leading to growing problems with inequality in access, especially for the UC campuses. The demise of affirmative action and the problematic inequality in col-lege access for low-income Latinos/as have been major concerns for California, and both merit attention here.

California was the first state to ban affirmative action. The state entered the debates on affirmative action in the 1970s when UC Davis Medical School's admissions practices became a national issue. The Supreme Court's 1978 decision on *Regents of the Univer-sity of California v. Bakke* established the framework for affirmative action—outlawing quotas but allowing consideration of race—that has held up legally since that time. The University of Michigan's *Gratz* and *Grutter* decisions in the early 2000s upheld the use of affirmative action as means of overcoming past discrimination but suggested a time horizon of 25 years for the policy. However, citizens in California had already voted to outlaw affirmative action, and Michigan was soon to follow.

The issue of providing fair access after the demise of affirmative action proved an especially difficult problem for the UC system. The UC Board of Regents issued SP-1 and SP-2 in 1995, banning affirmative action in admissions and contracting. Litigation against the ban, *Castaneda v. Regents of the University of California,* upheld the ban, and in 1997, California voters passed Proposition 209, effectively codifying the UC ban across the state (Chapa & Horn, 2007). In 2001, the Board of Regents rescinded both SP-1 and SP-2; but by that point, Proposition 209 made that decision largely symbolic.

In the UC system, attention was paid to the different types of SAT scores (Rothstein, 2002); but with excessive demand, the system simply did not adjust sufficiently. In fact, UC stands in marked contrast to the University of Texas, which adapted to similar constraints by adopting a top 10% plan providing access to students based on class rank—an approach that was more successful in maintaining existing levels of racial and ethnic diversity across the system (Chapa & Horn, 2007). There has been a decline in representation of African Americans and Latinos/as in the UC system in this decade (Gándara, 2002, 2005; Gándara, Orfield, & Horn, 2006), which occurred in Texas as well. The difference is that Texas was able to respond and adapt more effectively under its 10% plan than California was able to do under its subsequently adopted and more anemic 4% plan for admission to UC.

The decline in access in the state and the fall from the top to the lower half of states in college enrollment rates have corresponded with declines in access for California's underrepresented students (Gándara, Orfield, & Horn, 2006; Orfield, 1988). In fact, there has been extensive research on inequalities in opportunity in California, with most of these studies focusing on issues related to access to academic advising and advanced courses (McDonough, 1997; McDonough & Fann, 2007; Tierney, Corwin, & Colyar, 2005; Tierney & Hagedorn, 2002). The new access research has been particularly powerful in revealing the role of culture within schools. For example, Tierney and Venegas (2007) examined how high schools convey to students whether college is a possibility, including whether they provide information on college options and student aid. New cultural patterns of reproducing an undereducated working class had evolved, especially in urban and rural parts of the state.

The underlying problem of public finance—how the state coordinates public funding to build campuses and fund students—received relatively little attention from proponents of access or the antitax public. Researchers have raised the topic of student aid (Fitzgerald & Kane, 2003) and the affordability of community colleges (Zumeta & Finkle, 2007). However, most commentary remained critical of increasing tuition and grants as a coordinated strategy for expanding supply and improving affordability. Until recently, tuition at public colleges in California had been low compared with other states, but balancing appropriations with tuition and grants, a strategy that has worked in other states (Hearn & Anderson, 1989, 1995; St. John, 1991a, 2006), has not received serious attention in California.

Demographic Change

California is unique in the United States; it has the largest population, is the most racially and ethnically diverse, and has the largest Gross State Product (GSP). But the demographic context is complex and influenced by countervailing trends. The labor force has more of a bimodal distribution of education than most states, with a high percentage of people with college degrees *and* a high percentage without high school. In 2010, some 37.7% of adults (aged 25 to 64) had attained at least an associate's degree, while 19.3% had not completed a high school credential (U.S. Census Bureau, 2011). In addition, the ethnic diversity of the state reflects both its position on the Mexican border, with a growing Latino/a population, and its position on the Pacific Coast, with a relatively high Asian population.

California also has had two economies that depend on two different patterns of immigration: Latino/a immigrants, many of whom are illegal, providing low-cost labor, and educated workers from other states and nations to fuel the state's high-technology economy. These conditions add to extremes in socioeconomic status, diversity, and social class. These demographic factors help frame the state's issues in K–12 and higher education policy.

Diversity in the State's Population

California has *become* a "majority minority state," meaning that White Californians have constituted less than half of the total state population since the 1990s. By 2006, more than 36% of California's population was made up of Latinos/as and nearly 13% comprised Asian Americans. In contrast, only about 6% identified as African American, down from about 8% in 1992, and less than 1% were Native Americans (St. John & Moronski, in press). This racial balance is important to keep in mind in trying to understand the policy discourse on race and access. These trends also suggest that the growing class differentiation in California may have racial undertones.

An Undereducated Working Class

The growing immigrant population coming across California's southern border has increased the percentage of the population that is undereducated. The state has a large undereducated population and, at the same time, plentiful jobs for citizens with college degrees. The percentage of the population that graduated from high school has stagnated relative to other states: the percentage of the population with a high school diploma was approximately equal to the national average at 79% in 1992; by 2008, California increased its graduation rates by 2% but failed to keep pace with the rest of the nation (85%) (St. John & Moronski, in press). The census number includes GED recipients, which is a difficult path to bachelor's completion. These undereducated adults work for low wages in agriculture, construction, and other trades and hold down wages for the traditional working class in the state.

Immigration in Response to Demand of Educated Workers

At the same time, California has a higher percentage of adults (between the ages of 25 and 64) with a bachelor's degree or above than the nation as a whole (St. John & Moronksi, in press). This is important to recognize because California also has a global, knowledge-based, innovation-driven, high-technology economy that depends on an educated labor force. California has attracted college-educated workers from the rest of the United States and from Asia, a pattern that contributed to new racial inequalities and economic disparities. In addition, California has had a relatively large Asian population since the late 19th century, when Chinese immigrants provided labor for railroads and other infrastructure development. Since the internment of Japanese during World

War II (Newton, 2006), California has had an open-access education system for Asian Americans.

CALIFORNIA'S EDUCATIONAL POLICIES

The transitions in California's public policies and educational outcomes are complex and interrelated. Whereas a substantial portion of the problem with growing inequality and decline in opportunity in the state seems to be linked to tax constraints, the inability of the state to adjust state finance policies to new contexts has also accelerated the decline. It is not a pretty story, and it could have been better had the state recognized the structural problems created by tax revenue constraints and adapted public policies.

As discussed earlier, California has a history of leadership in higher education finance and K–12 education. Both of these historic leadership roles have been in decline in recent decades. In fact, it is important to consider policy trends in both areas in relation to enrollment trends.

High School Reform

In 1992, California was among a minority of states that required two math courses for high school graduation (Figure 7.1). The state added Algebra I as a minimum requirement for graduation in 2003 and a mandatory exit exam in 2006. With the improvements in preparation, a similar improvement in college participation rates would be expected. As we will show later in this chapter, California did not experience the enrollment gains these policies might have intended.

Ban on Affirmative Action

With the passage of Proposition 209 in 1996, California became the first state to ban affirmative action. Demographic trends are central to understanding the vote, given the shift of Whites to minority status soon after the election, which helps explain the protectionist attitudes that became prevalent among Whites. However, Whites were no

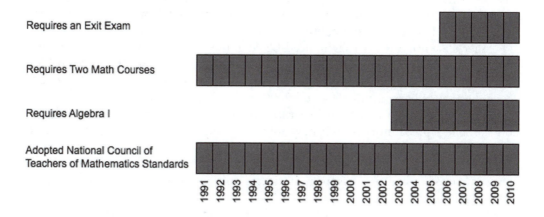

Figure 7.1 California High School Graduation Requirements

Source: © 2011 Projects Promoting Equity in Urban and Higher Education, NCID at the University of Michigan.

longer the majority; the arguments opposing affirmative action (e.g., Connerly, 2000; Montgomery, 2000) had to appeal to large numbers of minority voters for the measure to pass, especially given the strong liberal arguments for affirmative action. Latinos/as, given their growing numbers in the state, were the group with the most to gain if there had not been a shift in admissions policy; however, many of them could not vote because of their undocumented legal status.

The different view of racial preference that emerged among a majority of voters was not without racist overtones. Prejudice against Mexican Americans has a long history in California, dating back to their segregation within the state's public school system in the early 19th century, a situation that changed when Earl Warren, a liberal Republican, was governor (Newton, 2006).[3] This politically charged context should not be overlooked in examining reasons for the decline in access in California education.

Financing of Higher Education

The financing of higher education in California, a historic topic of national interest (e.g., Hansen & Weisbrod, 1967, 1969), has undergone change in recent decades. There has been an erosion of the old model of low tuition and high grant aid but not a full-scale restructuring, leaving the state in a weaker competitive position among U.S. states with respect to its capacity to educate its youth within its current tax structure.

California held to low tuition through the end of the 20th century (Figure 7.2), although it was recognized that this strategy rewarded wealthy families whose children attended the highly subsidized UC campuses. Tuition charges in California's public colleges were starting to catch up with the nation in the 2000s, but they still lagged behind. In 2008, for example, California's average charge (averaged across full-time equivalents [FTEs] in the public system) was half of the national average. It is in the context of low public tuition that California's commitment to student aid seems generous.

California's funding per FTE in public higher education was consistently higher than the national average from 1992 to 2008, although the gaps substantially narrowed in 2006 and 2008 (Figure 7.3). Higher subsidies per student are a necessity in a state that maintains low tuition if the state seeks to maintain quality and competitive public campuses over the long term. The consequence in California appears to be its inability to expand the system's infrastructure to accommodate increased demand. There has been a tendency for institutions to substitute tuition revenues for losses in state subsidies.

Further, state funding per FTE on need-based grants rose in California between 1992 and 1998, at which point it caught up with the national average. State funding fell behind the national average again in 2002, after a 2-year drop, and rose to a level substantially above the national average in 2004 and 2006 (Figure 7.4). It is important to recognize that California's grant programs are awarded on both merit and need.[4] Students who do not take college preparatory courses may not be eligible for merit-based grants, so advising for students in high school is a critical issue in increasing access to college in California (McDonough & Calderone, 2006). In addition, the purchasing power of need-based grants is related to college costs; in recent years, tuition has risen much more quickly than Cal Grant allocations.

California grant spending has been much higher than the national average relative to tuition (Figure 7.5). Between 1994 and 2000, California had an extreme upward trajectory on this ratio, which is typically associated with improved college enrollment rates (St. John, Williams, & Moronski, 2010). Although in theory low tuition and high grants

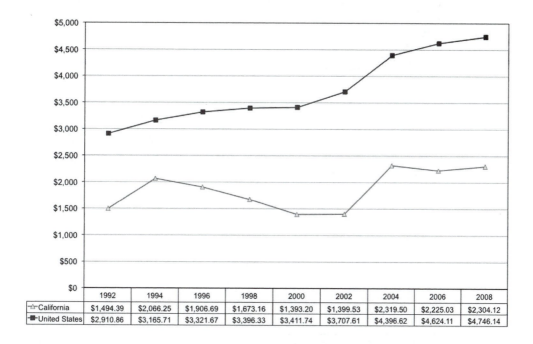

	1992	1994	1996	1998	2000	2002	2004	2006	2008
California	$1,494.39	$2,066.25	$1,906.69	$1,673.16	$1,393.20	$1,399.53	$2,319.50	$2,225.03	$2,304.12
United States	$2,910.86	$3,165.71	$3,321.67	$3,396.33	$3,411.74	$3,707.61	$4,396.62	$4,624.11	$4,746.14

Figure 7.2 Trends in Weighted Average Tuition Charges by the California Public Higher Education System, 1992–2008 (In 2008 Dollars)

Source: Data from NCES Integrated Postsecondary Education Data System © 2011 Projects Promoting Equity in Urban and Higher Education, NCID at the University of Michigan.

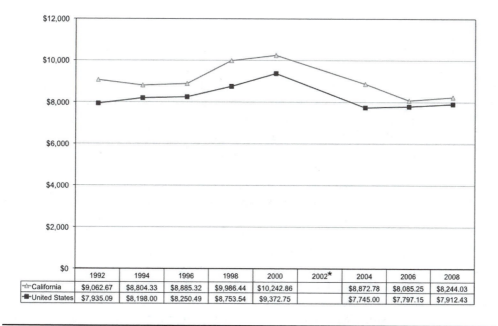

	1992	1994	1996	1998	2000	2002*	2004	2006	2008
California	$9,062.67	$8,804.33	$8,885.32	$9,986.44	$10,242.86		$8,872.78	$8,085.25	$8,244.03
United States	$7,935.09	$8,198.00	$8,250.49	$8,753.54	$9,372.75		$7,745.00	$7,797.15	$7,912.43

Figure 7.3 Trends in California and U.S. Average Annual Amount of State and Local Appropriations per FTE for Public Higher Education (In 2008 Dollars)

Source: Data from NCES Integrated Postsecondary Education Data System © 2011 Projects Promoting Equity in Urban and Higher Education, NCID at the University of Michigan.

* This data is missing in the Integrated Postsecondary Education Data System (IPEDS).

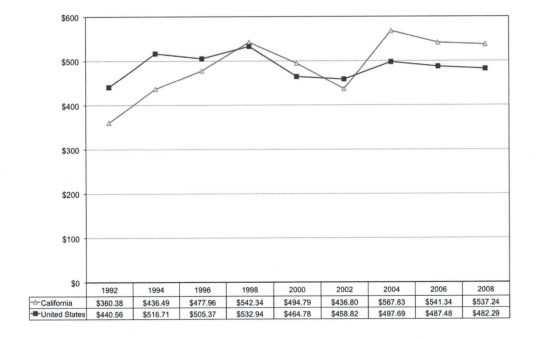

	1992	1994	1996	1998	2000	2002	2004	2006	2008
California	$360.38	$436.49	$477.96	$542.34	$494.79	$436.80	$567.83	$541.34	$537.24
United States	$440.56	$516.71	$505.37	$532.94	$464.78	$458.82	$497.69	$487.48	$482.29

Figure 7.4 Trends in California and U.S. State Need-Based Undergraduate Grants per FTE (in 2008 Dollars)

Source: Data from NCES Integrated Postsecondary Education Data System © 2011 Projects Promoting Equity in Urban and Higher Education, NCID at the University of Michigan.

(in relation to tuition) are the best possible combination for students, this combination of policies loses its practical value for students when their opportunity to enroll (i.e., the enrollment capacity of institutions) is constrained. Had California shifted to a high-tuition, high-aid strategy decades earlier, it would have been possible to expand the public system, moving toward goals set in the 1987 revision of the state's master plan.

California actually rates higher than most other states in need-based aid funding per FTE student in higher education in relation to tuition charges. Owing to the history of low tuition charges in public institutions, the state directed most of its aid funding revenues to students in private colleges. Since California grant programs limit the amount of an award by institution type, the maximal dollar award at the public colleges is far lower than that for private colleges. Unless the maximal amount of an award for a student attending a public postsecondary institution increases, the need gap left for low-income students will increase as public tuition rises. The federal stimulus funding for Pell grants filled this gap in part, but this only blunted the intended effect of the stimulus. It was also only a stop-gap solution to a longer-term problem; in 2011 the stimulus funds were no longer available, leaving the state on the hook.

Through the years studied, California continued to fund its public colleges at a higher level per student than the average for other states. This pattern has held up in spite of the fact that the heavily subsidized UC system has not grown as fast as community colleges or state universities. The problems with this model as it evolved in California were (1) a comparatively higher taxpayer cost per student in the public system; (2) difficulty expanding access, given the high direct subsidies to existing colleges; and (3) the inability to adapt to tax

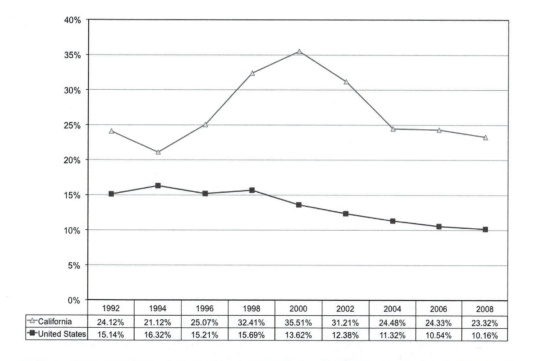

	1992	1994	1996	1998	2000	2002	2004	2006	2008
California	24.12%	21.12%	25.07%	32.41%	35.51%	31.21%	24.48%	24.33%	23.32%
United States	15.14%	16.32%	15.21%	15.69%	13.62%	12.38%	11.32%	10.54%	10.16%

Figure 7.5 Trends in California and U.S. Ratios of Need-Based Grants as a Percent of State Tuition

Source: Data from NCES Integrated Postsecondary Education Data System and National Association of State Student Grant & Aid Programs © 2011 Projects Promoting Equity in Urban and Higher Education, NCID at the University of Michigan.

revenue constraints. The most recent round of budget shortfalls has brought rapid change to the state, especially with respect to tuition charges, a development we discuss below.

TRENDS IN EDUCATION OUTCOMES

In California as in most other states, there is a correspondence between changes in policy and education outcomes. This section examines indicators of outcomes related to high school preparation, followed by trends in college continuation rates and diverse representation within the state's system of higher education.

College Preparation

The implementation of more rigorous requirements for high school graduation has corresponded with improvements in outcomes related to academic preparation in California. Given the great difficulties facing the state's economy and budgets in recent years, the gains in high school outcomes are noteworthy.

High School Graduation Rates

California's high school graduation rates improved from 1996 through 2005 but have declined since, especially for minority students (Figure 7.6). The percentage of African Americans graduating from high school dropped from 61% in 2005 to 54% in 2008; Latino/a graduation rates dropped from 61% to 58% during the same period, and 64%

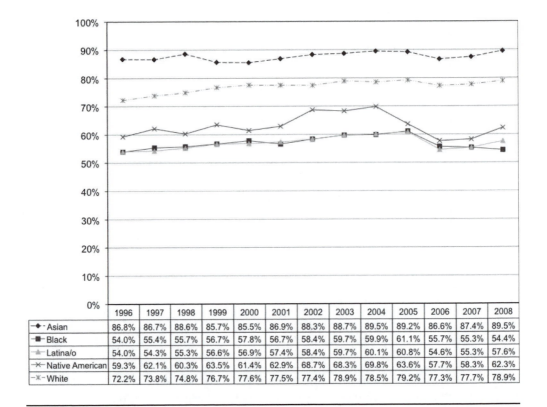

	1996	1997	1998	1999	2000	2001	2002	2003	2004	2005	2006	2007	2008
◆ · Asian	86.8%	86.7%	88.6%	85.7%	85.5%	86.9%	88.3%	88.7%	89.5%	89.2%	86.6%	87.4%	89.5%
■ Black	54.0%	55.4%	55.7%	56.7%	57.8%	56.7%	58.4%	59.7%	59.9%	61.1%	55.7%	55.3%	54.4%
▲ Latina/o	54.0%	54.3%	55.3%	56.6%	56.9%	57.4%	58.4%	59.7%	60.1%	60.8%	54.6%	55.3%	57.6%
✕ Native American	59.3%	62.1%	60.3%	63.5%	61.4%	62.9%	68.7%	68.3%	69.8%	63.6%	57.7%	58.3%	62.3%
✳ White	72.2%	73.8%	74.8%	76.7%	77.6%	77.5%	77.4%	78.9%	78.5%	79.2%	77.3%	77.7%	78.9%

Figure 7.6 Trends in California Public High School Graduation Rates by Race/Ethnicity

Source: Data from NCES Common Core Data © 2011 Projects Promoting Equity in Urban and Higher Education, NCID at the University of Michigan.

of the American Indian cohort graduated in 2005, contrasted to a low of 63% in 2007. On the other hand, graduation rates for Whites and Asian Americans remained stable, 88% in 2005 and 89% in 2009. These declines correspond to the implementation of new high school graduation requirements, and the stark differences are probably related to the capacity of high schools to adjust. If that is the case, it is possible that there will be improvements after several years, during which time the K–12 system will have an opportunity to adapt to the new expectations.

Test Scores

California students have made progress on test scores. The state has consistently had a higher percentage of students taking the SAT than the national average (Figure 7.7); with 46% of high school students taking the SAT in 1992, California's rate was 4 percentage points higher. In 2004 through 2008, the rates of taking the test were nearly equal to the U.S. average. Even with the increase in graduation rates and the percentage of graduates taking the SAT, which tends to bring down SAT scores, the average SAT math score in the state was higher than the national average from 1992 to 2004 and equal to the U.S. average of 518 in 2006 and 515 in 2008 (Figure 7.8). On the other hand, the verbal scores on the SAT have been consistently lower than the national average (Figure 7.9), but the gap narrowed from 1992 through 2004, before widening again from 2006 to 2008.

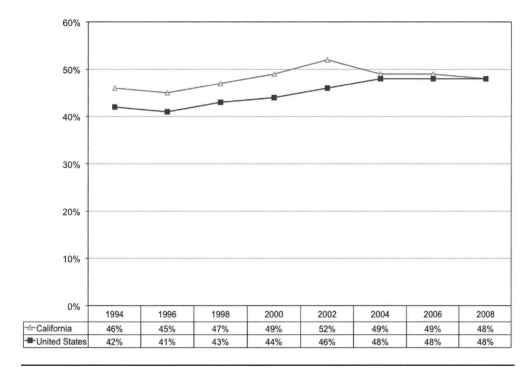

	1994	1996	1998	2000	2002	2004	2006	2008
⊸△⊸California	46%	45%	47%	49%	52%	49%	49%	48%
⊸■⊸United States	42%	41%	43%	44%	46%	48%	48%	48%

Figure 7.7 Trends in the Percent of California and U.S. Students Who Took the SAT

Source: Data from The College Board © 2011 Projects Promoting Equity in Urban and Higher Education, NCID at the University of Michigan.

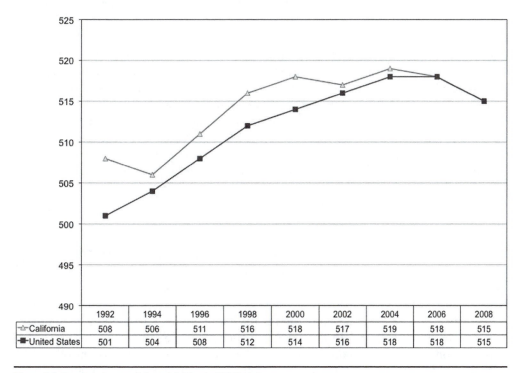

	1992	1994	1996	1998	2000	2002	2004	2006	2008
⊸△⊸California	508	506	511	516	518	517	519	518	515
⊸■⊸United States	501	504	508	512	514	516	518	518	515

Figure 7.8 Trends in Average U.S. and California SAT Math Scores

Source: Data from The College Board © 2011 Projects Promoting Equity in Urban and Higher Education, NCID at the University of Michigan.

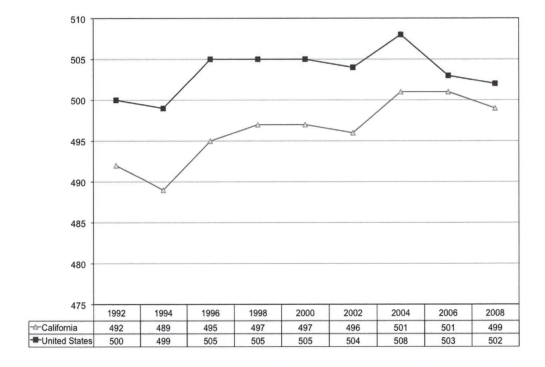

Figure 7.9 Trends in Average SAT Verbal Scores in California and the United States

Source: Data from The College Board © 2011 Projects Promoting Equity in Urban and Higher Education, NCID at the University of Michigan.

California education has faced serious funding challenges in recent decades, given the constraints on property taxes (Proposition 13), historically the primary source of funding for public education, and spending constraints on other state tax revenues: state tax revenues normally account for a larger share of school funding as local property tax revenues decline. With improved high school graduation rates and SAT scores, academic preparation was not an explanation for college access challenges in the state. The changes in graduation requirements appear to have worked as a means of preparing a higher percentage of students for college, but college enrollment rates did not keep pace with the nation.

Higher Education Access

College Continuation Rates

In the 1960s, California had the highest college continuation rate of any state in the nation, but this had changed by 1992. In the mid 1990s (1994 and 1996), California's rate of college continuation plunged below the national average and remained below that rate through 2006 (Figure 7.10). However, there was a sharp increase in the college continuation rate between 2004 and 2008, surpassing the national rate. These trends in California raise questions about the relative role of academic preparation in access.

As demonstrated throughout the chapters in this volume, the rate of enrollment is not the only critical issue: equity in representation is also important. Our analyses in this subsection consider how well California maintained a diverse student population in the

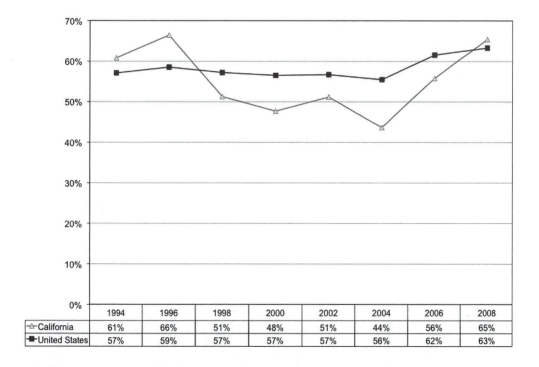

	1994	1996	1998	2000	2002	2004	2006	2008
California	61%	66%	51%	48%	51%	44%	56%	65%
United States	57%	59%	57%	57%	57%	56%	62%	63%

Figure 7.10 Trends in the California and U.S. College Continuation Rates

Source: Data from Postsecondary Education Opportunity © 2011 Projects Promoting Equity in Urban and Higher Education, NCID at the University of Michigan.

face of the political assault on affirmative action and the overall decline in opportunity. If we assume that a greater proportion of underrepresented students are on the margins in terms of qualifying for admission (the assumption made by critics of affirmative action), then we would expect that African Americans and Latinos/as would be the groups suffering the most substantially with regard to college enrollment opportunity.

Racial Representation in Public 4-Year Institutions

Asian Americans were most substantially overrepresented in public 4-year institutions, where they maintain representation at nearly twice their level in the population (Figure 7.11). There was a substantial decline in representation of Whites in 4-year institutions, from 0.96 in 1992 to 0.88 in 2008. In contrast, representation of African Americans rose from 0.68 to 0.85, indicating substantial gains in the 4-year sector; Latinos/as and American Indians also made gains in representation. From the overall trend in 4-year institutions, it does not appear that imposing the ban on affirmative action influenced trends in racial representation.

The core issue in the debates about access for diverse groups centered around admissions to the most elite campuses—the Berkeley and Los Angeles campuses of UC. Fundamentally, college access is about access both for whom and to what. Substantial progress for African American and Hispanic students is an important trend, but it also matters where they attend. There is overwhelming evidence of increased inequality at the UC Berkeley and UCLA campuses (Orfield, Marin, Flores, & Garces, 2007). For example,

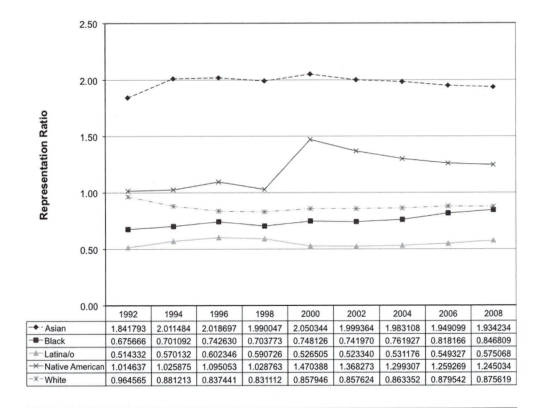

	1992	1994	1996	1998	2000	2002	2004	2006	2008
Asian	1.841793	2.011484	2.018697	1.990047	2.050344	1.999364	1.983108	1.949099	1.934234
Black	0.675666	0.701092	0.742630	0.703773	0.748126	0.741970	0.761927	0.818166	0.846809
Latina/o	0.514332	0.570132	0.602346	0.590726	0.526505	0.523340	0.531176	0.549327	0.575068
Native American	1.014637	1.025875	1.095053	1.028763	1.470388	1.368273	1.299307	1.259269	1.245034
White	0.964565	0.881213	0.837441	0.831112	0.857946	0.857624	0.863352	0.879542	0.875619

Figure 7.11 Racial/Ethnic Representation in California Public 4-Year Postsecondary Institutions as a Proportion of the State Population

Source: Data from NCES Integrated Postsecondary Education Data System and U.S. Census Bureau © 2011 Projects Promoting Equity in Urban and Higher Education, NCID at the University of Michigan.

the engineering programs at UC Berkeley have had great difficulty enrolling underrepresented freshmen engineering students. This is not to argue that campus diversity is not important to campus officials or to policy discourse in general, but system access is more directly related to the costs and benefits of various public investment policies.

Prior analyses of trends in enrollment in the UC campuses found a slightly different pattern. Asian Americans were substantially overrepresented in the UC system before Proposition 209, and their representation increased in the 2000s (St. John & Moronski, in press). In fact, their representation at UC was more than 2.5 times their representation in the population from 1994 to 2006. The White representation ratio was only 0.86 in 1994, before the ban on affirmative action was first implemented (in 1998), and it dropped to 0.82 in 2004 and 2005. The problem has been African American and Latino/a representation in the UC system after the ban on affirmative action: Africans Americans dropped from a representation ratio of 0.51 in 1994 and 1996 to a ratio of 0.39 in 1998, the first year after the ban, and hit a low of 0.33 in 2000 and 2002, when the ban's full effects were being realized. The drop for Latinos/as has been less severe (9 percentage points over the period), but they had lower representation to start with; their ratio dropped from 0.44 in 1994 to 0.35 in 2004 and 2005.

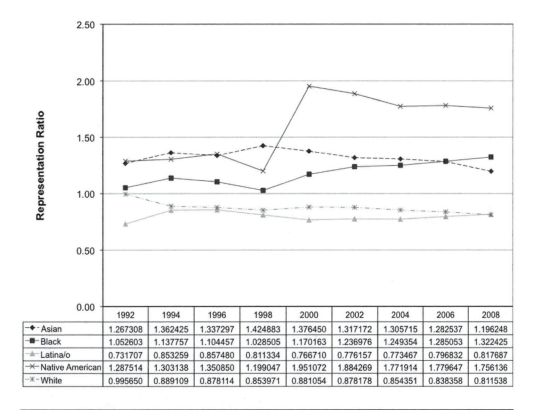

	1992	1994	1996	1998	2000	2002	2004	2006	2008
Asian	1.267308	1.362425	1.337297	1.424883	1.376450	1.317172	1.305715	1.282537	1.196248
Black	1.052603	1.137757	1.104457	1.028505	1.170163	1.236976	1.249354	1.285053	1.322425
Latina/o	0.731707	0.853259	0.857480	0.811334	0.766710	0.776157	0.773467	0.796832	0.817687
Native American	1.287514	1.303138	1.350850	1.199047	1.951072	1.884269	1.771914	1.779647	1.756136
White	0.995650	0.889109	0.878114	0.853971	0.881054	0.878178	0.854351	0.838358	0.811538

Figure 7.12 Racial/Ethnic Representation in California Public 2-Year Postsecondary Institutions as a Proportion of the State Population

Source: Data from NCES Integrated Postsecondary Education Data System and U.S. Census Bureau © 2011 Projects Promoting Equity in Urban and Higher Education, NCID at the University of Michigan.

Public 2-Year Colleges

African Americans and Native Americans made substantial enrollment gains in the California community college system by 1998 (Figure 7.12). In 2008, African Americans were represented in community colleges at 1.3 times their rate of representation in the state's population and Native Americans were represented at 1.8 times their rate in the state. White representation declined after 1992, while Latino/a representation increased; the two groups had nearly equal representation ratios in 2008 (0.81 for Whites and 0.82 for Latinos/as).

College Completion

There was modest improvement in the 6-year graduation rate within public 4-year colleges and universities (Figure 7.13). This rate for Blacks improved from 35% in 2002 to 44% in 2008. Whereas the gains for other groups were more modest, there was an overall pattern of improvement. In 2004, the completion rates were 71% for Asian Americans, 67% for Whites, 53% for Native Americans, and 52% for Latinos/as. In spite of the substantial gain, African Americans continued to have the lowest graduation rates in California's public colleges and universities.

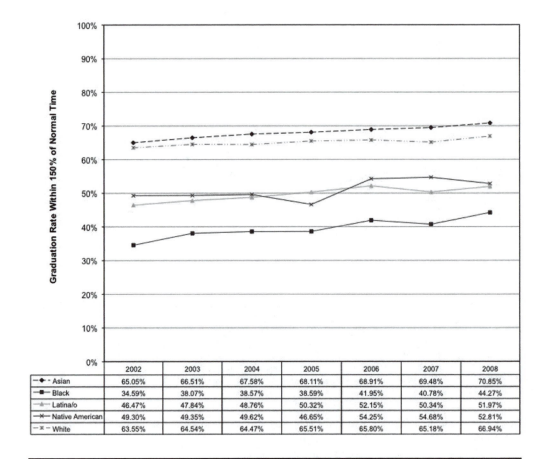

	2002	2003	2004	2005	2006	2007	2008
Asian	65.05%	66.51%	67.58%	68.11%	68.91%	69.48%	70.85%
Black	34.59%	38.07%	38.57%	38.59%	41.95%	40.78%	44.27%
Latina/o	46.47%	47.84%	48.76%	50.32%	52.15%	50.34%	51.97%
Native American	49.30%	49.35%	49.62%	46.65%	54.25%	54.68%	52.81%
White	63.55%	64.54%	64.47%	65.51%	65.80%	65.18%	66.94%

Figure 7.13 Trends in Graduation Rates in California Public 4-Year Postsecondary Institutions

Source: Data from NCES Integrated Postsecondary Education Data System © 2011 Projects Promoting Equity in Urban and Higher Education, NCID at the University of Michigan.

In contrast to the public 4-year colleges, the California community college system experienced a precipitous drop in 3-year completion[5] rates after 2004. In 2004, the completion rates for underrepresented groups ranged from 33% for Asian Americans to 18% for African Americans (Figure 7.14). It is possible that these serious problems were related to cuts in funding in the community colleges that constrained enrollment and increased tuition in 2004–2005 (California Community Colleges Chancellor's Office, 2005), a development that had an apparent impact on degree completion rates.

CURRENT ISSUES IN CALIFORNIA

California has been a bellwether state for higher education policy and postsecondary opportunity. Consider the response of the College Board when the state of California threatened to eliminate the use of the SAT in college admissions because it did not adequately assess what students need—particularly writing—to succeed in college. The College Board set out to reformulate the test, which now includes a writing assessment. Not many states wield that sort of power; therefore few can influence postsecondary

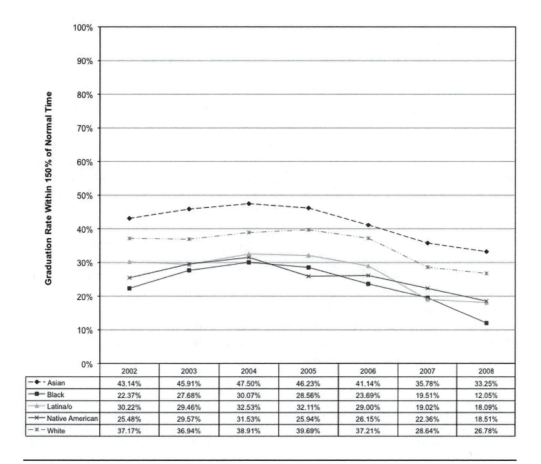

Figure 7.14 Graduation Rates in California Public 2-Year Postsecondary Institutions

Source: Data from NCES Integrated Postsecondary Education Data System © 2011 Projects Promoting Equity in Urban and Higher Education, NCID at the University of Michigan.

	2002	2003	2004	2005	2006	2007	2008
Asian	43.14%	45.91%	47.50%	46.23%	41.14%	35.78%	33.25%
Black	22.37%	27.68%	30.07%	28.56%	23.69%	19.51%	12.05%
Latina/o	30.22%	29.46%	32.53%	32.11%	29.00%	19.02%	18.09%
Native American	25.48%	29.57%	31.53%	25.94%	26.15%	22.36%	18.51%
White	37.17%	36.94%	38.91%	39.69%	37.21%	28.64%	26.78%

opportunity like California. The state has been, and in some ways continues to be, the model of a liberal state. It is one of the most culturally diverse states in the nation with both the largest community college system and some of the most elite public universities in the nation. California has been on the front lines of many of the important political challenges facing higher education in the United States, including both affirmative action and in-state residency status for undocumented students. California has also maintained, until very recently, a strong commitment to a low-tuition strategy, particularly in the community college and the state college systems, combined with a generous means-tested financial aid program.

This section briefly reviews recent policy developments in the state and considers the degree to which the liberal model is sustainable in the largest and one of the fastest-growing states in the country. Specifically, we consider three key policy developments in California higher education that in many ways will define the future direction of the state: the DREAM Act (Development, Relief and Education for Alien Minors), the institutional capacity of the postsecondary system, and the rising cost of college for students and their families.

The DREAM Act and Access for Undocumented Students

California was among the first of the 10 states that passed legislation allowing undocumented students to qualify for in-state tuition at public colleges and universities (Flores, 2010). In 2002, the state legislature passed a version of the federal DREAM Act that provided access to in-state tuition at the California State University (CSU) and California Community College (CCC) systems. It did not, however, go as far as to provide undocumented students a path to citizenship, which was included in the language proposed at the federal level. In 2011, California policymakers extended the provisions of the law to allow undocumented students to qualify for private scholarship programs and institutional aid provided by the CSU and CCC systems (Around the Capitol, 2011). As of the writing of this chapter, California policymakers have not passed a set of provisions allowing undocumented students to qualify for the Cal Grant programs.

In many ways, California's commitment to the DREAM Act is consistent with its liberal approach to college access and opportunity. However, failure to open state financial aid to undocumented students and the omission of a legal path to citizenship are both notable limitations for a vulnerable population. The families of undocumented students are least likely to be able to afford even the lowest-cost institutions in the state, meaning that, for many, without access to the Cal Grant, college remains beyond their reach. But the more important challenge, which is not unique to California, is that without a path to citizenship, undocumented students who earn a degree will find it extremely difficult to find employment in the United States.

Postsecondary System Capacity

California remains the largest and one of the fastest-growing states in the United States. Between 2000 and 2010, the state's population grew 10%, to more than 37 million people (U.S. Census Bureau, 2011). Much of that growth is in the Latino community. In 2000, some 32% of California residents identified as Hispanic/Latino; in 2010, that percentage had grown to more than 37%. To put that into perspective, of the more than 3.5 million new Californians, 3.2 million identify as Hispanic/Latino. Latinas/os represented 22% of the student population in 2000 and 27% in 2010, with much of that enrollment in the community college sector.

Today, there are more students seeking entry into the California public higher education system than there are spaces to accommodate them. Where the overall population has grown by 10% since 2000, public college enrollments have only grown by 7.6% (National Center for Education Statistics, 2011). California projects substantial growth in community college enrollments but warns that without sufficient state support, as many as 400,000 students may be turned away in the coming years (Wilson, Fuller, & Angeli, 2009).

The Rising Cost of Public Higher Education

The days of low tuition and high aid in California may be numbered. In 2009, the UC system raised tuition a staggering 32% in response to a $650 million funding cut from the state (Bachman, 2011). Over the past 6 months, the system has announced two increases amounting to more than a 17% tuition increase. CSU has experienced similar increases as well. In November 2010, the trustees approved a tuition increase of 10% and in July announced an additional increase of 12% (Megino, 2011). The challenge for community colleges is slightly different. While these 2-year institutions continue to maintain low tuition and fees, students may find access prohibitive because of the costs associated with attendance by out-of-state students (Zumeta & Finkle, 2007).

Additionally, the state has modified eligibility for the Cal Grant program, meaning that some students will lose eligibility and a number of institutions will no longer be eligible to receive those funds. In 2011, the state passed legislation that requires all Cal Grant renewals to meet the same eligibility requirements as initial applications, which will mean that students whose status has changed may lose funding (California Student Aid Commission, 2011). At the same time, institutions with high student loan borrowing rates and 3-year cohort default rates in excess of 24.6% will no longer be eligible to receive Cal Grants. Both of these limitations have the potential to limit opportunity for lower-income students and families in a state where the public system lacks the capacity to serve all eligible students.

CONCLUSIONS

The California case offers a stark contrast between a proud past of liberal progressive development leading to arguably the nation's best system of education by the 1970s and a financially troubled system that lacks a sustainable strategy for meeting growing student demand for postsecondary opportunity. A transformation has occurred in the financial conditions in the state, but the state's capacity to finance the system consistent with the 1960 master plan has seriously eroded.

The question facing policymakers, researchers, and voters in California is: Can the state sustain its commitment to a liberal approach to higher education access? Californians are now confronted by a harsh new reality. The system has not expanded to meet the growing demand for many years. The conversion of Merced Junior College into the 10th UC campus was a long overdue response, given the parameters set forth in the master plan, but it remains a small improvement at one level of the system. Much more will need to be done if the state hopes to keep higher education accessible for the growing and increasingly diverse state population. Questions for discussion and debate are posed in Text Box 7.1.

Text Box 7.1 Discussion Questions About the California Case

1. How serious a problem is the ban on affirmative action for California's public system of public higher education?

2. Should improvement in K–12 education be a priority over public funding for higher education in the allocation of tax dollars in California? Why?

3. Given the tax constraints, what are the alternative ways for the state of California to expand access and increase opportunities for degree completion in California higher education?

4. What criteria should be used to assess alternative strategies (e.g., extent of access, net taxpayer costs, quality of education, or equality in access)?

5. Of the evaluation criteria you think are important for the state, which should have the highest priority? Why?

6. Do the constituent groups have different interests with respect to strategies for promoting expansion in access, and what value would you place on criteria for evaluating options (e.g., antitax constituencies, underrepresented racial/ethnic and income groups in the state, middle-income families with an interest in replicating opportunity across generations, current students, or college and university faculty)?

7. How does the research (reviewed in Part I or from your own reviews) inform your judgment about alternative approaches to expanding access and improving degree completion in California?

8. Given the restructuring of the financing of higher education now underway in California, do you think California will continue to improve access?

8

THE MARKET MODEL

The Minnesota Case

Minnesota adopted the high-tuition and high-grant market model for the financing of public and private higher education in the early 1980s after a crisis in state funding. While it has often been characterized as a model for other states to follow, there is wide recognition that is difficult for states to maintain the strategy (Hossler, Lund, Ramin-Gyurnek, Westfall, & Irish, 1997). In Minnesota's case, the model has been followed relatively consistently through both conservative and liberal gubernatorial administrations, although there are now serious limitations to it given the rising tuition costs. This case study reviews the development and current operation of the Minnesota model.[1]

In the early 1980s Minnesota had three state systems—the University of Minnesota System, Minnesota State University System, and the Minnesota Community College System. The state also had a thriving private sector comprising mostly small liberal arts colleges, like the University of St. Thomas and Carlton College. Largely as a consequence of planning for an enrollment drop that did not occur, the higher education system faced serious financial challenges, along with competition between sectors for state funding when it developed the market approach, which included mechanisms for coordinating state funding for campuses, tuition, and student grant aid for public and private higher education.

DEVELOPMENT OF MINNESOTA'S MARKET MODEL

Minnesota had a long history as a progressive state in terms of financing higher education, with a planning system in place long before the market-based funding model was established in 1984. Like many states, Minnesota was challenged by higher than expected enrollment growth in the 1970s combined with severe revenue shortfalls in the 1980s. The progressive tradition of the state had emphasized high-quality education to stimulate economic development. Unlike other midwestern states with an industrial base, Minnesota had well-established research centers in the 1980s, emphasizing medical research and computer technologies. The emphasis on excellence in the science, technology, engineering, and math (STEM) fields was well established in planning for higher education.

Policy Developments Leading to the Market Model

Like many states, Minnesota responded to studies predicting a decline in enrollment after 1978 (e.g., Carnegie Commission on Higher Education, 1973). In 1977 the Minnesota Higher Education Coordinating Board (MHECB) implemented an enrollment bulge policy by freezing basic appropriations at 1977 levels (Minnesota Higher Education Coordinating Board, 1982). Although such plans seemed rational at the time, given the many reports claiming that higher education had unreasonable plans for growth (e.g., Cheit, 1971, 1974; Balderston, 1974), institutional adaptations to the policy were largely unanticipated.

The University of Minnesota System had a well-established research capability. Recognizing that the new context created a new set of opportunities, the university capped enrollment and focused on raising quality. The system began to focus on generating revenue from other sources, including its hospital operation. During this period there were also many special line-item allocations from the state for specific projects (St. John, 1991a). Education researchers viewed this as an opportunity to test new approaches to managing internal costs and tuition charges. For example, the system experimented with a differential pricing model (Berg & Hoenack, 1987). Researchers at the university were also engaged in supporting the MHECB.

In contrast, the state universities and community colleges seized opportunities for growth, letting enrollment rise during the expected bulge as a means of generating new revenue. The state universities absorbed excess demand generated by qualified students denied access to UM due to the enrollment cap. However, by 1982 it became clear that the average revenue per student had substantially declined in the state universities owing to the constraints on state funding. The community colleges also experienced enrollment gains, but that was not as serious a problem because they relied less on state funding.

In 1979, the MHECB formed a task force to study enrollment and financing policy with funding from the Ford Foundation. In 1981, the task force invited national experts to discuss funding challenges in public postsecondary education and student financial aid. The task force considered financing alternatives, including average cost funding, fixed and variable funding, student financial aid, and other approaches. After some deliberation, the task force (Minnesota Higher Education Coordinating Board, 1982) recommended a strategy that included (1) providing incentives for innovation and resource management, encouraging the governing boards to anticipate changes in conditions, (2) providing resources in an equitable manner, assuring fairness in funding across sectors of higher education, (3) recognizing differing costs patterns, including the higher cost of STEM field education, (4) ensuring quality using identifiable measures of performance, and (5) encouraging increased productivity.[2]

The Minnesota Model

Minnesota adopted a new approach to funding in fiscal year 1984 (St. John, 1991), establishing average cost funding for each institution based on an analysis of a 12-cell matrix (high-, medium-, and low-cost programs at the lower division, upper division, and graduate levels), with average costs based on full year enrollment (fall enrollment adjusted for within-year attrition) in each of the cells. Studies of costs at peer institutions were used as a basis for setting the funding target in each cell. In addition, the state set a goal of one-third funding from tuition and two-thirds from state appropriation. At the time, most states had not yet allowed tuition to rise to even 20% of costs, so this was a relatively high tuition model. There was also an explicit link between tuition and student aid policy in the new Minnesota plan. Need-based student grant aid covered students' costs minus Pell grants and expected student and family contributions. Following implementation, MHECB funded studies of the impact of the new policies on enrollment by low-income students, which documented the positive impact of the program (Hearn, Sand, & Urahn, 1985; Minnesota Higher Education Coordinating Board, 1987).

Other problems occurred as the MHECB sought to build and hold together a political coalition in support of reform. They sought to replace line-item funding with a general budget allocation on the new average cost formula and set new goals for state funding to maintain the two-thirds state support, but the legislature did not endorse the necessary funding increases (St. John, 1991b). When the new financial model was implemented in 1988, a state auditor uncovered financial mismanagement, resulting in the resignation of the UM President (St. John, 1991b). At a time of tax revenue shortfalls, the university had failed to "inform the governor or legislature about excess revenues from the hospital. When the information finally became public, in 1988, the University of Minnesota's system quality improvement campaign, called 'A Commitment to Focus,' ran into political problems and was withdrawn from legislative consideration" (p. 275). Yet in the midst of this controversy, the MHECB managed to launch a center in Rochester, Minnesota, involving cooperation between the university, states colleges, and the community college system.

Perhaps the most remarkable feature of the Minnesota model is that it has held together for nearly three decades, albeit with changes along the way. Hearn and Anderson (1989, 1995) conducted two studies of implementation, documenting that continued collaboration between researchers and policymakers played a role in maintaining the basic model in a policy environment. The ability to sustain political commitment to the model resulted from political support for all sectors, a coalition that has been difficult to hold together in most other states (Hossler et al., 1997). Coordinating mechanisms built into the Minnesota model included an emphasis on funding targets that assured adequate funding for campuses, a balance of tuition and student aid ensuring stability in the ability to meet demand as the state's share of funding gradually declined, and student aid sufficient to fund low-income students who enrolled in both public and private colleges.

The Evolution of Strategy

While Minnesota embraced a liberal market approach to funding of higher education, it was never easy for the MHECB to hold together political coalitions to fully support the model (Hearn & Anderson, 1989, 1995). As the model evolved, it proved necessary to make adjustments to the percent of costs subsidized by the state. Over time, Minnesota's governors and legislatures frequently lacked the will to fund the coordinated scheme. The MHECB was dissolved and replaced by the Minnesota Office of Higher Education (MOHE), an agency with less overall budget authority and a more limited focus on administration of state financial aid programs. The higher education system office took on the direct responsibility for proposing budgets and lobbying for its own state funding. Student grant aid became less central to the shared agenda of all three systems. There was an effort to develop a policy center at the University of Minnesota that would provide analyses for the state, but this vision was never fully realized.[3] As a consequence of these systemwide changes, tuition rapidly rose to more than one third of average costs. There were also changes in the basic precepts of the student grant program, which undermined its effectiveness, especially with respect to student debt and student outcomes.

The Student Aid Strategy in 2010

By 2010, MOHE had developed a new scheme for coordinating state grants and tuition charges, using the logic of both explicit and implicit assigned responsibility. The model explicitly assigned family responsibility as the ability to pay, based on federal need analysis methods; taxpayer responsibility through aid to colleges and students; and student responsibility for a work/loan burden. In addition, students had an implicit responsibility for the costs of attendance beyond expected work/loan contributions, grants, loans, and other sources.

Since the creation of the average costs strategy, Minnesota had awarded state grants after Pell grants, reducing its obligation by the amount of money students received from that program (Hearn & Anderson, 1995). The 2010 strategy made explicit a student obligation to assume loans and work at a level approaching $8,000 per student even before the Pell grant was taken into account (Figure 8.1)—an extremely high amount to expect from low-income students whose families qualified for full Pell funding. Further, the maximum grant (Pell plus state grant) was capped at $16,000. Because the state cap subtracted the grant award from its maximum award, the neediest students received a lower state grant than students in the lower-middle-income group. Thus the new award scheme was not optimal for students in the lowest income group in terms of choice of institution or the purchasing power of their grant packages.

Perhaps the most serious problem with the new model was that the explicit work/loan burden in Minnesota was substantially higher than the federal standards established in the Pell formula. Using the federal methodology, the student contribution is calculated at 50% of assets above $2,500. A second problem was that there was evidence that

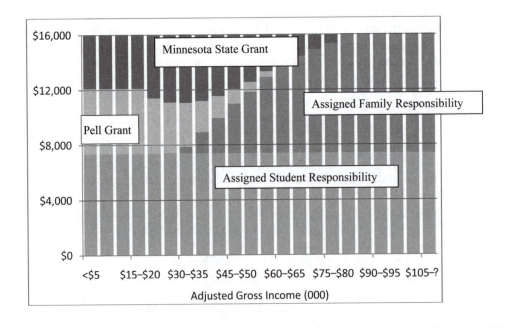

Figure 8.1 Paying for College: Students, Families, Taxpayers, and the State Grant Model
Source: Lydell, 2008.

Table 8.1 Average Cumulative Debt for Students Who Borrowed, 2007–2008, for the United States and Minnesota

College Type	United States	Minnesota
Public 2-year	8,700	9,900
Public 4-year	14,500	16,900
Private 4-year	18,900	20,400
Private for profit/proprietary	14,100	18,700

Source: http://nces.ed.gov/pubs2010/2010181rev.pdf, Tables 5.7 and 7.1.

student borrowing, especially by lower- and lower-middle income families, was excessive in Minnesota because of the combination of explicit and implicit costs. In 2007–2008, Minnesota had participated in a national study of student borrowing (Table 8.1). That year Minnesota students enrolled in each type of institution had substantially higher debt than the national average for students enrolled in similar types of institutions, even community college students.

TRENDS IN K–16 POLICIES AND OUTCOMES

Minnesota has had a distinctive history in K–12 education as well as in the market system used to finance higher education. The patterns of change in academic preparation, college access and diversity, and college completion are reviewed below.

High School Preparation Policies

In the national discourse, inequalities in academic preparation are often used as an argument for inequality in college access. In spite of problems with the public financing of higher education in the past decade, Minnesota has continued to have an exemplary record in K–12 preparation and outcomes and is a leading state in the implementation of policies supporting college preparation (Figure 8.2). The state implemented math

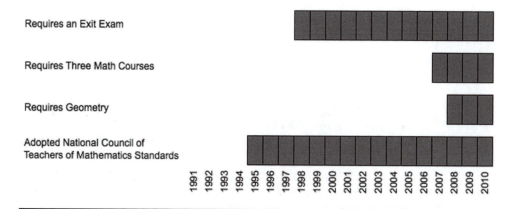

Figure 8.2 Minnesota High School Graduation Requirements

Source: © Projects Promoting Equity in Urban and Higher Education, NCID at the University of Michigan.

standards in 1995 and required an exit examination in 1997. Three math courses were required for graduation for the high school class of 2007. Geometry was added as a requirement for the graduating class of 2008, a requirement higher than that for other states examined as case studies.

In addition, Minnesota can claim more than a quarter century of dual enrollment policies, encouraging high school students to enroll in community colleges for credit (Selix, 2010). These policies affect college enrollment rates reported by community colleges, but since most of these students do not continue enrollment after high school, it is more appropriate to exclude these students when examining persistence by first-time freshmen enrolling in community colleges, because high school student enrollment can artificially depress college completion rates in public 2-year institutions (St. John & Musoba, 2010).

COLLEGE FINANCE

Minnesota incrementally abandoned its historic commitment to fully funding need-based grant aid as a means of financing its postsecondary education market model. Further, Minnesota is a state with an exemplary history of academic preparation. Therefore this case provides a unique window on the impact of reductions in student need-based grants and the emergence of high-tuition and high loans. We trace Minnesota's trends in public finance, enrollment rates, and diversity below.

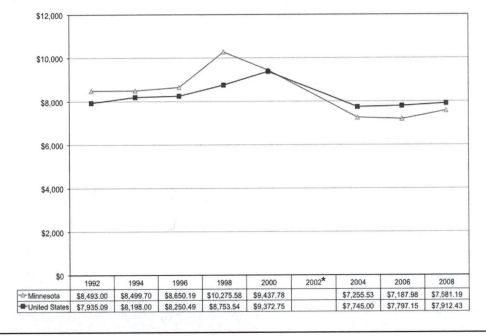

	1992	1994	1996	1998	2000	2002*	2004	2006	2008
Minnesota	$8,493.00	$8,499.70	$8,650.19	$10,275.58	$9,437.78		$7,255.53	$7,187.98	$7,581.19
United States	$7,935.09	$8,198.00	$8,250.49	$8,753.54	$9,372.75		$7,745.00	$7,797.15	$7,912.43

Figure 8.3 Trend in Minnesota's Average Annual Amount of State and Local Appropriations per FTE for the Public Higher Education System Compared With the National Average (in 2008 Dollars)

Source: Data from NCES Integrated Postsecondary Education Data System © 2011 Projects Promoting Equity in Urban and Higher Education, NCID at the University of Michigan.

*This data is missing in the Integrated Postsecondary Education Data System (IPEDS).

State Funding of Public Higher Education

Minnesota's state and local appropriations per FTE student to public colleges were higher than the national average in the 2000s but lower than average from 2004 to 2006 (Figure 8.3). The average appropriation declined from a high of $10,275 per FTE student in 1997 (in 2008 dollars) to $7,581 in 2008. Some of the decline in funding per student is related to rapid expansion in enrollment in lower-cost 2-year colleges, but the most substantial changes were attributable to real reductions in state funding.

Tuition Charges in Minnesota Colleges and Universities

Public sector tuition charges in Minnesota grew substantially faster than the national average between 1992 and 2006 (Figure 8.4). The average tuition charge weighted by average FTE student across the different types of public college (St. John, 2006) was higher but close to the national average in 1992—$3,460 in Minnesota compared with $2,911 in the United States as a whole (in 2008 dollars)—but substantially greater than the national average in 2008 ($6,657 in Minnesota compared to $4,746 in the United States). The jump in tuition between 2000 and 2008 corresponds with the decline in state funding, illustrating how tuition has been used to make up for decreases in state subsidies in Minnesota.

Declining State Need-Based Grants

If increases in public tuition charges are coordinated with increases in student grants, inequalities are unlikely to increase (St. John, 2003, 2006). State grant funding per FTE

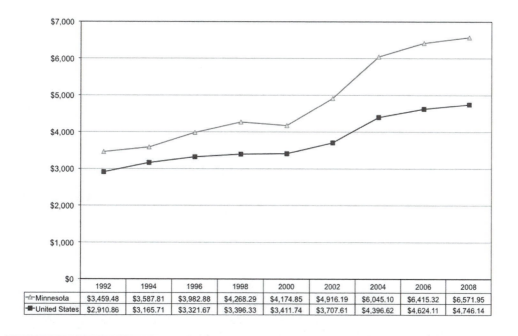

	1992	1994	1996	1998	2000	2002	2004	2006	2008
Minnesota	$3,459.48	$3,587.81	$3,982.88	$4,268.29	$4,174.85	$4,916.19	$6,045.10	$6,415.32	$6,571.95
United States	$2,910.86	$3,165.71	$3,321.67	$3,396.33	$3,411.74	$3,707.61	$4,396.62	$4,624.11	$4,746.14

Figure 8.4 Trend in Minnesota's Average Amount of Undergraduate In-State Tuition and Fees for the Public Higher Education System

Source: Data from NCES Integrated Postsecondary Education Data System © 2011 Projects Promoting Equity in Urban and Higher Education, NCID at the University of Michigan.

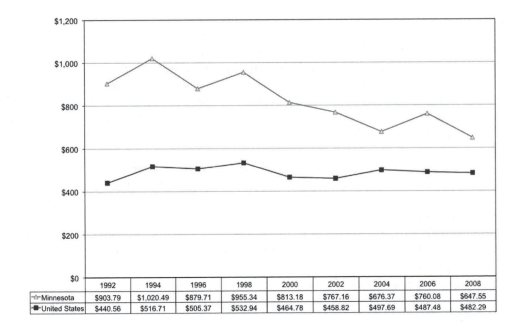

	1992	1994	1996	1998	2000	2002	2004	2006	2008
Minnesota	$903.79	$1,020.49	$879.71	$955.34	$813.18	$767.16	$676.37	$760.08	$647.55
United States	$440.56	$516.71	$505.37	$532.94	$464.78	$458.82	$497.69	$487.48	$482.29

Figure 8.5 Trend in Minnesota's Need-Based Undergraduate Grants per FTE Compared With the National Average (In 2008 Dollars)

Source: Data from National Association of State Student Grant & Aid Programs © 2011 Projects Promoting Equity in Urban and Higher Education, NCID at the University of Michigan.

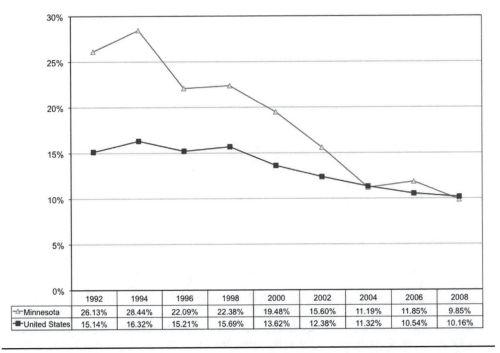

	1992	1994	1996	1998	2000	2002	2004	2006	2008
Minnesota	26.13%	28.44%	22.09%	22.38%	19.48%	15.60%	11.19%	11.85%	9.85%
United States	15.14%	16.32%	15.21%	15.69%	13.62%	12.38%	11.32%	10.54%	10.16%

Figure 8.6 Trend in Minnesota Need-Based Grants as a Percent of State Tuition Compared With the National Average

Source: Data from NCES Integrated Postsecondary Education Data System and National Association of State Student Grant & Aid Programs © 2011 Projects Promoting Equity in Urban and Higher Education, NCID at the University of Michigan.

student in Minnesota's public and private higher education system began to drop even before subsidies to colleges (Figure 8.5).[4] In 1992, state grant funding per FTE student was more than double the national average ($904 compared with $441 in the United States). This average dropped, declining to an average of $748 per FTE student by 2008—still high compared with the national average of $482. However, this illustrates that during a period when tuition charges in Minnesota public colleges and universities increased and state support of institutions rose, student aid awards declined. The increased net price paid by students was clearly a factor in the increased student borrowing.

Decline in Grants in Relation to Tuition

The ratio of need-based grant funding per FTE student as a percent of tuition reveals just how much the Minnesota model has eroded (Figure 8.6). In 1992–1994, when the old market model was still a centerpiece of state policy, the state grant funding per FTE student in public and private colleges was more than 25% of the weighted average tuition in public colleges, and the ratio was more than 10 percentage points above the national average; in 2004, Minnesota's ratio had dropped to the national average, and by 2008 it was slightly below.

TRENDS IN STUDENT OUTCOMES

The three types of outcomes influenced by changes in state policies on preparation and higher education finance are high school graduation (directly related to preparation requirements), college access (affected directly by finance policies and dual enrollment and indirectly by other preparation policies), and degree completion (affected directly by campus policies and practices and state finance policies and indirectly by state academic preparation requirements). Trends related to these three types of outcomes are summarized below.

High School Graduation

According to the pathways theory of change (Figure 3.1) and the review of related research (Chapter 3), we suggest that there is a direct and significant relationship between state policies on graduation and both achievement on test scores and high school graduation rates. We examine trends in these outcomes below.

Student Academic Achievement

Minnesota has consistently had high test scores compared with other states. In 2008, 70% of the high school class took the ACT, compared with 47% nationally (Figure 8.7). The composite ACT score has been consistently higher in Minnesota than the United States as a whole; in Minnesota, the average score rose from 21.8 to 22.9 between 1994 and 2010, whereas the national score increased from 20.8 to 21.0 (Figure 8.8). The rise in the ACT composite score in 2006 corresponds with the implementation of three math courses for graduation, and the increase in the upward trajectory in 2008 suggests a positive association between test scores and requiring geometry for graduation. We recommend caution in make causal assertions based on convergence of trends but recognize that this prospect is also consistent with prior research (Chapter 3).

High School Graduation Rates

Unlike many other states, Minnesota had substantial improvement in high school graduation rates for African Americans between 1996 and 2008, rising from 52% to 65%, a

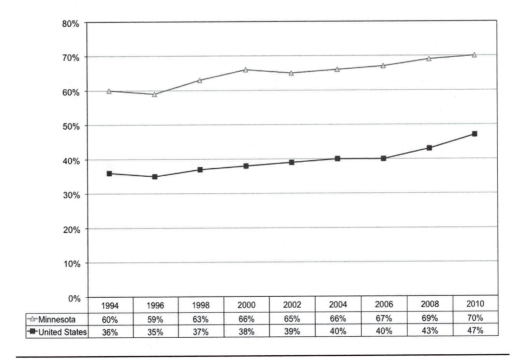

	1994	1996	1998	2000	2002	2004	2006	2008	2010
Minnesota	60%	59%	63%	66%	65%	66%	67%	69%	70%
United States	36%	35%	37%	38%	39%	40%	40%	43%	47%

Figure 8.7 Trends in Percent of Minnesota and U.S. Students Who Took the ACT

Source: Data from ACT, Inc. © 2011 Projects Promoting Equity in Urban and Higher Education, NCID at the University of Michigan.

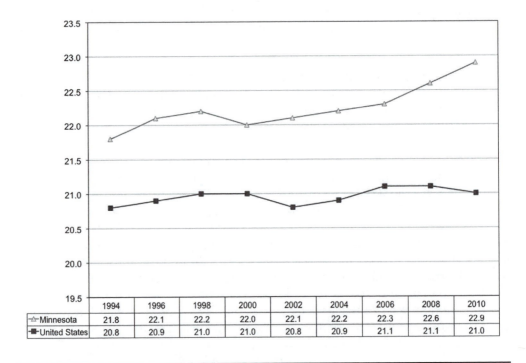

	1994	1996	1998	2000	2002	2004	2006	2008	2010
Minnesota	21.8	22.1	22.2	22.0	22.1	22.2	22.3	22.6	22.9
United States	20.8	20.9	21.0	21.0	20.8	20.9	21.1	21.1	21.0

Figure 8.8 Trends in Average Composite ACT Scores in Minnesota and the United States

Source: Data from ACT, Inc. © 2011 Projects Promoting Equity in Urban and Higher Education, NCID at the University of Michigan.

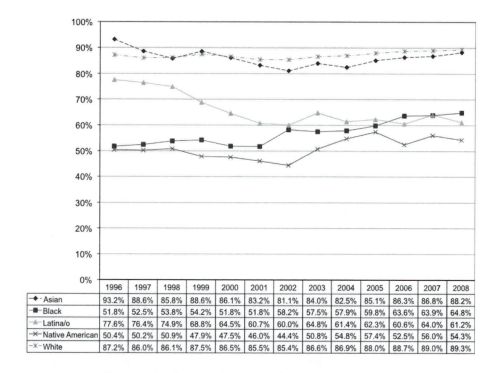

Figure 8.9 Trends in Minnesota Public High School Graduation Rates by Race/Ethnicity

Source: Data from NCES Common Core Data © 2011 Projects Promoting Equity in Urban and Higher Education, NCID at the University of Michigan.

13 percentage point gain (Figure 8.9). Programs in Minnesota that provide opportunities for dual enrollment in community colleges may be one of the factors contributing to these gains; however, not all groups had similar gains. There was a slight gain in high school graduation rates for Native Americans, but the rates actually declined over the 12-year period for Whites, Asian Americans, and Hispanics.

Access and Diversity

Access and diversity are closely intertwined policy issues that interact with the distribution of diverse groups within states. In Minnesota, most of the African American population is concentrated in the Twin Cities, along with campuses located in that city (community colleges, city campuses part of the state university system or the University of Minnesota, private colleges, and proprietary colleges). There is geographic access for minorities in Minnesota, but academic access is influenced by preparation, while the ability of prepared students to pay for college is dependent on federal, state, and institutional aid.

College Enrollment

College continuation rates—the number of high school graduates in the spring of a year, divided by the number of college freshmen from the state enrolling anywhere in the United States—increased faster in Minnesota than in the nation as a whole (Figure 8.10)

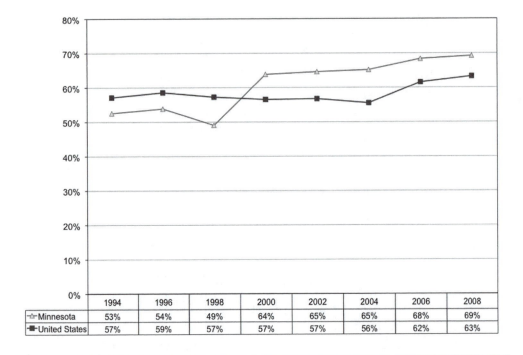

Figure 8.10 Trends in Minnesota's College Continuation Rate Compared With the National Average

Source: Data from Postsecondary Education Opportunity © 2011 Projects Promoting Equity in Urban and Higher Education, NCID at the University of Michigan.

and was substantially higher in Minnesota in the early 2000s. However, the gains in access in Minnesota are somewhat deceptive, given the patterns of diversity within the state system.

Diversity in Public 2-Year Colleges

The gains in access for African Americans in Minnesota were driven by patterns in the 2-year colleges (Figure 8.11) and private proprietary colleges. African American representation in community colleges grew from 122% of their percentage of the state population in 1992 to 186% in 2008, with most of the growth occurring after 2000. American Indians and Asian Americans also had modest increases in their representation in public 2-year colleges, while Whites had a slight drop and Latinos/as had a very substantial drop, from a ratio of 1.2 in 1997 to 0.86 in 2008.

Diversity in Public 4-Year Institutions

In contrast to community colleges, Minnesota's public 4-year college system had only modest changes in racial representation (Figure 8.12). The most substantial drop in the representation ratio was among Asian Americans, whose participation declined from a high of 1.73 in 1994 to a low of 1.2 in 2004 and rose slightly thereafter to 1.3 in 2008. Native American representation increased from 0.63 in 1992 to 1.0 in 2008. There was a substantial decline in representation of Latinos/as, dropping from 81% of the representation in the state population to 37% after the 2000 census, for which Hispanic classification categories had been altered. In contrast, representation of African Americans

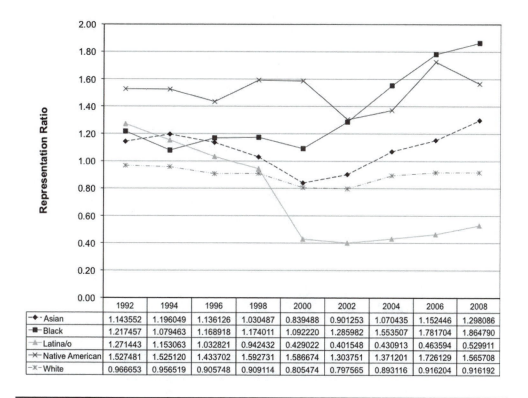

	1992	1994	1996	1998	2000	2002	2004	2006	2008
◆ Asian	1.143552	1.196049	1.136126	1.030487	0.839488	0.901253	1.070435	1.152446	1.298086
■ Black	1.217457	1.079463	1.168918	1.174011	1.092220	1.285982	1.553507	1.781704	1.864790
▲ Latina/o	1.271443	1.153063	1.032821	0.942432	0.429022	0.401548	0.430913	0.463594	0.529911
✕ Native American	1.527481	1.525120	1.433702	1.592731	1.586674	1.303751	1.371201	1.726129	1.565708
✳ White	0.966653	0.956519	0.905748	0.909114	0.805474	0.797565	0.893116	0.916204	0.916192

Figure 8.11 Trends in Racial/Ethnic Representation in Minnesota Public 2-Year Postsecondary Institutions as a Proportion of the State Population

Source: Data from NCES Integrated Postsecondary Education Data System and U.S. Census Bureau © 2011 Projects Promoting Equity in Urban and Higher Education, NCID at the University of Michigan.

fluctuated but did not change substantially, and representation of Whites remained relatively steady, hovering around 96%.

The overall pattern of enrollment distribution suggests a differential impact of high school improvement and college net prices across racial groups, especially between 2006 and 2008. Representation of Whites in public 4-year colleges was higher in 2006 and 2008 than in prior periods in this trend analysis. The opposite is true for Latinas/os and African Americans: they were less well represented in public 4-year colleges than in the 1990s. High school improvement probably had a muted impact on these groups owing to differences in family incomes and ability to pay for the higher costs of enrollment in public 4-year institutions.

Constrained Gains in Access

The gains in access evident in the 2000s in Minnesota were limited to community colleges and proprietary institutions—institutions that became increasingly overrepresented by African Americans. This pattern of constrained access does not appear to be related to economic factors—the rise in tuition and decline in state funding for grants—but rather to problems in preparation. In spite of the erosions at the edges of Minnesota's market approach, the state has expanded access in a period of constrained state resources.

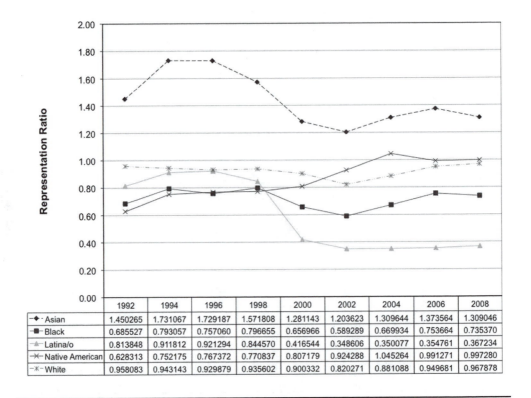

	1992	1994	1996	1998	2000	2002	2004	2006	2008
Asian	1.450265	1.731067	1.729187	1.571808	1.281143	1.203623	1.309644	1.373564	1.309046
Black	0.685527	0.793057	0.757060	0.796655	0.656966	0.589289	0.669934	0.753664	0.735370
Latina/o	0.813848	0.911812	0.921294	0.844570	0.416544	0.348606	0.350077	0.354761	0.367234
Native American	0.628313	0.752175	0.767372	0.770837	0.807179	0.924288	1.045264	0.991271	0.997280
White	0.958083	0.943143	0.929879	0.935602	0.900332	0.820271	0.881088	0.949681	0.967878

Figure 8.12 Trends in Racial/Ethnic Representation in Minnesota Public 4-Year Postsecondary Institutions as a Proportion of the State Population

Source: Data from NCES Integrated Postsecondary Education Data System and U.S. Census Bureau © 2011 Projects Promoting Equity in Urban and Higher Education, NCID at the University of Michigan.

Graduation Rates in Minnesota's Higher Education System

College completion rates are related to family background, academic preparation, initial college choices, and student financial aid. State polices can affect degree completion rates through initiatives that improve preparation and college finance strategies that meet student need. Graduation rates are calculated at 150% of the expected graduation time (3 years for 2-year programs and 6 years for 4-year programs), which means that part-time students could graduate in the expected time period.

Public 2-Year Colleges

In 2002, the 3-year graduation rates in Minnesota's community colleges ranged from about one-third of Whites to 12.7% of African Americans. Although there were gains in preparation and initial college access for African Americans, these gains did not lead to improved attainment; completion rates for African Americans as a group dropped, especially after 2005 (Figure 8.13), and by 2008 the 3-year completion rate for African Americans was only 7.5%. Other groups remained stable. Although some of the gain in African American enrollment could be due to inner-city enrollment during high school, it is evident that these constrained gains in access are not followed by completion of 2-year degrees or access to 4-year colleges and universities.

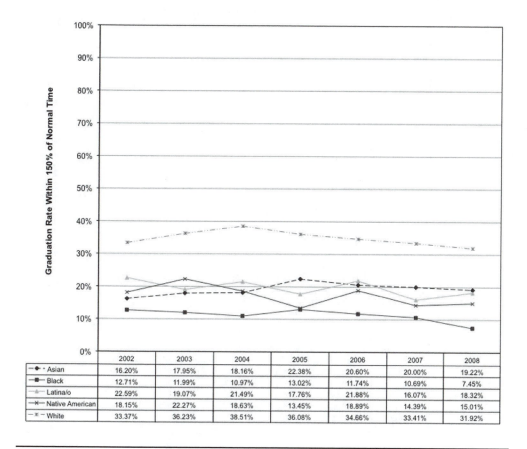

Figure 8.13 Trends in Graduation Rates in Minnesota Public Two-Year Postsecondary Institutions by Race/Ethnic Group

Source: Data from NCES Integrated Postsecondary Education Data System © 2011 Projects Promoting Equity in Urban and Higher Education, NCID at the University of Michigan.

Public 4-Year Institutions

In contrast to public 2-year colleges, Minnesota's public 4-year colleges and universities demonstrated improved degree completion rates for every racial/ethnic group between 2002 and 2008, although there was a widening of the gaps among groups (Figure 8.14). In 2002, 43% of Whites graduated, compared with 32.2% of Blacks (a 10.8 percentage point gap) and 24.2% of Native Americans (an 18.8 percentage point gap). In contrast, in 2008, 57.1% of Whites graduated, compared with 39.8% of Blacks (17.3 percentage point gap) and 29.6% for American Indians (27.5 percentage point gap). Both Asian Americans and Hispanics had graduation rates over 50% in 2008. These trends indicate differential progress in improving degree attainment.

Constrained Access and Limited Attainment

Looking across these sets of trends, it is apparent that in the early 2000s Minnesota made gains in high school preparation, especially for African Americans; targeted gains in college access for African Americans, principally at 2-year institutions; but had declining degree completion rates for African Americans in community colleges. Further study of dual enrollment, student aid, and college support services would be needed to discern the

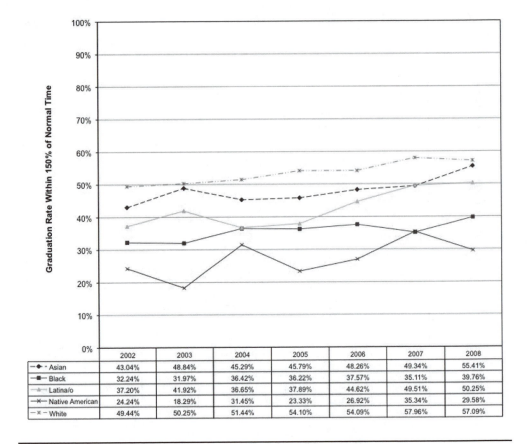

Figure 8.14 Trends in Graduation Rates in Minnesota Public Four-Year Postsecondary Institutions

Source: Data from NCES Integrated Postsecondary Education Data System © 2011 Projects Promoting Equity in Urban and Higher Education, NCID at the University of Michigan.

reasons for these atypical patterns in Minnesota. In spite of erosion in need-based grants, the Minnesota model worked relatively well for most groups through the Great Recession.

CURRENT ISSUES IN MINNESOTA

Minnesota has embraced a high tuition/high aid model for the funding of higher education and to date they have fared reasonably well. In 2010, 31.2% of Minnesota adults above age 25 had attained a bachelor's degree or above—almost 4% higher than the national average of 27.4% (U.S. Census Bureau, 2011). Tuition rates across the two public systems—particularly in the University of Minnesota System—have been higher than other states in the region, but the maximum awards for the state grant program kept pace with rising tuition to maintain an affordable college education for low-income students. In 2011, in-state students paid $12,288 for tuition and fees at the Twin Cities campus of UM (National Center for Education Statistics, 2011). That rate is nearly 30% higher than 4 years earlier and is comparable with rates at the other Big Ten universities. The Minnesota State College and University (MNSCU) System, meanwhile, is a relative bargain for in-state students at approximately $7,000 per year.

The maximum state grant for 2011 is set at $10,488 for attendance at a 4-year public institution. The program is means tested, and in 2010 the average award was approximately $1,100. All of this might suggest that the market model has worked reasonably well. However, as in other states across the country, state budget deficits and growing cuts to higher education are placing tremendous strain on institutions, which has been passed along to students and their families. The key policy issues facing Minnesota are related to its market orientation and strong commitment to a high tuition/high aid approach to funding higher education. In Minnesota as in many states, academic expectations in high school will ratchet up in the coming years, which will have implications for access directly in terms of admission but also indirectly, if conservative policymakers are correct, as a market mechanism to increase students' qualifications for merit-based aid, particularly at the institutional level. Johnstone (2001) warns that the danger inherent in the high tuition/high aid model is that the state will fail to keep its promise in terms of aid; this is where the Minnesota case is beginning to show some strain. Finally, like other states trying to reign in what they consider out-of-control expenses in public higher education, Minnesota has cut funding substantially and committed a small portion of those cuts to performance funding. Each of these policies is important to consider, both in the context of the Minnesota case and relative to the challenges facing other states across the country.

Graduation Requirements and High-Stakes Testing

Minnesota, like many states across the country, has been increasing the requirements it places on students in order to earn a high school diploma. For a number of years, Minnesota has required students to complete 21.5 Carnegie units—most of which are in English (4), Math (3), Science (3), and Social Studies (3.5). Current students are required to complete algebra and geometry as part of the math sequence and a biology course in science. The class of 2015 will be required to complete the same minimum number of courses but will have to add algebra II to the math sequence and either chemistry or physics in science. These requirements are in close alignment with the 4-year college standard and assume students are currently avoiding more difficult courses and are therefore not maximizing their education in high school.

In addition to ratcheting up the rigor of the course requirements, Minnesota is adopting a mandatory exit exam. Students slated to graduate from high school between 2010 and 2014 will either be required to pass minimum competency exams in reading, writing, and math or an alternative set of requirements. Beginning with the class of 2015, all students will be required to test as proficient on the three sections of the Minnesota GRAD test. Research on mandatory exit exams suggests the policy may negatively impact high school completion rates in the state. The combination of more rigorous course requirements and a mandatory exit exam may allow fewer students to gain entry to college but better prepare those that make it.

Cuts to the Minnesota State Grant

Generally speaking, Minnesota has kept its promise. Tuition is high, but so is the aid for low-income students; however, this may be in jeopardy. In 2010, demand for state grants increased beyond estimates and the program was underfunded (Minnesota Office of Higher Education, 2011). The state utilized 2011 funds to cover the deficit, but the consequence is that that state will not be able to grant full awards. In order to cover a projected $44 million shortfall, the governor intends to eliminate summer tuition support for transition programs and temporarily increase the expected family contribution (EFC). During 2011, higher education is projected to receive cuts of $293 million or 11% of state-based funding (Minnesota Budget Project, 2011). It is not likely that state revenues or public support for higher education will improve in the coming years.

Performance Funding

Minnesota is not a state with a history of performance funding for higher education. However, in 2011 amid a budget shortfall of more than $6 billion, the state shifted 1% of total appropriations for the University of Minnesota and MNSCU to performance funding. These resources will be contingent upon improvements in graduation rates, institutional diversity, and other state priorities. Research on performance funding has generally found that the modest amounts states set aside does not have a significant effect on institutional behavior, and the same may be expected for Minnesota. Performance funding is perfectly aligned with the market orientation of Minnesota higher education policy. It identifies the goal but allows institutions to develop the most cost-effective strategies to achieve the goal. Unfortunately performance funding typically favors campuses most capable of achieving the benchmarks, which are institutions that frequently serve more privileged students. The consequence may be that fewer resources will be allocated to campuses most likely to serve underrepresented students. See Text Box 8.1 for questions about the Minnesota situation.

Text Box 8.1 Questions About the Minnesota Case

1. What role did researchers play in the development of Minnesota's market model?

2. How does institutional self-interest influence the advocacy and adaptive strategies in Minnesota colleges and universities?

3. What role did public trust of higher education play in the capacity of legislatures to develop and sustain fair approaches for funding higher education in Minnesota?

4. Is debt burden an indicator of the weaknesses of the market model and/or were there changes in Minnesota's approach to public funding that increased student reliance on borrowing?

5. How did changes in Minnesota's funding model influence the racial distribution of students in the higher education system?

6. How did changes in racial/ethnic differentials in high school graduation rates relate to differentials in college opportunities in Minnesota?

7. What roles do educational preparation and financial aid play in the completion rates of Minnesota college students?

8. How important is a state's commitment to funding need-based student aid to the success of the market model? How did Minnesota develop and sustain the commitment to funding student aid given the competitive behaviors of institutions?

9. How do you anticipate performance funding will change the patterns of outcomes (distribution of enrollment and degree completion) in Minnesota institutions?

9

MERIT AID

The Florida Case

The Georgia HOPE program became a model that many southern—and a few northern—states adapted to fit the higher education systems in their states (Heller & Rasmussen, 2002). Proponents of merit grants argue that these programs retain high-achieving residents in the state and improve access, arguments for which there is some empirical support (e.g., Dynarski, 2002). But merit programs are also associated with inequality, and they make it more difficult for low-income residents to attend 4-year colleges if they do not meet the academic requirement for scholarship eligibility (Chapter 5). Given the wide use of merit grants as a model for expanding college access and encouraging academic preparation (Bishop, 2004), it is important for policymakers to ponder the strengths and limitations of merit grants as a political strategy for financing access to higher education.

Florida provides a useful illustration of the merit aid strategy because it emulated features of the Georgia HOPE program but made modifications to provide multiple points of access to higher education institutions of different types, including 2-year programs. The state also took steps to align the Bright Futures program with the state's K–12 reforms, which focus on expanding academic preparation. The Florida case provides a good example of adaptation of innovation as well as the use of merit grants as part of a comprehensive state-level reform strategy promoting improvement in preparation and college access. Yet the Florida Bright Futures program has been controversial, with strong and vociferous support coupled with serious critiques from both Florida citizens and external experts.[1]

The Florida Bright Futures program has been in place for more than a decade and has served more than 550,000 students. It offers three different award levels to students: the Florida Academic Scholarship (FAS), which covers 100% of the cost of a 4-year degree at a public university for an "A" student; the Florida Medallion Scholars (FMS) award, set at 75% of the cost of a 4-year degree for "B" students or 100% at a community college; and the Florida Gold Seal Vocational (FSV) award, intended to cover 75% of the cost of a vocational degree program (Office of Student Financial Assistance, 2011). The program is funded by state lottery receipts and has been so well utilized that in 2011 it cost more than the lottery earned. Students meet the qualifications through a combination of high school GPA and SAT scores. In addition, students are expected to complete the Florida high school graduation requirements and achieve proficiency on the Florida Comprehensive Assessment Test (FCAT). In order for students to maintain their awards, they must achieve a minimum GPA and credit requirements in college that differ depending on the level of the award.

While the program was implemented in 1997 to promote academic preparation for college, reward high school students, and encourage more of them to enroll in college, critics argue that it undermines college access for low-income and minority students.

Critics question whether Bright Futures merits continuation. Cuts to higher education funding for colleges coupled with increased tuition have effectively driven up the cost of the Bright Futures program. An underlying problem was the fairness of spending on higher education; but whatever methods the state used to support colleges and universities, the campuses in the state were left to craft viable financial strategies. This case study reviews the features of the Bright Futures program, along with arguments for and against continuing the program, before reviewing trends in key state indicators as a way of building an understanding of the impact of implementing this new program.

THE BRIGHT FUTURES GRANT IN CONTEXT

During the 1970s, Florida had a major historically black college (Florida A&M University), a land grant university (Florida State University), two major public universities (University of Florida), several regional public universities (e.g., Florida International, Central Florida, and Florida Atlantic), all organized under the umbrella of the State University System of Florida's Board of Governors, along with a community college system.[2] There were 28 districts in the Florida Community College System, many of which represented multiple counties.[3] There is a long history of articulation between 2-year colleges and state universities in Florida, making it easy for students to maintain dual enrollment in a community college and a number of 4-year institutions as a cost-saving strategy. By 2010, some community colleges in Florida had developed 4-year degree programs as a lower-cost alternative to the state college system, as we describe later in the chapter.[4] The state had a history of funding both merit- and need-based grants but was not among the leading states in either type of program.

Florida was one of the early states to adopt more rigorous graduation requirements for high school graduation. By 1997, when the state started Bright Futures, Florida had a mandatory state exit exam, required three math courses for graduation, and had adopted national math standards. In 1998, it implemented algebra as a minimum requirement for graduation. Thus there was an alignment between what was generally considered a rigorous high school standard and Bright Futures.

Program Features of Bright Futures Merit Grants
Precursor programs (e.g., Florida Undergraduate Scholars Fund, or FUSF), which operated prior to 1997, were intended to combat brain drain and reward college preparedness. In a Commission of Education report to the legislature, the goals of Bright Futures when implemented in 1997 were to

- encourage college preparedness (aligned to state university admissions); and
- combat the deflating value of FUSF's flat awards by offering an award amount equal to tuition. (Winn, 2005)

Over time, other explanations for the program have been articulated in the press and other media—including improving college access for prepared students and reducing brain drain—rationales that had been used by other states to promote merit programs (Cohen-Vogel & Ingle, 2007). The persistent rationales for the program have been to encourage academic preparation and reward students who met a predefined set of academic criteria. Both outcomes—improvement in preparation and increased retention of prepared students at state institutions—are emphasized in arguments frequently used by supporters of continuation and full funding of the program.

The reward criteria reflect the academic intent, but the program also provided support for students to enroll in technical programs. The Florida Bright Futures program is awarded to Florida residents who enroll in eligible public and private programs within 3 years of high school graduation. The Bright Futures program has the following components:

- *Florida Academic Scholars (FAS).* Requires a 3.5 GPA; 1270 SAT/28 ACT or IB diploma; National Merit, Achievement, National Latino Scholar, or Home Education; and 75 hours of public service when a college prep HS diploma is chosen. The award was set at 100% of tuition plus $600 per year for education expenses.
- *Academic Top Scholar.* Awarded to one top-ranked initial FAS per county.
- *Florida Medallion Scholars (FMS).* Requires HS standard diploma or GED, 3.0 GPA in 15 college prep courses, plus 970 SAT/20 ACT but no community service. The first year, recipients receive $1,500 for education expenses in addition to 100% of tuition and fees at any postsecondary institution.
- *Gold Seal Vocation Scholars (GSV).* Requires HS standard diploma or GED, 3.0 GPA in 15.5 HS core courses, minimum 3.5 GPA in three vocational courses and no community service. Award equals 75% of tuition and fees.
- To maintain their awards, students must maintain a 3.0 GPA for FAS and 2.75 for FMS and GSV with at least 6 hours per term. Award equals 75% of tuition and fees.
- Students who attend private institutions receive an amount equivalent to what they would have received for a public institution.

The award criteria essentially set preparation thresholds for students in different high school tracks, encouraging an alignment between type of academic preparation and the financial opportunity to enroll in college. Merit grant programs are not explicitly designed to meet financial need.[5] Low-income students are the most likely to respond to embedded financial incentives. For example, students with grades above 2.75 but below 3.0 might consider taking a vocational course if they have financial need, an option in the Bright Futures program but not in some other state and federal grants.

The financial incentives created by Florida's Bright Futures are complex, attempting to align different patterns of student preparation with enrollment in different types of colleges and programs. Although the GPA requirements to maintain grants can influence major choices (Hu, 2008), these intermediate program effects are not a primary focus of this review.[6] Given the extensive commentary on the program in the popular press, we focus on the potential effects of the program on preparation (the initial program intent) and on equity in college access (an unintended consequence of the program). Bright Futures may improve upon HOPE from an access perspective, given the range of awards and eligibility criteria, but the trade-off is that the program is complex, which may make it difficult for students to understand whether they are eligible or which program best fits their situation. Ultimately the lack of a clear signal to students regarding their likely net cost of college may have a negative effect on college participation relative to HOPE.

Critiques and Reform Efforts

While the intent of the Bright Futures program was to encourage academic preparation, most of the criticism has focused on enrollment effects. We expect that the effect of the program on academic preparation has an indirect effect on enrollments, particularly regarding the choice of institution attended. The literature includes the following commentary:

- Scholars and the press have documented the gap in awards for African Americans and Latinos/as compared with Whites, arguing that the program adds to disparities in the opportunity to enroll in college (Dynarski, 2002, 2004; Heller, 2002, 2004a, 2004b)—an issue that has been widely reported (Miller, 2008; National Center for Fair and Open Testing, 2008).
- There has also been criticism of the program because of the standards used for qualification. Some reports have argued that the scores required for awards are too low (Kormanik, 2002).
- Research indicates that low-SES families benefit less from Bright Futures than high-SES families in Florida (Heller, 2004a; Stranahan & Borg, 2004) for two reasons: fewer students from low-income families choose to attend college, even when they finish high school; and fewer low-SES students qualify for the programs. When they do qualify, it is for the less generous variations of the program.
- The indexing of awards to tuition may influence tuition increases, thus constraining funding for public universities (Colavecchio-Van Sickler, 2007), an argument made a decade earlier about the Pell grants by Secretary of Education Bennett (1987).
- The program is criticized in the press as a reverse Robin Hood program (Braun, 2008), generating money from low-income families through the lottery to pay for the college costs of students from wealthy families.

The Florida lottery revenue agency, the Education Enhancement Trust Fund, prioritizes Bright Futures over discretionary allocations to educational institutions (i.e., subsidies to schools and colleges). To the extent that college tuition charges rise, the Bright Futures funding rises and resources for discretionary distribution decline. Thus raising tuition can reduce allocations to colleges, which in turn could increase demand on the Education Enhancement Trust Fund for the Bright Futures scholarships. This pattern became more problematic in the late 2000s, given the decline in other sources of tax revenue used to fund public education in Florida.

There have been efforts to revise the Bright Futures program since its inception, with issues ranging from addressing inequalities to raising requirements for awards (Adams, 2007). However, the state has found it difficult to amend the program because of its popularity, especially among middle-income students and their voting parents (Kronholz, 2003). For example, a recent legislative attempt to limit awards to science fields ran into organized student protests (Morales, 2008). The only modification approved to date has been to place more emphasis on advanced placement courses and testing.

The Florida Bright Futures program provides financial rewards to students who take specific precollege courses and receive high grades in these courses, but it doesn't specify which courses students should take. Since only the number of advanced math courses is specified, it is possible for students to avoid difficult courses if they are near the threshold of qualifying for the program.

College students are among the most politically active advocates for the program because they depend on the grants. Yet advocacy for the program on the part of college students is appropriately viewed as being in their own self-interest. In contrast, most of the criticisms of the program raise issues related to social justice and inequality. In order to untangle these arguments, it is necessary to examine trends in preparation and college access as well as to review changes, if any, in other policies that could influence preparation or college enrollment by diverse groups of students.

There is a serious capacity issue in the state, a situation that has fueled some of the movement to create the state college system and enable community colleges to award baccalaureate degrees. With this limited capacity for growth, keeping more talented students in the state of Florida (reducing the brain drain) could reduce access to 4-year colleges, especially for low-income students who qualify for a 4-year college but do not earn the Bright Futures award. This could result in reduced college continuation rates for high school students. Given these complexities, it is important to examine a range of enrollment outcomes related to the program.

Why Examine Bright Futures?

With the exception of Doyle's (2006) analysis of the diffusion of merit aid programs, the literature on programs like Bright Futures tends to overlook the intent and outcomes related to the implementation of merit aid. Doyle tests several competing theories for why states adopt merit aid programs and finds that states with low college continuation rates tend to adopt merit programs and that, contrary to the policy rationale, states with low rates of students leaving the state for college are more likely to adopt merit programs. Given this finding, it is possible to conclude that there is a wide gap between the espoused intent of states adopting merit grant programs and the actual outcomes in the state before implementing the grants.

We analyze trends of key indicators below as a relatively straightforward method of examining policy intent in relation to outcomes, which may, in turn, provide insights into how the timing of other policies, such as graduation requirements, might also influence the intended outcomes.

In the analysis of trends below, we try to fill gaps in understanding of the Florida Bright Futures program. In particular, we examine the implementation of the program in relation to other policies that can also influence preparation and enrollment.

Information Gaps

Two themes about the Bright Futures program emerge from the academic literature, but gaps are evident in this work to date:

- First, the Bright Futures program has been characterized as an "innovation" that was implemented as part of a diffusion process concentrated largely in the southeastern United States (Cohen-Vogel & Ingle, 2007; Cohen-Vogel, Ingle, & Levine, 2008; Ingle & Cohen-Vogel, 2007). With the exception of Doyle (2006), the literature tends to overlook the intent and outcomes related to the implementation.

- There are studies that focus on the effects of merit aid on access (Dynarski, 2002; Heller & Marin, 2002, 2004), but these studies focus primarily on college enrollment and overlook the impact on preparation, a major intent of the program.

The policy reports on Bright Futures prepared by state agencies in Florida have focused on indicators of preparation, affordability, and enrollment (e.g., OPPAGA Program Review, 2003) and retention (OPPAGA Program Review, 2004). These reports indicate there have been improvements in preparation and enrollment, but do they not consider other programs and policies that could influence these outcomes, nor do they consider the unintended consequences of the program. For example, prior studies indicate that merit programs that create academic thresholds for eligibility for student aid could discourage some low-income students from graduating from high school (St. John, 2006).

Filling the Gaps

Preparation and enrollment outcomes are thought to relate directly to the intent of the Bright Futures program, but other types of state funding and K–12 requirements can also influence these outcomes; it is important to think critically about the timing of changes in outcomes. The analyses of representation by racial/ethnic groups consider full-time equivalent (FTE) enrollment rather than first-time enrollment rates; as a consequence, they provide an indicator of enrollment that includes all students and indicate retention as well as initial enrollment. Changes in representation using these measures could be related to implementation of the Bright Futures program, but there are also other state education and public finance policies that could influence these outcomes. We consider these policies along with Bright Futures, avoiding the false impressions that can be created by focusing on a single program—a limitation of most state policy research. State policies are implemented in complex contexts in which numerous policies are already in place. It is shortsighted to consider only one program, because the mix of policies in place at any given time influences outcomes observed in a state.

TRENDS IN POLICY IMPLEMENTATION

There is a substantial body of research in higher education that links public policies to education outcomes. In this section, we examine trends in education policy and higher education finance in Florida, including but not limited to the Bright Futures program.

State Policy Related to Academic Access

Like many other states, Florida has undergone a revision in high school graduation policy. Florida also revised its college admissions policies with respect to affirmative action, as did Texas, Washington, and California. This also affects the academic pathways between high school and college.

High School Graduation Requirements

Florida has regular, accelerated, and special diploma options (Florida Department of Education, 2004), consistent with the tradition of comprehensive high schools in the United States. However, there is variability in the extent to which the courses required for each of the high school diplomas are available to all students. Research that controls for state context using time-series data indicates that raising state graduation requirements

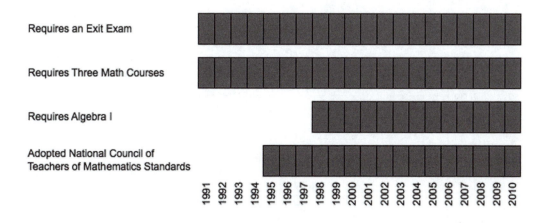

Figure 9.1 Florida High School Graduation Requirements

Source: © Projects Promoting Equity in Urban and Higher Education, NCID at the University of Michigan.

is positively associated with higher math achievement on SAT tests but lower high school graduation rates (St. John, 2006). The implementation dates for graduation requirements are discussed below (Figure 9.1).

Three math courses have been required for graduation since 1990, and state exit exams have been required for graduation since 1991, both implemented well before the trends examined. Math content standards consistent with NCTM were implemented in 1995. The requirement that students must pass algebra I to graduate was implemented in 1998. It is possible that stricter standards could depress graduation rates, a pattern evident in Florida as it was nationally before 2000 (St. John, 2006). However, the fact that SAT math scores have been lower than the national average is not consonant with national research, which typically finds a positive association between increased math requirements and state average SAT test scores (St. John, 2006).

College Admissions

In 1999, by executive order Governor Jeb Bush banned affirmative action in Florida and instead guaranteed access to state universities to the top 20% of a high school's graduating class (Blair, 1999). The transition from race-conscious admissions to alternative methods has been controversial. The percentage enrollment plans in Texas and California were initially criticized by the U.S. Civil Rights Commission (Blair, 1999) and by the Harvard Civil Rights Project (Denniston, 2003), arguing that these plans would probably be worse than race-conscious affirmative action. However, research on implementation of the Texas Top 10 Percent program indicates that it has worked relatively well (Chapa & Horn, 2007) to mitigate potential losses of talented minority youth from higher education. The Florida version is not nearly as simple as the Texas plan and, as a result, may actually create barriers for students, particularly during the choice phase of the admissions process. In Texas, the top 10% of every high school graduating class are guaranteed admission to the institution of their choice, meaning that every student could attend UT Austin if that were their preference. In Florida, students are not guaranteed admission to any specific institution or to an institution of their choice. Rather, they are guaranteed

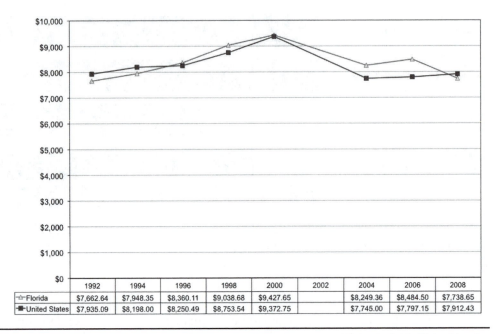

	1992	1994	1996	1998	2000	2002	2004	2006	2008
Florida	$7,662.64	$7,948.35	$8,360.11	$9,038.68	$9,427.65		$8,249.36	$8,484.50	$7,738.65
United States	$7,935.09	$8,198.00	$8,250.49	$8,753.54	$9,372.75		$7,745.00	$7,797.15	$7,912.43

Figure 9.2 Florida Average Annual Amount of State and Local Appropriations per FTE for the Public Higher Education System (in 2008 Dollars)

Source: Data from NCES Integrated Postsecondary Education Data System © 2011 Projects Promoting Equity in Urban and Higher Education, NCID at the University of Michigan.

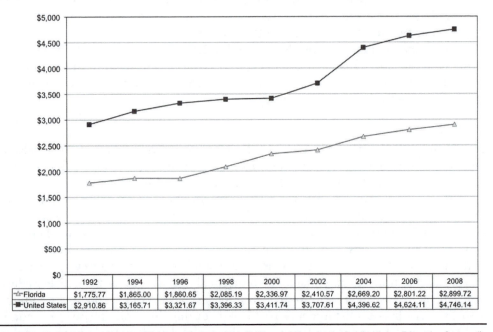

	1992	1994	1996	1998	2000	2002	2004	2006	2008
Florida	$1,775.77	$1,865.00	$1,860.65	$2,085.19	$2,336.97	$2,410.57	$2,669.20	$2,801.22	$2,899.72
United States	$2,910.86	$3,165.71	$3,321.67	$3,396.33	$3,411.74	$3,707.61	$4,396.62	$4,624.11	$4,746.14

Figure 9.3 Florida Average Amount of Undergraduate In-State Tuition and Fees for the Public Higher Education System (in 2008 Dollars)

Source: Data from NCES Integrated Postsecondary Education Data System © 2011 Projects Promoting Equity in Urban and Higher Education, NCID at the University of Michigan.

a spot in the system as long as they apply to a range of institutions. This level of uncertainty makes it difficult for students to make informed decisions about their future educational pathways.

State Financing of Postsecondary Education

State Appropriations for Public Higher Education

State appropriations per FTE improved relative to inflation between 1992 and 2003 but dropped in 2004 (Figure 9.2). Florida also made major cuts in the most recent budget (Braun, 2008). The problem evident in these trends is the lack of coordination between state subsidies and tuition—both rose after 1998 when the Bright Futures program was implemented.

Public Tuition Charges

The weighted average public tuition charge in Florida remained relatively flat from 1992 to 1996, adjusted for inflation (Figure 9.3). However, tuition charges increased faster than inflation in Florida after 1996. Public tuition increases can decrease enrollment by low-income students if there is not adequate need-based grant aid; even then, there is some indication that tuition has a stronger effect than grant programs (Heller, 1999).

Increases in tuition after 1997 correspond with the implementation of Bright Futures. However, the rate of increase in public tuition in Florida has been substantially below the national average, especially after the year 2000. So it cannot be concluded that implementing Bright Futures had an impact on tuition increases.

Funding for Non-Need-Based Grants

Examining trends in funding for the non-need (mostly merit) grants in Florida, it is evident that funding per FTE increased substantially between 1992 and 2008, with a peak in funding per student in the year 2000 (Figure 9.4). The initial rise was between 1996 and 2000, when funding more than doubled, from $301 to $656. In addition, there was a decline in FTE funding for non-need grants between 2000 and 2002, but this reached a new high of $696 per FTE in 2008.

Public funding for non-need grants is associated with improved enrollment rates (Dynarski, 2002; St. John, 2006) but with decreased high school graduation rates (St. John, 2006)—the former is consistent with the espoused theory of change but the latter runs counter to the theory unless the merit program coincided with higher academic expectations. The trends in Florida provide evidence of both these patterns. In addition, there was a decline in SAT math test scores of Florida students, while math scores increased nationally, introducing another possible linkage: It is possible that some Florida students avoided taking more advanced courses in high school as a means of keeping their grades high enough to qualify for a Bright Futures scholarship, which resulted in lower SAT scores. These scores may also reflect the growing proportion of high school students attending college who may not have done so in years past.

Need-Based Grant Aid

Need-based student financial aid is linked to improvement in college enrollment rates, especially for low-income students (Heller, 1997; Leslie & Brinkman, 1988; St. John, 2006). State funding for need-based grant aid is extremely low in Florida; it was less than

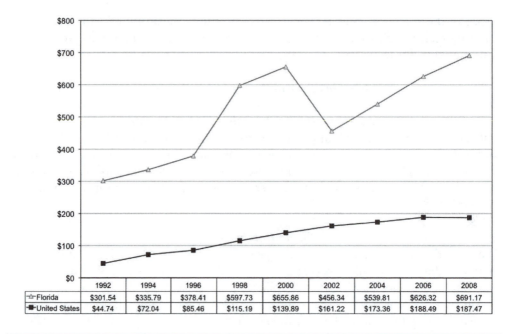

Figure 9.4 Trends in Florida State Non-Need-Based Undergraduate Grants per FTE (in 2008 Dollars)

Source: Data from National Association of State Student Grant & Aid Programs © 2011 Projects Promoting Equity in Urban and Higher Education, NCID at the University of Michigan.

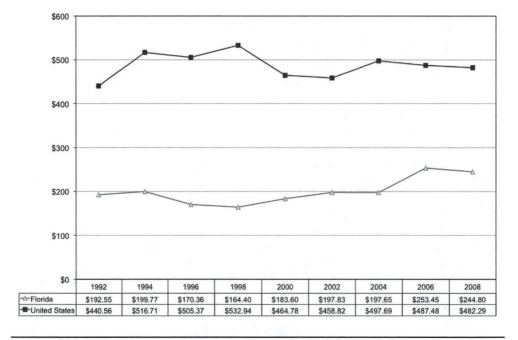

Figure 9.5 Trends in Florida State Need-Based Undergraduate Grants per FTE (in 2008 Dollars)

Source: Data from National Association of State Student Grant & Aid Programs © 2011 Projects Promoting Equity in Urban and Higher Education, NCID at the University of Michigan.

$200 per FTE between 1992 and 2008 (Figure 9.5). This trend is troubling given the rise in tuition. The consequences of this trend are appropriately considered in relation to tuition, which rose more rapidly than need-based aid.

Ratio of Need-Based Grant Funding to Average Tuition Charge

Although Florida has not emphasized need-based aid, it has continued funding it. For the United States as a whole, the ratio between need-based aid and tuition declined from 15.1% in 1998 to 10.2% in 2008; for Florida, the decline was from 10.8% to 8.4% (Figure 9.6).

TRENDS IN STUDENT OUTCOMES

In theory, a merit program like Bright Futures could improve preparation by providing incentives for preparation, while the follow-through on the state's commitment to funding could improve access to 4-year institutions while also improving quality. Although the research partially supports these propositions (Chapters 4–6), other policies in states also influence these outcomes. If other state funding strategies are altered to accommodate the grant program—for example, increasing tuition owing to the decline in state support to colleges—then it is possible these other changes could offset the impact of the grant program. Building an understanding of the timing of the implementation of grants and other policies is central to untangling the ways implementation of Bright Futures influenced student outcomes.

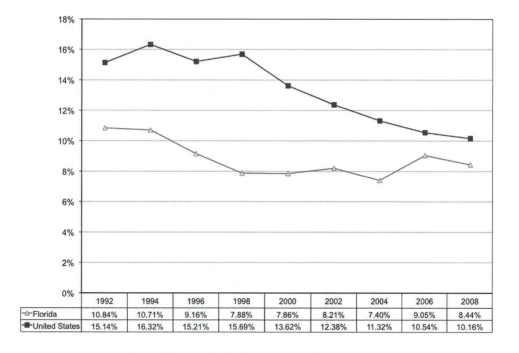

	1992	1994	1996	1998	2000	2002	2004	2006	2008
Florida	10.84%	10.71%	9.16%	7.88%	7.86%	8.21%	7.40%	9.05%	8.44%
United States	15.14%	16.32%	15.21%	15.69%	13.62%	12.38%	11.32%	10.54%	10.16%

Figure 9.6 Trends in Florida Funding Per FTE for Need-Based Grants as a Percent of State Tuition Charges

Source: Data from NCES Integrated Postsecondary Education Data System and National Association of State Student Grant & Aid Programs
© 2011 Projects Promoting Equity in Urban and Higher Education, NCID at the University of Michigan.

Trends in College Preparation

The intent of the Bright Futures program was to improve high school preparation through financial incentives to work harder in school. Of course it does not matter how hard one works if the requisite courses are not available. We examine trends in high school graduation, SAT scores, and ACT scores below.

High School Graduation Rates

If Bright Futures had an influence on high school graduation rates, it should have been evident after 2000: the Bright Futures program was implemented for seniors in 1998, when students in the class of 2000 were sophomores (Figure 9.7). It should be noted that high school graduation rates declined for every racial/ethnic group except Whites in Florida between 2000 and 2009. The combination of policies implemented apparently benefited Whites more than other groups, possibly because predominantly White suburban high schools were better prepared to offer the new college preparatory curriculum when it was first implemented.

In 2008, less than half of the African American students graduated high school; however, this rate was higher than it had been for the previous 10 years. For Latinas/os, the high school graduation rate dropped after 1996, rose somewhat in 2003 and 2008, but remained lower than the 1996 high of 63.3%. The graduation rate for Asian American

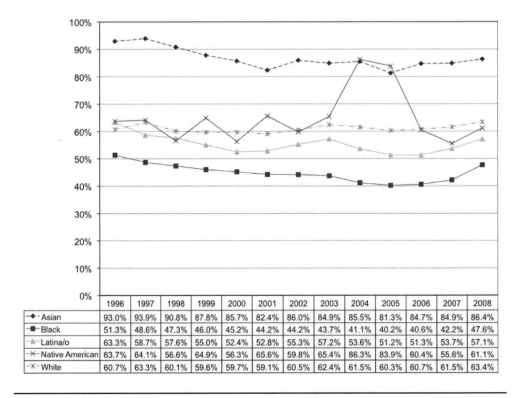

	1996	1997	1998	1999	2000	2001	2002	2003	2004	2005	2006	2007	2008
Asian	93.0%	93.9%	90.8%	87.8%	85.7%	82.4%	86.0%	84.9%	85.5%	81.3%	84.7%	84.9%	86.4%
Black	51.3%	48.6%	47.3%	46.0%	45.2%	44.2%	44.2%	43.7%	41.1%	40.2%	40.6%	42.2%	47.6%
Latina/o	63.3%	58.7%	57.6%	55.0%	52.4%	52.8%	55.3%	57.2%	53.6%	51.2%	51.3%	53.7%	57.1%
Native American	63.7%	64.1%	56.6%	64.9%	56.3%	65.6%	59.8%	65.4%	86.3%	83.9%	60.4%	55.6%	61.1%
White	60.7%	63.3%	60.1%	59.6%	59.7%	59.1%	60.5%	62.4%	61.5%	60.3%	60.7%	61.5%	63.4%

Figure 9.7 Trends in Florida Public High School Graduation Rates by Race/Ethnicity

Source: Data from NCES Common Core Data © 2011 Projects Promoting Equity in Urban and Higher Education, NCID at the University of Michigan.

students, though the highest across groups, also dropped between 1998 and 2008. The graduation rate for Native Americans varied substantially over time. In contrast, the graduation rate for Whites hovered around 60% throughout the period but was higher in 2008 (63.4%) than it was in 1996 (60.7%). Given all this variation, it simply is not possible to make a claim about a direct relationship between high school graduation rates and Bright Futures implementation, but the general pattern fits with research on the correlation between implementation of more rigorous graduation requirements and declines in graduation rates (Chapter 4).

SAT Scores

Since high school grades are an intermediate outcome that can be positively influenced by the possibility of receiving a Bright Futures award,[7] it is important to consider trends in the percentage of students taking college entrance exams and their scores on these tests. Trends in SAT participation in Florida (Figure 9.8) indicate an increase in the percentage of high school seniors taking the test between 1998 and 2008. The percentage of students taking the exam peaked in 2006 at 67% but declined afterward, to 54% in 2008.

Since the Bright Futures program requires the SAT, the increase in the number of students taking the exam after 2000 could be an artifact of the new policy, especially since the rate of participation increased faster in Florida than it did nationally until 2006. However, the drop in the rate after 2006 raises questions about the long-term efficacy of the scholarship program as an incentive for improving test-taking rates.

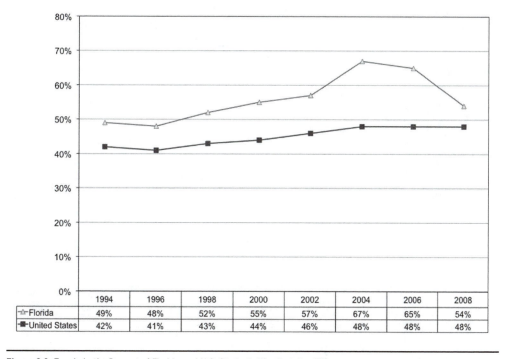

	1994	1996	1998	2000	2002	2004	2006	2008
Florida	49%	48%	52%	55%	57%	67%	65%	54%
United States	42%	41%	43%	44%	46%	48%	48%	48%

Figure 9.8 Trends in the Percent of Florida and U.S. Students Who Took the SAT

Source: Data from The College Board © 2011 Projects Promoting Equity in Urban and Higher Education, NCID at the University of Michigan.

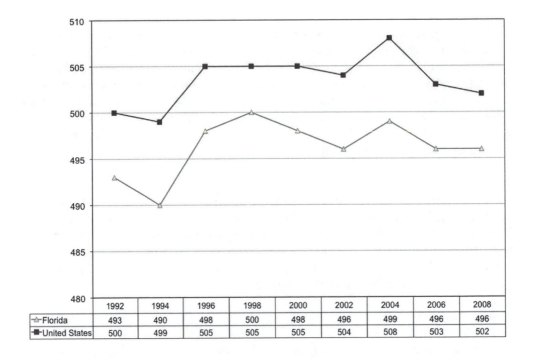

	1992	1994	1996	1998	2000	2002	2004	2006	2008
Florida	493	490	498	500	498	496	499	496	496
United States	500	499	505	505	505	504	508	503	502

Figure 9.9 Trends in Average SAT Verbal Scores in Florida and the United States

Source: Data from The College Board © 2011 Projects Promoting Equity in Urban and Higher Education, NCID at the University of Michigan.

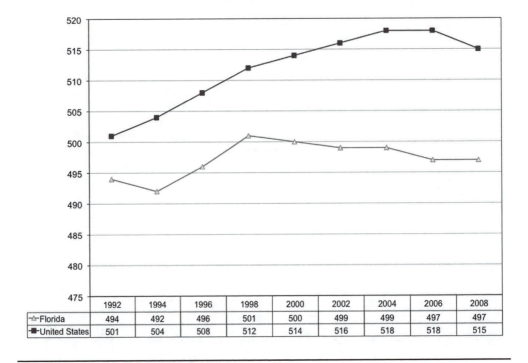

	1992	1994	1996	1998	2000	2002	2004	2006	2008
Florida	494	492	496	501	500	499	499	497	497
United States	501	504	508	512	514	516	518	518	515

Figure 9.10 Trends Average SAT Math Scores in Florida and the United States

Source: Data from The College Board © 2011 Projects Promoting Equity in Urban and Higher Education, NCID at the University of Michigan.

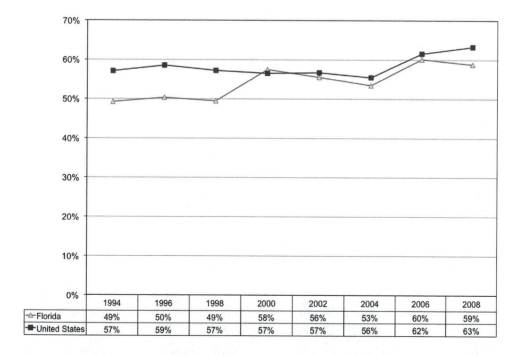

	1994	1996	1998	2000	2002	2004	2006	2008
Florida	49%	50%	49%	58%	56%	53%	60%	59%
United States	57%	59%	57%	57%	57%	56%	62%	63%

Figure 9.11 Trends in College Continuation Rate for the State of Florida and the United States

Source: Data from Postsecondary Education Opportunity © 2011 Projects Promoting Equity in Urban and Higher Education, NCID at the University of Michigan.

The scores of Florida students on the SAT verbal (Figure 9.9) and math (Figure 9.10) tests declined after 1998 compared with the national average; at the same time, the number of test takers in Florida changed at about the same rate as the national average. The average verbal score recovered in 2004 but declined again in 2006. The state scores improved relative to the national averages between 1994 and 1998, but the gap did not narrow substantially thereafter.

In contrast, math scores in Florida declined slightly after 1998, a time period when they improved nationally, indicating that Florida lagged behind in the quality of academic preparation in mathematics. The gap in scores for Florida compared to the United States as a whole after the implementation of Bright Futures should be a reason for concern across the state.

Trends in College Enrollment and Diversity

A second intent of Bright Futures is to improve retention of high-achieving Floridians in the state. Although we do not have a direct measure of this outcome, both continuation rates and the diversity of racial representation provide related indicators. College continuation rates measure the percentage of resident students who enroll in both in-state and out-of-state universities.

College Continuation Rates

Trends in college continuation for Florida are similar to the national college continuation rates (Figure 9.11) although consistently lower (except in 2000). Florida's rate climbed

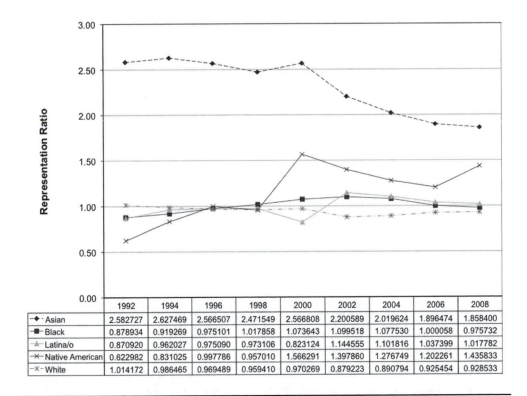

	1992	1994	1996	1998	2000	2002	2004	2006	2008
Asian	2.582727	2.627469	2.566507	2.471549	2.566808	2.200589	2.019624	1.896474	1.858400
Black	0.878934	0.919269	0.975101	1.017858	1.073643	1.099518	1.077530	1.000058	0.975732
Latina/o	0.870920	0.962027	0.975090	0.973106	0.823124	1.144555	1.101816	1.037399	1.017782
Native American	0.622982	0.831025	0.997786	0.957010	1.566291	1.397860	1.276749	1.202261	1.435833
White	1.014172	0.986465	0.969489	0.959410	0.970269	0.879223	0.890794	0.925454	0.928533

Figure 9.12 Trends in Racial/Ethnic Representation in Florida Public 4-year Postsecondary Institutions as a Proportion of the State Population

Source: Data from NCES Integrated Postsecondary Education Data System and U.S. Census Bureau © 2011 Projects Promoting Equity in Urban and Higher Education, NCID at the University of Michigan.

between 1992 and 2000 and declined after that. From this trend, there is no reason to expect that the Bright Futures program contributed to improvement in college continuation rates. The continuation rate includes students from Florida who enrolled out of state, so we cannot make judgments about the brain drain from these data.

The overall continuation rate improved in Florida after 1998, when the gap between the state's rate and the national rate was small. There was a gain in enrollment rates between 1998 and 2000, counter to the national trend, which began a slight decline in 2000 but rose again between 2006 and 2008. It is possible that the Bright Futures program contributed to this upward bump between 2000 and 2006. In addition, the continuation rate was slightly higher in 2000, 2002, and 2004 than it had been between 1994 and 1998. However, the fact that both high school graduation and college continuation rates declined in Florida after 2000 is problematic. We expect continuation rates to decline as high school completion rises because the continuation rate is calculated with the proportion of students who complete high school in the denominator.

Diversity in Public 4-Year Colleges

The trends in racial representation in public 4-year colleges (Figure 9.12) differ from the overall pattern. In 2006, both African Americans and Latinos/as were better represented

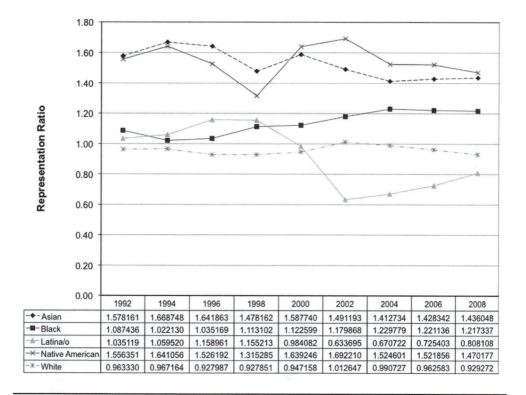

	1992	1994	1996	1998	2000	2002	2004	2006	2008
Asian	1.578161	1.668748	1.641863	1.478162	1.587740	1.491193	1.412734	1.428342	1.436048
Black	1.087436	1.022130	1.035169	1.113102	1.122599	1.179868	1.229779	1.221136	1.217337
Latina/o	1.035119	1.059520	1.158961	1.155213	0.984082	0.633695	0.670722	0.725403	0.808108
Native American	1.556351	1.641056	1.526192	1.315285	1.639246	1.692210	1.524601	1.521856	1.470177
White	0.963330	0.967164	0.927987	0.927851	0.947158	1.012647	0.990727	0.962583	0.929272

Figure 9.13 Trends in Racial/Ethnic Representation in Florida Public 2-year Postsecondary Institutions as a Proportion of the State Population

Source: Data from NCES Integrated Postsecondary Education Data System and U.S. Census Bureau © 2011 Projects Promoting Equity in Urban and Higher Education, NCID at the University of Michigan.

in public 4-year colleges than they had been in 1992; however, this shift did not exactly parallel implementation of Bright Futures. The representation of Latinos/as in public 4-year colleges actually declined in 2000,[8] the first observation point after implementation, but improved after that. There could have been a lag in time owing to changes in student preparation or a dip related to changes in the methods of counting immigrants, but the shift may also be related to other factors (see the discussion of admission policies below). Further, the overall pattern of increased representation for both groups was evident between 1992 and 1998, before implementation of Bright Futures, although representation of African Americans improved the most between 2000 and 2002. The percentage of Whites in public 4-year colleges declined modestly after 2000, while the representation of Native Americans improved substantially. There was a steady pattern of improvement in the representation of African Americans between 1994 and 2002, and between 2004 and 2006 the gap narrowed for African Americans compared with Whites.

Public 2-Year Colleges

Asian Americans and Native Americans were consistently overrepresented in public 2-year colleges compared with other groups during this entire period, but both groups showed a one-year dip in 1998, the first year Bright Futures was implemented (Figure 9.13).

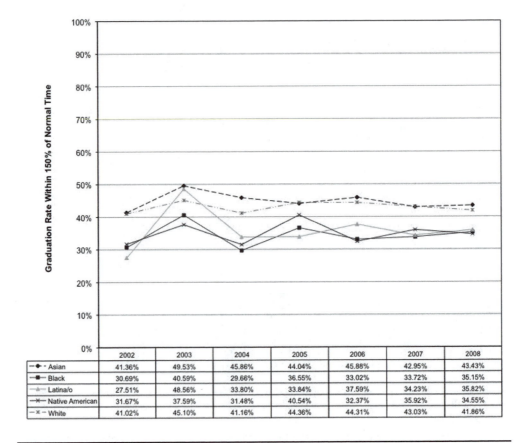

	2002	2003	2004	2005	2006	2007	2008
Asian	41.36%	49.53%	45.86%	44.04%	45.88%	42.95%	43.43%
Black	30.69%	40.59%	29.66%	36.55%	33.02%	33.72%	35.15%
Latina/o	27.51%	48.56%	33.80%	33.84%	37.59%	34.23%	35.82%
Native American	31.67%	37.59%	31.48%	40.54%	32.37%	35.92%	34.55%
White	41.02%	45.10%	41.16%	44.36%	44.31%	43.03%	41.86%

Figure 9.14 Trends in Graduation Rates in Florida Public 2-year Postsecondary Institutions

Source: Data from NCES Integrated Postsecondary Education Data System © 2011 Projects Promoting Equity in Urban and Higher Education, NCID at the University of Michigan.

The overrepresentation of African Americans in public 2-year colleges declined to nearly equaling their share of the state population in 1994 and 1996 but increased steadily after 1998 and was slightly more than 120% of their share of the population in 2004 to 2006. The representation of Whites increased slightly in 2002 to a rate equaling their share of the state's population, but it declined thereafter and fell to 81% in 2008. There was a dramatic drop in Hispanic representation between 2000 and 2002, but increases were seen after that.

Degree Completion

Degree completion rates were lower for 2-year college students than overall, but there was also a relatively consistent pattern of Whites and Asians graduating at a higher rate than students from underrepresented groups, especially after 2006 (Figure 9.14). This pattern is consistent nationally and persists throughout all of our cases.

Graduation rates for all groups were higher in public 4-year colleges than in private 2-year colleges, but there was still a consistent pattern of higher completion rates by Whites and Asians than by the underrepresented groups (Figure 9.15). Further, the graduation rates for Asians and Native Americans were higher in 2008 than in 2002 but

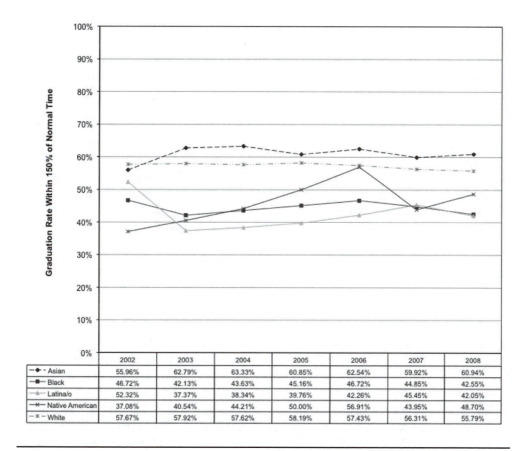

Figure 9.15 Trends in Graduation Rates in Florida Public 4-year Postsecondary Institutions by Racial/Ethnic Group

Source: Data from NCES Integrated Postsecondary Education Data System © 2011 Projects Promoting Equity in Urban and Higher Education, NCID at the University of Michigan.

slightly lower for other groups including Whites; however the gap in completion rates between Asians and Whites compared with African Americans and Latinos/as widened during the period. Implementation of Bright Futures and higher graduation requirements did not appear to have an equalizing impact on degree completion in Florida's 4-year institutions.

THE CURRENT POLICY CONTEXT

It is important to consider whether changes to the program are likely to diminish its potential impact. Florida, like many states in the southern United States, has focused heavily on merit aid programs both to create an incentive for stronger preparation in high school and to keep top academic talent in the state, largely through the Bright Futures scholarship program, the key higher education policy issue. We consider how recent changes to the program will impact college access across the state. Second, and in many ways related, we consider the changing high school graduation requirements. Increasing course requirements coupled with a mandatory exit exam for high school completion raises the bar. Successful students are likely to be better prepared for college, but for others the path may be considerably more challenging. Third, the state of Florida led the way in an ambitious effort to expand access to baccalaureate education through community colleges. In 2010, Florida announced the creation of the Florida State College system, which comprises the tier of community colleges granted the ability to provide 4-year programs.

Changes to the Bright Futures Scholarship

The success of the Bright Futures scholarship program may be the cause of its undoing. When Florida launched the program in 1997, it cost taxpayers approximately $70 million, paid for by the state lottery; in 2010 the program cost the state $437 million (Travis, 2011). The full award, granted to the students with an "A" average in high school, was worth the full cost of attending a 4-year public institution for a maximum of 7 years. The cost of the program exploded for two reasons—tuition and fees have risen considerably over the decade and more students are attending college and qualifying for the program. Florida, by all accounts, is among the most reasonably priced public systems of postsecondary education in the country. However, it has seen the cost of tuition and fees rise dramatically in the past 4 years; public university tuition rates alone have risen by more than 40%, more than doubling since the program was first launched (National Center for Education Statistics, 2011). In 2001 Florida public colleges and universities enrolled more than 730,000 students; this figure grew by 30%, to 930,000 enrolled full or part time by 2011. These two sets of pressures have forced policymakers to think about whether the model is sustainable. In 2010, the lottery brought in $100 million less than the total cost of the program; the state used stimulus dollars to offset the expense (Travis, 2011).

The program has been scaled back twice in recent years. Prior to 2008, the awards for both the Florida Academic Scholars (FAS) and the Gold Seal Vocational (GSV) programs covered the equivalent of 110% of the cost for up to 132 and 90 hours respectively. In 2009, three changes were made to the program: maximum awards covered only 100%, the FAS could extend for up to 120 hours instead of 132, and those who lost eligibility could have their award restored only if eligibility was lost through not meeting the GPA requirement during the first year (prior to that, a student could restore the award at any time for either GPA or insufficient number of credits). A second set of changes was recently put into place. In prior years, students had up to 7 years to complete a degree program; beginning in 2010 they have 5. The more critical change, however, relative to the merit aid program, is that the academic criteria are changing so that the standard is higher and fewer students will be eligible. The minimum SAT for the FAS will increase modestly over the next 4 years from 1270 to 1290, but the increase is much more substantial for the GSV, which will go from 970 to 1170 in the year 2014.

The immediate concerns about the rising costs of the Bright Futures program were eased in 2010 when the board of governors and the legislature chose not to provide increases in Bright Futures awards beyond current levels. In 2011, the board of governors announced a 15% tuition increase, with the following clarification: "The increases approved Thursday by the Board of Governors are in a category called differential tuition. Florida's merit-based Bright Futures scholarships don't include money to cover differential tuition. Nor do pre-paid tuition contracts purchased after July 1, 2007" (*Orlando Sentinel*, 2011). The new agreement was reached because of the severe cuts sustained in public universities after the Recession of 2009. It provides a means for 4-year institutions to move down the path toward privatization.

High School Graduation Requirements

Florida high school students face two important requirements to earn a high school diploma. First, they are required to complete a certain number of courses in the core academic subjects and in some cases specific courses are identified. Second, Florida requires that students pass a minimum competency examination in reading and math, the Florida Comprehensive Assessment Test (FCAT), in order to earn their diploma. The state has made changes to both requirements, and the changes may have implications for students' access to college.

Florida has a three-tier high school graduation system: the 24-hour program, an accelerated 3-year program starting in 10th grade; an 18-hour college preparatory program; and a similar 3-year career prep program. The number of credits has not changed, but the specific courses in math and science will change. In 2010, students on either of the first two paths will be required to complete the same number of math courses (four), but two of those courses must be algebra I and geometry. In science, the state has required three credits, at least two of which include a lab component, but in 2010 they specified that one of those courses must be biology I. Beginning with the 9th grade class of 2012, high school graduates in these two tracks will also be required to complete algebra II, either chemistry or physics, and at least one additional higher-level science course. These changes raise the course rigor bar for students and may potentially keep some students from finishing high school—a critical first step toward earning the Bright Futures scholarship.

Changes to the FCAT may prove to be a more critical barrier for some students. Prior to 2010, FCAT minimum scores were set at a single level. Students who did not meet the minimum threshold were required to retake the test. The minimum threshold for the test, which is administered during the 10th grade, was below grade-level proficiency. Beginning in 2011, the minimum scores will be set to align with basic grade level proficiency, which the Florida Senate Pre-K–12 Appropriations Committee (2009) estimates will negatively impact high school graduation rates. Their estimates suggest if the same standard had been applied to the 10th grade class in 2008, some 40% more would have failed the FCAT for the first time. The changes to both the course requirements and the FCAT are likely to have an impact on students' eligibility for the Bright Futures scholarship indirectly through high school graduation rates.

The Community College Baccalaureate and the Florida State College System

In addition to asking whether students were either prepared to succeed in college or could afford to pay for it, Florida policymakers have been confronted with the question of whether they had sufficient capacity in the system to meet the growing demands for postsecondary education in the state. This is particularly true in the 4-year public sector. Unlike other large states in the nation, Florida has lacked a mid-tier, regional 4-year state college system. Students either entered directly into one of the nine universities or attended a community college, many with the intent to transfer. Over the past 10 years, the state has attempted to meet its growing demand for baccalaureate education by providing targeted programs in high-need disciplines like nursing and teaching through community colleges throughout the state. The community college sector has rationalized these decisions as an extension of their historic commitment to providing access in communities where people live and work. In 2010, Florida policymakers passed legislation to create a governance structure for the Florida College System, comprising 28 former community colleges. This new breed of institution will offer a mix of 2-year and 4-year degrees and will help the state meet the growing demand.

The question remains whether or not the baccalaureate degree programs offered through the college system are of a quality comparable with those provided at the universities throughout the state—or whether they should be. Prior to the 2010 legislation, all new baccalaureate programs offered at community colleges had to be approved by the state department of education. With the passage of the new legislation, the colleges approve their own programs through their respective boards. This policy offers the potential to make baccalaureate education more readily available to a broader cross section of the state's population. Policymakers are frequently frustrated with the growing cost of college and see community colleges as a more cost-effective alternative; however, it is not clear at this point whether community colleges can meet the demands of accrediting agencies in terms of the quality of their programs and continue to offer baccalaureate education at much lower tuition charges than their university counterparts, even when you consider the added local tax support these institutions receive.

CONCLUSIONS

Whereas the immediacy of concerns about the costs of the Bright Futures program have subsided in the past few years due to the political compromises reached in the state, the basic challenge continues: funding a complex higher education system in a troubled state economy. Therefore the state's obligations through Bright Futures may be subject to further change as the political processes of lobbying and advocacy intersect with the annual budget preparation process at the state and institutional levels. With the agreement to decouple future tuition increases in 4-year colleges from the state's commitments on future maximal awards under Bright Futures, we are concerned that cost will become an increasingly important barrier in Florida, much as it has in other states.

As Florida's public colleges and universities move through the economic hardships in the aftermath of the Great Recession of 2008, they will probably face constrained state support. Senior institutions are likely to be confronted by challenges to coordinate tuition increases with campus financial aid policies. They also have an implied obligation to the many students who started high school thinking that Bright Futures would pay their tuition if they met the achievement standards. In contrast, public 2-year colleges are faced with different challenges as they continue to develop low-cost 4-year degrees as an alternative to the Board of Governors' universities. Questions are posed in Text Box 9.1.

Text Box 9.1 Questions About the Florida Case

1. Given the research on student outcomes and the national political discourse (Part I), how would you assess the long-term stability for the Florida Bright Futures Program? Would you consider other models for the financing of higher education in states?

2. What alternatives does the state have with respect to the its strategy for financing higher education?

3. If you were advising a budget committee at a state university with mostly local students near one of the state's major cities, what advice would you give regarding future strategies for balancing tuition increases, allocations to student aid, and commitments to faculty salary increases? Consider how they might balance the interests of students, faculty, and the long-term well-being of the institution.

4. If you were advising a community college board about strategies for financing new four-year degree programs, what options would you examine? Should they consider different charges for upper-division and lower-division courses, raising prices to capture more resources for student grants, or other strategies for competing for local students with the state universities?

5. If you were advising a high school student who was at the margin of qualifying for Bright Futures, would you advise them to take advanced math courses (e.g. pre-calculus or calculus) if you thought it would put them at risk of not qualifying for a Bright Futures award?

6. Given the alterations in Bright Futures and the development of new market-based strategies in institutions, is Florida's limited investment in need-based grants overly problematic for low-income students?

7. Florida has chosen to address its capacity constraints at the four-year degree level by allowing community colleges to offer baccalaureate degrees and to create a state college system from a subset of those institutions. How would you address the capacity challenge?

10

COMPREHENSIVE STRATEGY

The Indiana Case

Indiana was the first state to develop a comprehensive approach to improving educational opportunities for low-income students. The Twenty-First Century Scholars Program (TFCS) was modeled after the "I have a dream" program in New York City schools. Any low-income student who took a pledge to prepare for college would receive a promise of financial aid equal to tuition; in addition, programs would be created so that the families of the students could learn how to help them prepare for and succeed in college. Governor Evan Bayh signed the program into legislation in 1990, but it was controversial and began as an unfunded mandate. In 1990, the Lilly Endowment partnered with the state by funding the parent component, and eventually the state funded its grant obligation. TFCS has been treated as a national model (Advisory Committee on Student Financial Assistance, 2002), with features of the program being replicated in other states.

The Twenty-First Century Scholars program operates as a hybrid merit and need-based aid program. In 8th grade, eligible students sign a pledge that they will achieve a minimum 2.0 GPA in high school, avoid drugs, alcohol, or other illegal activities, apply to and gain acceptance to a college in the state, and file the FAFSA on time (State Student Assistance Commission of Indiana, 2011). To be eligible, students must qualify for the free or reduced-cost lunch program at the time of the pledge and must sign the pledge. If eligible students meet their obligations, the state guarantees them a full 4 years of tuition at a public university or a comparable amount to be used at a participating private institution in Indiana (St. John, Musoba, Simmons, & Chung, 2002), even if their families' finances change.

The financial aid guarantee provided by TFCS has certainly been an important part of the Indiana story and the gradual improvements in access in the 1990s compared with other states. However, while the total grant commitment—to fund tuition—was substantial, the actual increase in per-student cost over the state's base grant was modest, because a relatively small proportion of students qualified, and the state of Indiana also funded a generous need-based grant program in the late 1990s and early 2000s. Indiana had also made changes in high school graduation requirements to increase the number of high school students who were prepared to go on to college. That the guarantee provided an incentive for academic preparation in an environment that already encouraged and supported it is a part of the story not frequently told (Lumina Foundation, 2008).

Although TFCS has received substantial attention because of its apparent impact on improvement in college enrollment in the late 20th and early 21st centuries, the more remarkable story is that the state also developed and maintained an integrated approach to education reform that included early reading reform, professional development for teachers, new standards for high school graduation, and a coordinated approach to need-based student aid that was integrated with educational policy and promoted fair access for all students. In fact, Indiana was historically—and still is—more conservative in education and social policy than other midwestern states that had been early models of progressivism (e.g., Illinois, Michigan, Minnesota, and Wisconsin). Because of this, it would not have been possible to maintain the state's commitment to low-income students had the state not engaged in reforms supporting all students.

THE INDIANA STORY

Until recently, Indiana could be characterized as both conservative and progressive. It was part of the Northwest Territories, a region that evolved into progressive traditions with Wisconsin, Michigan, Illinois, and other states in the region. Unlike the others, Indiana did not seek to have the highest-quality or best-funded universities; rather, its conservative and liberal politicians sought to expand opportunity, an issue that became especially important as the rust belt industries of steel and auto manufacturing declined. The comprehensive approach that evolved in the state was research-based and aimed at using tax dollars well rather than outpacing peer states. With the election of a neoconservative governor in the late 2000s, some of the foundations built in the late 1990s and early 2000s have been dismantled (see current policies below), but the story of how the comprehensive approach evolved is important because it provides a model for collaboration between policymakers and researchers in efforts to expand opportunity.

Indiana's public higher education system developed a distinct set of generally accessible public colleges. There are two strong state research university systems—Indiana University and Purdue University—that have their own branch campuses. Purdue had the state's engineering school while Indiana had the state's medical school, and both systems were geographically distributed around the state. The Purdue and Indiana University systems provided geographic access to 4- and 2-year degree opportunities. There were also joint Indiana and Purdue campuses in Indianapolis and Fort Wayne. Some thought that Indiana had an exemplary model of 4-year degree access. Indiana's state universities—Ball State, Indiana State, and the University of Southern Indiana—were independent of these two large state systems. The state also had well-established independent colleges, including the University of Notre Dame and several liberal arts colleges.

In the early 1990s there was not a public 2-year college system in the state. Ivy Tech, the state's technical college system, had historically awarded technical certificates but not college degrees. Vincennes University, a regional public 2-year college in the southwestern corner of the state, was the 2-year college, but it had a residential feel and was not by any standard a community college, given that it was not geographically accessible to most Indiana state residents. Transfer students generally came from the regional campuses of IU and

Purdue. Based on a review of access in the state, Gary Orfield (1997) argued the Indiana provided better access to 4-year degrees than states with separate 2- and 4-year systems.

The state had a sound K–12 system but ranked low on test scores (St. John & Musoba, 2010). Major developments during the 1990s and early 2000s in policies affecting preparation, access, and college completion, which comprised Indiana's comprehensive approach, along with the role of research informing these policies, are discussed before reviewing trends in policies and outcomes.

A Period of Change

The Indiana Commission for Higher Education was formed in 1971 and was made up of a 14-member board of gubernatorial appointees representing the Congressional districts of the state, a faculty representative, and a student representative. The commission was charged with the responsibility to

- define the educational missions of Indiana's public colleges and universities;
- plan and coordinate Indiana's state-supported system of postsecondary education;
- review budget requests from public institutions and the State Student Assistance Commission (SSAC); and
- approve or disapprove the establishment of new programs or expansion of campuses for public institutions.[1]

Coordinating agencies play different roles in different states. Historically, Indiana's agency had a strong research capability, a tradition established by George Weathersby, who left his faculty position at Harvard to become commissioner in 1976. The state had developed a student record system for public higher education and coordinated with the Independent Colleges of Indiana, Inc., and analyses included students in private colleges. Weathersby had been staff director for the National Commission on the Financing of Postsecondary Education in the early 1970s and had helped design a strong need-based grant system. The independent colleges had a strong lobbying presence in Indianapolis for the state's need-based grant programs. Purdue, Indiana, the state universities, and Ivy Tech also actively lobbied for funding, but in spite of these pressures the ICHE maintained a rational budgeting formula into the 1990s.

Stan Jones, a former state legislator and student body president at Purdue University, was appointed commissioner in 1995 and served through 2000. He was the first appointee who did not come from a background in higher education. During his term as commissioner, Jones was credited as the architect of several major initiatives, including

- creating and expanding Twenty-First Century Scholars, a scholarship program aimed at increasing the number of low-income students attending and completing higher education;
- developing the Community Colleges of Indiana, the state's community college system;
- forming the Indiana Education Roundtable, a bipartisan consensus-building group of key policymakers focused on improving student achievement P–16;
- establishing the Core 40 as Indiana's required high school curriculum, an effort to improve student preparation for college and workforce success; and
- developing Reaching Higher, the commission's strategic plan focused on significantly increasing college graduation rates.

During these years the various branches of government collaborated on the development of a comprehensive, coherent set of strategies. During most of this period the two houses of the legislature were divided—one Democrat and the other Republican. The superintendent was an elected Republican. Stan Jones was appointed by a Democratic governor, and the statehouse remained Democratic until the end of his term. The Indiana Education Policy Center, an independent research organization housed at Indiana University, collaborated with the ICHE, the governor's office, legislative staff, and foundations in the state (i.e., Lilly Endowment and Lumina Foundation) on research supporting and informing policy development throughout most of this period (St. John, in press; St. John, Loescher, & Bardzell, 2003; St. John & Musoba, 2010; Theobald, 2003).[2] The IEPC was a trusted source of research but generally did not make specific recommendations in their reports; rather, analyses of policy options were provided to inform positions and an effort was made to maintain political neutrality. In fact, the credibility of the research was dependent on providing balanced analyses, especially given the split control of the legislature.

Indiana's Balanced Approach

Indiana's balanced approach to providing access to higher education began to develop even before Stan Jones's appointment as commissioner. The cornerstone of the approach was the Twenty-First Century Scholars program. At the time, Stan Jones was a state legislator who supported the unfunded initiative; he then served as a special assistant on education to Governor Bayh. The key feature of the Twenty-First Century Scholars program was the pledge taken by low-income students in the federally subsidized lunch programs. Students agreed to take the steps to prepare for college, remain drug-free, and apply for college and financial aid, while the program committed scholarships equaling tuition at a public college (and an amount equaling the tuition and state institutional subsidies in private colleges). After implementation, a balanced approach to preparation and access emerged in Indiana that provided the basis for the pathways to change model (Figure 4.1).

Another important feature of Indiana's balanced approach was coordination with high school preparation. Under the leadership of Dr. Suellen Reed, superintendent for public instruction in Indiana from 1992 to 2008, the state had developed an honors diploma. When Jones became commissioner of ICHE in 1995, he advocated for the Core 40 in all high schools as a step toward preparing students for enrollment in 4-year colleges. By the late 1990s, all high schools were required to provide the full Core 40 curriculum. A school finance committee was created comprising representatives from the governor's office, legislative staff for education and budget committees, and a representative of the Indiana Department of Education. With analytic support by the Indiana Education Policy Center (Theobald, 2003), the committee developed a funding formula that provided supplemental funding to schools with low-income students and incentive funding for schools to improve the percentage of students graduating with Core 40 and honors diplomas.

In the years before Jones was appointed commissioner, there has been a concerted effort to build an infrastructure that supported encouragement services. Don Hossler, a professor at Indiana University, was actively engaged as a researcher supporting development of the early college information programs in the state, which led to the creation of the Indiana Career and Postsecondary Advancement Center (ICPAC), charged with providing information and encouragement services throughout the state (Hossler & Schmit, 1995). ICPAC assumed coordination of the support services for Twenty-First Century Scholars but also provided information to all potential college students in the state. ICPAC collected surveys from all middle-school students, providing data used for several studies on college preparation and success in Indiana (e.g., Hossler, Schmit, & Vesper, 1999). Eventually these surveys were linked to the individual student data collected by the state, and the survey data for the high school class of 1999 was linked to college enrollment data to provide a basis for evaluating the impact of the program on college enrollment and choice of institution (St. John, Musoba, Simmons, & Chung, 2002).

Through the late 1990s and early 2000s, the support services provided for Scholars expanded (Evenbeck, Seabrook, St. John, & Murphy, 2004). There were regional centers across the state that provided mentoring for parents and students; an extensive telephone network was provided; both students and parents had opportunities to visit college campuses; and an evaluation was conducted to consider the effectiveness of the Twenty-First Century Scholars Program, which quickly became a model for other federal initiatives including GEAR UP (Gaining Early Awareness and Readiness for Undergraduate Programs) and the federal 21st Century Scholars college readiness intervention program.

The primary challenge for Indiana was to ensure funding for the aid guarantee as part of the annual budget process. Over time, a series of tactics emerged. Nick Vesper, formerly a researcher with the Indiana Education Policy Center (IEPC), took a research position with the State Student Aid Commission of Indiana (SSACI) in 1995. He provided access for researchers at the IEPC to the extensive student aid data provided as part of the state system, making it possible to develop a series of studies assessing the impact of state grants on retention (St. John, Hu, & Weber, 1999, 2001). Vesper had also helped to create a funding scheme for state grants that differentiated amounts for students based on their diploma type: 100% of the base award for students with the honors diploma; 90% of funding for high-need students with Core 40; and 80% funding for the regular diploma. Central to the new funding policy was that the maximum base award for the neediest students would be set at the prior year's tuition charge if the program was fully funded; Twenty-First Century Scholars already had the full commitment to student aid funding.

The full funding of the differentiated aid award scheme—a hybrid merit- and need-based aid—was held together by both conservatives favoring the merit features and liberals supporting the need-based features. Whereas the studies of student persistence may not have been persuasive to legislators in debates about maintaining full funding for student aid, they did lead to formation of an informal working group to examine higher-education finance composed of staff from the governor's office. Researchers in the policy center worked with the committee to examine alternative policies. A set of state indicators was developed for a report comparing Indiana's financing strategy to peer states using federal databases (St. John, Simmons, Hoezee, Wooden, & Musoba, 2002).[3] The report was released with a press statement by the governor's office in 2002; it encouraged the co-ordination of financial strategies, similar to the Minnesota model. For a few years, funding for student aid was maintained at a high level because of the informal indexing of aid to tuition and the attention given to research on comparison states. In spite of these efforts, it was not yet clear whether Indiana's legislature would sustain a commitment to fund fully its need-based student aid programs as a means of maintaining fairness in public finance.

The study of the 1999 high school cohort in Indiana found that Twenty-First Century Scholars were substantially more likely to enroll in the newly developing public 2-year colleges or in private colleges (St. John, Musoba, Simmons, & Chung, 2002). In fact, many of the private colleges recognized that the Twenty-First Century Scholars brought substantial resources with them, and some began to actively recruit and retain them. In contrast, the public campuses did not substantially alter their recruitment procedures to attract Scholars, nor was there much evidence of campus-based efforts to provide academic support to these students (Lumina Foundation, 2008).

Limitations of Indiana's Model

Indiana's comprehensive model depended on financial incentives for schools, colleges, and students that were embedded in the finance system, but there had been little formal consideration of retention. In fact, the Indiana campuses had a weak record of providing support services for Scholars, and Scholars' persistence did not differ significantly from that of other low-income students who had enrolled in college without the support of the program (Lumina Foundation, 2008). In fact, research showed that most low-income, first-generation students in Indiana could have benefited from additional support of the type provided by Washington State Achievers, another state-level program (St. John, Hu, & Fisher, 2011).

Yet, there was a history of projects focusing on retention in Indiana. In particular, the Lilly Endowment made substantial grants to Indiana's colleges and universities to promote persistence. At a planning meeting hosted by Indiana University in 2004 to discuss the future of retention projects, Don Hossler presented a review of the literature on persistence, finding that there had been only limited prior research using generally accepted standards evaluating interventions in persistence (Patton, Morelon, Whitehead, & Hossler, 2006). Representatives of many of the Indiana campuses claimed to have developed proven approaches. In response, an external expert was chosen by the campuses to review the evaluation studies of these various strategies. John Braxton's report reached a similar conclusion about the research by Indiana universities: few had actually documented impacts on persistence using generally accepted research methods (Braxton, McKinney, & Reynolds, 2006).

The Indiana Project on Academic Success (IPAS) was an attempt to model a research-based approach to improving retention (Musoba, 2006; St. John, McKinney, & Tuttle, 2006). A research team used state and national data systems to track students in the 2000 high school cohort from preparation through college to inform campus-based interventions by public and private colleges. There was substantial research evidence that interventions in orientation programs, learning communities, supplemental instruction services, and leadership education improved retention on campuses; some of these projects went to scale within institutional systems (Hossler, Gross, & Ziskin, 2009; St. John & Musoba, 2010). These projects may have modeled a new direction in state efforts to improve retention, but there has not been follow-up research; it is not clear whether more recent efforts to emphasize retention at the state level (e.g., Jones's "Reaching Higher" or performance funding) will improve retention in the public system.

TRENDS IN STATE POLICY AND FUNDING

Indiana made substantial gains in college access during the late 1990s and early 2000s. The roles and impact of policies on preparation, access, and retention are examined below.

Academic Preparation Policies

The changes in high school graduation requirements are illustrated in Figure 10.1. Indiana had implemented math standards and a requirement of at least two math courses for graduation by 1991 and started requiring an exit exam in 2000. A study of implementation of the exit exams revealed negative effects on high school completion by special education students (Manset & Washburn, 2000); in subsequent years the policy was changed to accommodate special needs students. The Core 40 diploma, which required algebra I, was the default

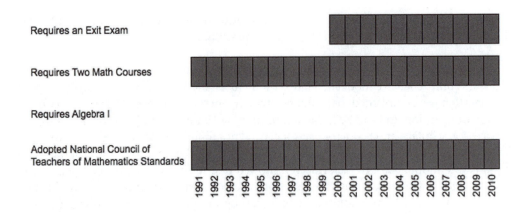

Figure 10.1 Indiana High School Graduation Requirements

Source: © Projects Promoting Equity in Urban and Higher Education, NCID at the University of Michigan.

curriculum. With parental approval, students could opt for a regular diploma type; however, student aid was substantially lower for students who did not complete the Core 40 program.

One distinctive feature of Indiana's approach was that all high schools were required to offer advanced diplomas and were funded for this extra effort before the college preparatory curriculum (Core 40) became Indiana's default curriculum. As illustrated in Indiana's balanced model, K–12 policies can have an indirect effect on college enrollment through improved preparation, as evidenced by modest gains in test scores in Indiana.

Another unique feature of Indiana's approach was development of a statewide organization to encourage academic preparation, especially for low-income students. The combination of guaranteed aid through Twenty-First Century Scholars and encouragement programming through ICPAC was significantly associated with improved enrollment rates by low-income students, as demonstrated by research on Twenty-First Century Scholars (e.g., St. John, Musoba, Simmons, & Chung, 2004). However, making the investment necessary to carry through with guarantees of need-based aid for Scholars and to fully fund need-based grant aid for all students has a substantial direct effect on enrollment and diversity. Trends in state finance, enrollment, and diversity by type of institution are examined below.

State Financing of Higher Education

There was a surge in public funding for student grant aid in Indiana during the early 2000s. But the ethos of the state suddenly shifted from its historic conservative progressive tradition to a neoconservative position on public finance. The election of Mitch Daniels as governor in 2005 ushered in a new era of tax cuts and rollbacks in funding for higher education and other public services. Scott Gillie, Executive Director of Encouragement Services, Inc., and founding director of ICPAC, recently observed "the proportion of tax revenue for higher education in Indiana was the same in 2010 as 1952."[4] These conditions have taken a toll on the financing of college access.

Funding for Public Colleges and Universities

When it became apparent in the early 2000s that the state did not have the tax dollars to expand access under its existing model, the policy indicators were developed to provide

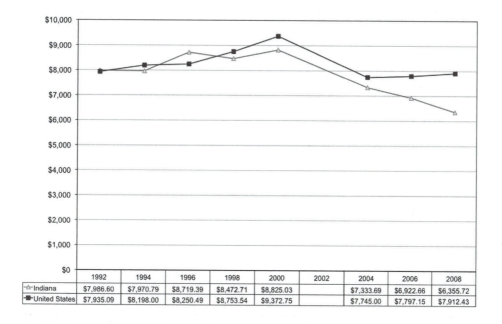

	1992	1994	1996	1998	2000	2002	2004	2006	2008
Indiana	$7,986.60	$7,970.79	$8,719.39	$8,472.71	$8,825.03		$7,333.69	$6,922.66	$6,355.72
United States	$7,935.09	$8,198.00	$8,250.49	$8,753.54	$9,372.75		$7,745.00	$7,797.15	$7,912.43

Figure 10.2 Trends in Indiana's Average Annual Amount of State and Local Appropriations per FTE for the Public Higher Education System Compared With the National Average (in 2008 Dollars)

Source: Data from NCES Integrated Postsecondary Education Data System © 2011 Projects Promoting Equity in Urban and Higher Education, NCID at the University of Michigan.

comparisons to other states in the region, including Kentucky (e.g., St. John, Simmons, Hoezee, Wooden, & Musoba, 2002). The intent of an informal bipartisan committee was to find a way to use available tax dollars to continue to expand opportunity in all types of institutions. At the time, the funding for the main campuses of Purdue and Indiana Universities was very low compared to other Big Ten institutions. It was important to keep per-student expenditures within the range of less well funded rivals, so there was relatively open discussion, at least among personnel engaged in budgeting for higher education, that the two key variables were state appropriations and tuition.

In 2000 and 2001, when the indicators research was being conducted, the state was on a trajectory toward decreased funding per student (Figure 10.2). It was recognized that the new community college system could increase enrollment at lower average cost. During the same period, the national trend line was downward, but there was a near leveling of financial support for public colleges nationally, which was not the case in Indiana; in 2008, Indiana had largest negative gap in funding compared with the national level of any period studied.

Public College Tuition Charges

In-state undergraduate tuition charges in Indiana were higher than the national average throughout the period (Figure 10.3), but the gap grew. Between 2000 and 2004 tuition charges grew faster in Indiana than in the nation as a whole, but both rates have flattened out. In Indiana, the leap in tuition charges corresponded with the downward trajectory in state appropriations. However, tuition leveled thereafter as state appropriations continued to decline, so the goal of maintaining educational funding for Indiana institutions became more elusive.

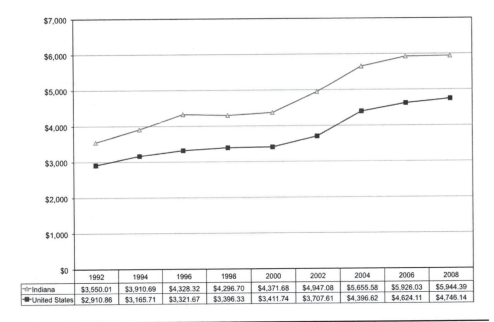

	1992	1994	1996	1998	2000	2002	2004	2006	2008
Indiana	$3,550.01	$3,910.69	$4,328.32	$4,296.70	$4,371.68	$4,947.08	$5,655.58	$5,926.03	$5,944.39
United States	$2,910.86	$3,165.71	$3,321.67	$3,396.33	$3,411.74	$3,707.61	$4,396.62	$4,624.11	$4,746.14

Figure 10.3 Trends in Indiana and the United States, Weighted Average Amount of Undergraduate In-State Tuition and Fees for the Public Higher Education System (in 2008 Dollars)

Source: Data from NCES Integrated Postsecondary Education Data System © 2011 Projects Promoting Equity in Urban and Higher Education, NCID at the University of Michigan.

State Funding for Need-Based Grants

The rise in tuition charges raised the state's cost of funding Twenty-First Century Scholars. There was a substantial rise in state funding for need-based grants in the early 2000s, as the state made efforts to fully fund the program and meet the guarantees made through Twenty-First Century Scholars (Figure 10.4). Reflecting on the trends in need-based grants in Indiana, Scott Gillie observed, "Regarding 2002, I think 2000 was the aberrant year. The [upward] slope of the line is nearly linear, if you take out 2000. The drop in need-based aid more recently reflects the conservative politics of the governor and legislature and, sadly, electorate."[5] There was a decline in state funding for need-based grants in 2008. Regardless of the cause of this dip in funding—and the politics of any coalition are difficult to hold together—the former balance of conservatism and progressivism shifted to the new conservative ideology in Indiana, a pattern evident in the decline in funding for state need-based grants, which continues.

The Relationship Between Public Tuition Charges and Need-Based Student Aid

The central feature of Indiana's comprehensive approach was coordination of tuition charges and need-based student aid. When the state fully funded the range of grant programs, the added costs of the Twenty-First Century Scholars program were relatively modest. In years when the state did not fund the base grant program sufficiently, like 2000 and 2008, the ratio of tuition to grants dropped (Figure 10.5).

The drop in this ratio between 2006 and 2008 was extreme. Suddenly this ratio was lower in 2008 than at any time during the years examined. By 2008, Indiana had departed from its comprehensive approach based on coordination of tuition and need-based student aid and was in danger of becoming a high-tuition low-aid state.

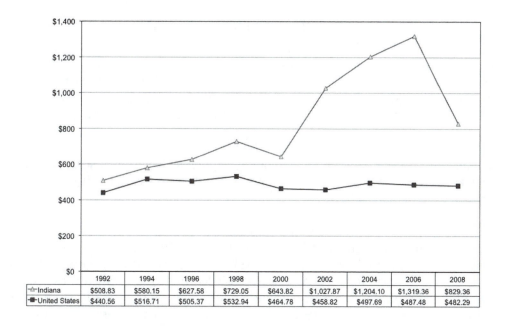

	1992	1994	1996	1998	2000	2002	2004	2006	2008
Indiana	$508.83	$580.15	$627.58	$729.05	$643.82	$1,027.87	$1,204.10	$1,319.36	$829.36
United States	$440.56	$516.71	$505.37	$532.94	$464.78	$458.82	$497.69	$487.48	$482.29

Figure 10.4 Trends in Indiana and U.S. State Need-Based Undergraduate Grants per FTE (in 2008 Dollars)

Source: Data from National Association of State Student Grant & Aid Programs © 2011 Projects Promoting Equity in Urban and Higher Education, NCID at the University of Michigan.

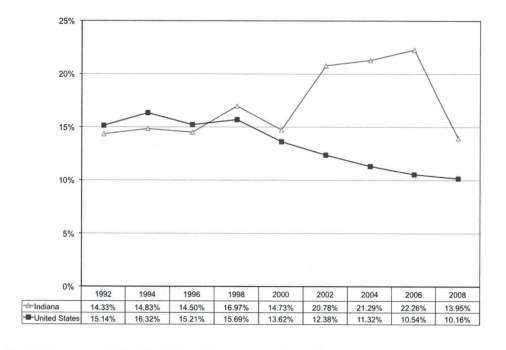

	1992	1994	1996	1998	2000	2002	2004	2006	2008
Indiana	14.33%	14.83%	14.50%	16.97%	14.73%	20.78%	21.29%	22.26%	13.95%
United States	15.14%	16.32%	15.21%	15.69%	13.62%	12.38%	11.32%	10.54%	10.16%

Figure 10.5 Trends in the Ratios of Need-Based Grants per FTE Compared With the Weighted Average Public Tuition Share for Indiana and the United States

Source: Data from NCES Integrated Postsecondary Education Data System and National Association of State Student Grant & Aid Programs © 2011 Projects Promoting Equity in Urban and Higher Education, NCID at the University of Michigan.

TRENDS IN STUDENT OUTCOMES

Indiana's case provides evidence of a relationship between coordinated public investment and improvement in opportunity. The case illustrates that it takes decades to build a new trajectory, but policy changes can occur rapidly. The case also illustrates that swings in student outcomes don't always shift immediately with radical changes in policy. Cultures that support improvement in education take time to develop and change.

Academic Preparation

The linkages between high school graduation requirements and high school achievement outcomes are well established (Chapter 4). We examine trends in graduation rates and test scores in Indiana below.

High School Graduation Rates

The K–12 reforms implemented in Indiana in the late 1990s and 2000s neither improved graduation rates nor reduced inequalities across racial/ethnic groups (Figure 10.6). Graduation rates for Asian Americans exceeded 100% for 7 of the 13 years, while graduation rates of Whites hovered around 74%. Graduation rates for Latinos/as and African Americans oscillated during the 13-year period but were lower in 2008 than in 1996. Graduation rates for Native Americans also varied substantially across the period

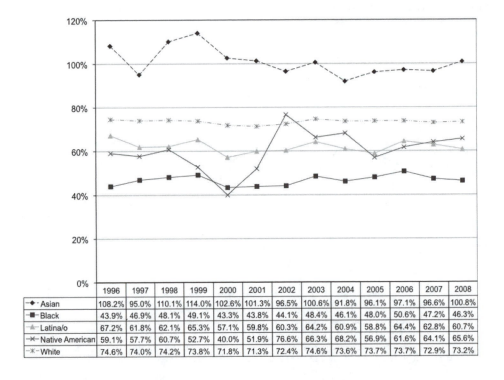

	1996	1997	1998	1999	2000	2001	2002	2003	2004	2005	2006	2007	2008
Asian	108.2%	95.0%	110.1%	114.0%	102.6%	101.3%	96.5%	100.6%	91.8%	96.1%	97.1%	96.6%	100.8%
Black	43.9%	46.9%	48.1%	49.1%	43.3%	43.8%	44.1%	48.4%	46.1%	48.0%	50.6%	47.2%	46.3%
Latina/o	67.2%	61.8%	62.1%	65.3%	57.1%	59.8%	60.3%	64.2%	60.9%	58.8%	64.4%	62.8%	60.7%
Native American	59.1%	57.7%	60.7%	52.7%	40.0%	51.9%	76.6%	66.3%	68.2%	56.9%	61.6%	64.1%	65.6%
White	74.6%	74.0%	74.2%	73.8%	71.8%	71.3%	72.4%	74.6%	73.6%	73.7%	73.7%	72.9%	73.2%

Figure 10.6 Trends in Indiana Public High School Graduation Rates by Race/Ethnicity

Source: Data from NCES Common Core Data © 2011 Projects Promoting Equity in Urban and Higher Education, NCID at the University of Michigan.

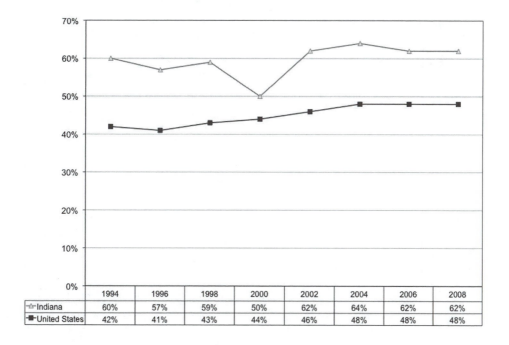

	1994	1996	1998	2000	2002	2004	2006	2008
Indiana	60%	57%	59%	50%	62%	64%	62%	62%
United States	42%	41%	43%	44%	46%	48%	48%	48%

Figure 10.7 Trends in Percentages of Indiana and U.S. Students Who Took the SAT

Source: Data from The College Board © 2011 Projects Promoting Equity in Urban and Higher Education, NCID at the University of Michigan.

but were higher in 2008 than in 1996. The gaps in graduation rates between Whites and Asians compared with African Americans and Latinos/as grew during the period.

SAT Test Scores

The participation rates in the SAT were generally higher in Indiana than the United States as a whole (Figure 10.7). Ironically, there was a dip in participation rates in 2000, the cohort studied for the baseline in the Indiana Project on Academic Success. SAT participation rose after 2000 and more than 60% of seniors had taken the exam between 2002 and 2008.

SAT score gaps narrowed between Indiana and the national average from 1992 to 2008 (Figure 10.8). In 1992 there was a 14-point differential in verbal scores compared with a 6-point gap in 2008. There was also a narrowing of the gap in SAT math scores (Figure 10.9). In 1992 Indiana had an average of 487 compared to a national average of 501, a 14-point differential. In 2008 the differential was 8 points, 508 in Indiana compared with 516 nationally.

College Access and Diversity

The Indiana case first gained national attention because of gains in college continuation rates (e.g., Hossler, Schmit, & Vesper, 1999; St. John, Musoba, Simmons, & Chung, 2002). In 1994, Indiana was below the national average in college continuation rate—55% in Indiana compared with 57% in the United States as a whole (Figure 10.10). For the next decade, the rate climbed in Indiana while it declined in the United States overall, reaching 62% in Indiana in 2004 compared with a U.S. average of 56%. Between 2004 and 2008, the U.S. continuation rate grew at a faster rate than in Indiana, but Indiana maintained a moderately higher overall percentage.

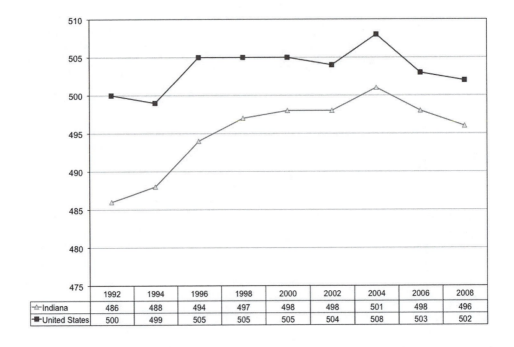

	1992	1994	1996	1998	2000	2002	2004	2006	2008
Indiana	486	488	494	497	498	498	501	498	496
United States	500	499	505	505	505	504	508	503	502

Figure 10.8 Trends in Average Indiana and U.S. SAT Verbal Scores

Source: Data from The College Board © 2011 Projects Promoting Equity in Urban and Higher Education, NCID at the University of Michigan.

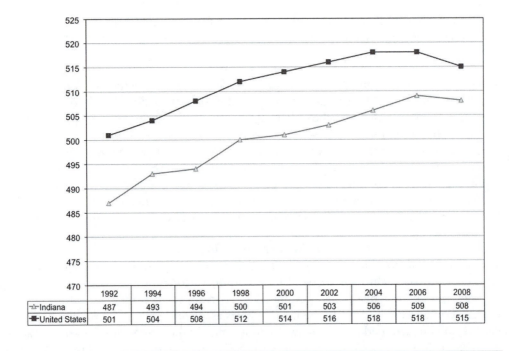

	1992	1994	1996	1998	2000	2002	2004	2006	2008
Indiana	487	493	494	500	501	503	506	509	508
United States	501	504	508	512	514	516	518	518	515

Figure 10.9 Trends in Average Indiana and U.S. SAT Math Scores

Source: Data from The College Board © 2011 Projects Promoting Equity in Urban and Higher Education, NCID at the University of Michigan.

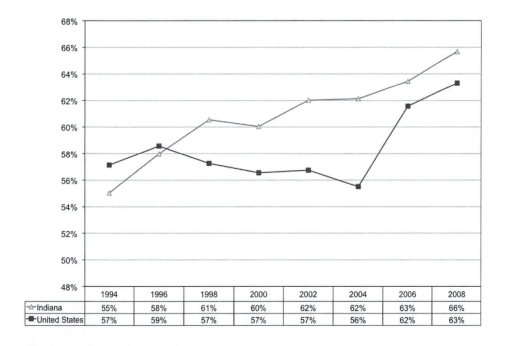

Figure 10.10 Trends in Indiana's College Continuation Rate Compared With the National Average

Source: Data from Postsecondary Education Opportunity © 2011 Projects Promoting Equity in Urban and Higher Education, NCID at the University of Michigan.

As the 2-year college system developed, the participation of African Americans began to rise (Figure 10.11). African Americans and Native Americans had been more heavily represented in the old Ivy Tech system, but the enrollment of African Americans rose after 1996 while Native American participation declined after 2000. There was a rise in Latino/a participation in this sector in the late 1990s, but enrollments declined in 2000 and after. There was a slight drop in representation of Whites and a rise in representation of Asian Americans, although both groups were underrepresented relative to their share of Indiana's population.

Whites maintained proportional representation in Indiana's public colleges and universities throughout the period (hovering around 0.99 and 1.0 on the representation ratio), while there was a slight rise in African American representation (Figure 10.12). During this period the regional campuses of Indiana and Purdue Universities were much more engaged in developing programming for low-income and minority students than were the flagship campuses in spite of efforts to encourage partnerships with urban high schools during the period (St. John & Musoba, 2010). The financial yield of students who could pay a substantial portion of tuition cost was a major consideration for Indiana University at the time (Hossler, 2004, 2006), but arguments that the Twenty-First Century Scholars brought substantial tuition subsidies had little impact on enrollment management strategies.[6] Consistent with statewide trends, there was also a drop in participation among Latinos/as in Indiana's population.

Degree Completion in Indiana Higher Education
Degree completion rates can be influenced by many factors, including individual background, academic programs and college life, support services on campuses, and public

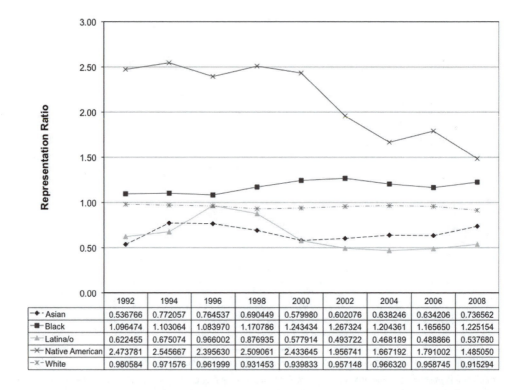

	1992	1994	1996	1998	2000	2002	2004	2006	2008
Asian	0.536766	0.772057	0.764537	0.690449	0.579980	0.602076	0.638246	0.634206	0.736562
Black	1.096474	1.103064	1.083970	1.170786	1.243434	1.267324	1.204361	1.165650	1.225154
Latina/o	0.622455	0.675074	0.966002	0.876935	0.577914	0.493722	0.468189	0.488866	0.537680
Native American	2.473781	2.545667	2.395630	2.509061	2.433645	1.956741	1.667192	1.791002	1.485050
White	0.980584	0.971576	0.961999	0.931453	0.939833	0.957148	0.966320	0.958745	0.915294

Figure 10.11 Trends in Racial/Ethnic Representation in Indiana Public 2-Year Postsecondary Institutions as a Proportion of the State Population

Source: Data from NCES Integrated Postsecondary Education Data System and U.S. Census Bureau © 2011 Projects Promoting Equity in Urban and Higher Education, NCID at the University of Michigan.

policy. Other than sustaining a commitment to financially support institutions and students, a practice that creates stability in students' perceived ability to be able to pay the costs of college, the impact of state policies is often modest and indirect. Individual campuses can design and test interventions that seek to improve retention rates and/or reduce inequalities in those rates, but research on systematic interventions remains scant (Patton et al., 2006; Hossler, Siskin, & Gross, 2009). In theory, the academic preparation standards of states have an indirect effect, depending on other factors influencing the quality of preparation in high schools. It has also been hypothesized that technical assistance and research support for campuses can also have an impact through support of innovation on campus, but research to date regarding these interventions has only considered specific cases and has not looked at reform in relation to trends (e.g., Hossler, Gross, & Ziskin, 2009; St. John & Musoba, 2010).

Public 2-Year Colleges

The 6-year completion rates for all groups were extremely low in the public 2-year sector. The completion rates for Whites dropped between 2003 and 2008, from 17% to 11.9%, but this rate was higher than for any other group in 2008, when only about 4% of African Americans and Hispanics graduated (Figure 10.13). Given the overrepresentation of African Americans, these trends are particularly troubling.

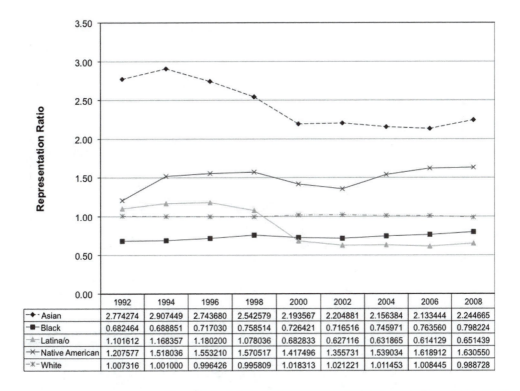

	1992	1994	1996	1998	2000	2002	2004	2006	2008
Asian	2.774274	2.907449	2.743680	2.542579	2.193567	2.204881	2.156384	2.133444	2.244665
Black	0.682464	0.688851	0.717030	0.758514	0.726421	0.716516	0.745971	0.763560	0.798224
Latina/o	1.101612	1.168357	1.180200	1.078036	0.682833	0.627116	0.631865	0.614129	0.651439
Native American	1.207577	1.518036	1.553210	1.570517	1.417496	1.355731	1.539034	1.618912	1.630550
White	1.007316	1.001000	0.996426	0.995809	1.018313	1.021221	1.011453	1.008445	0.988728

Figure 10.12 Trends in Racial/Ethnic Representation in Indiana Public 4-Year Postsecondary Institutions as a Proportion of the State Population

Source: Data from NCES Integrated Postsecondary Education Data System and U.S. Census Bureau © 2011 Projects Promoting Equity in Urban and Higher Education, NCID at the University of Michigan.

Public 4-Year Colleges

In contrast to community colleges, the completion rates in public 4-year colleges improved between 2002 and 2008 for all groups except Native Americans (Figure 10.13). Completion rates for both African Americans and Whites improved by about 3 percentage points, but there was still a 20 percentage point differential in 2008, with 53.2% of Whites completing compared to 33% of African Americans. There was more substantial improvement for Asians American (64.8% in 2008), the group with the highest completion rate, and Latinos/as (43.9 % in 2008).

Private Nonprofit Colleges and Universities

While most groups made only modest gains in retention rates in Indiana's independent colleges from 2002 to 2008, there was a 5 percentage point gain for African Americans, to 50.7%, and a three percentage point gain for Latinos/as, to 71.8%. There was also expansion in enrollment rates for African Americans in independent colleges, so these gains in completion rates contributed to the narrowing of the retention gaps in Indiana.

Innovations at independent colleges appear to have contributed to the reduction in the gap. The IPAS reform at Indiana Wesleyan University provides one illustration of the sorts of strategies that may have contributed to reduction in the degree attainment

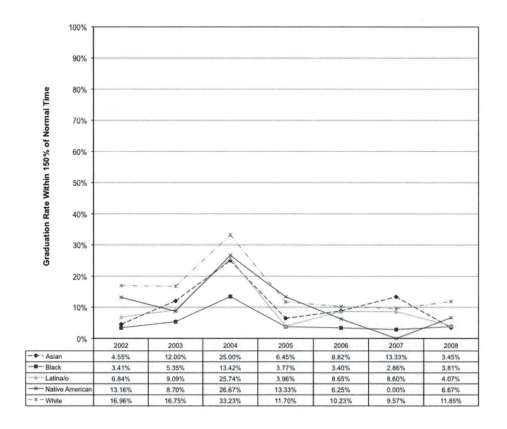

	2002	2003	2004	2005	2006	2007	2008
Asian	4.55%	12.00%	25.00%	6.45%	8.82%	13.33%	3.45%
Black	3.41%	5.35%	13.42%	3.77%	3.40%	2.86%	3.81%
Latina/o	6.84%	9.09%	25.74%	3.96%	8.65%	8.60%	4.07%
Native American	13.16%	8.70%	26.67%	13.33%	6.25%	0.00%	6.67%
White	16.96%	16.75%	33.23%	11.70%	10.23%	9.57%	11.85%

Figure 10.13 Trends in Graduation Rates in Indiana Public 2-Year Postsecondary Institutions by Racial/Ethnic Group

Source: Data from NCES Integrated Postsecondary Education Data System © 2011 Projects Promoting Equity in Urban and Higher Education, NCID at the University of Michigan.

gap (St. John & Musoba, 2010). The core campus had a well-documented pilot test of an engaged-leadership strategy for undergraduate education (Pattengale, 2008; Reynolds, Gross, Millard, & Pattengale, 2010) that was taken to scale within the multi-campus system and resulted in elimination of the gap in retention rates for African Americans compared to Whites (Carey, 2008). Clearly, more research is needed on interventions that focus on improving retention rates and reducing gaps in completion so that successful intervention methods can be disseminated.

CURRENT ISSUES

The Indiana strategy for postsecondary access and success has been, by most accounts, comprehensive, but it is proving difficult to sustain given shifts in political attitudes in the state. The state utilized a balanced framework for identifying and addressing the challenges students faced when engaging in the college choice process; for more than 2 decades, the state initiated substantial changes that addressed both access and persistence barriers. The Twenty-First Century Scholars program was the signature initiative designed both to eliminate costs as a barrier for low-income families and to engage

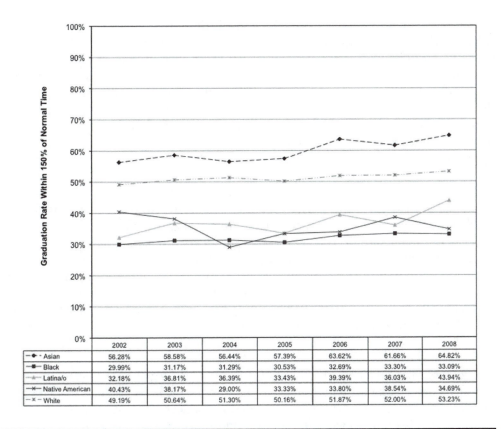

	2002	2003	2004	2005	2006	2007	2008
Asian	56.28%	58.58%	56.44%	57.39%	63.62%	61.66%	64.82%
Black	29.99%	31.17%	31.29%	30.53%	32.69%	33.30%	33.09%
Latina/o	32.18%	36.81%	36.39%	33.43%	39.39%	36.03%	43.94%
Native American	40.43%	38.17%	29.00%	33.33%	33.80%	38.54%	34.69%
White	49.19%	50.64%	51.30%	50.16%	51.87%	52.00%	53.23%

Figure 10.14 Trends in Graduation Rates in Indiana Public 4-Year Postsecondary Institutions by Racial/Ethnic Group

Source: Data from NCES Integrated Postsecondary Education Data System © 2011 Projects Promoting Equity in Urban and Higher Education, NCID at the University of Michigan.

students earlier in the choice process. The Core 40 diploma was established to raise the academic threshold for preparation, which it was hoped would lead to successful completion of a college education. While this is an important feature of the Indiana case, part of the story is still to be written. In 2011, all students will be required to complete the Core 40 unless their parents opt them out. Access to postsecondary education has improved dramatically in Indiana since the inception of the Twenty-First Century Scholars and Core 40, but there is one subset of the student population that has not found higher education to be accessible—Latino/a students. In 2011, the state passed an anti–DREAM Act bill, precluding undocumented students from being granted in-state tuition. Public higher education is experiencing substantial financial cuts, and only some of this money is being returned to institutions through performance funding. For 2001–2013, 5% of funds have been set aside for performance funding for improvement in degree completion, credit-hour production, and research productivity (Harnisch, 2011).

From a funding perspective, Indiana fared well relative to other states in the 1990s and early 2000s. While the state contribution to higher education declined in 2009, the loss was offset by federal stimulus dollars (Palmer, 2011). Higher education felt modest effects of declining state support in 2010 but will face a slightly more substantial reduction in 2011, when the federal stimulus dollars are no longer available. The total 2-year reduction is approximately 2.5% of the base, which, even after adjusting for inflation, is a cut of less than 8%. Since 2006, tuition and fees have risen by approximately 17%, which is less a concern in Indiana, where need-based aid has been indexed to the cost of tuition. Finally, in 2011, the state will take a portion of the cuts to postsecondary education and make an additional 5% of state appropriations available as an incentive for improved outcomes. All three of these policies have the potential to impact opportunity for students, but we suspect that the effects may be mixed.

P16 Curriculum Alignment Class of 2011

Beginning in 2011, the Core 40 curriculum became the minimum requirement for admission into the public 4-year college sector. From a system alignment perspective, this policy may actually simplify the signals sent to students and parents and make it clearer what is expected to be successful in college. It does, however, suggest that students who choose to opt out of the Core 40 will be forced to follow a more circuitous path into baccalaureate education, if they so choose, through the Ivy Tech system or the regional university campuses. It is not yet clear how well that consequence is and will be explained to students and parents during the opt-out process.

DREAM Act

College access has been at the forefront of the Indiana strategy for postsecondary access and success, but recent legislation signed by Governor Mitch Daniels suggests that access may remain a contentious issue when considering undocumented students. In 2011, the state passed legislation explicitly prohibiting undocumented students from qualifying for in-state tuition (Martin, 2011). The barriers to access for undocumented students are substantial, and the tuition rate is just one of many. In most states that allow in-state tuition for undocumented students, those students do not qualify for state aid programs. Even for those who can afford to pay the full in-state tuition rate, there is no path to citizenship that will allow them to seek gainful employment once they have earned a college degree.

Performance Funding

Performance funding is a commonly attempted strategy for tying state funding to postsecondary outcomes, but it is not frequently thought of relative to college access. In theory this policy may have an effect on access in two ways. First, to the extent that performance funding affects the cost of providing public higher education, low-income students may be affected. In the case of Indiana, performance funding is being implemented at a time when cuts to higher education have been substantial. The most recent cut reallocates 5% of state appropriations to provide incentives for improving graduation rates and time to degree (Wray, 2011). In this case, performance is directly tied to cuts in base appropriations, which have a negative effect on institutions and may affect tuition rates. Second, the effect of the performance funding model depends on how the program is structured. In Indiana, the metrics are based on improvement in key outcomes, which will favor, on average, institutions with the greatest room for improvement. In this case the main campuses for Indiana and Purdue Universities are likely to fare less well because they are already the top-performing public institutions in the state. The complicating factor, however, for any of the public sector institutions, is that it can be difficult to improve upon outcomes when state support declines.

CONCLUSIONS

Indiana's higher education system has made substantial gains in access in recent decades and more modest improvements in retention, especially in private nonprofit colleges. But Indiana could also be a state perched on the edge of decline. As the California case illustrates, declines in education outcomes follow cuts in state investment. Indiana has cut funding for higher education institutions and students. It could be difficult for the colleges and universities to improve equity and retention even with "performance funding" when total support declines. The heralded Indiana system had an embedded set of progressive incentives in the older K–16 finance system that encouraged improvement in preparation and access along with a private nonprofit sector that was highly responsive to funding incentives. In the near future, Indiana is likely to become a testing ground for judging the impact of reduced funding coupled with explicit "performance" incentives. Questions about the Indiana case are presented in Text Box 10.1.

Text Box 10.1 Questions About the Indiana Case

1. How do Indiana's strategies for improving preparation and access compare with those of the other states studied?

2. How did Indiana achieve coordination of public finance and college preparation strategies?

3. What is the proper role of universities in the higher education policymaking process? Can they provide impartial and unbiased research on questions of policy import when they are self-interested institutions?

4. How did different types of postsecondary institutions in Indiana respond to financial incentives for improving postsecondary opportunity in the state?

5. What roles did policymakers, legislative and executive staffs, and researchers play in crafting coordinated K–16 strategies in Indiana?

6. What role has litigation and legislation played in access for Latinos/as in Indiana?

7. Did Indiana's comprehensive approach reduce inequalities in educational opportunities? Did the influence of state policies differ across the sectors of the state's higher education system?

8. How do the new policies—reductions in funding for students and institutions, the anti-DREAM legislation, and performance funding—alter the comprehensive strategy in Indiana?

9. Given the direct and indirect relationships between policies and outcomes, how do you expect recent policy changes are likely to influence educational outcomes in Indiana?

10. How were policy indicators used in Indiana to inform policy decisions about the financing of higher education?

11

UNFETTERED NEOLIBERALISM

The Michigan Case

In some ways, Michigan's public universities (and, to a lesser extent, community colleges) are the envy of the nation because of the constitutional autonomy they enjoy. Leaders across New York State, for example, looked to the University of Michigan when a state-wide commission was considering how best to position the state's public higher education for the future. Critics argue, however, that the lack of a coordinating body at the state level creates inefficiencies, which ultimately drive up the costs of college (Vedder & Denhart, 2007) and make higher education less financially accessible to low-income students and their families (Cunningham, Erisman, & Looney, 2008). In the case of Michigan, it seems both sets of claims are essentially true. The University of Michigan (UM) ranks among the top public universities in the nation (U.S. News & World Report, 2011) and is among the top-ranked research universities in the World (Quacquarelli Symonds Limited, 2011). Michigan State University (MSU) also ranks among the American Association of Universities (AAU). Combined, UM, MSU, and Wayne State University (WSU) conduct more than $1 billion in federally funded research annually (Anderson & LaSalle, 2007).

At the same time the cost of attending a public 4-year institution in Michigan is substantially higher than the national average. The College Board (Baum & Ma, 2009) reported that average in-state tuition at public 4-year colleges across the country was $6,590 in 2008; the average in Michigan was approximately $8,500, with only one institution (Saginaw Valley State University) falling below the national average (President's Council—State Universities of Michigan, 2009). Some of these more recent problems are attributable to the lack of a cohesive and comprehensive state policy framework that could tether the trajectory of the state's system as governors respond to new issues promoted by Republicans and Democrats in the neoliberal period. The Michigan case starts with an examination of constitutional autonomy and its implications for public higher education as part of the policy context, considers recent trends in policies and outcomes, and returns to more recent policy developments before reaching a few conclusions and raising a few questions for readers.

THE POLICY CONTEXT

In addition to discussing the history of constitutional autonomy, we consider the political context for education prior to 2000, when school districts maintained substantial autonomy over curriculums while the state shifted funding for K–12 education away from property taxes in favor of per-pupil funding from a centralized school aid fund. One of the major policy decisions introduced in the early 1990s was a merit-based state scholarship program advanced by Governor John Engler; we discuss its creation, evolution, and eventual demise. We then consider the important policy changes that have placed considerable pressure on K–12 schools and, to a lesser extent, higher education institutions. During the mid-2000s, Governor Jennifer Granholm convened a statewide commission on higher education and economic growth, and the recommendations from that body established a public policy agenda that in some ways continues to serve as the framework for higher education policy in Michigan.

Constitutional Autonomy for Michigan Higher Education

In order to understand higher education in Michigan, it is important to consider the state's historic commitment to the establishment of constitutional autonomy for public universities. It may be both the most important and celebrated feature of the Michigan system and the policy that creates the most serious challenges.

It is difficult to know whether Michigan would be better off with a coordinating board (or separate boards for community colleges and public universities), because these structures have never existed in the state. In 1850, the state of Michigan held a constitutional convention where the University of Michigan was granted autonomy from the influences of the legislature. As Bracco (1997) points out, the purpose of distinguishing the University of Michigan as the first constitutionally autonomous public university was to prevent legislators from meddling in the curricular and administrative decisions best made by institutional leaders.

Michigan Agricultural College (now MSU) was founded shortly after the 1850 constitutional convention but was not granted the same special distinction until the next convention in 1908. Today, under Michigan's Constitution (circa 1963), all public universities enjoy the same autonomy. Article VIII, Section III of Michigan's Constitution reads: "The power of the boards of institutions of higher education provided in this constitution to supervise their respective institutions and control and direct the expenditure of the institution's funds shall not be limited to this section" (Public Sector Consultants, 2003, p. 3).

The constitution provides for the state board of education to plan and coordinate educational policies, but those powers have been limited over time. In 2006, the superintendent of public instruction sought to exert his influence over public higher education by specifying requirements for teacher education programs in university-based schools of education. The state board of education has also been charged with providing "leadership and general supervision for community colleges" (Bracco, 1997, p. 10), though the community colleges each fall under the leadership of a local board.

Voluntary Collaboration

Although Michigan higher education has never fallen under the formal coordination of a state agency, both the public 4-year universities and the community colleges organize voluntarily under the umbrella of state lobbying organizations. The Presidents Council of the State Universities of Michigan has been in existence since the middle part of the 20th century, when it was literally a forum for the presidents of the public universities to consult with one another on their state policy priorities. Michigan is home to 15 public university campuses with 13 presidents and 2 chancellors (for the branch campuses of the University of Michigan at Dearborn and Flint), who make up the board of the Presidents Council. The state has not articulated a set of expectations for how the campuses should collaborate, but the council has chosen to seek many of the same benefits one might expect from a system, collaborating on cost-savings initiatives for purchasing, property insurance, and healthcare (Daun-Barnett, 2008a); however, the presidents of their respective universities differ on important policy issues, including the distribution of state funding for higher education.

In addition to the board of presidents and chancellors, the Presidents Council convenes meetings of leaders across 12 functional areas within the institutions, from chief information officers to institutional researchers and directors of student affairs. The provosts, for example, meet to review and approve curricular changes and degree programs across the institutions three times per year. Directors of admissions partnered to introduce electronic transcript sending capabilities for high schools and for the respective campuses to receive those transcripts. Representatives from the general counsel's offices convene to consider the range of legal issues facing campuses and, from time to time, discuss strategies to defend the principle of constitutional autonomy for higher education.

The challenge to voluntary coordination is that there is no mechanism to force resolution on contentious policy differences, which frequently pit the "big three" research universities against the remaining 10 institutions—leaving the branch campuses in a unique middle space where they are legally a part of the University of Michigan, but their interests and concerns more closely align with the regional serving institutions. Campuses within highly coordinated systems also differ on important policy issues, but the final say rests with the system chancellor rather than with a vote among member presidents.

The Michigan Community College Association (MCCA) represents the presidents of the 28 community colleges across the state and seeks to influence the state's policy agenda for higher education, much like the Presidents Council. The executive directors for the Presidents Council and the MCCA are registered lobbyists and are responsible for educating legislators and legislative staff about the important role of higher education and advocating for either expanding funding for higher education or—as has been the case for the past decade—fighting to minimize the level of cuts the state would impose on public higher education.

Occasionally, MCCA and the Presidents Council collaborate for a common cause, but frequently the two are at odds with one another regarding the policy priorities for higher education in the state. One of the recent and perhaps more contentious debates was whether to allow community colleges to offer applied baccalaureate degree programs where demand is high and 4-year institutions are unwilling or unable to meet the demand. MCCA began a campaign to promote the community college baccalaureate and partnered with the Michigan Department of Labor and Economic Growth to assess the need for offering 4-year degrees and the interest in doing so among community college presidents. Twenty-three of the 28 community colleges wanted to offer baccalaureate degrees; of those, 17 identified nursing as the program they would most like to offer (Muffo,

Voorhees, & Hyslop, 2008). The executive director of the MCCA serves on the board of the national Community College Baccalaureate Association (CCBA) and the debate continues more than 3 years after it began. Community colleges see the baccalaureate degree as an extension of their mission to increase access within their local communities, while 4-year universities worry that the move undermines the value of baccalaureate education if attempted within the existing community college infrastructure or that it will drive up the costs at community colleges to reflect a new set of curricular standards (Boulus & Daun-Barnett, 2008).

One issue that has brought the two organizations together has been the implementation of performance funding for higher education. On several occasions, Michigan policymakers have initiated performance funding programs intended to improve institutional outputs, but those measures tend to change as frequently as the term-limited legislature. Both the Presidents Council and MCCA oppose performance funding, particularly during a period of persistent cuts to higher education. The current performance funding program offsets a modest portion of a 22% cut to state higher education appropriations, meaning that institutions are being asked to do more with even less. Opposition from these two groups reflects different concerns. The universities view these schemes as infringing upon their constitutional autonomy and express frustration that the expectations change frequently and apply equally across very different institutions. The community colleges oppose performance funding largely because no matter the measures legislators introduce, the 2-year institutions believe the measures will not accurately reflect the work they do; stated differently, community colleges perform poorly on all metrics of student success on average.

The Political Landscape

Like all states, higher education does not operate in a vacuum. The K–12 policy context is as important to college access in Michigan, since the policies directly impact postsecondary education. There are two key policies that have affected K–12 education in Michigan. First, Proposal A was passed under Republican John Engler's administration in the mid-1990s to equalize funding for schools. Proposal A decreased the overall tax burden for the average family in Michigan and narrowed the gap in funding per student between the highest- and lowest-funded districts, but it also placed important constraints on districts, particularly during periods of declining state revenues, as has been the case in Michigan for nearly a decade. Second, in 2006 Michigan adopted a set of high school course requirements for graduation beginning with the class of 2011. The change in policy was initiated as part of a statewide commission on higher education and economic growth convened in 2004. To that point, Michigan was one of six states with no common graduation requirements; but beginning with the graduating class of 2011, it has among the most rigorous set of requirements across the nation.

The Engler Administration

Proposal A

In 1993, amid growing concern over high and steadily increasing property tax rates, the Michigan legislature passed Public Act 145, repealing property taxes as the primary funding for K–12 education with no alternative to replace local revenues. At that point, 55% of funding for K–12 education came from local property taxes (Michigan Senate

Fiscal Agency, 1996), which were a third higher than the national average, and funding per pupil differences was as high as 3:1 between the highest- and lowest-funded districts. Governor Engler proposed replacing the $7 billion in lost revenue with a 2% increase to the sales and use tax rate, a $6 million state education tax (SET) on property, a $0.50 per package tax increase on cigarettes, and a real estate transfer tax. The proposal passed in March of 1994 by a wide margin.

Proposal A established a minimum foundation grant that raised the floor for districts that had substantially lower funding per pupil. For example, in 2003 the foundation grant was set at a minimum of $6,700 per pupil (Office of Revenue and Tax Analysis, 2002). The shift provided a more equitable distribution of school aid funding, but it did not eliminate the gaps between the highest- and lowest-funded districts. Today, districts like Bois Blanc Pines and Bloomfield Hills spend twice as much as Benton Harbor or Genesee schools—an improvement over 1993 but still a substantial gap. The tradeoff to Proposal A was a set of school reforms including school choice, creation of charter public schools, and lengthening the school year. By 2003, a total of 189 public charter schools were operating across the state, serving more than 72,000 students, and the full foundation grant follows the student. In 2010, the cap on the number of public charter schools was increased substantially as the state attempted to align its policies with the priorities of the federal Race to the Top competition.

Proposal A has had very real implications for K–12 education in the state of Michigan and has indirectly affected higher education as well. The legislation moved a step toward greater funding parity for schools, but in the process it limited a district's ability to raise funds locally. The intermediate school district maintains some discretion to raise property taxes to be distributed equally across individual school districts, but few have been successful at raising additional revenues in this way. Shifting these resources to the state School Aid Fund (SAF) has provided some guarantee of minimal funding for districts, but because this money is guaranteed, it places greater pressure on the shrinking proportion of the state budget that is discretionary, which includes higher education. State revenues have declined steadily between 2006 and 2011 and support for higher education has dropped considerably. Because the sales tax was increased to provide alternative revenues for schools, there is little appetite to increase state taxes to maintain support for higher education, and only the community colleges have access to local tax support.

The Michigan Merit Scholarship

Michigan is a state that may be accurately described as a high-tuition low-aid state, meaning that a substantial portion of the cost of postsecondary education is passed on to students, with little aid to offset the higher than average tuitions. In June 1999, Governor John Engler signed House Bill No. 4666, creating the Michigan Merit Award program. Michigan used a portion of its annual tobacco settlement revenues to pay for the program. Every eligible student received $2,500 to attend an approved postsecondary institution in the state of Michigan or $1,000 to attend an equivalent institution outside the state. According to Sec. 4 (1) of the bill, "the goal of the board is to increase access to postsecondary education and reward Michigan high school graduates who have demonstrated academic achievement" (Justia US Law, 2010).

Eligibility was defined for any student who (1) passed all four sections of the Michigan Educational Assessment Program (MEAP)—reading, writing, math, and science; (2)

passed two or three of the areas and received an overall score on a standardized college admissions exam in the top 25%; or 3) passed two or three sections and received a qualifying score on a nationally recognized job skills assessment test as designated by the board. The American Civil Liberties Union (ACLU) brought suit against the state of Michigan (*White v. Engler,* 2001) claiming that eligibility defined solely upon test scores was discriminatory and in violation of Title VI of the Civil Rights Act of 1964 (American Civil Liberties Union, 2000). Heller and Shapiro (2001) found that only 12% of African American students qualified for the award, compared with more than 53% of White students. Further, they showed that 93% of all awards were based upon criterion 1, meaning the alternatives did very little to mitigate any potential bias of the MEAP. Despite the evidence demonstrating the disparate impact of the MEAP, plaintiffs dropped the case against the state because it had been decided that individuals could not bring claims of disparate impact under Title VI of the Civil Rights Act of 1964.

The merit scholarship should be placed in context. As controversial as it was, it was a one-time award of as much as $2,500 in a state with modest need-based aid programs (including the tuition grant, which is designated for students attending private institutions only). Even if more low-income and underrepresented minority students qualified for the program, it would cover only a modest portion of the total cost of attending a public university in Michigan. In the end, the Michigan Merit Scholarship was too poorly conceived and inadequately funded to improve students' chances for access or success in college. However, the program was popular among middle-class voters who expected their sons and daughters to earn the award, so any changes in financial aid strategy could build upon this foundation rather than introducing a new program.

The Granholm Administration
The centerpiece of Governor Jennifer Granholm's higher education agenda was the appointment of a commission on higher education. In addition, her administration took steps to alter the Michigan merit program in ways that were slightly more generous but that used a very different merit mechanism for eligibility.

The Cherry Commission on Higher Education and Economic Growth
The Cherry Commission was announced by Governor Granholm in March 2004, charged with the task of identifying the best approaches to double the number of college graduates in the state within 10 years. Lieutenant Governor John Cherry chaired a group of 41 commissioners including 8 college presidents, 2 district superintendents, presidents of the state board of education, the Michigan Education Association, the Detroit Regional Chamber, and the Henry Ford Museum, as well as an array of education, business, and public policy leaders from across the state. In addition to the voting members, the commission included a dozen state policymakers, directors of special interests, the governor's executive leadership team, a policy director, two senior policy advisors, a logistics management firm, and a team of graduate student researchers. In addition to doubling the numbers of college graduates in the state in 10 years, the commission was charged with improving alignment between higher education and the emerging employment opportunities in the state's economy and to build a dynamic workforce with talents and skills for the 21st century (Lieutenant Governor's Commission on Higher Education and Economic Growth, 2004). The commission met for the better part of 6

months and issued a report to the governor in December 2004 with a slate of 19 broad recommendations, most of which represented the plurality of voices participating in the commission's work.

Of those 19 recommendations, two were particularly surprising, though for different reasons. The first was the call for a statewide set of high school graduation course requirements. Michigan was one of six states at the time without a set of common course requirements. A half-year of civics was the only course required by the state. It was not surprising that the issue was brought to the commission; most states had already adopted course requirements (National Center for Education Statistics, 2005), and a number of interest groups were advocating for a policy (ACT, 2000; American Diploma Project, 2002). However, the idea was dismissed by one state senator participating in the preparation work group. The legislature had considered similar legislation a few years earlier and they lacked political support to establish course requirements at that time. After two white papers by the research staff and successive presentations by ACT and Achieve, support among commissioners had shifted and graduation requirements became one of the signature recommendations in the final report.

The second surprise recommendation called for the creation of community compacts for educational attainment. The idea was not a part of the initial briefing paper and was never taken up in the work group sessions. It first became a topic of conversation during the second full commission meeting, where a number of commissioners noted the importance of tailoring strategies to the needs of local communities. The lieutenant governor proclaimed during that meeting that he sensed a "sea change" in terms of thinking on how best to tackle the issues facing higher education, and he acknowledged and recognized the importance of a community-centered approach. The participation work group considered the issue more extensively and it became one of the final recommendations to the governor.[1]

The commission report is important because for more than 5 years it served as a blueprint or a common agenda for higher education policy. However, in many ways it is as important to consider what was left off the agenda in order to understand the current situation in Michigan. Before the Cherry Commission was formed, the National Center for Public Policy in Higher Education (NCPPHE) issued its second report card of the states, called *Measuring Up*, and the report had been discussed among state leaders at the National Governor's Association annual meeting. *Measuring Up* graded states on six key areas—preparation, participation, affordability, completion, benefits, and learning, The *Measuring Up* report served as the basic organizing structure for the work of the Cherry Commission, but Governor Granholm and her staff responsible for forming the commission left affordability and learning off the table.

The most obvious limitation of the Cherry Commission was that it failed to address college affordability. During the first meeting of the commission, Governor Granholm addressed the group, framed the nature of the problem and the importance of the commission, and explained her rationale for leaving funding off the table. She acknowledged to the group that funding was important, but she did not want the commission to constrain its recommendations to what was financially possible. She suggested the best ideas should be brought to the table and then they would find the necessary funding. With seven presidents from public institutions, all of whom had experienced successive cuts in state appropriations, it may have been difficult to avoid talking about funding and, in fact, during a number of work group meetings, the funding theme reemerged.

Leaving affordability out of the organizing structure prevented the commission from even considering ways to rethink student aid, performance funding, or a range of other higher education finance issues that can impact the cost of college. For example, the National Governors' Association had identified promising state practices to coordinate appropriations, tuition, and financial aid policies; contain costs; and focus attention on need-based aid for students. There was no natural place for an extended conversation on finance by the commission because it was left out of the work group structure (Austin, Burkhardt, & Jacobs, 2004); however, a small subgroup was charged to consider financial aid, independent of the formal commission process, and the result was the reformulation of the Michigan Merit Scholarship into the credit-contingent Promise Scholarship.

Student learning was left off the agenda as well, but the context was different. The impact of college cost and student financial aid on students' postsecondary access and success was well established with a number of effective models to consider. With respect to student learning, there was no consensus on how to assess whether and what students were learning. The testing agencies were developing tools to assess general skills, but there was no uniform standard, and there were no state models from which to draw. In 2008, NCPPHE continued to issue incomplete grades for student learning because they lacked sufficient data to compare across states (National Center for Public Policy and Higher Education, 2008). The closest the commission came to addressing student outcomes was to recommend improved institutional completion measures, reflecting the unique missions of each institution and then disaggregating by relevant subgroups.

As a consequence of the flawed political process, state leaders established an agenda for higher education policy that was both widely regarded and regrettably incomplete. Although no formal body was convened to carry forward the recommendations of the commission, the governor's office and the state board of education continued to push pieces of the agenda, and the changes made to education policy during this period were linked back to the final report. Failing to address affordability created two problems for the state. First, in order to double the numbers, more low income, first generation, and underrepresented students would need to attend college—and these are the groups most sensitive to price. Second, failure to address persistent cuts to higher education appropriations and anemic financial aid policies limited the ability of higher education to expand its capacity to meet the growing needs of students, particularly in community colleges where demand was strongest.

Local Control of the High School Curriculum

In 2006 Michigan shifted from leaving high school graduation requirements to local discretion to adopting what is arguably among the most rigorous set of requirements in the nation. Legislation calls for the class of 2011 to complete at least three math courses (including algebra I, geometry, and algebra II), 3 years of science (including one biological science and one physical science course), 4 years of English, and 4 years of social studies. The class of 2016 will be required to add 2 years of a foreign language to the list (Michigan Department of Education, 2006). Of course it is too early to know whether the policy helps or hurts student success in the long term. Experience tells us that, at least in the near term, more rigorous requirements will prevent some students from completing high school—a pattern that will likely improve as the system adjusts to prepare students earlier for the increased demands.

The requirements are likely to increase the level of preparation students receive for a 4-year college education, but there is no guarantee the higher education system will be able to accommodate the growing proportion of high school graduates prepared for postsecondary education. At the same time, the focus on a college preparatory standard prevents career and technical education (CTE) programs from developing more robustly, perhaps even aligning to applied degree programs at community colleges. We are concerned that the detrimental effects of failing to earn a high school diploma outweigh the potential gains in preparation, particularly given that community colleges continue to operate as open enrollment institutions.

Shift to the Promise Scholarship

The subgroup of the Cherry Commission asked to consider an alternative financial aid strategy proposed eliminating the contentious Michigan Merit Scholarship, with a more generous merit aid program designed to create an incentive for postsecondary success. Effective December 21, 2006—just over 2 years after the final recommendations were issued by the commission—the Michigan Merit Scholarship was replaced by the Michigan Promise Grant Act (Act 479; 2006), beginning during the 2006–2007 school year. The Promise Scholarship was similar to its predecessor with a few important exceptions:

1. Students were eligible for a total of $4,000, which was an increase over the $2,500 offered under the Merit scholarship.
2. Students were required to take only the Michigan Merit Exam (MME), which replaced the MEAP, and they were no longer required to achieve a certain level of proficiency to earn the award.
3. All or part of the award was contingent upon successful completion of 2 years (or its equivalent 60 college credits) while earning at least a 2.5 GPA. (Michigan Department of Treasury, 2006)

From a policy perspective, all three changes were improvements over the previous program—increasing the award by 60%, eliminating the testing proficiency requirement, and creating an incentive to complete college. When students demonstrated proficiency on the Michigan Merit Exam (MME), they received the first two $1,000 disbursements at the beginning of the first 2 years in postsecondary education; the remainder of their award was granted once they had successfully earned 60 college credits and achieved a 2.5 GPA. If students were unable to demonstrate proficiency on the MME, they received no money up front but qualified for the entire award after completing the 60 credit/2.5 GPA requirements.

The amount of the award was motivated by the lieutenant governor's desire to guarantee 2 years of community college for every student. At the time of the Commission, the average tuition and fees at a Michigan community college was approximately $2,000 per year. The scholarship was not linked to fluctuations in tuition and fees—which was more problematic for students attending public universities where the average tuition in Michigan exceeded the national averages by more than $2,000 (Baum & Ma, 2011). We have no evidence demonstrating whether or not the program had any impact on access or success, because within 3 years of its passage, the Promise Scholarship was eliminated, meaning that there is no longer a signature financial aid program in Michigan.

TRENDS IN POLICY DECISIONS

The track record for college access and success in Michigan has been decidedly mixed. The roles and impact of policies on preparation, access, and retention are examined below.

Academic Preparation Policies

As a state that emphasized local control of schools, Michigan was slow to implement course requirements for higher education. Once it made the decision, the state adopted a rigorous standard reflecting both the priorities of Achieve, Inc., and basic expectations of the ACT college admissions test. The two most challenging requirements are in math and foreign languages. Michigan is the third of seven states in the process of requiring all students to complete algebra I, geometry, and algebra II. The foreign language requirement will apply to the graduating class of 2016 and will require all students to complete two credits in a language other than English.

The state adopted math standards in 1995 because it was a requirement for continued federal funding for federal education programs (Figure 11.1). The exit exam went into effect for 11th graders in 2008. The new graduation requirements did not go into effect until 2011. Before that time Michigan had been a local-control state, a policy pattern typically associated with high achievement outcomes (St. John, 2006).

State Financing of Higher Education

Michigan has had economic problems for most of the 21st century, including high unemployment due to the decline of the auto industry. These conditions have constrained tax revenues, altering the funding strategies used to support colleges and college students. Trends in public financing are summarized below.

State Funding of Public Institutions

In the 1990s, state appropriations for higher education in Michigan were similar to the national average, but in the 2000s a gap opened (Figure 11.2). In 2008, the weighted state appropriations per FTE were $6,773, compared with $7,912 in the United States as a whole—a $759 differential. This decline was attributable to tax revenue shortfalls that spanned both Republican and Democrat administrations.

Tuition Charges by Public Colleges and Universities

The weighted average tuition charge in Michigan was comparable to the national average in the 1990s, before the decline in state funding (Figure 11.3) but declined near the turn of the 21st century. As tuition increased in Michigan through the 2000s, the gap between the Michigan average and the national average grew to $1,566. On a per student basis, Michigan public higher education had substantially higher general education-related revenue (the combination of tuition and state subsidies) than the national average between 1990 and 2010.

Need-Based Student Aid

Need-based aid in Michigan was comparable to national average in 1992 but began to diverge through the 1990s (Figure 11.4). The growth in the gaps between Michigan investments in need-based aid and those of the nation after 1998 are the result of a shift in financial aid philosophy as the state adopted the Michigan Merit Scholarship under

Requires an Exit Exam

Requires Three Math Courses

Requires Algebra I

Adopted National Council of
Teachers of Mathematics Standards

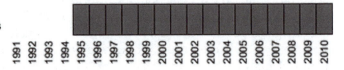

Figure 11.1 Michigan High School Graduation Requirements

Source: © Projects Promoting Equity in Urban and Higher Education, NCID at the University of Michigan.

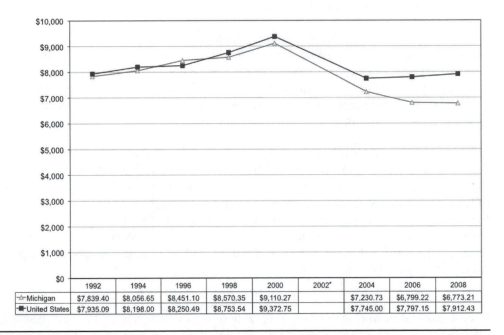

	1992	1994	1996	1998	2000	2002*	2004	2006	2008
Michigan	$7,839.40	$8,056.65	$8,451.10	$8,570.35	$9,110.27		$7,230.73	$6,799.22	$6,773.21
United States	$7,935.09	$8,198.00	$8,250.49	$8,753.54	$9,372.75		$7,745.00	$7,797.15	$7,912.43

Figure 11.2 Trends in Michigan and U.S. Average Annual Amount of State and Local Appropriations per FTE for the Public Higher Education (in 2008 Dollars)

Source: Data from NCES Integrated Postsecondary Education Data System © 2011 Projects Promoting Equity in Urban and Higher Education, NCID at the University of Michigan.

*This data is missing in the Integrated Postsecondary Education Data System (IPEDS).

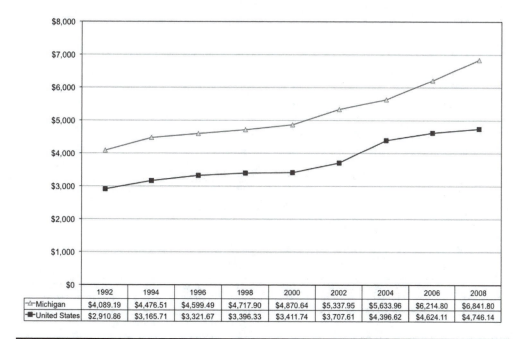

	1992	1994	1996	1998	2000	2002	2004	2006	2008
Michigan	$4,089.19	$4,476.51	$4,599.49	$4,717.90	$4,870.64	$5,337.95	$5,633.96	$6,214.80	$6,841.80
United States	$2,910.86	$3,165.71	$3,321.67	$3,396.33	$3,411.74	$3,707.61	$4,396.62	$4,624.11	$4,746.14

Figure 11.3 Trends in Michigan and U.S. Averages for Weighted Averages for Undergraduate In-State Tuition and Fees for Public Higher Education (in 2008 Dollars)

Source: Data from NCES Integrated Postsecondary Education Data System © 2011 Projects Promoting Equity in Urban and Higher Education, NCID at the University of Michigan.

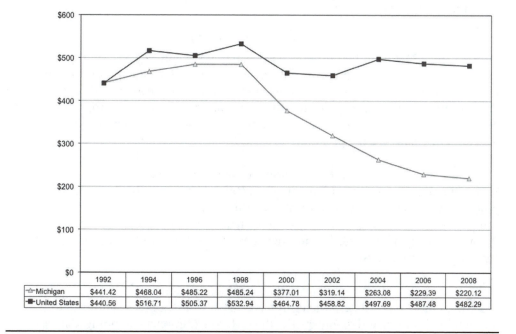

	1992	1994	1996	1998	2000	2002	2004	2006	2008
Michigan	$441.42	$468.04	$485.22	$485.24	$377.01	$319.14	$263.08	$229.39	$220.12
United States	$440.56	$516.71	$505.37	$532.94	$464.78	$458.82	$497.69	$487.48	$482.29

Figure 11.4 Trends in Michigan and U.S. State Need-Based Undergraduate Grants per FTE (in 2008 Dollars)

Source: Data from National Association of State Student Grant & Aid Programs © 2011 Projects Promoting Equity in Urban and Higher Education, NCID at the University of Michigan.

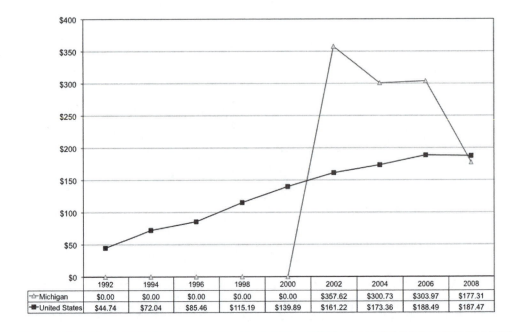

	1992	1994	1996	1998	2000	2002	2004	2006	2008
Michigan	$0.00	$0.00	$0.00	$0.00	$0.00	$357.62	$300.73	$303.97	$177.31
United States	$44.74	$72.04	$85.46	$115.19	$139.89	$161.22	$173.36	$188.49	$187.47

Figure 11.5 Trends in Michigan State Non-Need-Based Undergraduate Grants per FTE (in 2008 Dollars)

Source: Data from National Association of State Student Grant & Aid Programs © 2011 Projects Promoting Equity in Urban and Higher Education, NCID at the University of Michigan.

the Engler administration, combined with the fact that need-based aid did not adjust according to changes in tuition.

Non-Need (Merit) Aid

Prior to 1999, Michigan had no non-need-based aid (Figure 11.5). The rapid increase after 2000 reflects the adoption of the Michigan Merit Scholarship, funded largely by tobacco settlement funds. It is unclear what caused the decline after 2002, but it may be that fewer students were eligible after the first year or that a greater proportion of students attending postsecondary education after that period were nontraditional students who did not qualify for the program.

The Ratio of Tuition to Need-Based Grants

With high tuition and low funding for grants, Michigan has not had an explicit focus on promoting financial access, as illustrated by the ratio of state need-based grant funding compared to tuition (Figure 11.6). Historically low compared to other states, this ratio dropped steadily after 1998. In the Michigan model, campuses had responsibility for ensuring financial access.

A State in the Middle of Change

More than most other states, Michigan has a history of delegating authority to schools through local control and to universities through constitutional autonomy. The relatively recent changes in graduation requirements altered the history of local control, but the state still has not taken on a strong role in coordinating higher education nor adopted

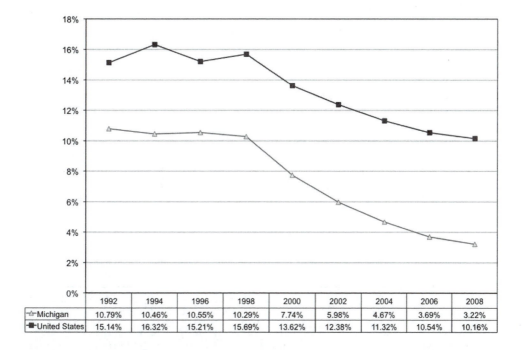

	1992	1994	1996	1998	2000	2002	2004	2006	2008
Michigan	10.79%	10.46%	10.55%	10.29%	7.74%	5.98%	4.67%	3.69%	3.22%
United States	15.14%	16.32%	15.21%	15.69%	13.62%	12.38%	11.32%	10.54%	10.16%

Figure 11.6 Trends in Michigan Need-Based Grants per FTE as a Percent of the Weighted Average State Tuition Compared With the U.S. Average

Source: Data from NCES Integrated Postsecondary Education Data System and National Association of State Student Grant & Aid Programs © 2011 Projects Promoting Equity in Urban and Higher Education, NCID at the University of Michigan.

performance funding strategies as has been the case in some other states in the region (Chapters 8 and 10). The state had provided competitive funding for higher education, but this changed in the 1990s. The rise in tuition and decline in grants substantially increased net costs before institutional aid for residents attending public colleges and university.

TRENDS IN STUDENT OUTCOMES

The track record for college access and success in Michigan has been decidedly mixed. The roles and impact of policies on preparation, access, and retention are examined below. Historically, Michigan has been a progressive state with a commitment to funding its postsecondary institutions. However, the shift toward more neoliberal ideologies has resulted in a set of policy priorities that may effectively undermine access and exacerbate gaps by racial and ethnic groups.

Changes in Academic Preparation

High School Graduation Rates
It is difficult to assess whether Proposal A finance reform in 1994 influenced graduation rates. The rates for Asian Americans exceeded 100% for 3 of the 13 years as an artifact of immigration, while graduation rates of Whites fluctuated from a low of 73.2% in 2002 to

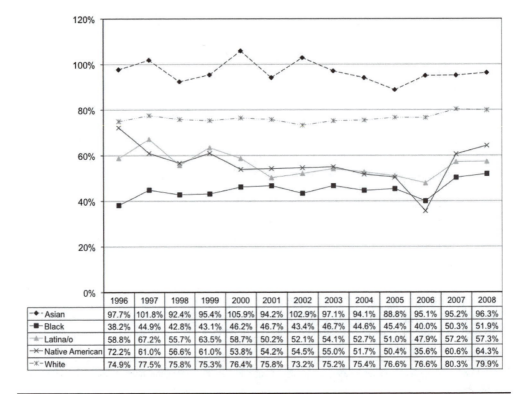

	1996	1997	1998	1999	2000	2001	2002	2003	2004	2005	2006	2007	2008
◆ Asian	97.7%	101.8%	92.4%	95.4%	105.9%	94.2%	102.9%	97.1%	94.1%	88.8%	95.1%	95.2%	96.3%
■ Black	38.2%	44.9%	42.8%	43.1%	46.2%	46.7%	43.4%	46.7%	44.6%	45.4%	40.0%	50.3%	51.9%
▲ Latina/o	58.8%	67.2%	55.7%	63.5%	58.7%	50.2%	52.1%	54.1%	52.7%	51.0%	47.9%	57.2%	57.3%
✕ Native American	72.2%	61.0%	56.6%	61.0%	53.8%	54.2%	54.5%	55.0%	51.7%	50.4%	35.6%	60.6%	64.3%
✳ White	74.9%	77.5%	75.8%	75.3%	76.4%	75.8%	73.2%	75.2%	75.4%	76.6%	76.6%	80.3%	79.9%

Figure 11.7 Trends in Michigan Public High School Graduation Rates by Race/Ethnicity

Source: Data from NCES Common Core Data © 2011 Projects Promoting Equity in Urban and Higher Education, NCID at the University of Michigan.

80% in 2008 (Figure 11.7). All groups improved from 2006 to 2008, before changes in the graduation requirements and financial aid took effect. African Americans experienced a slow but steady improvement from 1996 to 2008 but remained well below White and Asian American students. Graduation rates for Native Americans also varied substantially across the period but were higher in 2008 than in 1996. The gaps in graduation rates between Whites and Asians compared with African Americans was at its narrowest point in 2008 but was still approximately 28 percentage points. It is too early to assess the impact of the new high school graduation requirements on completion rates.

ACT Tests

Michigan has a long history as an ACT state; it adopted the ACT as the 11th grade test in 2008 and, prior to 2008, it had higher than average percentages of students who took the ACT (Figure 11.8) *and* a higher composite average score (Figure 11.9). These trends illustrate that under local control, Michigan schools outperformed the national average. In 2008, after Michigan required the ACT of all students, the percentages of Michigan students jumped as expected and Michigan's average ACT composite score dropped substantially. The drop is probably explained by the jump from 67% taking the test to 100%. However, given the changes in college continuation noted below, there could be even more serious problems in Michigan education.

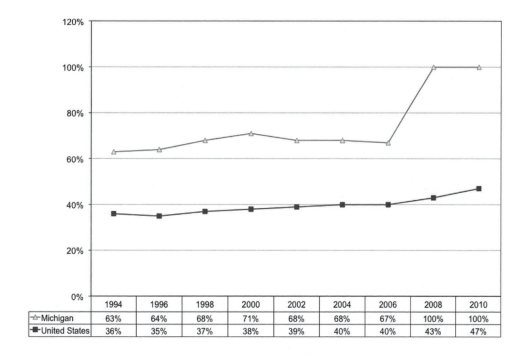

	1994	1996	1998	2000	2002	2004	2006	2008	2010
Michigan	63%	64%	68%	71%	68%	68%	67%	100%	100%
United States	36%	35%	37%	38%	39%	40%	40%	43%	47%

Figure 11.8 Percent of Michigan Students Who Took the ACT Compared With the U.S. Average

Source: Data from ACT, Inc. © 2011 Projects Promoting Equity in Urban and Higher Education, NCID at the University of Michigan.

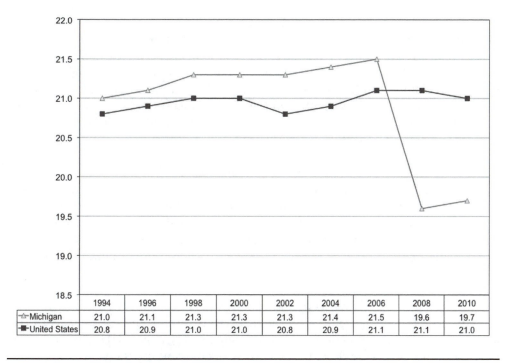

	1994	1996	1998	2000	2002	2004	2006	2008	2010
Michigan	21.0	21.1	21.3	21.3	21.3	21.4	21.5	19.6	19.7
United States	20.8	20.9	21.0	21.0	20.8	20.9	21.1	21.1	21.0

Figure 11.9 Trends in Average Composite ACT Score in Michigan and the United States

Source: Data from ACT, Inc. © 2011 Projects Promoting Equity in Urban and Higher Education, NCID at the University of Michigan.

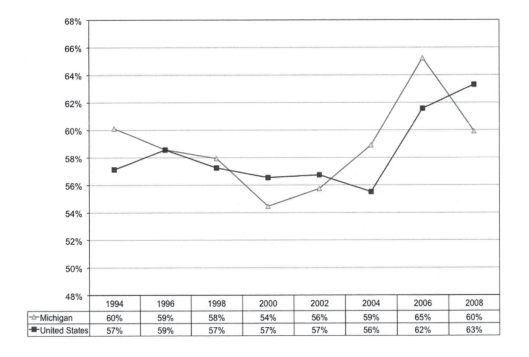

	1994	1996	1998	2000	2002	2004	2006	2008
Michigan	60%	59%	58%	54%	56%	59%	65%	60%
United States	57%	59%	57%	57%	57%	56%	62%	63%

Figure 11.10 Trends in Michigan and U.S. College Continuation Rates

Source: Data from Postsecondary Education Opportunity © 2011 Projects Promoting Equity in Urban and Higher Education, NCID at the University of Michigan.

College Access and Diversity

The pathways theory of change (Figure 4.1), logic, and prior research suggest that financial policies have a direct effect on college enrollment and high school preparation policies have an indirect effect. In Michigan, the first class of graduates under the new high school requirement had not completed high school at the time of our study, so it is reasonable to assume that differentials in college continuation and diversity are attributable to the combination of state finance policy, the passage in 2006 of Proposal 2 banning affirmative action, and institutional student aid.

College Continuation Rate

Between 2002 and 2006, Michigan made substantial gains in college continuation, outpacing the U.S. average, but this rate dropped substantially in 2008 (Figure 11.10). The decline may be attributable to the financial strategies used in the state or to the adoption of the ban on affirmative action. Whatever the reason, the correspondence between trends and outcomes raises questions about the viability of policies adopted in Michigan.

Diversity in Michigan Higher Education

With the exception of Native American students, who are overrepresented in 2-year colleges, every other group is underrepresented (Figure 11.11), although Hispanic and African American students are closer to reflecting population numbers.

Whites maintained similar representation in Michigan's public colleges and universities throughout the 1990s, but their numbers slowly declined after 2000, while there was

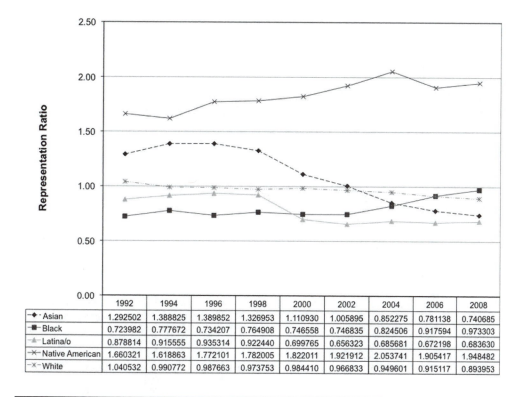

	1992	1994	1996	1998	2000	2002	2004	2006	2008
–◆· Asian	1.292502	1.388825	1.389852	1.326953	1.110930	1.005895	0.852275	0.781138	0.740685
–■– Black	0.723982	0.777672	0.734207	0.764908	0.746558	0.746835	0.824506	0.917594	0.973303
–▲– Latina/o	0.878814	0.915555	0.935314	0.922440	0.699765	0.656323	0.685681	0.672198	0.683630
–✕– Native American	1.660321	1.618863	1.772101	1.782005	1.822011	1.921912	2.053741	1.905417	1.948482
–✕– White	1.040532	0.990772	0.987663	0.973753	0.984410	0.966833	0.949601	0.915117	0.893953

Figure 11.11 Trends in Racial/Ethnic Representation in Michigan Public 2-Year Postsecondary Institutions as a Proportion of the State Population

Source: Data from NCES Integrated Postsecondary Education Data System and U.S. Census Bureau © 2011 Projects Promoting Equity in Urban and Higher Education, NCID at the University of Michigan.

a slight rise in African American representation (Figure 11.12). From an equity perspective, we expect to see convergence of the proportions by racial/ethnic group over time, and that is what we observe, although gaps remain. African American students remain highly underrepresented but have experienced an 8% increase from 1992 to 2008. Hispanic students once again showed overrepresentation in the 1990s and then dropped to rates similar to those of African American students through the 2000s.

Degree Completion in Michigan Higher Education

As we have discussed in prior chapters, the linkages between state policies and degree completion are less clear. We recognize that financial aid plays a role in allowing students to remain in school, but research on this relationship is mixed. Preparation may also be related, but that effect is evident whether and where students choose to attend college. Much of the difference observed across institutions and sectors is largely a function of who those institutions choose to admit, but some research suggests that institutions may be able to improve upon their success rates, at least at the margins.

Public 2-Year Colleges

The 3-year completion rates for community colleges were low across all groups. White students completed degrees at the highest rates, but fewer than 1 in 5 graduated with an

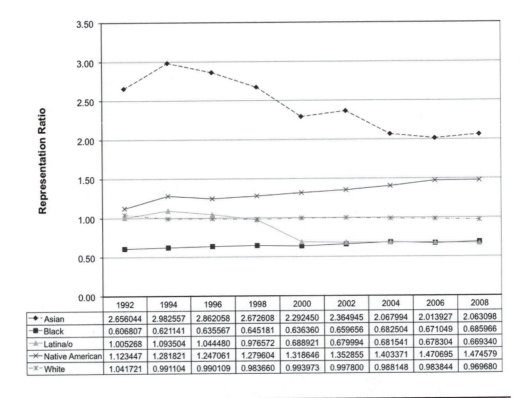

	1992	1994	1996	1998	2000	2002	2004	2006	2008
Asian	2.656044	2.982557	2.862058	2.672608	2.292450	2.364945	2.067994	2.013927	2.063098
Black	0.606807	0.621141	0.635567	0.645181	0.636360	0.659656	0.682504	0.671049	0.685966
Latina/o	1.005268	1.093504	1.044480	0.976572	0.688921	0.679994	0.681541	0.678304	0.669340
Native American	1.123447	1.281821	1.247061	1.279604	1.318646	1.352855	1.403371	1.470695	1.474579
White	1.041721	0.991104	0.990109	0.983660	0.993973	0.997800	0.988148	0.983844	0.969680

Figure 11.12 Trends in Racial/Ethnic Representation in Michigan Public 4-Year Postsecondary Institutions as a Proportion of the State Population

Source: Data from NCES Integrated Postsecondary Education Data System and U.S. Census Bureau © 2011 Projects Promoting Equity in Urban and Higher Education, NCID at the University of Michigan.

associate's degree in that time frame (Figure 11.13). Hispanic success rates at community colleges have been fairly consistent throughout the 2000s, hovering near 10%; African American students' success has been more erratic, with a high of 17.7% in 2004 and a low of 6.8% in 2008. These completion rates do not account for successful transfers to 4-year colleges, but even with that adjustment, fewer than half of students attending community colleges are successful.

Public 4-Year Colleges

In contrast to community colleges, the completion rates in public 4-year colleges improved, but the gaps between groups remain considerable (Figure 11.14). Approximately 60% of White students complete a bachelor's degree within 6 years, compared with only 36% of African American students. Both Latino/a and Native American students have experienced general trends upward, but they remain 6 to 12 percentage points behind White students at public 4-year universities.

CONTEMPORARY STATE CONTEXT

Michigan had a plan for higher education, but that plan was disjointed and never fully funded, in part owing to a contentious political climate but more directly to a declining

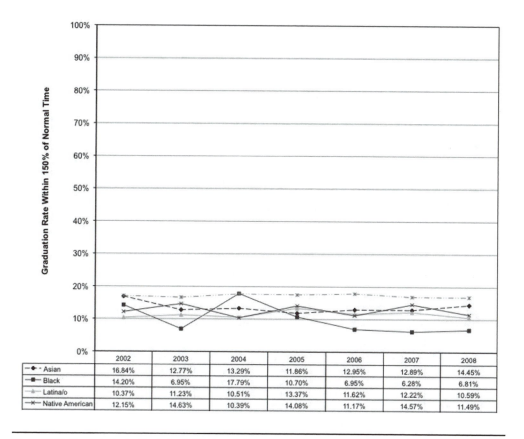

	2002	2003	2004	2005	2006	2007	2008
Asian	16.84%	12.77%	13.29%	11.86%	12.95%	12.89%	14.45%
Black	14.20%	6.95%	17.79%	10.70%	6.95%	6.28%	6.81%
Latina/o	10.37%	11.23%	10.51%	13.37%	11.62%	12.22%	10.59%
Native American	12.15%	14.63%	10.39%	14.08%	11.17%	14.57%	11.49%

Figure 11.13 Trends in Graduation Rates in Michigan Public 2-Year Postsecondary Institutions by Racial/Ethnic Group

Source: Data from NCES Integrated Postsecondary Education Data System © 2011 Projects Promoting Equity in Urban and Higher Education, NCID at the University of Michigan.

state economy that was showing signs of recession well before the rest of the nation. The plan was laid out in the final report of the Statewide Commission on Higher Education and Economic Growth, whose work was limited by a failure to consider either the cost of higher education or accountability for student learning. As a consequence, the approach addressed only pieces of the problem without an integrated strategy to tie the pieces together. In many ways, the case of Michigan serves as a counterpoint to those we have identified as successful. The one unique and promising development in Michigan relative to higher education policy actually has very little to do with state policy: utilization of the federal college access challenge grant, discussed below. Michigan, under the leadership of the Department of Education and the Michigan College Access Network, has begun catalyzing local strategies to improve college access and success. In addition, although it is too early to judge their direct impact, the changes in management of Detroit schools brought about by state financial management legislation are likely to influence the diversity of Michigan's 4-year institutions.

Phase II of the Graduation Requirements

The high school graduation requirement policies adopted subsequent to the Cherry Commission were spread out over time in an effort to allow the system to adjust. The

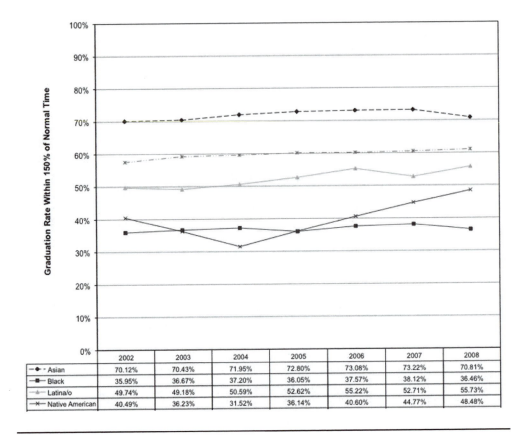

	2002	2003	2004	2005	2006	2007	2008
Asian	70.12%	70.43%	71.95%	72.80%	73.08%	73.22%	70.81%
Black	35.95%	36.67%	37.20%	36.05%	37.57%	38.12%	36.46%
Latina/o	49.74%	49.18%	50.59%	52.62%	55.22%	52.71%	55.73%
Native American	40.49%	36.23%	31.52%	36.14%	40.60%	44.77%	48.48%

Figure 11.14 Trends in Graduation Rates in Michigan Public 4-Year Postsecondary Institutions

Source: Data from NCES Integrated Postsecondary Education Data System © 2011 Projects Promoting Equity in Urban and Higher Education, NCID at the University of Michigan.

first phase of the policy was announced in 2006 and applied to the first cohort of high school graduates in 2011. It is possible that the higher standards will make it more diffi-cult for some students to complete high school, particularly those in large urban districts like Detroit and small rural communities like those in the central and northern portions of the state. Time will tell. In the meantime, the second phase of the increased gradu-ation requirements will begin with the 9th grade class of 2013, when two courses in a foreign language will be required. To put this decision into context, Michigan will be the 17th state in the nation to require at least one course in a foreign language (Council of Chief State School Officers, 2008); half of those states require only one course or allow students an option between a foreign language or another credit (including American sign language or computer science).

It is important to recognize that the adoption of these policies was presumed to be revenue-neutralwheninfactchangeslikethesemustbeaccompaniedbyappropriateresources to provide additional training and support to existing teachers, improved teacher education training programs for those entering the profession, and remedial support programs to help students who are challenged by the new, more rigorous curriculum. The challenge for foreign languages, like math and science, is that the requirement may necessitate hir-ing many more teachers with this background than are currently available. The state superintendent has made the reform of teacher preparation programs a central focus of his administration, but all of these changes are complicated by the lack of a central co-ordinating board for higher education. Some have suggested that Michigan create such a board (Cunningham, et al., 2008), but to do so would require an amendment to the state constitution.

The Loss of State Financial Aid Programs

The adoption of state graduation requirements may have important implications for students in the future, but the more fundamental challenge in Michigan is the growing cost of college for students and their parents. Since 2009, state appropriations for higher education have declined in real dollars by nearly 9% (Palmer, 2011). In 2011, the state announced an additional 15% cut to state appropriations. Some of that decline was offset by federal stimulus dollars, but those resources are no longer available and the state revenue picture has not changed. During the same period, average tuition and fees have risen by nearly 25%, to more than $9,100 per year for resident students (National Center for Education Statistics, 2011). The state has required that institutions raise their student aid commensurate with the increases in tuition, but there is no stipulation re-garding whether those resources should be targeted to serve high-need students.

The cost of tuition and fees has risen dramatically in recent years—a problem com-pounded by the fact that the state provides very little financial aid support for students and almost no aid targeted to financial need. In 2006, the Michigan Promise Grant Act (Act 479) was passed, effectively guaranteeing $4,000 to every Michigan high school graduate who completes a full 2 years of college (2006). The Promise Scholarship re-placed the less generous Michigan Merit Scholarship ($2,500) but was short-lived, hav-ing been eliminated in October of 2009. The state is now left with no signature financial aid program at a time when the price is rising at rates that far outpace either inflation or the growth of family income.

The Michigan College Access Network and the Growth
of Local College Access Strategies

If there is a bright spot in the Michigan college access strategy, it can be found in its utilization of the federal college Access Challenge Grant (CACG). In 2008, the U.S. De-partment of Education issued block grants to states to expand efforts to address col-lege access. The grant stipulated a one-third match of state resources as a condition of the grant application, and those resources were to be targeted toward efforts to increase the proportion of students going to and eventually succeeding in college. The Michigan approach has been unique relative to other states, and its strategy also has roots in the Cherry Commission. One of the recommendations suggested the creation of commu-nity compacts to assemble community partners and leaders to address the unique local challenges facing students and their families as they plan and prepare for college. The Kalamazoo Promise formally emblazoned the local strategy into the minds of state poli-cymakers who have passed legislation to create 10 Promise Zones across the state.

In 2009, the Michigan College Access Network (MCAN) launched an ambitious effort to expand on the local access strategy by seeding the organization of as many as 40 com-munities who are planning for or developing strategies to bring to scale existing efforts to improve access for local students. These place-based strategies have the advantage of bringing additional resources into the college access conversation, but the concern is what happens for students in those communities not served by the Local College Access Networks (LCAN). The genesis of these place-based strategies is economic development and, as such, they raise concerns for whether and to what extent these opportunities will be extended fully to those with the fewest advantages (Daun-Barnett & Holohan-Moyer, in press).

MCAN has become a model for connecting state-level policy strategy with local initiatives to find solutions to the problems associated with college access. The organization has raised several million dollars beyond the federal block grant to expand its reach across the state, which it has leveraged to bring community foundations actively into the college access conversation (beyond their traditional role to provide donor-generated scholarships to students). Whether a statewide network connecting state policy with local practice will translate into increased opportunities for postsecondary access and success is unclear, but to the extent that one of the primary barriers for students is access to information and support, the approach has potential.

Financial Managers in Action

Soon after his election, Governor Rick Snyder pushed for new tax cuts (Fitzsimmons, 2011) and legislation on emergency financial managers (Selweski, 2011). The most immediate education impact has been the appointment of a financial manager for the Detroit Public Schools (DPS) (Wattrick, 2011). Currently the state is pushing new-style market reforms in Detroit, following the models put in place in New York City and New Orleans. As is the case with other education reforms in Michigan, it is too early to judge the eventual impact of these changes. Although Detroit has declined in size over the past decade, the Detroit schools continue to enroll most of the state's African American students. The future of DPS and of the school reforms in the state will have a substantial, yet to be determined, influence on diversity at the University of Michigan and the state's other senior institutions.

CONCLUSIONS

While the University of Michigan may have earned the admiration of the nation's higher education community because of the position it took in the *Gratz* and *Grutter* Supreme Court cases, the state's voters soon banned affirmative action in Proposal 2 in 2006. The universities in the state suffer from a reactionary state political context that favors neoliberal interpretations of the rights of all in a state that lacks a coherent history and framework for the funding of colleges and students. The swing toward merit under a Republican governor and the repacking of this program under a Democrat governor took away much of the state's need-based aid, redistributing it to students who attended high schools with a college preparatory curriculum. While the state has implemented rigorous new graduation requirements for all high school students, it is still unclear whether these changes will improve diversity in the long term. We encourage readers to ponder the implications of the Michigan case. The Michigan case raises many questions about the consequences shifting the focus of higher education policy from access to and financing of higher education to the preparation of students for college, the neoliberal argument carried to an extreme (see Text Box 11.1).

Text Box 11.1 Questions About the Michigan Case

1. Is there a relationship between the historical autonomy of institutions in Michigan and the disjointed pattern of public funding for higher education in the state?

2. How are K–12 education reforms in Michigan related to recent changes in student test scores and other high school outcomes? Are the recent patterns likely to change substantially after the new high school graduation requirements are fully implemented?

3. What is the relationship between changes in Michigan's state grant and scholarship programs and the enrollment patterns in the state's postsecondary institutions?

4. What, if any, policy decisions appear related to the growing disparity in college graduation rates for Whites and African Americans in Michigan?

5. Is there hope that the improvements in college preparation will improve equity in Michigan's higher education system without changes in the state financing of higher education?

6. Are place-based college access strategies likely to increase postsecondary opportunities for students? Or will this approach simply reward communities that are already well positioned to provide these advantages?

7. What strategies should Michigan's public colleges and university use to encourage reform in the state's financing of higher education? It is currently a high tuition/low aid state and the declines in state revenue seem to be persisting longer than in the rest of the nation. What alternatives should be considered?

8. How would you expect the election of the new Republican governor—a strong antitax conservative—to affect the policy framework implemented in Michigan?

12

THE NEW PROGRESSIVE SOUTH

The North Carolina Case

Of the southern states, North Carolina has been a relatively consistent example of progressive change in higher education. From the development of the Research Triangle in the 1960s through the response to federal mandates to desegregation in 1978 and the state's investment in need-based student financial aid in the early 21st century, North Carolina has provided a model for the new South. This case describes some of the critical developments in the North Carolina system of higher education, the trends, policies and outcomes, and recent policy developments, before raising questions for readers.

A NEW PROGRESSIVE TRADITION

Historically North Carolina has taken a progressive stance toward public education. The state claims the first university founded as a public university to grant degrees (University of North Carolina) and the first public historically Black college founded as a liberal arts institution (North Carolina Central University). In recent years, the public 4-year and community college systems have taken steps to expand access and opportunity.

A 4-Year Public University System

The University of North Carolina is among the oldest and most esteemed public systems of higher education in the nation. It comprises 16 campuses—including the flagship research university at Chapel Hill—and an accelerated high school for gifted students. The University of North Carolina prides itself as the first public university in the nation (1789) and the only one to graduate students during the 18th century (University of North Carolina General Administration, 2011), which distinguishes it from the College of William and Mary in Virginia and Rutgers University in New Jersey, both of which were founded prior to UNC. The multicampus institution is overseen by a 32-member board of governors elected by the general assembly of the state. The board, in turn, elects a president for the institution, and each of the campuses is run by a chancellor. The chancellors report to the president of the institution and are responsible to 8-member boards of trustees for their respective campus. The 17 campuses serve more than 221,000 students, nearly a quarter of whom are graduate students (University of North Carolina General Administration, 2011).

The UNC system has demonstrated an openness to innovation within the campuses that strengthens higher education in the state. There has been system support for campuses to provide national leadership. We use a couple of illustrative examples: North Carolina's historical leadership in desegregation and the development of the North Carolina Covenant as a means of improving economic and racial diversity and as a stimulus for the improvement of student aid funding in the state.

Desegregation of the North Carolina System

The UNC system was one of systems that complied early after the federal government provided guidance for the desegregation of public systems of higher education (Williams, 1988). Several of the UNC historically Black colleges and universities (HBCUs), adopting the *Adams* guidelines for systemwide desegregation and the strengthening of developing institutions, had been involved in the federal Title III developing institutions program since its inception. For example, North Carolina A&T University was designated as exemplary of the advanced program under Title III and was one of the first HBCUs to plan for the development of doctoral programs (St. John, 1981).

Amalgamation of HBCUs into the North Carolina system helped provide a framework for the development of these campuses as well as for systemwide desegregation. This exemplary approach of system integration and development was a stark contrast to states like Alabama, Mississippi, and Louisiana, which maintained separate systems, resisted the *Adams* framework, and instead used the *Fordice* framework, which supported program development at HBCUs only if that new development could attract White students (St. John & Hossler, 1998). The success of the North Carolina model rests with full acceptance of HBCUs as partners systemwide in providing accessible college opportunities.

North Carolina's HBCUs continue to provide national leadership in advocacy for strengthening and developing these vital institutions. For example, in June 2010, North Carolina Central University hosted a national meeting on the future of HBCUs. An analysis completed for the symposium found that in spite of differences in preparation at the time of admission (HBCUs have largely taken on a developmental focus), HBCUs had similar graduations rates for African Americans as the public universities in the state (St. John, 2010). The trends in graduation rates from HBCUs illustrate a stable pattern of graduation for African Americans (45% in 2002 and 44% in 2007) at the majority at these colleges. After the symposium, NCCU issued a report, *Strengthening America's Historically Black Colleges and Universities: A Call for Action* (Nelms, 2011), calling for continued federal support for the HBCUs as a vital resource in a global period emphasizing increased achievement.

The Carolina Covenant and Commitment to Need-Based Student Aid

In 2003, the University of North Carolina at Chapel Hill implemented the *Carolina Covenant* as a comprehensive approach to improving access for and retention of underrepresented low-income students; it rapidly became a national model for ensuring student financial support. The Covenant guaranteed low-income students would receive sufficient grant aid to ensure that borrowing would not be necessary during college if they were willing to work 15 hours a week on College Work Study. At the time, the idea was that the new program would "send a message to young people harboring aspirations of

Table 12.1 Characteristics of UNC Carolina Covenant Scholars

	Fall 2004	Fall 2005	Fall 2006	Fall 2007	Fall 2008	Fall 2009	Fall 2010
Number of new covenant scholars	224	350	417	398	410	537	563
Average high school GPA	4.21	4.25	4.19	4.26	4.30	4.31	4.44
Average SAT scores	1209	1223	1198	1202	1206	1230	1232
State of origin: North Carolina	87%	89%	84%	87%	84%	84%	84%
North Carolina counties represented	68	74	72	77	74	78	76
Gender							
Female	69%	63%	61%	63%	60%	61%	64%
Male	31%	37%	39%	37%	40%	39%	36%
Students of color	63%	60%	63%	61%	61%	62%	57%
First-generation college graduate	55%	52%	57%	53%	55%	57%	56%

Source: Ort, Williford, and St. John, in press.

attending UNC: if they worked hard in high school and gained admission, lack of money would not be an obstacle to becoming a 'Tar Heel'" (Fiske, 2010, p. 17).

Although the financial aid guarantee provided by UNC received national attention and was widely replicated, the program also developed a comprehensive set of support services, including orientation, mentoring, academic workshops, special programming, cultural events, and other programs and services. Many of the institutions across the country that have adopted the aid guarantee overlooked the support services. The documented success of the program, summarized below, is attributable to both the guaranteed aid and the support services.

The Covenant came at a time when the test scores of admitted low-income students were rising (Table 12.1). The percentage of low-income minority students remained constant as the number of low-income students rose, illustrating an increase in the total number of low-income high-achieving students of color at UNC and success in recruiting high-achieving underrepresented students. This finding is consistent with the experience at Harvard, where the differences were attributed to more concerted efforts to expand outreach beyond traditional feeder schools (Avery et al., 2006). Owing to restrictions on the numbers of students who could be admitted from out of state, the gains in scores came largely from attracting higher-achieving North Carolina residents.

The success of the Carolina Covenant is demonstrated by the improved economic and racial diversity on the Chapel Hill campus and, ultimately, improvement in long-term outcomes—degree completion and employment. The early analysis indicates improved retention. A comparison of 4th-year retention by the 2004 cohort (i.e., the first Covenant group) to the 2003 ("control") cohort that entered the year before the establishment of the Carolina Covenant indicated a 5 percentage point gain for the Covenant students (Table 12.2). An additional analysis examined graduation rates, finding the greatest improvement in graduation rates for White males (33 percentage point gain from the 2004 cohort to the 2003 cohort), followed by Black males (20 percentage point gain) and Black females (12 percentage point gain); White females actually showed a slight drop in 4-year graduation (Ort, Williford, & St. John, in press). The cohort comparison indicates a reduction in the gap in retention and completion rates for African American and White males compared with females.

Table 12.2 Change in Retention Rates Among Covenant-Eligible Students in the 2003 (Control Group) and 2004 Cohorts at the University of North Carolina, Chapel Hill

Group	Enrolled in Year 4		
	2003 Control Group	2004 Cohort	Percentage Point Improvement
Covenant	84.3%	89.6%	5.3%
Other needy	87.6%	88.2%	0.6%
Non-needy	90.5%	91.6%	1.1%
All students	89.3%	90.5%	1.2%

Source: Ort, Williford, and St. John, in press.

With this kind of evidence of success, the UNC system has successfully lobbied the state to increase its funding of need-based grants for students in public 4-year colleges. These gains in state funding for grants (discussed below) have reduced the costs of maintaining the commitment to meeting tuition for UNC as well as improved funding for students at other campuses in the system.

Community College System

The community college system in North Carolina epitomizes the progressive shift in the state. The community college system was born during the tumultuous decade of the 1950s when desegregation efforts in the South were in full force and, as Wescott (2005) notes, the community colleges were never segregated, accepting both Whites and students of color from the beginning. For that reason, the North Carolina Community College System (NCCCS) is emblematic of the progressive shift in the state and across much of the South.

The mission of NCCCS narrowly defines the role of the community college relative to other systems across the country. Although Michigan allowed community colleges to operate largely independent of the state and Florida community colleges could broadly interpret their mission inclusive of access to baccalaureate education, North Carolina community colleges focus on technical and vocational preparation and training. According to NCCCS (2008, p. 2),

> The major purpose of each and every institution operating under the provisions of this Chapter shall be and shall continue to be the offering of vocational and technical education and training, and of basic, high school level, academic education needed in order to profit from vocational and technical education, for students who are high school graduates or who are beyond the compulsory age limit of the public school system and who have left the public schools.

Like most community college systems, NCCCS also provides academic pathways to the 4-year degree, allowing for systemwide articulation to the UNC system and agreements with private colleges across the state, but this is secondary to vocational and technical education.

The early establishment of the NCCCS is reminiscent of the dual public systems of Indiana and Purdue Universities in Indiana. In 1950, the North Carolina Superintendent of Public Instruction convened a statewide commission headed by Allan Hurlburt to consider the question of the establishment of postsecondary alternatives to 4-year institutions; 2 years later, the Hurlburt Commission issued its recommendation to create a state-funded system of community colleges (Wescott, 2005). The 1957 general assembly passed acts providing funding for both a community college system intended for the arts and sciences (reminiscent of public junior colleges) and a set of industrial education centers. These two systems operated largely independently for the first 5 years of their establishment. In 1962, Governor Terry Sanford convened the Commission on Education beyond High School. The Carlyle Commission (as it was known) called for the consolidation of these two systems under a single administrative unit in the state board of education, and a year later the system was officially established with 20 industrial centers and six junior colleges (North Carolina Community College System, 2008). In 1981, the Department of Community Colleges was moved out of the state board of education and established as a separate entity; in 1999 the name was changed to the North Carolina Community College System. According to recent figures, the system now comprises 59 institutions serving more than 358,000 students (National Center for Education Statistics, 2010).

POLICY CHANGES

In the early 2000s, North Carolina took a different path with respect to both K–12 and higher education policies than most other states. Below we review trends in policies on academic preparation and higher education finance before reviewing related outcomes.

Policy Trends in North Carolina

Coordination of Academic Preparation and College Access

Like most states in the United States, North Carolina adopted a comprehensive set of high school course requirements in the core academic subjects aligned with postsecondary expectations (Figure 12.1). By 1998, the state had adopted exit exams and 3 years of math, including a minimum of algebra. The difference is that North Carolina is among the first states to differentiate those requirements according to different postsecondary opportunities—a position that is set to change, as we describe in the final section of this chapter.

The North Carolina model raised math requirements for all students while maintaining a comprehensive approach to high school education and educational standards consistent with NCTM, the indicator noted in national reform efforts for academic preparation (Chapter 3). However, North Carolina has maintained multiple pathways consistent with the comprehensive high school model. In contrast, Michigan, Indiana, and other states have recently established their default state curriculum to be in alignment with admission into a 4-year college; North Carolina has provided multiple paths to a high school diploma while also providing a minimum standard for all, but without requiring a language and some advanced math for all students, like the Michigan approach.

It is still unclear which of the approaches to high school reform will prove the most effective with respect to graduation rates and narrowing gaps in opportunity. However,

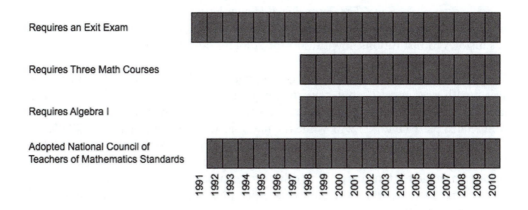

Figure 12.1 North Carolina High School Graduation Requirements

Source: © Projects Promoting Equity in Urban and Higher Education, NCID at the University of Michigan.

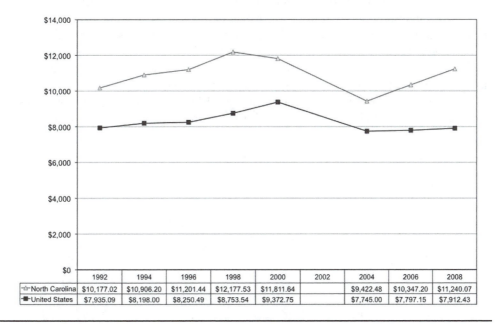

	1992	1994	1996	1998	2000	2002	2004	2006	2008
North Carolina	$10,177.02	$10,906.20	$11,201.44	$12,177.53	$11,811.64		$9,422.48	$10,347.20	$11,240.07
United States	$7,935.09	$8,198.00	$8,250.49	$8,753.54	$9,372.75		$7,745.00	$7,797.15	$7,912.43

Figure 12.2 North Carolina Average Annual Amount of State and Local Appropriations per FTE for the Public Higher Education System (in 2008 Dollars)

Source: Data from NCES Integrated Postsecondary Education Data System © 2011 Projects Promoting Equity in Urban and Higher Education, NCID at the University of Michigan.

given the early adoption of high standards in North Carolina, the trends in this state provide some evidence of the long-term effects of high school curriculum reform. While all three paths are aligned with postsecondary options, they are subject to criticism that they amount to tracks within schools, particularly with respect to the math curriculum, where the greatest amount of variation is possible. Indeed, the comparison of cases raises questions about which approach to curriculum alignment is most progressive ideologically and with respect to outcomes.

The Financing of Higher Education

In the 2000s, North Carolina managed to adhere to a public finance model of high public subsidies to institutions, low tuition for students, and high need-based student aid, counter to the other state cases.

The trends in state and local funding of higher education per FTE (Figure 12.2) have varied, with rises and falls, but have remained about $2,000 to $3,000 higher than the national average. In fact, public subsidies in North Carolina rose between 2000 and 2008, from $9,422 per FTE to $11,240, while the national average hovered around $7,800.

While the average in-state tuition charge in North Carolina rose between 1992 and 2008, it was consistently lower than the national average (Figure 12.3). In 2008, the weighted average tuition charge in North Carolina was slightly more than $1,400 below the national average, while the sum of tuition plus appropriations was substantially above the national average because of the appropriations.

North Carolina is unique because it shifted funds to expand need-based undergraduate aid (Figure 12.4). The state's growing commitment to meeting financial need is a response to a growing progressive sentiment in the state. Even with its historic commitment to maintaining low tuition in the public sector, NC invested little in need aid through the 1990s. Late in the decade, the state increased its investment substantially, and by 2006, North Carolina's investment per FTE in need-based aid substantially exceeded national averages. It has become the one state in the nation to embrace a low-tuition high-aid approach to public higher education finance.

The ratio of tuition to need-based grants per FTE in North Carolina rose from an extremely low rate in 1992 to a rate well above national averages over the next 116 years

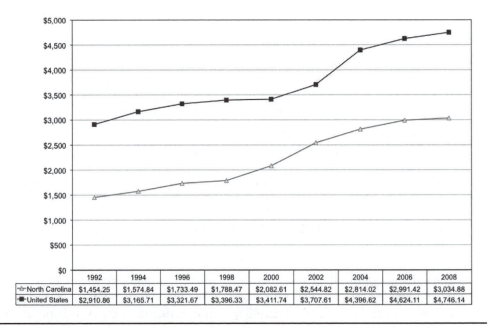

	1992	1994	1996	1998	2000	2002	2004	2006	2008
North Carolina	$1,454.25	$1,574.84	$1,733.49	$1,788.47	$2,082.61	$2,544.82	$2,814.02	$2,991.42	$3,034.88
United States	$2,910.86	$3,165.71	$3,321.67	$3,396.33	$3,411.74	$3,707.61	$4,396.62	$4,624.11	$4,746.14

Figure 12.3 Trends in Weighted Average Public Tuition Charged in North Carolina—Average Amount of Undergraduate In-State Tuition and Fees for the Public Higher Education System (in 2008 dollars)

Source: Data from NCES Integrated Postsecondary Education Data System © 2011 Projects Promoting Equity in Urban and Higher Education, NCID at the University of Michigan.

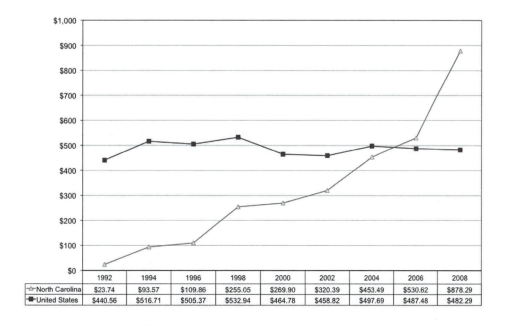

Figure 12.4 North Carolina State Need-Based Undergraduate Grants per FTE (in 2008 Dollars)

Source: Data from National Association of State Student Grant & Aid Programs © 2011 Projects Promoting Equity in Urban and Higher Education, NCID at the University of Michigan.

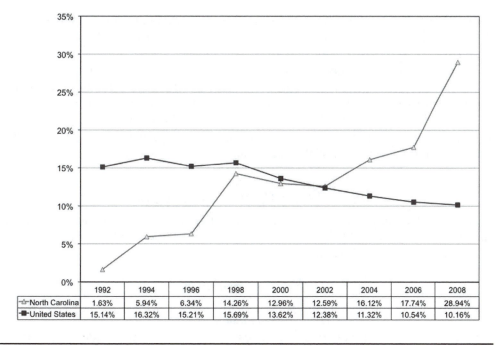

Figure 12.5 North Carolina Need-based Grants as a Percent of State Tuition

Source: Data from NCES Integrated Postsecondary Education Data System and National Association of State Student Grant & Aid Programs © 2011 Projects Promoting Equity in Urban and Higher Education, NCID at the University of Michigan.

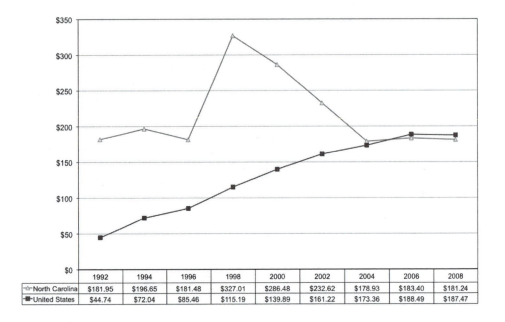

	1992	1994	1996	1998	2000	2002	2004	2006	2008
North Carolina	$181.95	$196.65	$181.48	$327.01	$286.48	$232.62	$178.93	$183.40	$181.24
United States	$44.74	$72.04	$85.46	$115.19	$139.89	$161.22	$173.36	$188.49	$187.47

Figure 12.6 North Carolina State Non-Need-Based Undergraduate Grants per FTE (in 2008 Dollars)

Source: Data from National Association of State Student Grant & Aid Programs © 2011 Projects Promoting Equity in Urban and Higher Education, NCID at the University of Michigan.

(Figure 12.5). The NC ratio funding for need-based grants to tuition rose to 28.9% of the weighted average in-state tuition in 2008, while the national rate declined gradually to 10.2%.

The rise in funding for need-based aid in the late 1990s and beyond coincided with a decline in non-need-based funding per FTE (Figure 12.6). Throughout the 1990s and into the first part of the 2000s, North Carolina was above the national average in terms of non-need-based grant aid, but between 1998 and 2004 the state experienced a substantial decrease in this form of aid as it increased need-based alternatives. Since 2004, North Carolina has remained slightly below national averages in non-need-based grants.

TRENDS IN STUDENT OUTCOMES

Trends in outcomes related to academic preparation, access and diversity, and degree completion are examined below. We also consider how these trends compare and contrast with changes in policy and funding.

Academic Preparation

High School Graduation Rates

Trends in high school graduation rates across North Carolina over time are consistent with the trends in other states (Figure 12.7). Asian American students graduate at the highest rates (82.1% in 2008), followed by White students (72%), and all three under-represented groups at just above 50%. Graduation rates for Whites improved during the period, while those for other groups did not. Thus it is possible that the reforms in

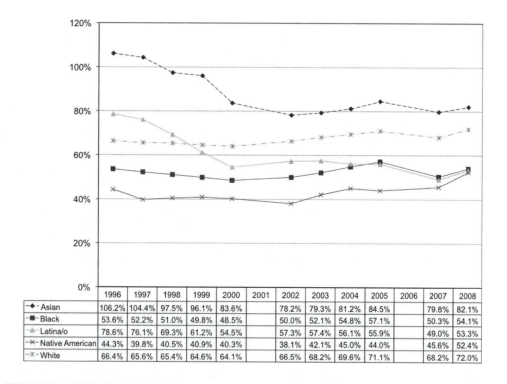

Figure 12.7 Trends in North Carolina Public High School Graduation Rates by Race/Ethnicity

Source: Data from NCES Common Core Data © 2011 Projects Promoting Equity in Urban and Higher Education, NCID at the University of Michigan.

high school had more substantially positive effects for Whites, possibly because they had better access to more advanced courses and better teachers. Such issues merit further exploration in North Carolina.

These trends demonstrate that in North Carolina racial/ethnic groups benefited differentially from the improvements in standards and high school graduation requirements implemented in the late 1990s. Whites had a modest consistent improvement in graduation rates after the new policies were implemented. Native Americans also showed improvement in this outcome. In contrast, there were declines in graduation rates for Asian Americans and Latinas/os, while the rate for African Americans remained relatively flat. The Black/White gap widened from 13 percentage points in 1996 to almost 18 in 2008. The precipitous decline in Latino/a graduation rates from 1996 to 2000 aside, the gap between White and Latino students grew from 4 percentage points in 2000 to almost 19 in 2008. These trends merit closer examination in relation to actual changes within high schools. In particular, it is important to consider whether the tracking patterns within high schools (i.e., diploma type by race) had an influence on these outcomes—a possible consequence of the multiple diploma pathways.

SAT Scores

North Carolina is an SAT state when it comes to college admission applications at selective colleges and universities. Nationally slightly fewer than half of all high school students take the SAT, but in North Carolina as many as 70% took the test in 2006, followed by a drop in 2008 (Figure 12.8). The percentage is consistent with other SAT states but suggests that over time, the proportion of students considering 4-year colleges has increased by almost 10 percentage points.

SAT Scores

State average SAT scores on both the verbal and math tests suggest that students are generally better prepared for college than they were nearly 20 years ago (Figure 12.9). On the verbal exam, North Carolina students scored 18 points lower than the national average, almost two standard deviations below the mean, in 1992. By 2008, the gap had been reduced to 6 points, while participation rates increased. A more dramatic shift occurred in math, where the gap was reduced from 22 to 4 points during the same period (Figure 12.10). It is difficult to ascertain whether these changes are a consequence of the rigorous high school curriculum, but it is certain that North Carolina has found a way to improve its preparation outcomes. At the very least, improved test scores coincide with the higher graduation requirements, a pattern evident nationally (Chapter 4).

Access and Diversity

The college continuation representation ratio—the number of graduating high school seniors in a state divided by the first-time freshmen residents enrolling the next year—provides an indicator of access that has logical linkages to both academic and financial policies. In North Carolina, college continuation was substantially below the national average in 1994, but it rose by 14 percentage points to be above the national average by

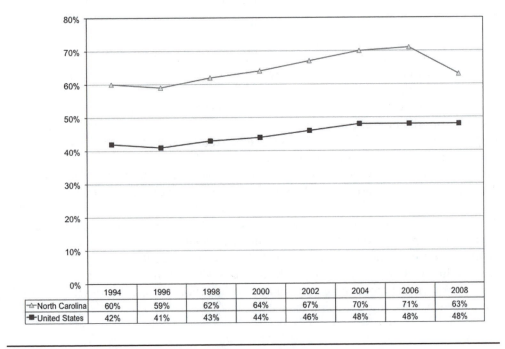

	1994	1996	1998	2000	2002	2004	2006	2008
North Carolina	60%	59%	62%	64%	67%	70%	71%	63%
United States	42%	41%	43%	44%	46%	48%	48%	48%

Figure 12.8 Trends in Percent of North Carolina Students Who Took the SAT

Source: Data from The College Board © 2011 Projects Promoting Equity in Urban and Higher Education, NCID at the University of Michigan.

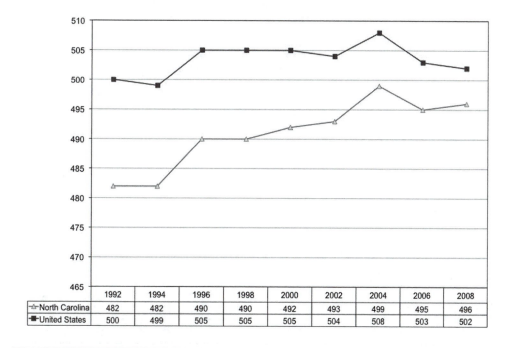

	1992	1994	1996	1998	2000	2002	2004	2006	2008
North Carolina	482	482	490	490	492	493	499	495	496
United States	500	499	505	505	505	504	508	503	502

Figure 12.9 Trends in Average SAT Verbal Score in North Carolina

Source: Data from The College Board © 2011 Projects Promoting Equity in Urban and Higher Education, NCID at the University of Michigan.

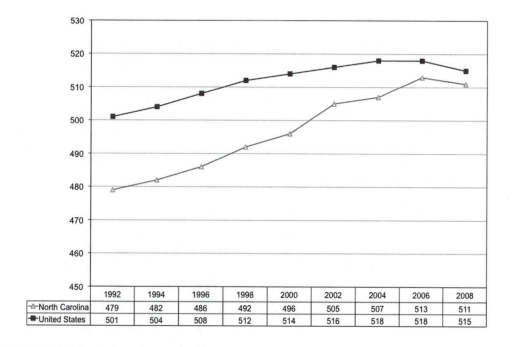

	1992	1994	1996	1998	2000	2002	2004	2006	2008
North Carolina	479	482	486	492	496	505	507	513	511
United States	501	504	508	512	514	516	518	518	515

Figure 12.10 Trends in Average SAT Math Score in North Carolina

Source: Data from The College Board © 2011 Projects Promoting Equity in Urban and Higher Education, NCID at the University of Michigan.

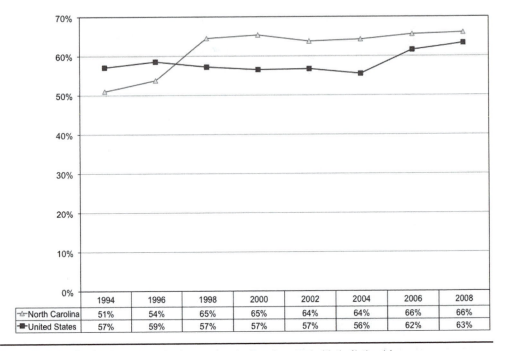

	1994	1996	1998	2000	2002	2004	2006	2008
North Carolina	51%	54%	65%	65%	64%	64%	66%	66%
United States	57%	59%	57%	57%	57%	56%	62%	63%

Figure 12.11 Trends in North Carolina's College Continuation Rate Compared with the National Average

Source: Data from Postsecondary Education Opportunity © 2011 Projects Promoting Equity in Urban and Higher Education, NCID at the University of Michigan.

1998; the rate remained about 65% to 66% through 2008 (Figure 12.11). The shift in the academic preparation standards corresponds with the early shift, indicating a rise in enrollment rates related to a decline in graduation rates (discussed above). But as high school graduation rates climbed in subsequent years, the continuation rate held steady.

From 2004 to 2008, there was no increase in the college continuation rate that corresponded with the increase in funding for student financial aid in the state. In fact, the national rates rose substantially during this period, narrowing the gap compared with North Carolina. However, the role of need-based student financial aid relates to equal opportunity for equally prepared students as well as to access as measured by enrollment rates (St. John, 2003, 2006, Chapter 5).

Trends in 2-year college enrollment rates are similar to the overall numbers with one exception: Native American students are more highly represented, suggesting that their enrollments in 2-year institutions may be driving their overall representation numbers (Figure 12.12). In some states, this overrepresentation in the community college sector might be a consequence of higher attendance rates at tribal colleges, but according to IPEDS, there are no tribal colleges in North Carolina.

Among 4-year public institutions, White and Native American students are slightly underrepresented and Black students are overrepresented. The interesting story here is the substantial decline in the proportion of Asian American students; in 1992, Asian American students were enrolled in public 4-year institutions at more than twice their percentage of the overall population, and that ratio had fallen to slightly more than 1.5 in 2008 (Figure 12.13).

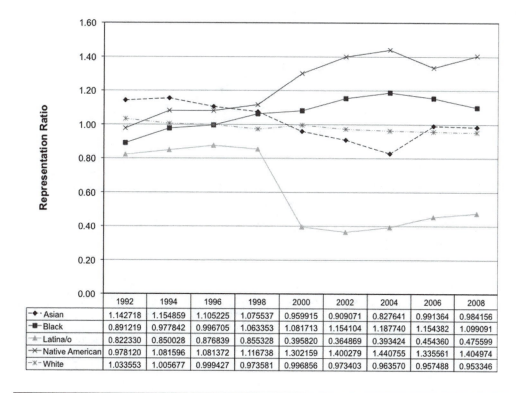

	1992	1994	1996	1998	2000	2002	2004	2006	2008
Asian	1.142718	1.154859	1.105225	1.075537	0.959915	0.909071	0.827641	0.991364	0.984156
Black	0.891219	0.977842	0.996705	1.063353	1.081713	1.154104	1.187740	1.154382	1.099091
Latina/o	0.822330	0.850028	0.876839	0.855328	0.395820	0.364869	0.393424	0.454360	0.475599
Native American	0.978120	1.081596	1.081372	1.116738	1.302159	1.400279	1.440755	1.335561	1.404974
White	1.033553	1.005677	0.999427	0.973581	0.996856	0.973403	0.963570	0.957488	0.953346

Figure 12.12 Trends in Racial/Ethnic Representation in North Carolina Public 2-Year Postsecondary Institutions as a Proportion of the State Population

Source: Data from NCES Integrated Postsecondary Education Data System and U.S. Census Bureau © 2011 Projects Promoting Equity in Urban and Higher Education, NCID at the University of Michigan.

Graduation Rates

The good news is that the gaps are not as great in comparing completion rates by racial/ethnic groups at community colleges (Figure 12.14). The bad news is that all groups graduate at very low rates, hovering between 10% and 20%. Gaps do remain, of course, with White students graduating at the highest rates (above 20%) and African American students earning degrees at a rate of 15%. Latino students graduate at higher rates than other underrepresented minority students, nearly equivalent to White students in 2008.

At 4-year public institutions, White and Asian American students earn bachelor's degrees within 6 years at comparable rates over time. Completion rates among African American and Latino/a students remain fairly constant at nearly 50%, with slight declines in recent years (Figure 12.15). Native American students have experienced greater fluctuations but saw an increase of 6 percentage points from 2007 to 2008—a number that is likely sensitive to relatively low enrollment rates.

CURRENT ISSUES

North Carolina is unique compared with other cases we have considered in this text. We have framed this case as an illustration of the new progressive South, and the

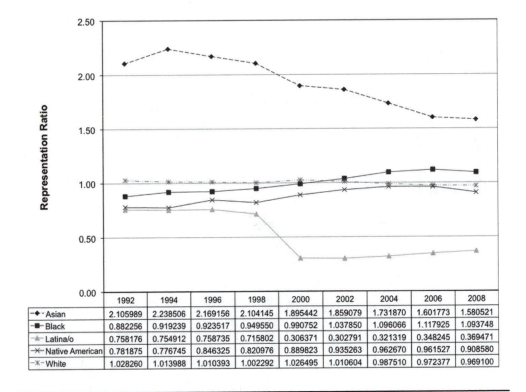

	1992	1994	1996	1998	2000	2002	2004	2006	2008
Asian	2.105989	2.238506	2.169156	2.104145	1.895442	1.859079	1.731870	1.601773	1.580521
Black	0.882256	0.919239	0.923517	0.949550	0.990752	1.037850	1.096066	1.117925	1.093748
Latina/o	0.758176	0.754912	0.758735	0.715802	0.306371	0.302791	0.321319	0.348245	0.369471
Native American	0.781875	0.776745	0.846325	0.820976	0.889823	0.935263	0.962670	0.961527	0.908580
White	1.028260	1.013988	1.010393	1.002292	1.026495	1.010604	0.987510	0.972377	0.969100

Figure 12.13 Trends in Racial/Ethnic Representation in North Carolina Public 4-Year Postsecondary Institutions as a Proportion of the State Population

Source: Data from NCES Integrated Postsecondary Education Data System and U.S. Census Bureau © 2011 Projects Promoting Equity in Urban and Higher Education, NCID at the University of Michigan.

developments in public funding of higher education reinforce this description. From 2006 to 2009, North Carolina increased its state support for public higher education appropriations by more than 26%. From 2009 to 2011, state contributions declined only once, which was more than offset by stimulus funding. During that period, funding for higher education grew by 9.4% and even when stimulus funds were not considered, the state contribution grew by 6.2% (Palmer, 2011). Few states in the country have been able to maintain that level of commitment to public higher education during this recessionary downturn. At the same time, tuition and fees at the UNC system are among the lowest in the country, averaging under $5,000 annually at the regional campuses and only $6,625 at Chapel Hill (National Center for Education Statistics, 2011). North Carolina is what we describe as a relatively low-tuition high-aid state.

In terms of maintaining its commitment to college access and success, North Carolina has seen developments in three key policy areas—academic preparation, college cost, and access to information and support. North Carolina was an early adopter of state course requirements for high school completion, which will be ratcheted up in the coming years. The state has continued its comprehensive support of the neediest students in the state both by keeping tuition low and maintaining its commitment to need-based aid. Finally, North Carolina has been a leader and pioneer in terms of developing the

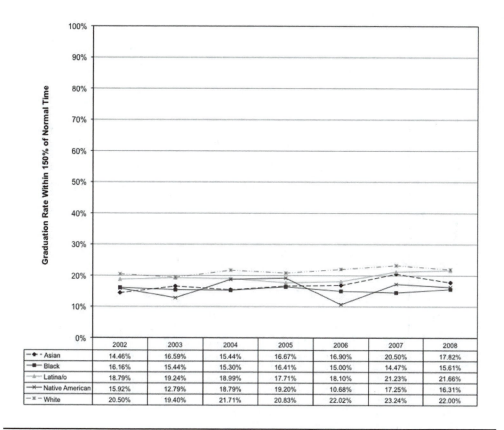

	2002	2003	2004	2005	2006	2007	2008
Asian	14.46%	16.59%	15.44%	16.67%	16.90%	20.50%	17.82%
Black	16.16%	15.44%	15.30%	16.41%	15.00%	14.47%	15.61%
Latina/o	18.79%	19.24%	18.99%	17.71%	18.10%	21.23%	21.66%
Native American	15.92%	12.79%	18.79%	19.20%	10.68%	17.25%	16.31%
White	20.50%	19.40%	21.71%	20.83%	22.02%	23.24%	22.00%

Figure 12.14 Trends in Graduation Rates in North Carolina Public 2-Year Postsecondary Institutions

Source: Data from NCES Integrated Postsecondary Education Data System © 2011 Projects Promoting Equity in Urban and Higher Education, NCID at the University of Michigan.

tools and resources to connect students and parents to the information and support they need to navigate college. Even with challenges to state budgets, North Carolina appears to be unwavering in its commitment to postsecondary access, which shows in its policy choices.

High School Graduation Requirements

To this point, North Carolina high school students have had the option to pursue one of four separate pathways to the high school diploma—career prep, college technical prep, college/university prep, and the occupational course of study (for students with "cognitive disabilities"). Beginning with the 9th grade class of 2009 (scheduled to graduate in 2013), the state has shifted to a college preparatory curriculum, the future-ready core, with an occupational alternative for those who qualify. The new consolidated curriculum will require all students to complete 4 years of English, 3 years of social studies, four math courses (including algebra I, geometry, and algebra II), and 3 years of science (including one physical, one biological, and one environmental science). In addition, it stipulates that while foreign language is not a requirement for a diploma, two courses are required for admission to UNC. The social studies requirement becomes more specific regarding U.S. history requirements for the graduating class of 2017. Like many of the

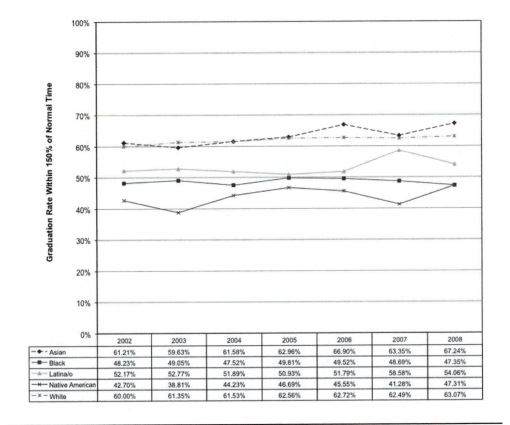

Figure 12.15 Trends in Graduation Rates in North Carolina Public 4-Year Postsecondary Institutions

Source: Data from NCES Integrated Postsecondary Education Data System © 2011 Projects Promoting Equity in Urban and Higher Education, NCID at the University of Michigan.

states highlighted in this text, North Carolina will transition to a more rigorous academic curriculum, which may pose a challenge for some students. If the experience in North Carolina is similar to that in other states, students who complete the more rigorous academic curriculum will be better prepared to succeed in college, which will have to be weighed against possible declines in high school graduation rates.

Maintaining Low Costs for College

Although North Carolinians may have concerns about the rising cost of college to students and parents (i.e., higher tuition), there are few states that have maintained such relative affordability, especially at its public flagship institution (Ferreri & Price, 2011). North Carolina has demonstrated that, at least relative to other states, it can keep tuition low and fund need-based aid sufficient to cover the remaining costs of college for the highest-need students. The state maintains three separate means-tested aid programs for students: the Community College Grant, the Education Lottery Grant, and the UNC Need-Based Grant. These programs reduce the costs of the Covenant and other campus-based programs that commit to meet the financial need of students. Two of these programs are targeted to North Carolina residents admitted to either a community college in the state or another eligible college in North Carolina, enroll in a minimum of two courses, and maintain satisfactory academic progress. The final program is need-based but is not limited to state residents; the only stipulation is that they attend one of the UNC institutions. The combination of these three programs allows the state to maintain its commitment to meeting the needs of low-income students and, unlike other states, extends its reach to out-of-state students who demonstrate a similar level of need.

Connecting Students and Parents to Information and Support

Since the creation of the College Access Challenge Grant (CACG), allocated by the U.S. Department of Education as a block grant to states, most states across the country have made efforts to address the informational needs of students and parents, particularly through the creation of comprehensive web portals. North Carolina was a leader in this movement and developed its strategy well before the CACG was introduced. Under the leadership of the College Foundation of North Carolina and the University of North Carolina system, the state has launched a comprehensive social marketing and process improvement plan for college admission. In 2001, CFNC partnered with Xap, Inc., to create a comprehensive web portal to consolidate all of the information and resources North Carolina students and parents need to navigate the college choice process. Unique to North Carolina perhaps as a result of fortunate timing, the North Carolina web portal is the primary place for students to submit their college applications online. In other states, the college applications may be available through a portal, but none requires students to use the portal to submit an electronic application. In conjunction with the portal, North Carolina has engaged in a social marketing campaign to encourage students and parents to use the web portal for all of their college choice questions. Finally, as an expansion of the popular College Goal Sunday designed to help students and parents complete the Free Application for Federal Student Aid (FAFSA), North Carolina has extended that program for an entire week and added the completion of college applications. These efforts raise awareness of college opportunity and streamline the choice process for students and parents. Initial findings suggest that the portal has become the point of entry for many North Carolina students into higher education—more than 300,000 online applications were submitted through the web portal in 2008 (College Foundation of North Carolina, 2009). To the extent that the college choice process is a primary barrier to college, it appears that North Carolina has developed a strategy to overcome the barrier with a great deal of potential.

CONCLUSIONS

North Carolina demonstrates an alternative pathway through the puzzle of the relationships between public policy and outcomes related to academic preparation, access, and academic success. We have characterized the state's policies as progressive as a comparative judgment related both to the history of desegregation in the South and recent policy changes that emphasize need-based student financial aid. In that comparative sense, the trends in policy reinforce such a narrative. Further, there has been a pattern of improvement in outcomes in North Carolina. Trends in outcomes do not always respond immediately to shifts in policy, a factor evident in North Carolina, across the state cases, and in the national patterns. Research that reviews policies in relation to outcomes provides the primary tool for policy analysis and the development of rationales for policy change. As a conclusion, we pose a few questions pertaining to the North Carolina case and the uses of policy indicators (Text Box 12.1).

**Text Box 12.1 Questions About the North Carolina Case and
the Use of Policy Indicators**

1. How do the policy developments in North Carolina reflect the liberal tradition of public policy in higher education? How does the North Carolina case compare with the California case?

2. Was the development of the Carolina Covenant a campus development that could have influenced the changes in public finance policies in the state? How might a case study research project be designed to test this proposition?

3. Does the concept of progressive policy differ from old liberal arguments about higher education?

4. What role do you think North Carolina's approach to desegregation played in the subsequent policies that supported higher education?

5. How do the trends in preparation outcomes in North Carolina correspond with policy changes on preparation and research on this topic?

6. How do the trends in access and diversity correspond with changes in preparation and diversity policies?

7. Are there relationships between trends in degree attainment and policies on preparation and public finance in North Carolina?

The Use of Policy Indicators

8. State and federal policies in K–12 education have used test scores and other indicators to hold schools "accountable" for their outcomes. From your analysis of the research and the cases, does the use of such indicators have some validity?

9. Given that policy indicators have been proposed as a policy lever in federal funding of higher education (e.g. prorating funding for student aid to reported outcomes), and that related performance funding is used in some states, do indicators provide a tool that can be used for public accountability in higher education?

10. If indicators can be used to somehow hold schools and colleges/universities accountable, can they also be used as a means of holding policymakers accountable for their decisions about education policy in relation to student outcomes?

11. How can public interest groups make use of policy indicators—trends in policy decisions and funding in relation to outcomes—as a means of public information for voters and activists?

12. When has policy trend data been misused in the development of public policy? How can researchers and policymakers develop safeguards to avoid the misuse of policy indicators?

Part III
Reframing Strategies

13

REFRAMING POLICY DECISIONS

The first serious question we face as a society when we ponder the future of higher education is: How can we adapt the rationales used to argue for a public role in higher education—along with the logics used in support of various policy preferences—as we engage in problem solving? John Rawls (1971, 2001) argued that fairness should guide public choices, especially the principles of basic liberties for all, while still grappling with existing differences (the least advantaged should receive preference). Although it has been argued that the two principles have merit as lenses for examining patterns of change in higher education (e.g., St. John, 2003, 2006), the current trajectory of public policy illustrates that different values are at work now than in the past. Amartya Sen (2009) offers choice theory as an alternative to the use of universal principles to guide public choices, providing a framework for bringing a greater emphasis on fairness into the policy discourse.

This chapter addresses policy decisions within the current trajectory of policy on higher education. We review the patterns that emerge across the analyses of trends at the state and federal levels. The overarching question for readers to consider is this: What adjustments to current policies are possible to improve fairness given the current ideological underpinnings of globalization?

PATTERNS OF CHANGE IN HIGHER EDUCATION

The big pattern of change in higher education has been the shift in the trajectory toward equal opportunity from the 1950s through the 1980s back to a period of greater inequality. The sad irony is that the period of national leadership from the founding of the U.S. Department of Education through the decades of K–16 reform strategies did not result in equality, although enrollment in higher education did expand at a lower cost per student for taxpayers (St. John, 2003, 2006). These developments are reasonably aligned with what could be construed as a compromise between neoconservative arguments for less public funding per student and neoliberal arguments expanding opportunity for all, irrespective of previous or current inequality. More minorities and Whites are going to college today than 30 years ago; they just aren't going to the same colleges, and they are still not going at the same rates. The economic stratification of colleges—the fact that middle-achieving low-income students are more likely to attend low-cost public or community colleges than their wealthier peers of similar achievement who can afford the full cost of elite public or private colleges—may be a consequence of these compromises.

American society has realized benefits in higher education for the investment made, but the critiques of education continue, along with the inequality and poor funding. The older arguments about a general social good coupled with cross-generation uplift have not been compelling enough to gain support for policies that maintain equality in opportunity and quality of education in the K–12 and higher education systems. Whereas we think the older values of social uplift and public investment should be given priority or at the very least a place in the conversation, we acknowledge the long-standing concern about taxpayer costs promoted as part of the neoconservative agenda (St. John, 1994a, 2003).

Regardless of the position readers take on the problems and paradoxes of the current policy trajectory in higher education and other social programs, there is a clash among the old liberal, conservative, neoconservative, and neoliberal arguments about the public role in education; as education becomes increasingly important as an economic engine in a global economy, those arguments are only going to intensify. A new image of the public good may be needed in the face of these ideological clashes. Our approach to this serious problem is to review the lessons learned from the study of policy trends and outcomes and to raise questions for readers of various persuasions to consider. Labaree (1997) recognized the tension among various ideologies more than a decade ago, with his competing goals framework for understanding the social goals of education. He contends that as a society, we hold three sets of expectations for education that are constantly in tension: the private good, which is encapsulated in our individualist notions of social mobility, and two separate public goods, one valuing social efficiency and the other democratic equality. Labaree contends that we have come to value social mobility at the expense of the other two goals and, as a consequence, have placed a premium on obtaining the credential rather than learning. Today, the ideological battles are largely fought between neoconservative defenses of private benefits and neoliberal support of stronger social efficiency, the result of which is political compromise devoid of meaningful representation for democratic equality.

The Federal Level

In 1980, when the U.S. Department of Education was formed, the neoliberal education agenda had already taken form: the Education Consolidation and Improvement Act of 1980 introduced the ideal of merging and rationalizing federal action as means of achieving greater good, possibly for less expenditure, and the Middle Income Student Assistance Act of 1978 lifted the income cap for student aid, creating challenges to funding Title IV programs for low-income students. The subsequent changes moved the United States further down a new trajectory that was forming under federal leadership:

- *A Nation at Risk* (U.S. Department of Education, 1983) introduced a new agenda for national standards and accountability that has been realized, albeit in a form different than imagined by those who envisioned it (e.g., Ravitch, 2010; see also Chapter 4). It pointed the finger squarely at high schools and left postsecondary education off the hook.

- The federal government student aid system shifted its student aid strategy from grants to loans, a policy that corresponded with rises in tuition and concomitant rises in student loan debt (Chapter 5).
- Degree completion rates slowed and inequalities in completion rates widened, but at a slower rate than would have been expected given the rise in tuition and the net costs of education (Chapter 6).

The increasing emphasis on academic preparation in high school and on postsecondary encouragement provided agendas for reformers. Federal research supported these new agendas and underlying problems with financial access, and economic stratification of higher education opportunity went without serious attention from federal policymakers or the researchers they funded. It wasn't until the Advisory Committee on Student Financial Assistance (2002), a congressional advisory group, did so, that a federal agency addressed these problems, which had taken shape decades earlier. Although agendas for improved preparation and the dissemination of trustworthy information to encourage preparation for postsecondary access provided a focal point for reform-minded educators and researchers, the underlying problems limiting financial access—the decline in federal grant aid and the inequality of K–12 schools—were difficult to address because they emphasized the need of underrepresented groups rather than rights for all. The argument we have seldom forcefully or effectively made is that individual self-interest is best served when the least advantaged in society are provided more targeted support to access opportunities like postsecondary education (Rawls, 1971, 2001).

In spite of these developments, many groups continue to advocate for reducing inequalities in educational opportunity, in part because of global competition (Chapter 3). Questions that merit attention by researchers and policy advocates who focus on federal policy are noted in Text Box 13.1.

These questions are stated as though it were possible to change the current trajectory in K–12 reform. While there are reasons to question the dominant reform

---

Text Box 13.1 Questions About Policy on Academic Preparation

1. How can the education reform agenda be reconstructed to address the inequalities in funding for schools?

2. How can we rethink P–16 education finance in ways that do not place K–12 and higher education in competition with one another for scarce and declining state revenues?

3. Does the evidence from states support arguments that the current market model of charters competing with public schools has been effective? Based on the comparison of states, do you think the federal framework in K–12 provides a sufficient basis for improving high school preparation?

4. How do the current education standards help or hinder the efforts to improve urban education?

5. Are the current accountability and testing standards working for urban, suburban, and rural schools? How can policy be better crafted to enable failing schools to improve the education they provide?

strategies—including evidence that urban public schools face curriculum constraints that make it difficult to compete with charter schools (St. John et al., in press), and charter schools do not yet outperform public schools (Ravitch, 2010)—it is indeed too soon to alter the agenda of raising high schools to college preparatory standards. Fortunately this agenda has not yet been implemented. There remains a need to ponder what the standards should be, including whether they should be differentiated to broaden the acceptable fields of preparation beyond science, technology, engineering, and math (STEM), along with how to craft policy to support movement toward those standards.

It is far more difficult to bring the financing of higher education back into a balance that encourages equalizing opportunities across racial and income groups in ways that are fairer to the least advantaged. The federal government played a major role in equalizing enrollment opportunities in the 1960s and 1970s, so there is a history showing that it is possible, but being realistic means recognizing both neoliberal values for all students (equal treatment) over targeting subsidies to those with the greatest needs and the neoconservative critique of additional taxation. Given these serious constraints on federal financing of higher education, we raise a few questions about student aid in Text Box 13.2.

Although there is an uneasy consensus between the neoliberals and neoconservatives with respect to education reform, there is no such consensus with respect to student financial aid. Much as the case has been with K–12 funding debates, funding conversations in higher education (including financial aid) are taking a back seat to discussions of accountability for student learning. Advocates of student financial aid must recognize the difficulty of arguing for more funding, the need to build coalitions across parties to

---

Text Box 13.2 Questions About Financial Aid

1. Has the average debt burden for college graduates risen to a level that makes it difficult for students to pursue careers in the public interest (i.e., teaching, public law, etc.)?

2. Are loan forgiveness policies sufficient to encourage enough students to pursue these careers?

3. Is it possible to maintain a commitment to grant funding that pays the cost of attendance minus family ability to pay (that is, to maintain high standard of equity)?

4. Is it possible to maintain a commitment to funding grants and subsidized loans to pay the costs of education minus expected family and student contribution (that is, to maintain a minimum standard of equity)?

5. Would collaboration with states, such as sharing the costs of grants, make it easier for the federal government to meet either the high or minimum standard for equity?

6. Do arguments for improving opportunities for higher education through reduced debt and increased grants offer a compelling case for using more federal tax dollars for student financial aid?

support reinvestment in student aid, and that the commitment to fund grants may require reductions in other federal programs, possibly even institutional support programs

State Policy on Finance and Accountability

States have the Constitutional responsibility for education. In the case of K–12 education, the right to equal access is established within most state constitutions and, to some extent, has been ensured by the 14th Amendment to the U.S. Constitution (Chapter 3), but access to higher education generally has remained at the level of an individual right, with no legal basis to litigate for equal financial access. For example, the *White v. Engler* case in Michigan (Chapter 11) was eventually dropped because intentional racial discrimination could not be proven in spite of substantial evidence of racial inequality in the awarding of aid due to differences in high schools (St. John & Chung, 2004). In other words, without a general consensus valuing equity within a state, there are no legal foundations to pursue equality in access to higher education.

State frameworks provide the basis for arguments about coherence in policy on higher education within a state. However, older frameworks are now confronted and even crumbling as a result of the new beliefs about equal rights to K–12 education and neoconservative arguments about cutting taxes. For example, California's historic master plan and Michigan's proud history of constitutional autonomy for 4-year colleges have not provided sufficient rationales for continuing historic funding patterns; the old arguments about the social and economic benefits of investment in higher education have not held up in relation to new arguments, resulting in high tuition with limited need-based aid in both states. The case states with newer frameworks—Minnesota, Florida, and Indiana—have withstood the negative effects of the new rationales somewhat better than California and Michigan but are contending with erosion of the public will to fund higher education at historic levels. Not only are tuition charges rising in public colleges as a consequence of the loss of state funding, many states are using new accountability and performance-funding mechanisms as means of monitoring and distributing declining amounts of subsidies to colleges and universities.

Below we compare the case states with respect to their policies on preparation, access, and college success, with an explicit focus on the role of state frameworks. We conclude each of the summary analyses with questions for readers.

Academic Preparation

All six case states had taken steps to raise high school graduation requirements, consistent with national trends and positions advocated in national research. Yet there were differences across the states in gains in access and equity during the period studied. The differences in outcomes illustrate some of the underlying complexities of interactions between state frameworks and newer arguments about education reform to prepare students for college.

Of the case states, only Michigan until recently has a history of local discretion in setting graduation requirements. There was a sudden shift from local control to a constrained state curriculum in Michigan that was like a shock wave that has already resulted in a drop in ACT scores attributable to use of this test as a state 11th-grade exam. The history of a state role in setting graduation requirements made it easier to make the transition in the other states. For example, Indiana had a history of requiring that schools offer a college preparatory curriculum before the new Core 40 requirements became the state's default curriculum. But all six case states had problems with the implementation of the new standards.

An underlying problem has been that critiques of state funding undermined support for the professional development needed to make the transitions in state requirements. In particular, schools in California and Michigan were adjusting to cuts in school funding at the same time they were implementing new curricula. More generally, the dual aspects of the current policy paradox—the push on schools to do more with less funding—has placed a strain on school reform. The research on states shows school funding has a positive effect on the preparation outcomes the new standards aim to effect (Daun-Barnett & St. John, 2012; St. John, 2006). Increased funding coupled with standards-based reform is needed.

There appears to be an indirect effect of higher education affordability on school preparation outcomes. Policies like Indiana's Twenty-First Century Scholars have demonstrated that early guarantees of student aid encourage preparation (Chapter 10). The linking mechanism relates to social-psychological perceptions of college affordability, but there is strong empirical evidence that availability of student aid also has an impact on preparation (Bishop, 2002, 2004; St. John, 2006).[1] Thus the cohesiveness of state frameworks matters in preparation: students and families develop their own expectations about engagement in high school based on their own observations and expectations about the future (St. John, Hu, & Fisher, 2011).

The question is not whether states will raise standards for education, but rather how well will they lay the groundwork for and support the development of a new American model of college preparatory high schools? The ways states construct cohesive frameworks matters. To stimulate reflection on these issues, we encourage readers to reflect on the questions based on the national data and state cases (Text Box 13.3).

Access and Diversity

College access is a complicated matter because of the racial and economic stratification in access to 4-year colleges. The national trends and state cases reveal that community colleges and for-profit colleges are accessible, although the costs and the amount of debt required for access vary across the two types of open-access colleges. In addition, the comparison of states reveals that both state frameworks and policy decisions matter. The trends in racial representation in 4-year colleges (Chapter 5) illustrate a narrowing of the gap in enrollment for African Americans and Whites this decade, but not for Latinas/os.

Text Box 13.3 Questions About Cases: Academic Preparation

1. Are variations over time in test scores and high school graduation rates within the state cases related to the implementation of new standards for graduation?

2. How can K–12 and higher education policies be better coordinated to ensure fairness in preparation for and access to 4-year colleges?

3. How can states strengthen the coherence of state K–12 frameworks and both academic and financial alignment with higher education?

The California master plan provided a guiding framework for the development of the state higher education systems in California that was followed and adapted across the United States. The other five states had the three types of public institutions—research universities, state colleges and universities, and community colleges—along with private colleges. However, there are great differences in the ways states coordinate state systems, ranging from voluntary coordination in Michigan to a coordinating council in California. The cohesion of the systems is important with respect to the forms of access provided, but having mechanisms for coordination is only part of the story of access and stratification.

Another part of the story is the financial mechanisms used to ensure equitable access and expand supply of opportunity. In California there is substantial racial and economic stratification across the three systems, a factor related to the slow expansion of state systems after 1980 and the constraints on tax revenues. Rather than using a market approach like Minnesota or Indiana, California adhered to the low-tuition strategy and constrained development of new systems, limiting capacity and causing drops in access. The Minnesota and Indiana models of coordinating need-based aid with tuition increases have proven workable, but the stability of these models depends on the will of legislative bodies to support students when funding for institutions declines. The Florida merit aid strategy offers an interesting contrast: the differentiated threshold of achievement functions as a form of coordination to support the expansion of access across institutional types, but this model also proved difficult to maintain when confronted by tax revenue constraints. In contrast, North Carolina took a distinctive path in the 2000s, adopting financial aid policies that promoted equal opportunity.

We characterized the North Carolina case as a new progressive model. In the early 20th century, the state managed to maintain low tuition for residents while raising state investment in need-based aid, counter to the pattern evident nationally and in most states. The University of North Carolina's Carolina Covenant provided the logic for expanding access, improving diversity, increasing test scores for minority students, and reducing gaps in retention and degree completion. Given that other states with high grant strategies, like Minnesota and Indiana, have backed away from this approach, it is important to see how well North Carolina can maintain support for high grants and whether this approach improves access and diversity while reducing gaps in retention. If the UNC example proves successful in North Carolina, then perhaps there will be increasing support for improving college affordability in other states.

In theory, using need-based student financial aid as a market mechanism creates incentives for private colleges to expand access and can, again in theory, drive down the total cost of higher education (i.e., subsidies per student for tuition reduction plus student aid). But even when state systems provide these incentives, as was evident in most of our state cases, the privatized systems generally did not equalize opportunity, especially in access to 4-year colleges. There was evidence in Indiana that when a stable state grant program was maintained over more than a decade, private nonprofit colleges expanded access for minority students and reduced the gaps in completion. While there was not equity in 4-year enrollment, the private colleges in Indiana did expand opportunity for African Americans, in contrast with national trends.

Another complicating factor is the effect of performance funding when these policies are implemented in contexts with declining state support for higher education, as has recently been the case in Minnesota and Indiana. As a policy mechanism, performance funding is closely aligned with neoliberal ideologies of fair treatment of all. The choices about which performance indicators merit additional funds are political and could have distributional effects on enrollment due to the redistribution of funds and the incentives. The efficacy of this policy mechanism can be undermined when total state funding for public higher education declines.

We examined the relationships between trends in policies and trends in related outcomes and have noted some of the patterns evident within and across states. Racial/ethnic representation within and across sectors in higher education varied substantially, sometimes in correspondence with policy shifts in state funding, as did the overall college continuation rate (ratio of high school graduates to college enrollees). We encourage readers to reflect on questions about the relationships between policies and outcomes (Text Box 13.4).

Text Box 13.4 Questions on State Cases:
State Policies in Relation to Race/Ethnic Representation

1. There were substantial differences in racial representation in public and private 4-year institutions across the case study states. How do state histories and financial strategies relate to trends in racial representation?

2. How do trends in racial representation in public 2-year colleges within states vary in relation to state finance policies?

3. How do state academic and financial aid policies correspond with changes related to the narrowing access gap for African Americans in private nonprofit 4-year institutions? In for-profit colleges?

4. What is the place of the for-profit sector in the U.S. system of higher education? How can they be leveraged to increase both access to college and successful completion of degrees? Is it problematic that African American students are so heavily overrepresented in these institutions?

5. How does the history of states (i.e., the frameworks used in K–16 education) relate to differences across states in patterns of access and racial representation?

6. How has the shift from differential high school graduation standards (vocational, regular, and college preparatory) to higher graduate standards for all (i.e., the new college preparation requirements variously implemented across states) influence the distribution of students across the sectors of higher education within states?

7. How do state policies on tuition subsidies for immigrants influence college access among a growing sector of the U.S. population?

8. How do your understandings of patterns of change inform your positions on:
   a. Strategies for funding of public institutions?
   b. Funding of merit and/or need-based aid programs?
   c. Coordination of K–12 and higher education funding strategies?
   d. Strategies for aligning high school graduation requirements with admission standards at different types of institutions?

College completion has become a new frontier for policy deliberations in states. When tuition rises and/or student aid declines, it is more difficult for students to pay for college. Students from low- and middle-income families often have to work and borrow more to pay the costs of attending, especially 4-year colleges. The overall downward trends in higher education finance could undermine college success rates. As states come up with new approaches for promoting retention, public officials need to compare the effects of the new strategies to the older ones being replaced to build an understanding of the effects of policy changes.

One mechanism being used to encourage retention is to change the ways subsidies are delivered to colleges and their students. Performance funding systems rewarding colleges for improvement in graduation rates are one of the mechanisms states have used to pursue this goal. Performance funding is usually limited to public colleges (with the exception of programs like Bundy aid in New York), and the effect of this form of targeted funding should be compared to the effects of total funding. The logic of formula funding eroded long ago in most states, but there is still a base rate of per student subsidies against which the newer funding schemes must be compared. It is difficult to untangle the effects of some forms of funding being directed to reward retention when overall state funding for colleges is declining. Such questions need to be asked as states move forward in this new era of promoting degree completion.

Using high need-based student aid in market systems was another method states used to promote retention. Private colleges have higher completion rates than public colleges, and high grants can have a positive effect on enrollment and completion at these campuses (e.g., the Indiana case). The rates of completion in private nonprofit colleges vary across states. It is possible that state frameworks—the historic combination of preparation strategies and financial aid programs—have differential effects on public and private 4-year colleges, but there is not yet much empirical evidence to confirm such a hypothesis. At this point, it is crucial to consider how high-aid market-based systems promote academic success in both public and private colleges.

There are also substantial gaps in completion rates between public 2-year colleges and private for-profit institutions. It is important to recognize that (1) some community colleges are developing 4-year degrees (e.g., Florida) and (2) for-profit colleges enroll a high number of underprepared students. So public 2-year and for-profit colleges are not directly comparable although they compete in similar markets. Many states provide aid to students in for-profit colleges (e.g., Indiana and Minnesota), so state aid could be a factor in addition to the federal aid from which both community colleges and for-profit institutions benefit.[2] Other factors related to differences between for-profit and public 2-year colleges may explain difference in their success rates.

Public colleges are the most critical group of institutions with respect to public strategies for improving retention and degree completion. In addition to performance funding, the alternative of using research with state data systems as a basis for informing interventions merits further testing. The limited evidence discussed in the Indiana case indicates this approach may have some merit (see also St. John & Musoba, 2010), but, as is the case with performance funding, there is no empirical evidence that research-based approaches make a difference.

Given the uncertainties about the future of state policies on retention, it is important to ponder differences in patterns of attainment across states—patterns that could be related to state frameworks along with differences over time within states. We encourage readers to consider a final set of question about the cases (Text Box 13.5).

> **Text Box 13.5 Questions About Academic Preparation
> and Human Capabilities**
>
> 1. Are the humanities (pondering the meaning of action and justice) and critical thinking (engaging in civic programs to support the public good) an important part of high school education along with preparation for science and math education in college?
>
> 2. How can market models of K–12 education be adapted to encourage liberal education that informs students about the range of advanced subjects and related career pathways at the same time as they build content-linked curriculums with career pathways?
>
> 3. What types of student and family support services are needed in high school to inform and support families as they navigate the new pathways between middle schools, high schools, and colleges?
>
> 4. How can college outreach help students and families as they adjust to the new system of education and make choices in preparing for college?

REFRAMING THE POLICY DECISION PROCESS

We raise these questions to encourage readers to ponder their own predispositions toward policy remedies, along with the ways past remedies relate to outcomes. Throughout this book we have been careful to consider recent research along with trends on state policy outcomes. Our thesis has been that policymakers react to trends when constructing policy but generally do not consider research on policy effects in crafting remedies to problems. Whereas most research focuses on the efficacy of one type of remedy or another (Chapters 4 through 6), it is also possible to construct policy research and technical support for change as processes involving learning-oriented research based on collaborations between researchers and policymakers.

Public Choice Framework

The idea that researchers can work with policymakers to bring the voices of citizens into policy is compelling but requires a shift in assumptions about justice and practice as well as the nature of the policymaking process. The idea that there are principles of justice that can inform research, the metaframework used in the scientific approach to educational research, leads to the idea that research on best practices can inform policy development. The analyses of trends in federal policy and state cases illustrate that this idealization of policy decisions has serious limitations. Based on the analysis of the roles and potential for policy research in promoting just social change (St. John, in press), we suggest an alternative framework, starting with alternative assumptions and followed by alternative concepts of the policy choice process and an illustrative example.

Although John Rawls's (1971, 2001) concepts of justice have applicability to deliberations on policy and finance in higher education, especially with respect to policy formation addressing inequality (St. John, 2003, 2006), they have serious limitations due to underlying assumptions about actual behavior, the social contract, and the relevance of a global perspective. Amartya Sen (1999) has long argued for a human capabilities approach to economics that focuses on the development of people rather than a human capital approach that reduces people to their economic products. The human capabilities approach provides a basis for arguing that access to quality K–12 education is a basic right, but the difference principle or an alternative that recognizes the interests of diverse groups is needed for a reconstructed understanding of equal opportunity.

In *The Idea of Justice,* Sen (2009) undertakes a comprehensive rethinking of Rawls's theory of justice adapted for the human capabilities concepts. He discusses the limitations of the Rawlsian approach, identifying three major problems.

First, Sen recognized the problems with Rawls's concept of reasonable behavior: "The mere acceptance of some principles as forming the right 'political conception of justice' does not resolve this issue if the theory of justice sought is to have any kind of applicability in choice of institutions in actual society" (p. 68). It is critically important to consider the intended goals of educational policy in relation to outcome, a basic concept guiding our approach in this book. Sen's argument introduces the idea that the extent of choice can differ within a society, which is a reason for considering outcomes and disparities across groups. We suggest an alternative assumption about the policy process: *Assessments of critical challenges and evaluation of policies should consider actual behaviors and outcomes rather than the intent of policy.*

Second, Rawls's social contract gave leeway to institutions based on intent of decision makers. Sen (2009) argued it is necessary to deal "with comparative assessment and not merely transcendental solutions…taking note of social realizations and not merely the demands of institutions and rules" (p. 70). He further argued that when "providing guidance in important problems of social justice" it was necessary to take "note of voices of membership" (p. 70). Thus he supports a more activist approach to addressing problems of inequality than Rawls. We suggest that a second assumption of an alternative view of policy decision is: *Comparative assessments of processes and outcomes within and across systems provide means of bringing diverse voices and experiences into policy deliberations.*

Third, Sen argued for "global assessment of fairness rather than *within* a society" (p. 72, italics in original). Sen departs from Rawls's notion that rights should be determined by nation states, reinforcing the capabilities approach for identifying human rights as a general standard consistent with the human rights movement during the global transition. This argument relates to the ongoing struggle to address the rights of immigrant groups and others disenfranchised by a nationalist frame within states and the nation. Specifically, if rights are universal and related to being human rather than legal status within nations, policies like the DREAM Act are as critical to addressing systemic inequalities as were the efforts to desegregate education in the 20th century. We propose a third assumption of an alternative perspective on policy: *A focus on policies that build the capabilities of people to contribute to the social good, recognizing differences within systems, has greater economic and social value than choices rationalized on the basis of efficiency.*

Sen's critiques provide a better, more workable basis for altering the ways we conceive of the relationships between policymaking, policy research, and integrating citizen's voices into the policy process. The three alternative assumptions have guided and informed our analyses and we encourage readers to consider problems within systems, rather than relying on principles and political arguments. We take this approach a step further by suggesting an alternative perspective on policy. We encourage readers to think

Table 13.1 Framing Action-Oriented Policy Research: Comparison of Sen's Concept of Voice and Social Choice With a Critical-Empirical Approach in Policy Research Coupled With Action Inquiry in Institutions

Sen's Voice and Social Choice	Critical-Empirical Approach to Research (Policy Level)	Action Inquiry (Institutional Level)	Reframing Action-Oriented Policy Decisions (Policy and Practice)
Focus on the comparative not just the transcendental	Focus on a social problem, including rights to quality education (or services) and equity in opportunity	Assessment using cohort data plus evaluation of reform to inform discussion of challenges	Focus on challenging recurrent social (and educational) problems
Recognition of the inescapable plurality of competing principles	Discern claims about linkages between policies and outcomes	Identify critical, recurrent, and unresolved social challenges	Identify critical unresolved issues that merit scrutiny and practical local solutions
Allowing and facilitating re-examination	Amass evidence (reviews, quantitative studies, and qualitative studies providing voices)	Organize teams to address challenges using action inquiry	Use evidence-based policy reform as framework for encouraging action inquiry
Permissibility of partial solutions	Examine evidence from research in relation to initial claims from divergent views	Build understanding of problem and look internally and externally for possible solutions	Recognize importance of problem solving in relation to constraints in policy and practice
Diversity of interpretation and inputs	Provide analysis of the relative effects of different possible solutions, considering divergent political views	Assess alternatives to the status quo and synthesize into possible solutions	Consider all feasible proposed solutions and promote informed policy choices and institutional strategies
Emphasize precise articulation and reasoning	Engage in reconstruction of theory and/or policy	Treat interventions as pilot tests, use evaluative studies as evidence to inform policy choices	Use research to inform policy adaptation (laws, regulations, and budgets); encourage adaptation to address challenges
Role of public reasoning in social choice	Use research to inform public policy and institutional decisions	Reconstruct intervention methods based on evidence and align strategies with institutional planning and budgeting	Public dissemination of research; partnerships with policymakers; and alliances with practitioners

Source: St. John, in press.

about how concepts of justice should be reframed as part of the process of addressing inequalities in educational opportunities.

Sen (2009) also provided an alternative perspective of bringing the voices of people affected by policy into the policy discourse through adaptation of social choice theory. He suggests a process approach to policy that provides means of addressing inequalities created by policy:

1. *Focusing on the comparative, not just the transcendental:* Sen argues that comparing conditions of groups affected by policy provides means of differentiating access and the practical reasons behind these differences.
2. *Recognition of the inescapable plurality of competing principles:* It is important to use a framework that concentrates on the relational and practical aspects of decisions and how principles conflict with each other.
3. *Allowing and facilitating reexamination:* Sen argues that it is not only necessary to consider the plurality of reasons for action and take note of the possibility of conflicts but also to reexamine critical issues as policies and their consequences unfold (examine whether policies intended to reduce inequality have results consonant with intent).
4. *Permissibility of partial solutions:* The strategies considered may not fully resolve conflict, so it is necessary to give further scrutiny to challenging problems through reassessment. It is possible solutions that initially looked plausible may become problematic when subjected to such scrutiny.
5. *Diversity of interpretation and inputs:* This involves the integration of the voices of those affected by policies and practices with the reasoning of experts as they interpret data. This makes visible the possibility of incompleteness in theory and actual barriers to human capabilities.
6. *Emphasis on precise articulation and reasoning:* Sen argues for creating room for fuller articulations and definitions of problems along with a focus on the poorest groups, consistent with Rawls's second principle.
7. *Role of public reasoning in social choice:* Recognize the role of championing positions and the use of public reasoning about various preferences and alternatives. (Abstracted from Sen, 2009, pp. 106–111.)

St. John (in press) reconstructed Sen's process approach to address the two-level process of policy and organizational change (Table 13.1) that recognizes the need for both evidence-based decisions at the level of government policy (a critical-empirical approach) and learning-oriented adaptation as a form of bottom-up reform within colleges and universities. Combining the two approaches suggests an action-focused orientation to policy decisions involving both policy and practice.

The case studies offer two examples of policy researchers working closely with state policymakers in a multilevel process of policy development: Minnesota's development of the market model, a process that engaged researchers and state officials (Hearn & Anderson, 1995), and Indiana's development of the comprehensive reform strategy. The process that evolved in Indiana is depicted in Table 13.2.

The Indiana Educational Policy Center (IEPC) was a nonpartisan research organization that worked with legislative staffs from across parties, the governor's staff, and

Table 13.2 Policy Research in Support of Higher Education Policy in Indiana, 1998–2007

Action-Oriented Policy Research	Research on Indiana's Student Aid Programs and Follow-up Support for Campus-Based Reform
Focus on challenging, recurrent social (and educational) problems Identify critical, unresolved issues that merit scrutiny and practical local solutions.	Indiana Education Policy Center (IEPC) developed a data agreement with the Indiana Commission for Higher Education (ICHE) on use of student record database in research on retention in higher education. Initial IEPC studies focused on differences in persistence by income and racial/ethnic groups in the state, with an explicit focus on the impact of state student financial aid programs. Later research focused on student aid and expanded to include the Twenty-First Century Scholars Program and the impact of alternative admission criteria.
Use evidence-based policy reform as a framework for encouraging action inquiry.	The Lumina Foundation funded follow-up studies of Twenty-First Century Scholars and the ICHE and Lumina funded studies of academic preparation and college success using College Board and state databases. The Indiana Project on Academic Success (IPAS) was created as a strategy for using these analyses to inform action inquiry projects at the state's college and university campuses.
Recognize the importance of problem solving in relation to constraints in policy and practice.	IPAS provided technical assistance to campus teams using action inquiry to address challenges they identified based on the research. Research support was also provided to campuses that started action inquiry with the evaluation of existing programs.
Consider all feasible proposed solutions and promote informed policy choices and institutional strategies.	The governor's office asked the IEPC to conduct and release studies addressing financial strategies for public higher education. In addition, IPAS provided encouragement for campuses to use research to inform campus decisions about policies and programs that promoted equity and academic success.
Use research to inform policy adaptation; encourage adaptation to address challenges.	During the 2000s, Indiana became a national leader in funding for student aid and made substantial gains in the academic success of high school students and college access. College success for underrepresented students remained an elusive goal.
Public dissemination of research; partnerships with policymakers and alliances with practitioners.	Throughout the process, studies were disseminated to legislative staff, the public through press releases, and scholars through academic publications in the field of higher education. Openness of research helped inform policy and make successes visible beyond state borders.

Source: Adapted from St. John, in press.

leadership of the Commission for Higher Education and the Indiana Department of Education. In the late 1990s, researchers at Indiana University conducted studies of high school students and their parents that informed the development of the Twenty-First Century Scholars program (e.g. Hossler & Schmit, 1995; Hossler, Schmit, & Vesper, 1999). In the early 2000s, the policy center developed a more direct role of working with policymakers on studies of higher education that focused on issues of inequality. For nearly a decade there was a strong collaborative relationship between researchers working with the IEPC and the Indiana Project on Academic Success (IPAS) and state officials who sought better strategies for promoting preparation, access, and degree completion. IPAS specifically introduced the action-inquiry process at campuses across the states as a means of using state and institutional data systems to support and inform efforts to improve retention on campuses across the state (St. John & Musoba, 2010; St. John & Wilkerson, 2006).

RETHINKING THE ROLES OF POLICYMAKERS, RESEARCHERS, AND CAMPUS OFFICIALS

The fact that strategies evolved over a couple of decades in two states that enabled universities to collaborate with state officials on crafting new policies does not mean this is a workable approach in all cases. The Michigan case provides a contrasting example: the National Forum for Higher Education at the University of Michigan provided research support for the Cherry Commission, but the state lacked a statewide database to conduct rigorous empirical analyses, graduate students conducted studies without guidance by seasoned researchers, and the policy research was treated in instrumental ways that promoted a neoliberal agenda without providing a cohesive framework. The fact that research collaboration occurs does not guarantee that an open discourse will evolve that can provide means of representing diverse voices in the policy process. In fact, it is rare to have the convergence of capable researchers and public officials who are willing to craft policies through engaging practitioners within colleges and universities to support change. It requires a process of evidence-based reform at the state level that is not only open to bottom-up innovation but actually supports it.

When the process works, it provides an alternative to the more typical use of research instrumentally to craft studies that support ideological positions. Although we recognize the difficulties, we encourage readers to engage in thinking about moving toward this evidence-based approach (Text Box 13.6).

Text Box 13.6 Questions About an Evidence-Based Approach to Policy Development

1. How can public forums be created in states for policy officials and researchers engaged in investigating the experiences of groups typically left out of the educational system? Can sufficient time be set aside to consider research and deliberate critically?

2. How can university research and even doctoral dissertations be framed to inform and assist states in the process of problem solving on critical issues?

3. How can institutional and state data systems be used to support action-inquiry focusing on improving opportunity rather than merely using these systems to monitor actions through public accountability?

4. Given the changing and combative political interests of elected officials, how can a stable inquiry-based approach to reform be developed in states?

14

REFRAMING THE SOCIAL GOOD

The second serious problem we face as a society when we ponder the future of higher education is: How can we generate a new understanding of the social good compatible with the political rationales of the current period? The idea of social good is a public construct, a commonly understood set of goals that guide public action. John Rawls (1971, 2001) argued there was a social contract that guided public choices about investment in education. More recent social theorists have concluded that there is no longer a social contract (Nussbaum, 2011; Sen, 2009). Recent analyses of dialogues about the social good among educational leaders in the early 2000s consistently demonstrate a valuing of economic rationales for investment in education over social uplift and issues of equity, although there are occasional voices of reformers advocating social justice for minorities and women in science and engineering (Pasque, 2010). In the present context, there is also increasing recognition of underrepresentation of males in higher education as a whole, especially minority males (Harper, Williams, Pérez, & Morgan, 2012). Inequalities in educational opportunity undermine the economic growth of the nation, especially given the inequalities in wealth distribution (Rampell, 2011), which should be a compelling argument for reconsidering the value of the current stance on taxation. Interjecting understanding of the role of policy and practice into the policy discourses on higher education represents a major challenge.

In this section we consider the underlying issues of human rights and capabilities as a means of understanding these daunting challenges. Using Nussbaum's (2000) concepts of human capabilities as a starting point, we encourage readers to ponder their own assumptions about the meaning of preparation, access, and academic success. As a conclusion, we discuss the human capabilities framework as means of reclaiming the social good through policy and practice in higher education.

EDUCATION AND HUMAN CAPABILITIES

Human development is at the core of the human capabilities approach to social policy. Rather than viewing education as a means of educating a workforce for global economic competitions, this view focuses on the minimum standards of education and social support as a basic right. We consider how core concepts related to human capability might inform the current debates about preparation, access, and persistence leading to college completion and academic success.

Human Capabilities

In her comparative research on women and social justice, Nussbaum (1999, 2000) recognized there were limitations to Rawls's concept of rights and liberties, especially when applied to the plight of women in developing countries. Previously, Rawls (1999) had argued that nations defined the rights of people influenced by faith traditions. In particular, Rawls demonstrated sensitivity to the Islamic traditions within nations. In contrast, Nussbaum (1999, 2000) recognized that women had basic rights to access health care and education if societies were committed to governing systems aligned with faith traditions, an argument she applied across nations. More recently, Nussbaum has adapted the human capabilities argument, refining it through analyses of political philosophy and religion (Nussbaum, 2004, 2008). In *Creating Capabilities: The Human Development Approach*, Nussbaum (2011) refined a set of human capabilities applicable across genders and nations, including: "*Senses, imagination, and thought*. Being able to use the senses, to imagine, think and reason—and to do things in a 'truly human' way, a way informed and cultivated by an adequate education" (p. 33). She argued that human capability standards represent goals for policy and that many elements of the list are not realized even in developed countries, including the United States. She recognized that a new standard was emerging in developed countries: "Currently, most modern nations, anxious about national profit and eager to seize or keep a share of the global market, have focused on a narrow set of marketable skills that are seen as having the potential of generating short term profit" (p. 115). She also argued for a more balanced view of education. This critique differs somewhat from her argument about education for women, which had focused on a standard of education necessary to support one's family.

Domains of Action

To the extent that Nussbaum's (2011) human capabilities list represents goals for human development in a global society, they also provide a starting point for thinking about the relationship between goals and fields of action in policy and practice. The concept of *fields*, a term used by Bourdieu (1980/1990), provides a way of viewing the domains of action in which people engage as they live in communities and learn in schools. Nussbaum also provides a vantage for thinking both within and beyond national boundaries in her arguments for capabilities related to the protection of species and environment (global/environmental) and cross-national discourses on rights and capabilities as goals and strategies. To facilitate the discussion of the ways humans behave within organizations, communities, and societies relate to human capabilities, St. John (in press) has reorganized the lists of capabilities into four domains: academic, social, health, and global. The term *global*, in this context, refers to human-constructed systems that have global influence, ecological systems that extend beyond nation states, and issues of human rights and dignity that extend beyond the boundaries of government.

The division of human capability into domains of action provides a basis for identifying the fields of action for policymakers, researchers, educators, and citizens. Viewing human capabilities as goals of action and fields as the domains of action provides a lens for viewing the relationships among individuals' actions in families and communities, professional action in organizations, and the pursuit of a greater justice in globalizing societies. Nussbaum's work provides insight into the ways capabilities relate to domains of action, but there is a need to focus on fields of action as such, in order to build a better understanding of the process of moving toward capabilities as goals. Since education has been our primary focus, especially with respect to capital formation, our thoughts on the other three domains of action are preliminary and therefore merit further exploration and examination.

Education is a distinct domain of practice. Originally Nussbaum (1999, 2000) argued that educating women to a level that provides them with the capability to support a family was an explicit standard for basic education. Her more recent work focuses on imagination and critical reason, recognizing that education "forms people's existing capacities into developed *internal capacities* of many kinds" (2011, p. 152, italics in original). She argues that a true education involves more than skills, and she is critical of the new melding of academic standards and workforce preparedness. Nussbaum also argues that critical thinking and the ability to imagine and build understanding are part of a minimum standard.

Academic Capital Formation

The introduction of human capabilities runs directly into the current debates about the educational pipeline. The concept of academic capital formation provides a frame that can be used to broaden the science, technology, engineering, and math (STEM) focus to include human capabilities and the broader concepts of education that Nussbaum urges. Academic capital formation has been defined as the knowledge needed for successful transitions through the educational process, from initial engagement in education through completion of advanced degrees for professions (including the professorate), and engaged scholarship and practice. These transitions involve engagement in social processes in families, schools, and communities, as well as the application of intellectual and mechanical abilities and talents (St. John, in press).

The current pipeline approach emphasizes STEM education over humanities, a position also argued by Diane Ravitch (2010). We recognize the essential importance of equity in opportunities to attain an education. In theoretical work on the concept of academic capital formation, St. John (in press; see also St. John, Hu, & Fisher, 2011) argues that in addition to promoting STEM preparation, education reform must also focus on:

- *Family engagement* in support of and advocacy for children
- *Academic preparation* in schools inclusive of balanced approaches to content and student engagement
- *Transitions to college* as a process of finding academic programs and career pathways
- *Engaged learning* in college, including opportunities to study with peers, engage in civic betterment, and research opportunities
- *Academic success,* including finding work congruent with acquired education and interests

Actualization of human capabilities and reduction of inequality within educational social institutions are not solely a matter of policy and regulation, but are also central to human action in families, communities, and professional organizations. The emergent theory of academic capital formation (St. John, Hu, & Fisher, 2011; Winkle-Wagner, Bowman, & St. John, 2012) provides a lens for understanding the role of social processes in educational attainment, but the transition into policy frameworks remains uncertain, especially given the limited, narrower concepts of the STEM pipeline that currently guide policy.

The core concepts of academic capital formation have been developed and tested in studies of the uplift processes among diverse, first-generation college students that reconstructed core assumptions from human capital (concerns about careers and college costs), social capital (networks, information and trust), and reproduction theory (i.e. Bourdieu's concepts of field, cultural capital, and habitus). The core argument is that education and family support help students build the academic capital needed to navigate educational and career pathways. Interventions through schools, community-based organizations (e.g., college pathways organizations), and colleges help create opportunities for students and families to build this social agency.

We have argued that a new trajectory of education reform has been established, one that differs substantially from the trajectory of the progressive century. A transformation of high schools from the old comprehensive approach to new college preparatory models is underway, along with efforts to expand college access and improve degree completion in privatized state systems of education that rely on tuition and loans in addition to public subsidies to colleges. In the previous chapter, we raised questions about this trajectory and how it might be altered to better achieve intended goals. The human capabilities framework provides a basis for asking readers about the values and visions that underlie the reforming pipeline.

Academic Preparation

Global competition in science and industry underlies arguments about the educational pipeline as currently constructed. The human capabilities framework provides an alternative way of thinking about the meaning of educational preparation, one situated in the basic rights of people along with the urgency of economic viability. In our view, this is not an argument that math and science education are not important, but instead an exploration of the broader purposes of education—that other academic disciplines may be of equal importance.

There is an urgency to consider the efficacy of college preparation as schools are being transformed to prepare all students for college. There are two complex aspects of the current transitions that potentially contradict each other (St. John, Masse, Lijana, & Bigelow, in press). On the one hand, the development of thematic, career-oriented high schools creates the necessity for families to ponder career pathways and the costs of higher education when they make choices about which high school their child will attend when the child is in middle school. In fact, high schools use their career-oriented themes as part of their marketing to students in middle schools. On the other hand, public schools have curricular constraints in the way they implement the new standards—constraints that charter schools do not have to contend with and that could undermine some of the thematic approaches needed for successful transition in the market economy. Currently we, as educators, face considerable challenges in helping students to effectively examine potential career pathways while in high school, and we are even less prepared to do so in middle school.

This new context is complicated for many students and their families. Parents generally do not have the same level of math education their children are expected to complete

Text Box 14.1 Questions About Fairness in Postsecondary Opportunity

1. Does emphasizing college preparation provide means for promoting a new standard for K–12 education as a basic human capability?

2. How can colleges adjust for prior inequalities in the opportunity to prepare (e.g., by attending quality schools) as means of promoting fairness in admissions? How do we incentivize or compel them to do so when the current system rewards less equity-minded strategies?

3. Recognizing that equal college access is not constitutionally ensured in states or at the national level, are there moral obligations to ensure fairness in academic and financial access?

4. Recognizing the complexity of state and national policies on financial access, are there moral obligations on states and the federal government for equalizing preparation and enrollment opportunities for illegal immigrants?

in high school (St. John et al., in press). The choice of high school is also complicated because many families lack the knowledge needed to choose among different thematic options. In the older model of the comprehensive high school, the first 2 years of college emphasized liberal arts education and were designed to provide a foundation for choosing majors.[1] Now students and parents are expected to choose between STEM, law, education, health, arts, and other specializations when they choose a high school. General preparatory education is not an option in some schools, and the notion that liberal arts education provides a foundation for informed choices of specialization has largely been marginalized.

In this context, there is reason to ponder the meaning of a constrained curriculum in relation to school choice and thinking through questions like the ones in Text Box 14.1.

Access and Life Transitions

Students make college choices, transfer decisions, and major choices based on aspirations, career goals, and family expectations, with information translated through personal lived experience (St. John, Hu, & Fisher, 2011). For students, the initial choice of college may be reconsidered based on social pressures from home and within college, alignment of personal interests with academic experiences, and financial pressures. Even with inequalities in schools and financial issues impeding access to 4-year colleges, current policies encourage high school graduates—and even dropouts—to enroll in some form of postsecondary education. The fact that the overall college participation rates are as high for African Americans as for Whites (Chapter 5) provides evidence that there is wide access; but the constraints on choice of institution, specifically a 4-year college, are serious and serve to perpetuate new forms of inequality.

The inequalities in K–12 schools have sustained effects throughout the college years. When 4-year colleges determine the quality of schools, they typically do so in ways that favor lower-ranked students from elite schools owing to an assumption that they had the benefit of a quality curriculum in spite of their test scores. In cases of equal achievement, if fairness were the primary criterion in college admissions, students who attended underperforming schools would have priority because of their prior disadvantage (St. John, in press). The alternative of the "top 10 percent" plan in Texas—an admission procedure that treated equally ranked students equally—worked well both in terms of diversity and the success of admitted students, but there were pressures on the University of Texas to retain a substantial number of admission spots for lower-ranked students in high-achieving schools (Chapa & Horn, 2007; Tienda & Nui, 2006).

The financial inequalities facing low-income students considering college are serious. Obviously the high net costs of attending make it difficult for low-income families to pay for a 4-year college without excessive borrowing, if it is possible at all. The prospects of finding employment at levels that would make it possible to pay off high debt are uncertain, which compounds the inequality. High college costs can discourage students and families from engaging in schools, thus creating barriers beyond those of preparation. The strategies currently being used to provide college preparation for all students (raising requirements for graduation) and access to 4-year colleges in most states (relying on high tuition and loans, subsidized and unsubsidized) do not address the existing inequalities and can, in fact, increase those created by disparities in family income.

There is an inherent conflict between a basic liberties approach emphasizing college preparation as a minimal standard if colleges do not have means of adjusting for prior inequalities, both financial and academic. It is not difficult to conceive of practical strategies for achieving fairness in college opportunities. We raise additional questions for our readers in Text Box 14.2.

Fair and Equal Opportunity to Persist to Degree Completion

The inequalities in opportunities to complete college are abundantly evident nationally (Chapter 6) and in the case study states (Part II), although private nonprofit colleges in some states have taken steps to narrow gaps in degree attainment. The financial, social,

---

Text Box 14.2 Questions About Academic Preparation and Human Capabilities

1. Are the humanities (pondering the meaning of action and justice) and critical thinking (engaging in civic programs to support the public good) an important part of high school education, along with preparation for science and math education in college?

2. How can market models of K–12 education be adapted to encourage liberal education that informs students about the range of advanced subjects and related career pathways at the same time as they build content-linked curriculums with career pathways?

3. What types of student and family support services are needed in high school to inform and support families as they navigate the new pathways between middle schools, high schools, and colleges?

4. How can college outreach help students and families as they adjust to the new system of education and make choices in preparing for college?

Text Box 14.3 Questions About Fairness in Postsecondary Opportunity

1. Does emphasizing college preparation provide means for promoting a new standard for K–12 education as a basic human capability?

2. How can colleges adjust for prior inequalities in the opportunity to prepare (e.g., by attending quality schools) as means of promoting fairness in admissions? How do we incentivize or compel them to do so when the current system rewards less equity-minded strategies?

3. Recognizing that equal college access is not constitutionally ensured in states or at the national level, are there moral obligations to ensure fairness in academic and financial access?

4. Recognizing the complexity of state and national policies on financial access, are there moral obligations on states and the federal government for equalizing preparation and enrollment opportunities for illegal immigrants?

---

and academic aspects of retention and degree attainment merit more attention across all sectors of higher education. The priority of equal opportunities for degree attainment has been a focal point in this book. In addition to suggesting an actionable approach to research on retention (Chapter 4), we have a few questions for readers in Text Box 14.3.

CONCLUSIONS

The history of the progressive century was characterized by tensions between economic development and social uplift, with a common understanding that both forces were good for society. This is not to argue there was ever a broad consensus on the relative value of both forces, but there was recognition that both forces had value in economic theory from the publication of the *Wealth of Nations* (Smith, 1776/2011) to the development of human capital theory (Becker, 1964, 1975). These values were explicitly recognized in Rawls's (1971, 2000) social contract. In fact, Rawls argued that taxation for education provided a mechanism for cross-generational uplift as part of the social contract.

Unfortunately, rather than taxing citizens to support new generations in attaining the college degrees and certificates students need to become productive citizens, American society has chosen to fund higher education through the use of loans, forcing students to choose between a college education and a high debt load. The financial aspects of the challenges facing higher education seem daunting. Many financial remedies have been suggested and tried; a few have produced substantial evidence of success, even in these difficult times with the pressures to reduce or constrain taxation. Higher education leaders can learn from these experiences through a new generation of research that explicitly considers the role of policy decisions in educational outcomes. We encourage researchers to address these applied problems.

The tensions between neoliberal and neoconservative rationales for reform are deep in all areas of public policy. The problems are serious in higher education because the focus on subsidies for all—like student loans and higher educational standards—has not reduced disparities in access to 4-year colleges. Privatization has added to underlying unfairness because provisions for equity (i.e., adequate funding for need-based programs) were not maintained: failure to raise the maximum awards for need-based aid redistributes benefits of funding up the income scale to those who have less unmet need—the net price after aid and expected family contribution. This pattern of public funding may redirect low-income students to lower-cost 2-year programs. While large percentages of minorities now enroll in public 2-year colleges, there are low completion rates in these institutions, with substantial disparities across groups. The neoconservative arguments for lower tax rates and against targeted programs have made it more difficult to address inequalities through public policy. Thus the loss of liberal rationales that argued directly for remedying inequalities (supplanted by neoliberalism's focus on individual rights) has been especially problematic in attempts to reduce disparities in recent decades.

While we raise questions about the moral basis on contemporary policy rationales for readers to consider, we also encourage readers to recognize it is important to craft strategies that promote greater equity given the prevailing arguments in the policy discourses on higher education now evident in states and nationally. It is crucial to recognize that the social inequalities in higher education opportunity are serious. Social and academic support are needed to empower a new generation of students to learn how to navigate the complex terrain of higher education, find employment that makes it possible to pay back the debt accrued, and support the next generation. Beyond uncovering challenges and raising questions, we also encourage a new generation of education leaders to embrace the challenges in research and activism that promote equal opportunity in higher education.

APPENDIX

POLICY INDICATORS

This appendix describes how several of the indicators from the Projects Promoting Equity in Urban and Higher Education were calculated.

THE GAP BETWEEN THE ACTUAL MAXIMUM PELL AWARD AND UNIVERSITY ATTENDANCE COSTS

This figure was calculated from data provided by two College Board reports: *Trends in College Pricing 2010* (Table 5a) and *Trends in Student Aid 2010* (Table 8). The maximum Pell award was then subtracted from the average public 4-year tuition, fees, and room and board costs to illustrate the funding gap for low-income students. All data were adjusted by the consumer price index (CPI) to account for inflation across years.

TRENDS IN AVERAGE STATE NEED-BASED AND NON-NEED-BASED UNDERGRADUATE GRANTS PER FTE (IN 2008 DOLLARS)

Data for these figures came from the National Association of State Student Grant & Aid Program's (NASSGAP) annual reports. NASSGAP provides the total amount states spend annually on need-based and non-need-based grants for undergraduates. We divided the total amount of each type of aid by the FTE (full-time equivalent) numbers provided by NASSGAP. Data were then adjusted by the CPI to account for inflation.

TRENDS IN AVERAGE ANNUAL AMOUNT OF STATE AND LOCAL APPROPRIATIONS PER FTE FOR THE PUBLIC HIGHER EDUCATION SYSTEM (IN 2008 DOLLARS)

The Integrated Postsecondary Education Data System (IPEDS) from the National Center for Education Statistics (NCES) was used to calculate state and local appropriations. FTE was calculated as full-time students plus one third of part-time students. In cases where an institution was either missing a value for FTE or appropriations the institution was dropped from the calculation of this statistic. To account for inflation, financial data were adjusted with the CPI.

TRENDS IN THE AVERAGE AMOUNT OF UNDERGRADUATE IN-STATE TUITION AND FEES PER FTE IN PUBLIC HIGHER EDUCATION SYSTEM (IN 2008 DOLLARS)

IPEDS was used to calculate a weighted tuition figure. Tuition and fees at public institutions in the state were weighted by the FTE of students attending each institution. Both 2- and 4-year public institutions were included. The CPI was used to adjust for inflation from year to year.

TRENDS IN THE AVERAGE PER FTE FUNDING OF NEED-BASED GRANTS AS A PERCENT OF THE AVERAGE PUBLIC COLLEGE TUITION CHARGE FOR FULL-TIME STUDENTS

These figures show the relationship between need-based grants and the average cost of in-state tuition and fees. To calculate the ratio, the amount of need-based grants per FTE was divided by the average amount of tuition. Twenty-five percent funding is considered the threshold that has an equalizing effect on enrollment opportunity for low- and middle-income students.

PUBLIC HIGH SCHOOL GRADUATION RATES FOR 9TH-GRADE COHORTS BY RACE/ETHNICITY

These figures use data from the NCES Common Core of Data (CCD). Ninth grade enrollments from three years prior were used to establish a base cohort. The number of graduates was then divided by the number of students in the corresponding 9th grade cohort to create a graduation rate. The limitation of this method is that it fails to take into account both student migration to different states and also students that either graduate in less or more than 4 years. Some imputation was done to account for missing data. The total number of students was known in each state, but the breakdown of students by race and ethnicity was missing for some years in some states. When these data were missing, the percentage of each race/ethnicity represented among the students was averaged for the years before and after the missing data. This percentage was multiplied by the total number of students, which was known in all cases, and the imputed numbers were then used to calculate a graduation rate.

TRENDS IN COLLEGE CONTINUATION RATE (RATIO OF HIGH SCHOOL GRADUATES TO FIRST-TIME FRESHMEN)

The college continuation rate is the percent of students that enrolled in college somewhere in the United States during the fall following high school graduation. It is important to consider the trend of high school graduation rates in interpreting this figure, since changes in that rate can influence the college continuation rate. The data for these figures come from Postsecondary Education Opportunity.

TRENDS IN THE PERCENT OF STUDENTS TAKING
THE SAT/ACT AND AVERAGE SCORES

SAT and ACT data come from the College Board and ACT Inc., respectively. In interpreting SAT figures, it is important to keep in mind that students in many states (especially in the Midwest) take the ACT. States with a lower rate of SAT participation generally have higher average verbal and math scores owing to student self-selection in taking the SAT. Similarly, many states have low ACT participation rates, whereas others use the ACT as a high school exit exam requirement and therefore have an almost 100% participation rate. The participation rate should always be considered in evaluating the average scores.

RACIAL/ETHNIC REPRESENTATION IN
POSTSECONDARY INSTITUTIONS AS A PROPORTION
OF THE UNITED STATES POPULATION

The indicator of racial/ethnic representation takes into account not only the percentage of a particular race/ethnicity enrolled in higher education but also the percent of that race/ethnicity in the state's population. This controls for demographic changes in the population. In other words, the representation indicator is a ratio of the percent of a particular race/ethnicity enrolled in higher education over the percent of that race/ethnicity in the population. A ratio equal to 1 would indicate equitable representation in higher education. A ratio greater than 1 indicates overrepresentation, and a ratio less than 1 indicates underrepresentation in higher education.

U.S. Census Bureau data were used to calculate the race/ethnicity percentages in the population. IPEDS data were used to calculate the percent of a particular race/ethnicity enrolled in higher education. FTE by race was calculated by the total number of full-time students plus one-third of part-time students. Some changes in representation between 1998 and 2000 may be due to changes in the way census data were reported.

TRENDS IN GRADUATION RATES IN
POSTSECONDARY INSTITUTIONS

Postsecondary graduation rate data came from IPEDS. These data are limited to first-time full-time freshmen so as to create a base cohort from which to calculate a graduation percentage rate. Graduation within 150% of normal time is what is reported to IPEDS. This typically means 4-year graduation rates for 2-year institutions and 6-year graduation rates for 4-year institutions. Graduation rates tend to be lower at 2-year institutions, since many students transfer to a 4-year institution before completing the requirements for a degree. IPEDS does provide transfer rates, but they are not included in the calculations we present in this book.

NOTES

PREFACE

1. http://www.ncid.umich.edu/promotingequity/data/main.html

CHAPTER 1

1. There are several private research universities and liberal arts colleges that truly are national or international in their marketing to students, so they do not have to be overly concerned about the education markets within their own states. However, even in these elite institutions, education professors often share a concern about state policy because it shapes the curriculum in teacher education and other subjects. In addition, administrators and professors in elite universities often share concerns with other educators about reducing inequalities in state education systems.

2. In the second edition of *Human Capital: A Theoretical and Empirical Analysis, With Special Consideration of Education,* Gary S. Becker (1975) discussed how portable student loans altered the basic cost-benefit framework for individual students.

3. The percentages of students of traditional college age who were enrolled in or had previously enrolled in higher education were nearly equal between 1973 and 1978 (St. John, 1994a, 1994b, 2003: St. John & Noel, 1989). In some of those years, the ratio was actually higher for Hispanics and African Americans than for Whites. For this brief period, there was relatively equal opportunity to enroll (or access). However, even during this period, the percentage of students who persisted was not equal—a condition related to inequalities in preparation as well as financial inequality.

4. For a more complete discussion of the history of education policy see St. John (2003) and St. John, Moronksi, and Williams (2010).

5. In two prior books, St. John (2003, 2006) refined John Rawls's theory of justice as a criterion for evaluating the effects of federal and state education programs. The *implied promise of fairness* in quality education can be viewed as a *basic right,* and an *equal opportunity* to achieve an education can be viewed as an adaptation of the *difference principle.*

6. Of course some readers may argue that we go too far when we argue that education, even a high school education, is a right. We invite those readers to ponder the linkages to market fairness. Regardless of where readers stand on the "should" and "ought" of education rights, it is important and necessary to consider how education markets and standards relate to fairness.

7. This restates the reconstruction of Rawls's "just savings principle" (1971, 1999) from *Refinancing the College Dream* (St. John, 2003), with an emphasis on adapting to market conditions within states.

8. The indicator of state need-based aid cited in these studies (St. John, 2006; St. John, Moronski, & Williams, 2010) was developed by dividing the total state expenditure on need-based aid by the number of

full-time-equivalent (FTE) students in public and private colleges, whereas tuition is a weighted average for public colleges only. The logic for this approach is (a) students can usually take need-based student aid to any public or private college in a state (which is why average funding per student is used as an indicator), and (b) the weighted average public tuition charge is the best indicator of the cost of education for resident students. Breakdowns of grant distribution by type of college (public or private) have not generally been available; we extend this approach in this volume.

9. We refer to charters and other new schools as *quasipublic* because they frequently use per student funding, as do public schools, but they were implemented to compete with public schools.

10. We use the term *quasipublic* to refer to schools like charter schools that are free of government control and regulation but funded in ways similar to typical public schools.

11. A decade ago, it was not yet clear that charters would be chosen as a privatization strategy over vouchers. Vouchers could have brought private schools, including Catholic schools, into the competitive environment. However, Catholic schools resisted vouchers, unwilling to adapt to the secular (nonreligious) requirements of public funding (Ridenour & St. John, 2003; St. John & Ridenour, 2000, 2001).

12. The Wisconsin Idea, developed during the Progressive Era (between 1890 and 1920), encourages contributions to the state by public universities. At the time, proponents of the Wisconsin Idea saw the state as "the laboratory for democracy," serving as a model for other states and the federal government.

13. See St. John (2009b) for a full statement of the postprogressive stance.

14. The major exception to this general rule is the research of Sheila Slaughter, a scholar who has consistently addressed the role of political ideology (e.g., Slaughter, 1991; Slaughter & Rhoades, 2004). We discuss her work as setting the stage for this book in Chapter 1.

15. Recall from earlier in this chapter that human capital theory argues that both the government and individuals make decisions about investment in education based on expected returns (G. S. Becker, 1964, 1975).

16. St. John (2009b) reviews the use of case methods in professional education. Our perspective in this book is informed by this prior work.

17. St. John directed the Indiana Education Policy Center (1997–2003). During his tenure, he worked with university researchers to design and execute studies that addressed policy and evaluation topics raised by policymakers in the state. The critical-empirical approach was used as a guiding framework in the Center.

CHAPTER 2

1. Subsequent chapters consider the emergence of preparation, access, and retention as a central focus of federal policy in higher education as part of our discussion of student aid. In each of these areas, we discuss roles of both policy decisions and research that seeks for inform those decisions.

2. The HEA is the major federal legislation in higher education. It is organized under a set of titles, or program areas. The HEA is discussed throughout Part I of this book because the program has defined the major federal programs in higher education. Authorized originally in 1965, the law has been reauthorized about every 4 years. The Education Amendments of 1972 and the Middle Income Student Assistance Act of 1978 are the reauthorizations that receive the most attention in the chapters that follow because of their impact of restructuring and redefining student aid programs.

3. Of course Carter also argued for lifting income caps for student aid, an argument that opened the way for neoliberal arguments about rights for all to become part of federal student aid policy (see Chapter 4). Carter reconstructed the older conservative arguments of southern Democrats with neoliberal arguments about human rights in the United States and internationally.

4. Slaughter's critique of academic capitalism focuses on capitalism as an economic force, in contrast with Marxism and socialism. The concept of academic capital formation (St. John, Hu, & Fisher, 2011; Winkle-Wagner, Bowman, & St. John, 2012) relates to the ways in which individuals develop knowledge and skills related to the navigation of education systems, combining concepts from theories of social, academic, and human capital.

5. These projections of future jobs indicate employment demand rather than pay. Part of the argument for expanding and reducing gaps in the STEM pipeline has been based on expected future earnings. We do not dispute arguments about earning differentials or gaps in the opportunity to prepare but propose that the pipeline approach is not perfectly aligned with employment opportunities for students.

6. This section substantially rewrites a portion of the conclusion to the volume (Powers & St. John, in press) to fit with the general arguments of this chapter.

7. The *Nine Points* were developed to guide the licensing of university technology. The document can be viewed at http://www.autm.net/Nine_Points_to_Consider.htm

8. Of course research indirectly subsidizes the education process through the buyout of faculty time for research and the employment of graduate students and postdoctoral students. In many academic fields the support for research is also integral to employment.

CHAPTER 3

1. Quality research includes both sound logic, consistent with theories commonly and appropriately used, and the accurate application of statistical methods. Serious statistical errors have been identified in studies of student preparation, access, and degree attainment (See Becker, 2004; Fitzgerald, 2004; Heller, 2004a). Common errors include the failure to consider critical variables logically related to outcomes, an omitted variable problem that distorts research findings. When studies with purposeful statistical and logical errors are used to construct arguments for new policies, the process of research and advocacy can be classified as "proofiness," or a misuse of statistics in support of political agendas.
2. It can be argued that, given Thomas Jefferson's philosophy, the University of Virginia was the first secular public university (Thelin, 2004a), but the shift toward secularization of knowledge did not occur on a large scale in American higher education until after the founding of land grant universities (Marsden, 1994).
3. Although the intent of market policies is to promote innovations (e.g., Chubb & Moe, 2000), according to Diane Ravitch (2010), the accountability policies were intended to constrain liberal innovation.
4. The federal government maintains a strong regulatory role across all areas of public action—an issue addressed in Chapter 6, along with federal funding for research and health benefits. These three policy issues are important in the governance of higher education.
5. In state studies to consider how adding college preparatory courses to graduation requirements influences graduation rates, it was found that raising the graduation requirement to a 4-year standard can reduce the percentage of students who graduate from high school.
6. Like many other policy researchers, the authors have worked with government agencies, foundations, and advocacy organizations on studies written up in policy reports that are part of a rationale-building process. The critical-empirical approach to policy analysis, used in this and other books by the senior author (St. John, 2003, 2006, 2009a, 2009b; St. John, Hu, & Fisher, 2010; St. John & Musoba, 2010) provides means of gaining an objective perspective on one's own original position (St. John, 2007).
7. The theory of the market used to advocate for portable grants and K–12 reform was that funding incentives would spark innovation (Chubb & Moe, 1990; Newman, 1971).

CHAPTER 4

1. The 1972 reauthorization of HEA, also renamed Supplemental Educational Opportunity Grants, or SEOGs.
2. At the time he was elected president in 1968, Nixon was extremely conservative for the period. Nixon promoted a social liberalism that emphasized a corporate role in health and student aid. For a thoughtful discussion of presidential speeches during this period, see Posselt (2009).
3. Carter had ushered in some of the elements of neoliberalism, including the Education and Consolidation Act of 1980, which reauthorized ESEA, and the Middle Income Student Assistance Act of 1978, which reauthorized the HEA but set the stage for the shift from grants to loans (St. John, 1994a).
4. HEW included most of the former Department of Education plus the programs now in the U.S. Department of Health and Human Services. The commissioner of education held a position roughly equivalent to that of the new secretary of education but with a higher-level appointment in the cabinet.
5. This text excerpt is from the introduction to the book and was written as a preamble, to which all authors were supposed to agree. In full disclosure, the senior author wrote the last chapter of the book on integrating finance systems for K–12 and higher education after the omission of the topic had been noted by a reviewer. The chapter discusses problems associated with integrating finance and provides a statement of limitations on the overall strategy.
6. Also missing in this conversation is a discussion of the capacity of higher education to accommodate a better-prepared cohort of students, particularly in the public sector. In recent years, states like California and Florida have turned students away from community colleges (National Center for Public Policy and Higher Education, 2008), in large part because they lacked the resources to expand capacity.
7. In full disclosure, the senior author was a "senior associate" at Pelavin Associates at the time. With his arrival as a postsecondary expert at the firm in 1985, the firm started to receive orders for postsecondary studies. This study of the enrollment gap was one of several the firm undertook. St. John directed studies of the

impact of student aid (e.g., St. John & Masten, 1990; St. John & Noel, 1987, 1989) and college costs (Kirshstein, Tikoff, Masten, & St. John, 1990).

8. Readers can refer forward to Table 4.2, which shows trends in high school graduation requirements. In 1990, no states had yet set this requirement. At the time, graduation requirements were usually considered a local policy matter determined by school boards. The comprehensive high school movement had provided access to advanced math within most school districts but not in all high schools.

9. Several authors published reports illustrating the problems with these claims: St. John (2002, 2003) and Fitzgerald (2004) published reports using Berkner and Chavez's statistics to illustrate that half of the college-qualified low-income students (using Berkner's own index) did not enroll in 4-year colleges. Lee (2004) published a reanalysis that showed large gaps in college enrollment rates for low-income students compared with middle- and high-income students. Becker (2004) and Heller (2004a) published reports documenting the statistical errors in the report.

10. There are statistical limitations with virtually all multivariate and causal research. These problems generally are not considered errors when researchers acknowledge the limitations, which was not the case with the NCES report.

11. Yet there has never been parity in high school graduation rates across racial/ethnic groups, so it was possible at the time that minority high school graduates were more likely to enroll in some type of college than were majority graduates. This condition may have created a perception of inequality by some majority students who did not enroll in college. Such factors could help to explain the anti–affirmative action movement that followed.

12. For example, Indiana started paying the costs of AP tests more than a decade ago (St. John & Musoba, 2010).

13. States with higher percentages of test takers usually have lower average scores (St. John & Musoba, 2010).

CHAPTER 5

1. The idea of a single standard for preparation is somewhat problematic (St. John, Masse, Lijana, & Bigelow, in press). Aligning the types of literacy and numeracy to collegiate standards by field seems more reasonable, given the different types of advanced literacy skills needed in interpretive and humanistic fields compared with STEM fields. When a single standard is required, education should be delivered to give every student a chance of success, which may require more emphasis on the improvement of high school curriculums.

2. We do not argue that the expanding access or globalization causes inequality, although they are correlated. Nor do we think that Phillip Altbach (2010) intended to argue that the relationship could be causal. Rather, we recognize the development and provide background for readers.

3. In the late 1970s, President Carter changed the basic systems model to zero-based budgeting (ZBB), a model that was easily manipulated by politics. By the start of the Reagan administration, strategic planning was widely used, symbolized by the "wall charts" of state education outcomes (First, 1992).

4. Diversity in private nonprofit and for-profit colleges also merits attention in the discourse on access. Supplemental information on trends in racial representation in these sectors can be found at http://www.ncid.umich.edu/promotingequity/data/main.html

5. This is a logical finding because public 4-year colleges are the most expensive per student for a state, given the cost of subsidies to institutions and students. In other words, at a given tax rate, it is less expensive for states to fund student grants and have more students enroll in 2-year and private colleges than to pay the full cost of those students in public 4-year colleges. In same study, we found that that average state tuition charges for public colleges during the sophomore year of college had a negative association with graduation rates. This illustrates the discouraging effects of tuition (St. John, Chung, Musoba, & Simmons, 2006).

6. In this study, both tuition and non-need grants were also positively associated with enrollment of middle-income students in 2-year colleges. Since these analyses control for the impact of high school curriculum completed and other background variables, they illustrate the marginal effects of state grants on moving students through the barrier of financial access.

7. Our conclusions about the role of research in policy differ from some of the specific arguments made by Hearn's analysis in *Higher Education: Handbook of Theory and Research* (1993). Hearn argued that student financial aid had been perpetuated in spite of lack of evidence of impact. The next year, St. John and Elliott (1994) reviewed research and trends, concluding that research had confirmed trends in outcomes. Even if there is evidence that finances have an impact on student outcomes, there is little evidence that the research has an impact on policy decisions except in the few instances noted in this and other chapters. So Hearn's basic position—that social process dominates over rationality in policy decisions—has held up over the decades.

CHAPTER 6

1. A crisis management approach seems to be prevalent in states, something akin to Klein's (2008) disaster capitalism. In this book, we try to hold to politically neutral positions but think it is important to raise issues for further inquiry into policy matters.
2. The terms *retention* and *persistence* have been used interchangeably. However, since the aim of state and federal policy is to improve degree attainment inclusive of transfer, we make this distinction for purposes of clarity. Some of the research discussed here as focusing on retention used the term *persistence* in reports.
3. The Higher Education General Information Survey predated the Postsecondary Education Data Systems that were used to develop the indicators used in this book.
4. Iris Oliver, an analyst who followed the GAP program (e.g., Oliver, 2009), indicated the source of the cut in an e-mail to St. John dated 3/10/11. She noted the continued efforts by foundations to fund graduation incentive grants.
5. The Gates Foundation launched a $35 million program to boost persistence, a development also related to the partnerships created through GAP. (http://www.gatesfoundation.org/press-releases/Pages/increasing-community-college-graduation-rates-101004.aspx)
6. Originally, Tinto (1987) argued that finances were an excuse for rather than a cause of dropout. The researchers cited adapted Tinto's theory to consider the effects of student aid along with other factors.
7. The federal standard for degree completion is based upon the assumption that an associate's degree program should take 2 years and a bachelor's degree program should require 4 years. At 150% of the time to degree, it is expected that an associate's degree student will finish in 3 years and a bachelor's student in 6 years.
8. Owing to space limitations, we could not include trends in degree completion in private institutions in the state cases (Part II). However, in a few instances we do discuss these trends because of the possible links to state policies.
9. The state cases in Part II do not include trends in degree completion in for-profit colleges. It is important to recognize, however, that the completion rates for certificates are consistently higher in for-profit colleges than for public 2-year colleges.

CHAPTER 7

1. Retrieved from http://igs.berkeley.edu/library/research/quickhelp/policy/finance/tax_spend_limits_2003.html
2. Retrieved from http://www.lao.ca.gov/2005/prop_98_primer/prop_98_primer_020805.htm, downloaded September 4, 2011.
3. Before the election of Ronald Reagan as governor in 1970, Republicans in California were liberal on many social issues and their party was a conservative one. The conservative roots of the Republican party were first established with the election of George Murphy as senator in 1964. The conservative contingent of the party started in Orange County, which had been the locale for the John Birch Society, a conservative organization founded in 1951. (http://en.wikipedia.org/wiki/John_Birch_Society)
4. California's Cal Grants have historically considered both merit criteria and financial need and therefore are a hybrid type of aid. Students must qualify for grants based on courses completed, test scores, and financial need. Students with no financial need do not qualify for the grants. The state does not have merit grant programs of the type examined in the next chapter.
5. If students attend part time, which is often case at 2-year colleges, they would typically take more than 2 years to graduate.

CHAPTER 8

1. This case was informed by research conducted as part of an early state case study analyzed in the *Journal of Higher Education* (St. John, 1991) along with subsequent collaboration on research on borrowing in Minnesota higher education conducted in collaboration with Education West.
2. In this context, James Hearn, a professor at the University of Minnesota, and David Longanecker, Deputy Commissioner of MHECB, developed a thought-provoking essay on the market model (1985). Hearn and Longanecker had been graduate students together at Stanford University, where they had been introduced to the market analysis model used by the National Commission on the Financing of Postsecondary Education (NCFPE) in a course taught by Greg Jackson. Jackson had been a student of George Weathersby, former research director for the NCFPE, and they had collaborated on related market-based research (e.g., Jackson & Weatherly, 1975; Weathersby, Jacobs, Jackson, St. John, & Tingley, 1977). Jackson used a simulation model developed by the NCPE for illustrative purposes when he taught courses on higher education policy and finance during this period.

3. James Hearn had left the University of Georgia to take a faculty position at UM and develop a policy center, making visits to the exemplary Indiana Education Policy Center and collaborating in meetings on the topic. For example, Hearn chaired a focused dialogue titled "University-Based Policy Research Centers" at the Association for Higher Education Forum in Sacramento in November 2000. It proved difficult to realize the goal of a new policy center, and Hearn eventually moved on to Vanderbilt University and later returned to the University of Georgia.

4. Minnesota does not report expenditures on non-need grant aid in the NASSGP/NCHELP annual report.

CHAPTER 9

1. In fact, two of the authors began the work on the Florida case as experts working with ENLACE Florida, an advocacy access group (i.e., St. John & Moronski, 2008). The discussion of the grant program that follows adapts text originally developed as a background paper for this advocacy group. The funder sought a balanced treatment of the program, given the arguments being made by both sides about this grant.

2. Interestingly, there were no state colleges comparable to California State or the SUNY College campuses.

3. In contrast, California community colleges were organized at the county level and did not have as strong a system.

4. For an example, see Miami Dade Community College's four-year degree programs: http://www.mdc.edu/main/academics/credit/.

5. A possible weakness of this program from a merit aid perspective is that, with multiple levels and varying criteria, it does not send a clear and simple message to students.

6. Given that the program requires college students to maintain a minimum GPA but does not require any specific courses during college, it is only logical that it could influence students at the margin for grades to avoid tough courses during college, a logic confirmed by Hu (2008).

7. At the margins, teachers might be persuaded by their inherent care for students to adjust grades for those who might be only slightly below the threshold for a Bright Futures award. In addition, some college preparatory high schools could informally adapt grading policies to increase the number of students who qualify.

8. This could be due to increased numbers of immigrants counted in the 2000 census, a pattern observed nationally.

CHAPTER 10

1. http://www.insideindianabusiness.com/newsitem.asp?id=33462

2. Before 1997, the IEPC had focused exclusively on K–12 policy. As part of the analytic support for the legislature during that period, IEPC analyzed school funding options, leading to enhancing the school funding formula per advanced high school diploma completed and other changes (Theobald, 2003). In the early 1990s, Don Hossler was actively engaged in using state data systems for research on postsecondary access (e.g., Hossler, Schmit, & Vesper, 1997). Between 1997 and 2004, when St. John was director, the policy center also engaged in research on college preparation, Twenty-First Century Scholars, higher education strategies, and retention in higher education (e.g., St. John & Musoba, 2010).

3. In fact, the indicators approach used in this book had its beginning in this project. Soon after, the Lumina Foundation funded a project using indicators to examine the impact of state need-based grant programs, and these indicators were eventually used in other projects and numerous doctoral dissertations.

4. E-mail from Scott Gillie to Edward P. St. John, Monday, November 28, 2011.

5. E-mail from Scott Gillie to Edward P. St. John, Monday, November 28, 2011.

6. As director of the Indiana Education Policy Center and the Indiana Project on Academic Success, St. John made many attempts to encourage outreach and partnerships with Indianapolis high schools. With Don Hossler's (Associate Vice President for Enrollment Management) encouragement St. John also made presentations to the president and board of regents in an effort to encourage a more targeted approach.

CHAPTER 11

1. The commission's report was released before the Kalamazoo Promise was announced. There was no discussion of Promise during the commission's proceedings, but since then "Promise Zones" in Michigan have been formulated. The goal is to replicate the success of Kalamazoo in 10 communities across the state. Policymakers link this outcome to the Cherry Commission, even though the actual strategy was not part of its recommendations.

CHAPTER 13

1. There is some disagreement in the literature about the relative effects of merit- (non-need) and need-based aid, but there is strong evidence that both forms have an influence. The amount of need-based aid available during students' sophomore year in high school is associated with improved outcomes (St. John, 2006). Both merit- and need-based aid have positive effects on college enrollment (Chapter 3). The structure of merit aid programs (e.g., the thresholds for awards) seems to make a difference in the impact of merit programs on preparation (see, for example, the Florida case, Chapter 8).

2. Our method of collecting and analyzing data on state student aid differentiated between need-based and non-need-based (mostly merit) aid but did not explore whether students in for-profit colleges could benefit from state aid. The impact of state aid on the success of students in proprietary colleges merits closer study.

CHAPTER 14

1. The major exception was engineering education, which usually required a more content-specific first 2 years of college.

REFERENCES

AACRAO. (2004). *Integrated Postsecondary Education Data System (IPEDS) Student Unit Records (UR)*. Retrieved from http://www.aacrao.org/federal_relations/IPEDS_UR.pdf

ACT. (2000). High school sophomores need help planning upper level courses, college and careers. News release. Retrieved from http://www.act.org/news/releases/2000/06–05–00.html

Adams, E. (2007, August 13). Campaign to change Bright Futures advances. *The Tampa Bay Tribune*. Retrieved from http://www.heraldtribune.com/article/20070813/NEWS/708130407/-1/xml

Adams v. Califano, 430 F. Supp. ll8 (D.C.D.C. 1977).

Adelman, C. (1999). *Answers in the tool box: Academic intensity, attendance patterns, and bachelor's degree attainment*. Washington, DC: National Center for Education Statistics.

Adelman, C. (2005). *Moving into town and moving on: The community college in the lives of traditional-age students*. Washington, DC: U.S. Department of Education.

Adelman, C. (2006, February). *The toolbox revisited: Paths to degree completion from high school through college*. Washington, DC: U.S. Department of Education.

Advisory Committee on Student Financial Assistance (2002). *Empty promises: The myth of college access in America*. Washington, DC: Author.

Advisory Committee on Student Financial Assistance. (2010). *The rising price of inequality*. Report prepared for Congress. Washington, DC: Author.

Alderete, K. (2006). *GEAR UP Evaluation project*. Austin, TX: National Council for Community and Education Partnerships.

Allen, W. R., Epps, E. G., & Haniff, N. Z. (Eds.). (1991). *College in black and white: African American students in predominantly White and in historically Black public universities*. Albany, NY: SUNY Press.

Allensworth, E., Nomi, T., Montgomery, N., & Lee, V. E. (2009). College preparatory curriculum for all: Academic consequences of requiring algebra and English I for ninth graders in Chicago. *Educational Evaluation and Policy Analysis, 31*(4), 367–391.

Altbach, P. G. (2010). Preface. In G. Goastellec (Ed.), *Understanding inequalities in, through, and by higher education* (pp. vii–ix). Boston: Sense Publishers.

Alvis, M. J., & Willie, C. V. (1987). Controlled choice assignments: A new more effective approach to school desegregation. *The Urban Review, 19*(1): 67–88.

American Association of Colleges of Nursing. (2010). *Nursing shortage fact sheet*. Washington, DC: Author.

American Civil Liberties Union. (2000, June 27). Civil rights groups sue over race bias in Michigan Merit Scholarship Program. ACLU.org. Retrieved from http://www.aclu.org/racial-justice/civil-rights-groups-sue-over-race-bias-michigan-merit-scholarship-program

American Diploma Project. (2004, December 10). *Ready or not: Creating a high school diploma that counts*. Washington, DC: Achieve, Inc., The Education Trust, Thomas B. Fordham Foundation. Retrieved from http://www.achieve.org/ReadyorNot

American Indian Higher Education Consortium. (2007). *American Indian Measures of Success (AIMS) fact book—2007 tribal colleges and universities report.* Retrieved from http://www.aihec.org/resources/AIMS.cfm

Anderson, P. L., & Salle, C. M. (2007). *Preliminary report: The economic benefits of the University Research Corridor.* Retrieved May 21, 2010, from http://www.urcmich.org/economic/URC_PreliminaryReport_May24.pdf

Archibald, D. A. (2004, October). School choice, magnet schools, and the liberation model: An empirical study. *Sociology of Education,* (October), 283–310.

Around the Capitol. (2011). *Student financial aid: Eligibility—California DREAM Act of 2011.* Retrieved from http://www.aroundthecapitol.com/Bills/AB_130/20112012/

Astin, A. W. (1975). *Preventing students from dropping out.* San Francisco: Jossey-Bass.

Attewell, P., Lavin, D., Domina, T., & Levey, T. (2007). *Passing the torch: Does higher education for the disadvantaged pay off across the generations?* New York: Russell Sage Foundation, American Sociological Association, Rose Monographs Series.

Austin, J., Burkhardt, J., & Jacobs, J. (2004). *Background briefing for commission members.* Retrieved from http://cherrycommission.org/docs/Resources/Background%20Briefing%20-%20Austin.pdf

Avery, C., & Hoxby, C. (2003). *Do and should financial aid packages affect students' college choices?* NBER Working Paper Series (9482), 70. Retrieved from http://www.nber.org/papers/w9482

Avery, C., Hoxby, C., Jackson, C., Burek, K., Poppe, G., & Raman, M. (2006). *Cost should be no barrier: An evaluation of the first year of Harvard's financial aid initiative.* NBER Working Paper Series (12029), 24. Retrieved from http://www.nber.org/papers/w12029

Bachman, R. (2011, July 18). UC regents approve 9.6% tuition hike. *Santa Barbara Independent.*

Bahr, P. R. (2007). Does math remediation work? A comparative analysis of academic attainment among community college students. *Research in Higher Education, 49*(4), 420–450.

Balderston, F. E. (1974). *Managing today's university.* San Francisco: Jossey-Bass.

Bastedo, M. N. (2009). Convergent institutional logics in public higher education: State policymaking and governing board activism. *Review of Higher Education, 32*(2), 209–234.

Baum, S., & Ma, J. (2009). *Trends in college pricing.* Trends in Higher Education Series. New York: College Board.

Baum, S., & Ma, J. (2011). *Trends in college pricing: 2010.* New York: College Board.

Baum. S., & Steele, P. (2010). *Who borrows most? Bachelor's degree recipients with high levels of debt.* Trends in Higher Education Series. Retrieved from http://advocacy.collegeboard.org/sites/default/files/Trends-Who-Borrows-Most-Brief.pdf

Bean, J. (1990). Why students leave: Insights from research. In D. Hossler & J. P. Bean (Eds.), *The strategic management of college enrollments* (pp. 147–169). San Francisco: Jossey-Bass.

Bean, J. P. (1980). Dropouts and turnover: The synthesis of a causal model of attrition. *Research in Higher Education, 12,* 155–187.

Bean, J. P. (1983). The application of a model of turnover in work organizations to the student attrition process. *Review of Higher Education, 6,* 127–148.

Becker, G. S. (1964). *Human capital: A theoretical and empirical analysis with special reference to education.* New York: Columbia University Press.

Becker, G. S. (1975). *Human capital: A theoretical and empirical analysis, with special consideration of education* (2nd ed.). New York: National Bureau of Economic Research.

Becker, W. E. (2004). Omitted variables and sample selection in studies of college-going decisions. In E. P. St. John (Ed.), *Public policy and college access: Investigating the federal and state roles in equalizing postsecondary opportunity.* Readings on Equal Education (Vol. 19, pp. 65–86). New York: AMS Press.

Bell, A. D., Rowan-Kenyon, H. T., & Perna, L. W. (2009). College knowledge of 9th and 11th grade students: Variation by school and state context. *The Journal of Higher Education, 80*(6), 663–685.

Bennett, W. J. (1986). Text of Secretary Bennett's speech on college costs and US student aid. *The Chronicle of Higher Education, 33*(13), 20.

Bennett, W. J. (1987, February 18). Our greedy colleges. *New York Times,* I 31.

Berg, D. J., & Hoenack, S. A. (1987). The concept of cost-related tuition and its implications at the University of Minnesota. *The Journal of Higher Education, 58,* 276–305.

Berkner, L., & Chavez, L. (1997). *Access to postsecondary education for the 1992 high school graduates.* Washington, DC: U.S. Department of Education, Office of Educational Research and Improvement.

Berkner, L., He, S., & Cataldi, E. M. (2002). *Descriptive summary of 1995–96 beginning postsecondary students: Six years later.* National Center for Educational Statistics, NCES 2003151. Retrieved from http://nces.ed.gov/pubs2003/2003151.pdf

Berkner, L., Horn, L., & Clune, M. (2000). *Descriptive summary of 1995–96 beginning postsecondary students: Three years later, with an essay on students who started at less-than-4-year institutions.* National Center for Educational Statistics, NCES 2000154. Retrieved from http://nces.ed.gov/pubsearch/pubsinfo.asp?pubid=2000154

Bettinger, E. (2004). How financial aid affects persistence. In C. Hoxby (Ed.), *College choices: The economics of where to go, when to go, and how to pay for it* (pp. 207–238). Chicago: University of Chicago Press.

Bettinger, E. P., & Long, B. T. (2009). Addressing the needs of underprepared students in higher education: Does college remediation work? University of Wisconsin Press. *Journal of Human Resources, 44*(3), 736–771.

Bifulco, R., Cobb, C. D., & Bell, C. (2009). Can interdistrict choice boost student achievement? The case of Connecticut's interdistrict magnet school program. *Educational Evaluation and Policy Analysis, 31*(4), 323–345.

Bishop, J. H. (2002, June). *A prospective policy evaluation of the Michigan Merit Award Program.* Prepared for the Kennedy School of Government conference: Taking Account of Accountability: Assessing Politics and Policy. Harvard University Press.

Bishop, J. H. (2004). Merit scholarships for the many: Doubling the number of high school students who work hard in high school. In R. Kazis, J. Vargas, & N. Hoffman (Eds.), *Double the numbers: Increasing postsecondary credentials for underrepresented youth* (pp. 87–100). Cambridge, MA: Harvard Education Press.

Black, S. E., & Sufi, A. (2002). *Who goes to college? Differential enrollment by race and family background.* NBER Working Paper Series (9310), 43. Retrieved from http://www.nber.org/papers/w9310

Blackmer, A. R., Bragdon, H. W., Bundy, M., & Harbison, E. H. (1952). *General education in school and college: A committee report by members of the faculty at Andover, Exeter, Lawrenceville, Harvard, Princeton, and Yale.* Cambridge, MA: Harvard University Press.

Bloom, A. (1987). *The closing of the American mind.* New York: Simon and Schuster.

Bloom, H. S., Thompson, S. L., & Unterman, R. (June 2010). *Executive summary. Transforming the high school experience: How New York City's new small schools are boosting student achievement and graduation rates.* New York: MDRC.

Bolman, L. G., & Deal, T. E. (1991/1996). *Reframing organizations: Artistry, choice, and leadership.* San Francisco: Jossey-Bass.

Boulus, M., & Daun-Barnett, N. (2008, October 11). *Community college baccalaureate: A solution in search of a problem.* Retrieved from http://pcsum.org/Portals/0/docs/Community%20College%20Baccalaureate-%20A%20Solution%20in%20Search%20of%20a%20Problem-FINAL.pdf

Bound, J., & Turner, S. (2002). Going to war and going to college: Did World War II and the G.I. Bill increase educational attainment for returning veterans? University of Chicago Press. *Journal of Labor Economics, 20*(4), 784–815.

Bourdieu, P. (1980/1990). *The logic of practice* (R. Nice, Trans.). Stanford, CA: Stanford University Press.

Bowen, H. R. (1978). *Investment in learning: The individual and social value of American higher education.* San Francisco: Jossey-Bass.

Bowen, H. R. (1980). *The costs of higher education: How much do colleges and universities spend per student and how much should they spend?* San Francisco: Jossey-Bass.

Bowen, W. G., & Bok, D. (1998). *The shape of the river: Long-term consequences of considering race in college and university admissions.* Princeton, NJ: Princeton University Press.

Bowen, W. G., Chingos, M., & McPherson, M. S. (2009). *Crossing the finish line: Completing college at America's public universities.* Princeton, NJ: Princeton University Press.

Bowman, P. J., & St. John, E. P. (2011). *Diversity, merit, and higher education: Toward a comprehensive agenda for the twenty-first century.* Readings on Equal Education, Vol. 25. New York: AMS Press.

Boyd, D., Lankford, H., Loeb, S., Rockoff, J., & Wyckoff, J. (2008). The narrowing gap in New York City teacher qualifications and its implications for student achievement in high-poverty schools. *Journal of Policy Analysis and Management 24*(4), 793–818.

Bozick, R., & Ingels, S. J. (2008). *Mathematics course taking and achievement at the end of high school: Evidence from the Education Longitudinal Study of 2002* (ELS: 2002). National Center for Educational Statistics, NCES 2008–319. U.S. Department of Education. Washington, DC: NCES.

Bracco, K. R. (1997). *State structures in governance of higher education.* San Jose, CA: California Higher Education Policy Center.

Braxton, J., McKinney, J., & Reynolds, P. (2006). Cataloguing institutional efforts to understand and reduce college student departure. In E. P. St. John (Ed.), *New directions in institutional research*, 130. San Francisco: Jossey Bass.

Braxton, J. M. (Ed.). (2000). *Reworking the student departure puzzle.* Nashville, TN: Vanderbilt University Press.

Breneman, D. W. (1994). *Liberal arts colleges: Thriving, surviving or endangered?* Washington, DC: The Brookings Institution.

Brodie, J. (1996). New state forms, new political spaces. In R. Boyer & D. Drache (Eds.), *States against markets: The limits of globalization* (pp. 383–398). London: Routledge.

Brown, M. C. II, Butler, J., & Donahoo, S. (2004). Desegregation and diversity: Finding new ways to meet the challenge. In E. P. St. John & M. D. Parsons (Eds.), *Public funding of higher education: Changing contexts and new rationales* (pp. 108–123). Baltimore: Johns Hopkins University Press.

• References

Brown v. Board of Education, 347 US 483 (1954).

Brown v. Board of Education, 349 US 294 (1955).

Bureau of Labor Statistics. (2004). *Consumer price index: All urban consumers* [online data file]. U.S. Department of Commerce. Retrieved from www.bls.gov/cpi/home.htm

Burke, J. C. (2005). *Achieving accountability in higher education: Balancing public, academic, and market demands.* San Francisco: Jossey-Bass.

Cabrera, A. F., Nora, A., & Castañeda, M. B. (1992). The role of finances in the persistence process: A structural model. *Research in Higher Education, 33*(5), 571–594.

Cabrera, A. F., Nora, A., & Castañeda, M. B. (1993). College persistence: Structural equations modeling test of an integrated model of student retention. *The Journal of Higher Education, 64*(2), 123–139.

Cahalan, M. W., Ingels, S. J., Burns, L. J., Planty, M., Daniel, B., & Owings, J. A. (2006). *United States high school sophomores: A twenty-two year comparison, 1980–2002.* National Center for Educational Statistics, NCES 2008–320. Washington, DC: U.S. Department of Education, National Center for Educational Statistics.

Calgano, J. C., & Long, B. T. (2008). *The impact of postsecondary remediation using a regression discontinuity approach: Addressing endogenous sorting and noncompliance.* NBER Working Paper Series (14194). Retrieved from http://www.nber.org/papers/w14194.pdf

California Community Colleges Chancellor's Office. (2005). *Addendum: Impact of student fee increase and budget changes on enrollment in California Community Colleges. Analysis of fee increase from $18 to $26 per unit.* Retrieved from http://www.cccco.edu/Portals/4/TRIS/research/reports/impact_study_18_26.pdf

California Student Aid Commission. (2011). *State budget reductions result in Changes to Cal Grant Program eligibility and cuts to Cal Grant awards.* Retrieved from http://www.csac.ca.gov/NEWS/05-05-11_Exec DirectorMsg_statebudgetreductionsincalgrants.pdf

Callan, P. M. (2002, February). *Coping with recession: Public policy, economic downturns and higher education.* National Center Report 02–2. Washington, DC: National Center for Public Policy and Higher Education.

Callan, P. M., & Finney, J. E. (Eds.). (1997). *Public and private financing of higher education: Shaping public policy for the future.* Phoenix, AZ: American Council on Education/Oryx Press.

Carey, K. (2008, April). *Graduation rate watch: Making minority success a priority.* Education Sector Reports. Washington, DC: Education Sector. Retrieved from http://www.educationsector.org/usr_doc/Graduation_Rate_ Watch.pdf

Carnegie Commission on Higher Education. (1973). *Priorities for action: Final report.* New York: McGraw-Hill.

Carnegie Council on Policy Studies in Higher Education. (1980). *Three thousand futures: The next twenty years for higher education.* San Francisco: Jossey-Bass.

Carnes, B. M. (1987). The campus cost explosion: College tuitions are unnecessarily high. *Policy Review, 40,* 68–71.

Carnevale, A. P. (2007). Confessions of an education fundamentalist: Why grade 12 is not the right end point for anyone. In N. Hoffman, J. Vargas, A. Venezia, & M. S. Miller, (Eds.), *Minding the gap: Why integrating high school with college makes sense and how to do it* (pp. 15–26). Cambridge, MA: Harvard Education Press.

Carnoy, M. (2001). *Do school vouchers improve student performance?* Washington, DC: Economic Policy Institute.

Carnoy, M., & Loeb, S. (2002). Does external accountability affect student outcomes? A cross-state analysis. *Education Evaluation and Policy Analysis, 24*(4), 305–331.

Ceja, M. (2006). Understanding the role of parents and siblings as information sources in the college choice process of Chicana students. *Journal of College Student Development, 47*(1), 87–104.

Chaney, B. (2010). *National evaluation of student support services: Examination of student outcomes after six years.* Washington, DC:

Westat.Chaney, B., Burgdorf, K., & Atash, N. (1997). Influencing achievement through high school graduation requirements. *Educational Evaluation and Policy Analysis, 19*(3), 229–244.

Chapa, J., & Horn, C. L. (2007). Is anything race neutral? Comparing "race-neutral" admissions policies at the University of Texas and the University of California. In G. Orfield, P. Marin, S. M. Flores, & L. Garces (Eds.) *Charting the future of college affirmative action: Legal victories, continuing attacks, and new research* (pp. 157–172). Los Angeles: Civil Rights Project, UCLA School of Education. Retrieved from http://www.civilrightsproject.ucla.edu/research/affirmativeaction/charting_aa.php

Chea, T. (2009, August). Budget cuts devastate California higher education. *Associated Press.* Retrieved from http://www.google.com/hostednews/ap/article/ALeqM5gjzoH4l6imyUZtTNQZkn2Kg4hsCAD99STNJ00

Cheit, E. F. (1971). *The new depression in higher education.* New York: Mc-Graw Hill.

Cheit, E. F. (1974). *The new depression in higher education—Two years later.* New York: McGraw Hill.

Chen, R., & Carroll, C. D. (2005). *First-generation students in postsecondary education: A look at their college transcripts.* Washington, DC: National Center for Education Statistics.

Chen, R., & St. John, E. P. (2011). State financial policies and student persistence at first institutions: A national study. *The Journal of Higher Education, 82*(5), 629–660.

Choy, S. P. (2002a). *Access & persistence: Findings from 10 years of longitudinal research on students.* Washington, DC: American Council on Education.

Choy, S. P. (2002b). *Findings from The Condition of Education, 2002: Nontraditional undergraduates.* Washington, DC: National Center for Education Statistics.

Chubb, J. E., & Moe, T. M. (1990). *Politics, markets, and America's schools.* Washington, DC: The Brookings Institution.

Chung, A.(2008a) The choice of for-profit college. [Dissertation.] Retrieved from http://mpra.ub.uni-muenchen.de/18971/1/MPRA_paper_18971.pdf

Chung, A. (2008b). For-profit student heterogeneity. Retrieved from http://mpra.ub.uni-muenchen.de/18967/1/MPRA_paper_18967.pdf

Chung, A. (2009). *The effects of for-profit college training on earnings.* Retrieved from http://mpra.ub.uni-muenchen.de/18972/1/MPRA_paper_18972.pdf

Clements, M. M., & Powers, J. B. (2011). Privatizing the intellectual commons: Ethical practice and the social contract for science in the United States. In J. B. Powers & E. P. St. John (Eds.), *Higher education, commercialization, and university-business relationships in comparative context. Issues in globalization and social justice: Comparative studies in international higher education.* AMS Monograph Series (Vol. 2). New York: AMS Press.

Clotfelter, C. T., Ladd, H. F., & Vigdor, J. L. (2007). *How and why do teacher credentials matter for student achievement?* NBER Working Paper Series (12828). Cambridge, MA: National Bureau of Economic Research.

Clune, W. H., & White, P. A. (1992). *School-based management: Institutional variation, implementation, and issues for further research.* New Brunswick, NJ: Rutgers University, Eagleton Institute of Politics, Center for Policy Research in Education.

Cohen, R., & Zelnik, R. E. (Eds.) (2002). *The free speech movement: Reflections on Berkeley in the 1960s.* Berkeley, CA: University of California Press.

Cohen-Vogel, L., & Ingle, K. (2007). When neighbors matter most: Innovation, diffusion and state policy adoption in tertiary education. *Journal of Education Policy, 22*(3), 241–262.

Colavecchio-Van Stickler, S. (2007, July 21). Not such a bright future: A lawsuit highlights a fierce tug of war over state's popular scholarship program. *St. Petersburg Times.* Retrieved from www.sptimes.com/2007/07/State/Not_Such_A_Bright_Future

Coleman, J. S. (1965). *Education and political development.* Princeton, NJ: Princeton University Press.

College Board. (2010). *Trends in student aid 2009.* Retrieved from http://trends.collegeboard.org/downloads/Student_Aid_2010.pdf

College Foundation of North Carolina. (2009). *An evaluation of North Carolina's College Planning Web Portal, CFNC.org.* Chapel Hill, NC: University of North Carolina General Administration.

Commission on the Future of Higher Education. (2006). *A test of leadership: Charting the future of US Higher Education. Report to the Commission on the Future of Higher Education.* Washington, DC: Department of Education.

Commission on the Reorganization of Secondary Education. (1918). *The cardinal principles of secondary education.* Washington, DC: Author.

Commission on the Skills of the American Workforce. (2007). *Tough choices, tough times: The report of the new Commission on Skills of the American Workforce.* Washington, DC: National Center on Education and the Economy.

Committee on Economic Development. (1973). *The management and financing of colleges.* New York: Author.

Conant, J. B. (1959). *The American High School Today.* New York: McGraw-Hill.

Conklin, K. D., & Curran, B. K. (2005). *Action agenda for improving America's high schools.* Sponsored by Achieve, Inc., and the National Governors Association. Retrieved from www.achieve.org/achieve.nsf/ActionAgenda_Overview?Open Form

Conley, D. (2005). *College knowledge: What it really takes for students to succeed and what it takes to get them ready.* San Francisco: Jossey-Bass.

Connerly, W. (2000). *A vision for America, beyond race: Intellectual ammunition.* Retrieved from www.heartland.org/ia/novdec00/connerly.htm

Conrad, C. F., Brier, E. M., & Braxton, J. M. (1997). Factors contributing to the matriculation of White students in public HBCUs. *Journal for a Just and Caring Education, 3*(1), 37–62.

Conrad, C. F., & Shrode, P. E. (1990). The long road: Desegregating higher education. *NEA Higher Education Journal, 6*(1), 35–45.

Constantine, J. M., Seftor, N. S., Martin, E. S., Silva, T., & Myers, D. (2006). *A study of the effect of the Talent Search program on secondary and postsecondary outcomes in Florida, Indiana, and Texas: Final report from phase II of the national evaluation.* Report prepared by Mathematica Policy Research for the U.S. Department of Education, Office of Planning, Evaluation, and Policy Development, Policy and Program Studies Service. Washington, DC: U.S. Department of Education.

Cook, W. A. (1912). A brief survey of the development of compulsory education in the United States. *The Elementary School Teacher, 12*(7), 331–335.

Council of Chief State School Officers. (2008). *Key state policies on PK-12 education: 2008.* Washington, DC: Author.

Cullen, J. B., Jacob, B. A., & Levitt, S. (2006). The effect of school choice on participants: Evidence from Randomized lotteries. *Econometrica, 74*(5), 1191–1230.

Cunningham, A., Erisman, W., & Looney, S. (2008). *Higher education in Michigan: Overcoming challenges to expand access.* Washington, DC: Institute for Higher Education Policy.

Cuomo, A., & Megna, R. L. (2011). *New York at a crossroads: A transformation plan for a new New York.* Retrieved from http://publications.budget.state.ny.us/eBudget1112/fy1112littlebook/BriefingBook.pdf

Dalton, B., Ingels, S. J., Downing, J., & Bozick, R. (2007). *Advanced mathematics and science coursetaking in the spring high school senior classes of 1982, 1992, and 2004.* National Center for Educational Statistics, NCES Statistical Analysis Report 07–312. Washington, DC: Institute of Education Sciences, U.S. Department of Education.

Data Quality Campaign. (2011). *Leveraging federal funding for longitudinal data systems—A roadmap for states.* Retrieved from http://www.dataqualitycampaign.org/build/arra_programs/

Daun-Barnett, N. (2008a). *Collaborating for efficiency and quality: A report from the President's Council, State Universities of Michigan.* Retrieved from http://pcsum.org/Portals/0/docs/Collaborating-Efficiency-Quality-2008.pdf

Daun-Barrett, N. (2008b). *Preparation and access: A multi-level analysis of state policy influences on the academic antecedents to college enrollment.* Unpublished doctoral dissertation, University of Michigan, Ann Arbor.

Daun-Barnett, N. (2011). The Kalamazoo promise: A new twist on tuition guarantees. *Journal of Student Financial Aid, 41*(1), 28-37.

Daun-Barnett, N. (2012). Access to college: A reconsideration of the National Education Longitudinal Study (NELS). *Educational Policy.* DOI: 10.1177/0895904811429290

Daun-Barnett, N., & Holohan-Moyer, I. (in press). Local college access strategies: Examining the equitable distribution of postsecondary access in Michigan. In G. Sunderman (Ed.), *Charting reform, achieving equity in a diverse nation.* Charlotte, NC: Information Age.

Daun-Barnett, N., & St. John, E. P. (2012). Constrained curriculum in high schools: The changing math standards and student achievement, high school graduation and college continuation. *Education Policy Analysis Archives, 20*(5). Retrieved from http://epaa.asu.edu/ojs/article/view/907

Deil-Amen, R., & Tevis, T. L. (2010). Circumscribed agency: The relevance of standardized college entrance exams for low SES high school students. *Review of Higher Education, 33*(2), 141–175.

Delaney, J., & Doyle, W. (2007). The role of higher education in state budgets. In K. Shaw & D. E. Heller (Ed.), *State postsecondary education research: New methods to inform policy and practice.* Sterling, VA: Stylus.

De Nies, J. (2010). President Obama outlines goal to improve college graduation rate in US: US ranks 12th globally, trailing Canada and Russia. Retrieved from http://abcnews.go.com/WN/president-barack-obama-outlines-college-education-goal-university/story?id=11359759

DesJardins, S., Ahlburg, D. A., & McCall, B. P. (2006). An integrated model of application, admission, enrollment, and financial aid. *The Journal of Higher Education, 77*(3), 381–429.

DesJardins, S. L., & McCall, B. P. (2009). *The impact of Washington State Achievers Scholarship on student outcomes.* Paper Presented at the 2009 Association for the Study of Higher Education Conference, Vancouver, BC.

Deutsch, A. (1917). A phase of compulsory education. *The School Review, 25*(2), 73–87.

Doyle, W. R. (2010). Does merit aid "crowd out" need-based aid? *Research in Higher Education, 51*(5), 397–415.

Dresch, S. P. (1975). A critique of planning models for postsecondary education: Current feasibility, potential relevance, and a prospectus for future research. *The Journal of Higher Education, 46,* 246–286.

Drury, S. B. (1997). *Leo Strauss and the American right.* New York: St. Martin's Press.

Dynarski, S. (1999, November). *Does aid matter? Measuring the effect of student aid on college attendance and completion.* NBER Working Paper Series (7422). Cambridge, MA: NBER.

Dynarksi, S. (2000). Hope for whom? Financial aid for the middle class and its impact on college attendance. *National Tax Journal, 53*(3), 629–662.

Dynarski, S. (2002, December). *The consequences of merit aid.* NBER Working Paper Series (9400). Cambridge, MA: National Bureau of Economic Research.

Dynarski, S. (2004). The new merit aid. In C. Hoxby (Ed.), *College choices: The economics of where to go, when to go and how to pay for it* (pp. 63–100). Chicago: University of Chicago Press.

Eckes, S., & Rapp, K. (2006). Charter school research: Trends and implications. In E. P. St. John (Ed.), *Public policy and equal educational opportunity: School reforms, postsecondary encouragement, and state policies on postsecondary education.* Readings on Equal Education (Vol. 21, pp. 3–36). New York: AMS Press.

Eckes, S., & Rapp, K. (2007). *Are charter schools using recruitment strategies to increase student body diversity?* Thousand Oaks, CA: Sage.

Education Commission of the States. (2000). *State funding for community colleges: A 50-state survey*. Denver, CO: Author.

Ehrenberg, R. G. (2002). *Tuition rising: Why college costs so much*. Cambridge, MA: Harvard University Press.

Evenbeck, S., Seabrook, P. A., St. John, E. P., & Murphy, S. (2004). Twenty-first century scholars: Indiana's program of incentives for college going. In R. Kazi, J. Vargas, & N. Hoffman (Eds.), *Double the numbers: Increasing postsecondary credential for underrepresented youth* (pp. 169–174). Cambridge, MA: Harvard Education Press.

Evens, J. (1970). The view from the state of California. *Change, 3*(5).

Etzkowitz, H. (2011). Whither the (entrepreneurial) university? In J. Powers & E. P. St. John (Eds.), *Higher education, commercialization, and university-business relationships in comparative context: Vol. 1. Issues in globalization and social justice: Comparative studies in international higher education*. AMS Monograph Series (Vol. 2). New York: AMS Press.

Feder, J. (2010). *Unauthorized alien students, higher education, and in-state tuition rates: A legal analysis*. Washington, DC: Congressional Research Service.

Felder, P. F. (2012). Prior socialization in academic capital formation: HBCU origins and their impact on doctoral student success. In R. Winkle-Wagner, P. J. Bowman, & E. P. St John (Eds.), *Expanding postsecondary opportunity for underrepresented students: Theory and practice of academic capital formation*. Readings on Equal Education (Vol. 26). New York: AMS Press.

Ferreri, E., & Price, J. (2011, April 3). NC shifting more higher education costs to students. *Charlotte Observer*, p. 2.

Finn, C., Manno, B., & Vanourek, G. (2000). *Charter schools in action: Renewing public education*. Princeton, NJ: Princeton University Press.

Finn, C. E., Jr. (1978). *Scholars, dollars, and bureaucrats: Federal policy toward higher education*. Washington, DC: The Brookings Institute.

Finn, C. E., Jr. (1988a). Judgment time for higher education in the court of public opinion. *Change, 20*(4), 35–38.

Finn, C. E., Jr. (1988b). *Prepared statement and attachments*. Hearing before the Subcommittee on Postsecondary Education, Committee on Education and Labor, House of Representatives, 100th Congress, 1st Session, No. 100–47, September 25. Washington, DC: U.S. Government Printing Office.

Finn, C. E., Jr. (1990). Why we need choice. In W. L. Boyd & H. J. Walberg (Eds.), *Choice in education: Potential and problems* (pp. 3–20). Berkeley, CA: McCutchan.

First, P. F. (1992). *Educational policy for school administrators*. Boston: Allyn and Bacon.

Fiske, E. B. (2010). The Carolina covenant. In R. D. Kahlenberg (Ed.). *Rewarding strivers: Helping low-income students succeed in college* (pp. 17–70) New York: Century Foundation Press.

Fitzgerald, B. F., & Kane, T. J. (2003, October). *Lowering barriers to college access in California and the nation: Opportunities for more effective state and federal student aid policies*. Paper presented at the conference of the Harvard Civil Rights Project and the University of California, Sacramento, CA.

Fitzgerald, B. K. (2004). Federal financial aid and college access. In E. P. St. John (Ed.), *Public policy and college access: Investigating the federal and state roles in equalizing postsecondary opportunity*. Readings on Equal Education (Vol. 19, pp. 1–28). New York: AMS Press.

Fitzgibbons, R. H. (1968). *The academic senate of the University of California*. Berkeley, CA: University of California, President's Office.

Fitzsimmons, E. G. (2011, February 17). Michigan governor proposes budget cuts and lower taxes. *New York Times*. Retrieved from http://thecaucus.blogs.nytimes.com/2011/02/17/michigan-governor-proposes-big-budget-cuts-lower-taxes/

Flores, S. M. (2010). State DREAM Acts: The effect of in-state resident tuition policies and undocumented Latino students. *Review of Higher Education, 33*(2), 239–283.

Florida Senate Pre-K–12 Appropriations Committee. (2009). *Bill analysis and fiscal impact statement: High school graduation requirements*. Retrieved from http://archive.flsenate.gov/data/session/2009/Senate/bills/analysis/pdf/2009s2654.ea.pdf

Fogel, R. W. (2000). *The fourth great awakening and the future of egalitarianism*. Chicago: Chicago University Press.

Fossey, R. E., & Bateman, M. (Eds.). (1998). *Condemning students to debt: College loans and public policy*. New York: Teachers College Press.

Friedman, M. (1962). *Capitalism and freedom*. Chicago: University of Chicago Press.

Friedman, T. L. (2005). *The world is flat: A brief history of the twenty-first century*. New York: Farrar, Straus, and Giroux.

Gándara, P. (2002). Meeting common goals: Linking K-12 and college interventions. In W. G. Tierney & L. S. Hagedorn (Eds.), *Increasing access to college: Extending possibilities for all students*. Albany, NY: SUNY Press.

Gándara, P. (2005). *Fragile futures: Risk and vulnerability among Latino high achievers*. Policy Brief. Princeton, NJ: Education Testing Service.

Gándara, P., Orfield, G., & Horn, C. (Eds.). (2006). *Expanding opportunity in higher education: Leveraging promise.* Albany, NY: SUNY Press.

Gladieux, L. E., & Wolanin, T. (1976). *Congress and the colleges: The national politics of higher education.* Lexington, MA: Lexington Books.

Gleason, P. (1995). *Contending with modernity: Catholic higher education in the twentieth century.* New York: Oxford University Press.

Glenny, L. A. (1971). *Coordinating higher education for the 70s: Multi-campus and statewide guidelines for practice.* Berkeley, CA: Center for Research and Development in Higher Education.

Glenny, L. A. (1973). *Trends in state funding in higher education: A preliminary report.* Denver: Higher Education Services Division, Education Commission of the States.

Glenny, L. A., Bowen, F. M., Meisinger, R. J., Morgan, A. W., Purves, R. A., & Schmidtline, F. A. (1975). *State budgeting in higher education: Data digest.* Berkeley, CA: Center for Research and Development in Higher Education, University of California, Berkeley.

Goldhaber, D. D., & Brewer, D. J. (2000). Does teacher certification matter? High school teacher certification status and student achievement. *Educational Evaluation and Policy Analysis, 100*(1), 129–145.

Gonzalez, J. (2011, February 27). Governors face challenges in improving college-completion rates: Lack of money, turnover in ranks are obstacles for ambitious goals. *Chronicle of Higher Education.* Retrieved from http://chronicle.texterity.com/chronicle/20110304a?pg = 22#pg22

Gratz v. Bollinger, 539 US 244 (2003).

Grubb, W. N. (1996a). *Learning to work: The case for reintegrating job training and education.* New York: Russell Sage Foundation.

Grubb, W. N. (1996b). *Working in the middle: Strengthening education and training for the mid-skilled labor force.* San Francisco: Jossey-Bass.

Grutter v. Bollinger, 539 US 306 (2003).

Habermas, J. (1984). *The theory of communicative* action (Vols. 1 & 2). Cambridge, UK: Polity Press.

Habermas, J. (1987). *The theory of communicative action: Vol. 2. Lifeworld and system: A critique of functionalist reasoning* (T. McCarthy, Trans.). Boston: Beacon Press.

Habermas, J. (1990). *Moral consciousness and communicative action.* Cambridge, MA: MIT Press.

Halstead, D. K. (1974). *Statewide planning in higher education.* Washington, DC: U.S. Government Printing Office.

Hammack, F. M. (2004). *The comprehensive high school today.* New York: Teachers College Press.

Hansen, W. L. (1983). The impact of student financial aid on access. In J. Froomkin (Ed.), *The crisis in higher education* (pp. 84–96). New York: Academy of Political Science.

Hansen, W. L., & Weisbrod, B. A. (1967). *An income net worth approach to measuring economic welfare.* Madison, WI: Institute for Research on Poverty, University of Wisconsin.

Hansen, W. L., & Weisbrod, B. A. (1969). *Benefits, costs, and finance of public higher education.* Chicago: Markham.

Harnisch, T. L. (2011). *Performance-based funding: A re-emerging strategy in public higher education funding.* A Higher Education Policy Brief. American Association of State Colleges and Universities. Retrieved from http://www.congressweb.com/aascu/docfiles/Performance_Funding_AASCU_June2011.pdf

Harper, S., Williams, C. D., Pérez D. II, & Morgan, D. L. (2012). His experience: Toward a phenomenological understanding of academic capital formation among Black and Latino male students. In R. Winkle-Wagner, P. J. Bowman, & E. P. St. John (Eds.), *Expanding postsecondary opportunity for underrepresented students: Theory and practice of academic capital formation.* Readings on Equal Education (Vol. 26). New York: AMS Press.

Harvey, D. (2005). *A brief history of neoliberalism.* New York: Oxford University Press.

Hearn, J. C. (1993). The paradox of growth in federal aid for college students: 1965–1990. In J. C. Smart (Ed.), *Higher education: Handbook of theory and research* (Vol. 9, pp. 439–460). New York: Agathon Press.

Hearn, J. C. (2001a). Access to postsecondary education: Financing equity in an evolving context. In M. B. Paulsen & J. C. Smart (Eds.), *The finance of higher education: Theory, research, policy, and practice* (pp. 439–460). New York: Agathon Press.

Hearn, J. C. (2001b). Epilogue to the paradox of growth in federal aid for college students: 1965–1990. In M. B. Paulsen & J. C. Smart (Eds.), *The finance of higher education: Theory, research, policy, and practice* (pp. 316–320). New York: Agathon Press.

Hearn, J. C., & Anderson, M. S. (1989). Integrating postsecondary education financing policies: The Minnesota model. In R. H. Fenske (Ed.), *Studying the impact of student aid on institutions* (pp. 55–74). New Directions for Higher Education, No. 62. San Francisco: Jossey-Bass.

Hearn, J. C., & Anderson, M. S. (1995). The Minnesota finance experiment. In E. P. St. John (Ed.), *Rethinking tuition and student aid strategies* (pp. 5–26). New Directions for Higher Education, No. 89. San Francisco: Jossey-Bass.

Hearn, J. C., & Holdsworth, J. M. (2004). Federal student aid: The shift from grants to loans. In E. P. St. John & M. D. Parsons (Eds.), *Public funding of higher education: Changing contexts and new rationales* (pp. 40–59). Baltimore: Johns Hopkins University Press.

Hearn, J. C., & Longanecker, D. (1985). Enrollment effects of alternative post-secondary pricing policies. *The Journal of Higher Education, 56*(5), 485–508.

Hearn, J. C., Sand, H., & Urahn, S. (1985). *Targeted subsidization of postsecondary enrollment in Minnesota: A policy evaluation.* Minneapolis: Center for Urban and Regional Affairs, University of Minnesota.

Heckman, J. J., & LaFontaine, P. A. (2007). *The American high school graduation rate: Trends and levels.* Cambridge, MA: National Bureau of Economic Research.

Heller, D. E. (1997). Student price response in higher education: An update to Leslie and Brinkman. *The Journal of Higher Education, 68*(6), 624–659.

Heller, D. E. (1999). The effects of tuition and state financial aid on public college enrollment. *Review of Higher Education, 23*(1), 65–89.

Heller, D. E. (2001). Trends in the affordability of public colleges and universities: The contradiction of increasing prices and increasing enrollment. In D. E. Heller (Ed.), *The states and public higher education policy: Affordability, access, and accountability* (pp. 11–38). Baltimore: The Johns Hopkins University Press.

Heller, D. E. (2004a). NCES research on college participation: A critical analysis. In E. P. St. John (Ed.), *Public policy and college access: Investigating the federal and state roles in equalizing postsecondary opportunity.* Readings on Equal Education (Vol. 19, pp. 29–64). New York: AMS Press.

Heller, D. E. (2004b). State merit scholarship programs. In E. P. St. John (Ed.), *Public policy and college access: Investigating the federal and state roles in equalizing postsecondary opportunity,* Readings on Equal Education (Vol. 19, pp. 99–108). New York: AMS Press.

Heller, D. E., & Marin, P. (Eds.). (2002). *Who should we help? The negative social consequences of merit scholarships.* Cambridge, MA: The Civil Rights Project, Harvard University.

Heller, D. E., & Marin, P. (Eds.). (2004). *State merit scholarship programs and racial inequality.* Cambridge, MA: The Civil Rights Project, Harvard University.

Heller, D. E, & Rasmussen, C. J. (2002). Merit scholarships and college access: Evidence from Florida and Michigan. In D. E. Heller & P. Marin (Eds.), *Who should we help? The negative social consequences of merit aid scholarships* (pp. 25–40) Cambridge, MA: The Civil Rights Project, Harvard University.

Heller, D. E., & Shapiro, D. T. (2001). *Legal challenges to high stakes testing: A case of disparate impact in Michigan?* Paper presented at the American Educational Research Association Annual Meeting, Seattle, WA.

Henry, M., Lingard, B., Rizvi, F., & Taylor, S. (2001). *The OECD, globalization and education policy.* Amsterdam: Pergamon Press.

Hoffer, T. B. (1997). High school graduation requirements: Effects on dropping out and student achievement. *Teachers College Record, 98*(4), 584–607.

Hoffman, N., Vargas, J., Venezia, A., & Miller, M. S. (Eds.) (2007). *Minding the gap: Why integrating high school with college makes sense and how to do it.* Cambridge, MA: Harvard Education Press.

Horn, L., Cataldi, E. F., & Sikora, A. (2005). *Waiting to attend college: Undergraduates who delay their postsecondary enrollment.* National Center for Educational Statistics, NCES 2005–152. Washington, DC: U.S. Department of Education, NCES.

Horn L., & Kojaku L. (2001). *High school academic curriculum and the persistence path through college: Persistence and transfer behavior of undergraduates 3 years after entering 4-year institutions.* National Center for Educational Statistics, NCES 2001–163. Washington, DC: U.S. Department of Education, NCES.

Horn, L. Nevill, S., & Griffith, J. (2006). *Profile of undergraduates in US postsecondary education institutions, 2003–04: With a special analysis of community college students.* Statistical Analysis Report. National Center for Educational Statistics, NCES 2006–184. Washington, DC: NCES.

Horn, L., & Nuñez, A. (2000). *Mapping the road to college: First-generation students' math track, planning strategies, and context of support.* National Center for Educational Statistics, NCES 2000153.Washington, DC: NCES.

Horn, L., & Peter, K. (2003). *What colleges contribute: Institutional aid to full-time undergraduates attending 4-year colleges and universities.* National Center for Educational Statistics, NCES 2003–157. Washington, DC: U.S. Department of Education.

Hossler, D. (1984). *Enrollment management: An integrated approach.* New York: College Entrance Examination Board.

Hossler, D. (1987). *Creating effective enrollment management systems.* New York: College Entrance Examination Board.

Hossler, D. (2004). Refinancing public universities: Student enrollments, incentive-based budgeting and incremental revenue. In E. P. St. John & M. D. Parsons (Eds.), *Public funding of higher education: Changing contexts and new rationales* (pp. 145–163). Baltimore: Johns Hopkins University Press.

Hossler, D. (2006). Student and families as revenue: The impact on institutional behaviors. In D. M. Priest & E. P. St. John (Eds.), *Privatization in public universities: Implications for the public trust*. Bloomington, IN: Indiana University Press.

Hossler, D., Bean, J. P., & Associates. (1990). *The strategic management of college enrollment*. San Francisco: Jossey-Bass.

Hossler, D., Gross, J. P. K., & Ziskin, M. (Eds.) (2009). *Enhancing institutional and state initiatives to increase student success: Studies of the Indiana Project on Academic Success*. Readings on Equal Education (Vol. 24). New York: AMS Press.

Hossler, D., Lund, J. P., Ramin-Gyurnek, J., Westfall, S., & Irish, S. (1997). State funding for higher education: The Sisyphean task. *The Journal of Higher Education, 68*(2), 160–190.

Hossler, D., & Schmit, J. (1995). The Indiana postsecondary-encouragement experiment. In E. P. St. John (Ed.), *Rethinking tuition and student aid strategies* (pp. 27–39). San Francisco: Jossey-Bass.

Hossler, D., Schmit, J., & Vesper, N. (1999). *Going to college: How social, economic, and educational factors influence the decisions students make*. Baltimore: Johns Hopkins University Press.

Hossler, D., Ziskin, M., & Gross, J. (2009). Getting serious about institutional performance in students retention: Research-based lessons on effective policies and practice. *About Campus, 13*(6): 2–11.

Hoxby, C. (2002). School choice and school productivity (or could school choice be a tide that lifts all boats?). NBER Working Paper Series, 8873, 75. Retrieved from http://www.nber.org/papers/w8873

Hoxby, C. (2004). Introduction. In C. Hoxby (Ed.), *College choices: The economics of where to go, when to go, and how to pay for it* (pp. 1–12). Chicago: University of Chicago Press.

Hu, S. (2008, May). *Merit-based financial aid and student enrollment in baccalaureate degree programs in science and engineering: What can Florida's Bright Futures program tell us?* Presented at the annual forum of the Association for Institutional Research (AIR), Seattle, WA.

Hu, S., & St. John, E. P. (2000, July). *Student persistence in a public higher education system: Understanding racial/ ethnic differences*. Policy Research Report No. 00–03. Bloomington, IN: Indiana Education Policy Center.

Inside Higher Education. (2011). *Obama signs short-term spending bill that kills LEAP Program*. Retrieved from http://www.insidehighered.com/news/2011/03/03/qt#252846

Institute of Education Sciences. (2011). *Statewide longitudinal data systems grant program*. Retrieved from http:// nces.ed.gov/programs/slds/

Institute of Governmental Studies. (2011, September 5). Tax and expenditure limitation in California: Proposition 13 & Proposition 4. UC Berkeley. Retrieved from http://igs.berkeley.edu/library/research/quickhelp/policy/ finance/tax_spend_limits_2003.html

Ishitani, T. T. (2003). A longitudinal approach to assessing attrition behavior among first-generation students: Time-varying effects of precollege characteristics. *Research in Higher Education, 44*(4), 433–449.

Jackson, G. A. (1978). Financial aid and student enrollment. *Journal of Higher Education, 49*(6), 548–574.

Jacob, B., & Lefgren, L. (2007). The effect of grade retention on high school completion. (NBER Working Paper Series, Vol. October). Cambridge, MA: National Bureau of Economic Research.

Jacob, B. A., & Lefgren, L. (2009, July). The effect of grade retention on high school completion. American Economic Association. *American Economic Journal: Applied Economics, 1*(3), 33–58.

Jacobs, F., & Tingley, T. (1977). *The evolution of eligibility criteria for Title III of the Higher Education Act of 1965: Appendix A. The development of institutions of higher education: Theory and assessment of impact of four possible areas of federal intervention*. Cambridge, MA: Harvard University Press.

Jencks, C., & Riesman, D. (1968). *The academic revolution*. Chicago: Doubleday.

Johnstone, D. B. (2001). Financing higher education: Who should pay? In P. G. Altbach, R. O. Berdahl, & P. Gumport (Eds.), *American higher education in the twenty-first century* (pp. 347–369). Baltimore: The Johns Hopkins University Press.

Justia US Law. (2010). Michigan Compiled Laws Chapter 390—Universities and Colleges Act 94 of 1999—Michigan Merit Award Scholarship. Retrieved May 10, 2012, from http://law.justia.com/codes/michigan/2010/ chapter-390/act-94-of-1999/

Kane, T. J. (1995). *Rising public college tuition and college entry: How well do public subsidies promote access to college?* NBER Working Paper Series (5146). Cambridge, MA: National Bureau of Economic Research.

Kane, T. J. (2003). *A quasi-experimental estimate of the impact of financial aid on college-going*. NBER Working Paper Series (9703), 65. Retrieved from http://www.nber.org/papers/w9703

Kane, T. J. (2004). *Evaluating the impact of the D.C. Tuition Assistance Grant Program*. NBER Working Paper Series (10658), 54. Retrieved from http://www.nber.org/papers/w10658

Katz, M. B. (2001). *The irony of early school reform: Educational innovation in mid-nineteenth century Massachusetts*. New York: Teachers College Press.

Kazis, R., Vargas, J., & Hoffman, N. (Eds.). (2004). *Double the numbers: Increasing postsecondary credentials for underrepresented youth*. Cambridge, MA: Harvard Education Press.

Kerr, C. (1963). *The uses of the university.* Cambridge, MA: Harvard University Press.

Kerr, C. (Ed.) (1978). *12 systems of higher education: 6 decisive issues.* New York: International Council for Educational Development.

Kerr, C. (1991, May). The new race to become Harvard or Berkeley or Stanford. *Change,* 8–15.

Kerr, C. (1994). *Higher education cannot escape history: Issues for the 21st century.* Albany, NY: SUNY Press.

Kerr, C. (2002). Shock wave II: An introduction to the 21st century. In S. J. Brint (Ed.), *The future of the city of intellect: The changing American university* (pp. 1–19). Palo Alto, CA: Stanford University Press.

Kim, D. (2008). The effect of financial aid on students' college choice: Differences by racial groups. *Research in Higher Education, 45*(1), 43–70.

Kipp, S. M., Price, D. V., & Wohlford, J. K. (2002). *Unequal opportunity: Disparities in college access among the 50 states.* Indianapolis, IN: Lumina Foundation for Education, New Agenda Series.

Kirp, D. L. (2003). *Shakespeare, Einstein, and the bottom line: The marketing of higher education.* Cambridge, MA: Harvard University Press.

Kirshstein, R. J., Tikoff, V. K., Masten, C., & St. John, E. P. (1990). *Trends in institutional costs.* Prepared for the U.S. Department of Education Office of Planning, Budget and Evaluation. Washington, DC: Pelavin Associates.

Kirst, M. W. (1998). *Bridging the remediation gap.* Bridge Project, Stanford University. Retrieved from www.standord.edu/group/bridgeporject/gap/remedgap.pdf

Kirst, M. W. (1999). *Babel of standards: Students face a confusing array of tests and assessments.* Stanford University. Retrieved from www.stanford.edu/group/bridgeproject/babel/babel.pdf

Kirst, M. W. (2001). *Overcoming the high school senior slump: New education policies.* Stanford University. www.standord.edu/group/bridgeproject/seniorslump/seniorslum.pdf

Kirst, M. W., & Venezia, A. (Eds.). (2004). *From high school to college: Improving opportunities for success in postsecondary education.* San Francisco: Jossey-Bass.

Klein, N. (2008). *The shock doctrine: The rise of disaster capitalism.* New York: Henry Holt.

Kornmanik, B. (2002, August 27). Bright Futures polices attached: Exam scores under fire as a scholarship basis. *The Florida Times-Union.* Retrieved from www.jacksonvill.com/tu-online/08702

Kozol, J. (1992). I dislike the idea of choice and I want to tell you why. *Educational Leadership, 50*(3), 90–92.

Kronholz, J. (2003, September 23). Merit scholarships expand as college expenses climb. *The Wall Street Journal Online.* Retrieved from http://www.nyu.edu/classes/jepsen/wsjSep2302.pdf

Krug, E. A. (1964). *The shaping of the American high school.* New York: Harper & Row.

Labaree, D. F. (1997). Public goods, private goods: The American struggle over educational goals. *American Educational Research Journal, 34*(1), 39–81.

L.A. Now. (2011, November 23). UC Davis chancellor: Police defied my orders by using pepper spray. Retrieved from http://latimesblogs.latimes.com/lanow/2011/11/uc-davis-pepper-spray-chancellor-police-defied-orders.html

Layzell, D. T., & McKeown, M. P. (1992). *State funding formulas for higher education: Trends and issues.* Paper Presented at the Annual ASHE Conference. Minneapolis.

Lazerson, M. (1997, March/April). Who owns higher education? *Change, 29*(2), 10–15.

Lazerson, M. (2001). The College Board and American educational history. In M. C. Johanek (Ed.), *A faithful mirror: Reflections on the College Board and education in America* (pp. xxv, 400). New York: College Board.

Lee, E. C., & Bowen, F. M. (1971). *The multi-campus university: A study of academic governance.* New York: McGraw-Hill.

Lee, E. C., & Bowen, F. M. (1975). *Managing multi-campus systems: Effective administration in an unsteady state.* San Francisco: Jossey-Bass.

Lee, J. B. (2004). Access revisited: A preliminary reanalysis of NELS. In E. P. St. John (Ed.), *Public policy and college access: Investigating the federal and state roles in equalizing postsecondary opportunity.* Readings on Equal Education (Vol. 19, pp. 87–96). New York: AMS Press.

Lee, J. B., & Carroll, C. D. (2001). *Undergraduates enrolled with higher sticker prices.* National Center for Educational Statistics, NCES 2001–171. Washington, DC: U.S. Department of Education and NCES.

Lee, M., & St. John, E. P. (2012). Academic capital formation among Hmong students: An exploratory study of the role of ethnic identity in college transitions. In R. Winkle-Wagner, P. J. Bowman, & E. P. St John (Eds.), *Expanding postsecondary opportunity for underrepresented students: Theory and practice of academic capital formation.* Readings on Equal Education (Vol. 26). New York: AMS Press.

Lee, V. E., Croninger, R. G., & Smith, J. B. (1997). Course-taking, equity, and mathematics learning: Testing the constrained curriculum hypothesis in US secondary schools. *Educational Evaluation and Policy Analysis, 19*, 99–121.

Lee, V. E., & Ready, D. D. (2007). *Schools within schools: Possibilities and pitfalls of high school reform.* New York: Teachers College Press.

Lee, V. E., & Ready, D. D. (2009, Spring). The US high school curriculum: Three phases of contemporary research and reform. *The Future of Children, 19*(1), 135–156.

Legislative Analyst's Office. (2005). *Proposition 98 primer.* Sacramento, CA: Author. Retrieved from http://www.lao.ca.gov/2005/prop_98_primer/prop_98_primer_020805.htm

Leslie, L. L. (1977). *Higher education opportunity: A decade of progress.* ERIC/AAHE Higher Education Research Report No. 3. Washington, DC: American Association for Higher Education.

Leslie, L. L., & Brinkman, P. (1987). Student price response in higher education: The student demand studies. *The Journal of Higher Education, 58*(2), 181–204.

Leslie, L. L., & Brinkman, P. T. (1988). *The economic value of higher education.* New York: Macmillan.

Levin, H. M., & McEwan, P. J. (2000). *Cost effectiveness analysis: Methods and applications* (2nd ed.). Thousand Oaks, CA: Sage.

Lindblom, C. E. (1959). The science of muddling through. *Public Administration Review, 19*(2), 79–88. Retrieved from http://www.archonfung.net/docs/temp/LindblomMuddlingThrough1959.pdf

Linsenmeier, D. M., Rosen, H. S., & Rouse, C. E. (2002). *Financial aid packages and college enrollment decisions: An econometric study.* NBER Working Paper Series (9228), 45. Retrieved from http://www.nber.org/papers/w9228

Lleras, M. P. (2004). *Investing in human capital: A capital markets approach to student funding.* Cambridge, UK: Cambridge University Press.

Lombardi, J. V., & Capaldi, E. D. (1996). Accountability and quality evaluation in higher education. In D. S. Honeyman, J. L. Wattenbarger, & K. C. Westbrook (Eds.), *Struggle to survive: Funding higher education in the next century.* Thousand Oaks, CA: Corwin.

Long, B. T. (2004). The impact of federal tax credits for higher education. In C. Hoxby (Ed.), *College choices: The economics of where to go, when to go, and how to pay for it* (pp. 101–168). Chicago: University of Chicago Press.

Lt. Governor's Commission on Higher Education and Economic Growth. (2004). *Final report of the Lt. Governor's Commission on Higher Education and Economic Growth.* Retrieved from http://www.cherrycommission.org/docs/finalReport/CherryReport.pdf

Lumina Foundation. (2008). *Indiana's Twenty-First Century Scholars program: A statewide story with national implications, results and reflections.* Indianapolis, IN: Author.

Lumina Foundation (2009). *Indiana's Twenty-First Century Scholars program: A statewide story with national implications.* Indianapolis, IN: Author. Retrieved from http://www.umich.edu/~mpas/LuminaReport.pdf

Lydon, J., & Morgan, R. (in press). The Bologna Process and the Lisbon Agenda: Implications for European Higher Education. In J. B. Powers & E. P. St. John (Eds.), *Higher education, commercialization, and university-business relationships in comparative context. Issues in globalization and social justice: Comparative studies in international higher education.* AMS Monograph Series (Vol. 2). New York: AMS Press.

Ma, J. (2003). *Education savings incentives and household saving: Evidence from the 2000 TIAA-CREF survey of participant finances.* NBER Working Paper Series (9505), 49. Retrieved from http://www.nber.org/papers/w9720

Manset, G., St. John, E. P., Hu, S., & Gordon, D. (2002). Early literacy practices as predictors of reading related outcomes: Tests scores, test passing rates, retention, and special education referral. *Exceptionality, 10*, 11–28.

Manset, G., & Washburn, S. (2000). Equity through accountability? Mandating minimum competency exit examinations for secondary students with learning disabilities. *Learning Disabilities Research and Practice, 15*(3), 160–167.

Manski, C. F., & Wise, D. A. (1983). *College choice in America.* Cambridge, MA: Harvard University Press.

Marksjarvis, G. (2010, December 5). Unemployment for college graduates and people over 45 hit highs. *Chicago Tribune.* Retrieved from http://newsblogs.chicagotribune.com/marksjarvis_on_money/2010/12/unemployment-for-college-graduates-and-people-over-45-hit-highs.html

Marmaduke, A. S. (Ed.) (1988). *Beyond the borders: A discussion of student financial aid and educational opportunity in Texas, New York, and the Pacific Rim.* Sacramento, CA: The Eureka Project, 1988.

Marsden, G. M. (1994). *The soul of the American university: From Protestant establishment to established nonbelief.* New York: Oxford University Press.

Martin, D. (2011, May 11). Ind. Gov. signs 80 bills into law, including budget. *Bloomberg Businessweek.* Retrieved from http://www.businessweek.com/ap/financialnews/D9N58MVG0.htm

Martorell, P. & McFarlin, I. (2007). Help or hindrance? The effects of college remediation on academic and labor market outcomes. *Review of Economics and Statistics, 93*(2), 436–454.

McConnell, T. R., & Mortimer, K. P. (1970). *The faculty in university governance.* Berkeley, CA: Center for Research and Development in Higher Education, University of California.

McDonough, P. M. (1997). *Choosing colleges: How social class and schools structure opportunity.* Albany, NY: SUNY Press.

McDonough, P. M., & Fann, A. (2007). The Study of Inequality. In P. Gumport (Ed.), *Sociology of Higher Education* (pp. 53–93). Baltimore, MD: The Johns Hopkins University Press.

McGrath, E. J. (1970). *Should students share the power? A study of their role in college and university governance.* Philadelphia, PA: Temple University Press.

McKeown, M. P. (1996). State funding formulas: Promise fulfilled? In D. S. Honeyman, J. L. Wattenbarger, & K. C. Westbrook (Eds.), *A struggle to survive: Funding higher education in the next century* (pp. 49–85). Thousand Oaks, CA: Corwin Press.

McLendon, M. K., Hearn, J. C., & Deaton, R. (2006). Called to account: Analyzing the origins and spread of state performance-accountability policies for higher education. *Educational Evaluation and Policy Analysis, 28*(1), 1–24.

McPherson, M. S. (1978). The demand for higher education. In D. W. Breneman & C. E. Finn Jr. (Eds.), *Public policy and private higher education* (pp. 143–146). Washington, DC: Brookings Institution.

McPherson, M. S., & Shapiro, M. O. (1991). *Keeping college affordable: Government and educational opportunity.* Washington, DC: The Brookings Institution.

McPherson, M. S., & Shapiro, M. O. (1998). *The student aid game: Meeting need and rewarding talent in American higher education.* Princeton, NJ: Princeton University Press.

Megino, N. (2011, July 16). CSU Tuition increases 12 percent. *Danville Patch.*

Mercer, C. (2008). Title III and Title V of the Higher Education Act: Background and reauthorization issues. U.S. Congressional Research Service RL31647. Retrieved from http://congressionalresearch.com/RL31647/document.php?study=Title+III+and+Title+V+of+the+Higher+Education+Act+Background+and+Reauthorization+Issues

Metcalf, K. K., & Paul, K. M. (2006). Enhancing or destroying equity? An examination of educational vouchers. In E. P. St. John (Ed.), *Public policy and equal educational opportunity: School reforms, postsecondary encouragement, and state policies on postsecondary education.* Readings on Equal Education (Vol. 21, pp. 37–74). New York: AMS Press.

Michigan Department of Education. (2006). *State of Michigan improved high school graduation requirements.* Retrieved from http://www.michigan.gov/documents/Final_HS_Grad_Requirements_One-Pager_5_158245_7.04.06.pdf

Michigan Department of Treasury. (2006). *Michigan Promise Scholarship Fact Sheet. The Michigan Merit Award Scholarship Act, MCL 390.1451 (1999).* Retrieved from http://www.michigan.gov/documents/mistudentaid/FactSheetPromiseFY07_192865_7.pdf

Michigan Senate Fiscal Agency. (1996). *School finance in Michigan before and after the implementation of proposal A: A comparison of FY 1993–94 and FY 1994–95 approaches to K–12 school funding in Michigan.* Retrieved from http://senate.michigan.gov/sfa/Publications/JointRep/FINPROPA/95COMP.HTML

Michigan State Legislature. (2006, December 21). *Michigan Promise Grant Act.* Retrieved June 14, 2008, from http://www.legislature.mi.gov/%28S%28exnku33psi2gky45e02vll45%29%29/documents/mcl/pdf/mcl-act-479-of-2006.pdf

Miller, K. (2008, April 23). Bright Futures top awards go primarily to whites. *Palm Beach Post.* Retrieved from http://www.palmbeachpost.com/localnews/content/local_news/epaper/2008/04/23/m1a_bfscholars_0423.html

Minnesota Budget Project. (2011). *Governor's budget cuts higher education as demand increases.* Retrieved from http://minnesotabudgetbites.org/2010/02/17/governors-budget-cuts-higher-education-as-demand-increases/

Minnesota Higher Education Coordinating Board. (1982). *Final report of the task force on future funding of postsecondary education.* Retrieved from http://www.leg.state.mn.us/docs/pre2003/other/830421.pdf.

Minnesota Office of Higher Education. (2011). *Minnesota state grant program parameters over time.* Retrieved from http://www.ohe.state.mn.us/pdf/faresearch/parameters.pdf

Moltz, D. (2009, March 29). Competing completion initiatives. *Inside Higher Education.* Retrieved from http://www.insidehighered.com/news/2009/05/05/completion

Montgomery, A. (2000, March 27). A "poison" divides us. Retrieved from http://dir.salon.com/politics2000/feature/2000/03/27/connerly/index.html

Morales, I. (2008, February 5). State universities protest Bright Futures Bill on line. *The Independent Florida Alligator.* Retrieved from http://www.alligator.org/articles/2008/02/05/news/uf_administration/brightfutures.txt

Morse, A., & Birnbach, K. (2010). *In-state tuition and unauthorized immigrant students.* Denver: National Conference of State Legislatures.

Moses, M. S. (2001, Spring). Affirmative action and the creation of more favorable contexts of choice. *American Educational Research Journal, 38*(1), pp. 3–36.

Moses, M. S. (2002). *Embracing race: Why we need race-conscious education policy.* New York: Teachers College Press.

Moses, M. S. (2006). Why the affirmative action debate persists: The role of moral disagreement. *Educational Policy, 20*(4), 567–586.

Moses, R. P., & Cobb, C. E. (2001). *Racial equations: Civil rights from Mississippi to the algebra project.* Boston: Beacon Press.

Muffo, J., Voorhees, R. A., & Hyslop, L. (2008). *An analysis of the feasibility for the bachelor's degree in applied science and technology in the state of Michigan.* Retrieved from http://www.michigan.gov/documents/dleg/pa_118_of_2007_Sec_408_230299_7.pdf

Musoba, G. D. (2006). Accountability v. adequate funding: Which policies influence adequate preparation for college? In E. P. St. John (Ed.), *Public policy and equal educational opportunity: School reforms, postsecondary encouragement, and state policies on postsecondary education.* Readings on Equal Education (Vol. 21, pp. 75–125). New York: AMS Press.

National Center for Education Statistics. (1970). *Projections of education statistics to 1979–80.* Washington, DC: Author.

National Center for Education Statistics. (1980). *Projections of education statistics to 1988–89.* By M. M. Frankel & D. E. Gerald. Washington, DC: Author.

National Center for Education Statistics. (2004). *National Educational Longitudinal Study 1988–2000.* Retrieved from Data Analysis System, http://nces.ed.gov/das/

National Center for Education Statistics. (2005). *Table 154—State requirements for high school raduation, in Carnegie units: 2004.* Retrieved from *http://www.nces.ed.gov/pubs2005/digest2005/*

National Center for Education Statistics. (2008). *Status and trends in education of American Indians and Alaska Natives: Enrollment in colleges and universities.* Retrieved from http://nces.ed.gov/pubs2008/nativetrends/ind_6_1.asp

National Center for Education Statistics (2009). *NAEP 2008 trends in academic progress.* Washington, DC: National Center for Educational Statistics. Retrieved from http://nces.ed.gov/nationsreportcard/pdf/main2008/2009479_1.pdf

National Center for Education Statistics. (2010). *The condition of education, 2010.* Retrieved from http://nces.ed.gov/programs/coe/2010/section1/indicator01.asp

National Center for Education Statistics. (2011*). Integrated postsecondary education data system.* Retrieved from http://nces.ed.gov/ipeds/

National Center for Fair and Open Testing (2007, July 11). *Florida scholarship bias challenged.* Retrieved from http://www.fairtest.org/florida-scholarship-bias-challenged

National Center for Public Policy and Higher Education. (2008). *Measuring Up 2008: The state-by-state report card for higher education.* Retrieved from http://measuringup2008.highereducation.org/

National Commission on the Financing of Postsecondary Education (1973). *Financing postsecondary education in the United States.* Washington, DC: Government Printing Office.

National Council of Teachers of Mathematics (1989). *Curriculum and evaluation standards for school mathematics.* Reston, VA: Author.

National Education Association (1894). *Report on the Committee of Ten.* Washington, DC: Author.

National Governors Association (2007). *Innovation: building a science, technology, engineering, and math agenda.* Washington, DC: Author.

National Research Council. (2011). *Incentives and test-based accountability in education.* Committee on Incentives and Test-Based in Public Education, M. Hout and W. W. Elliott (Eds). Washington, DC: The National Academies Press.

Nelms, C. (2010). *Strengthening America's historically Black colleges and universities: A call to action.* Paper presented at the NCCU Symposium Setting the Agenda for Historically Black Colleges and Universities, June 2–4, 2010, Durham, NC. Retrieved from http://www.nccu.edu/formsdocs/proxy.cfm?file_id=1447

Ness, E., & Tucker, (2008, Spring). Eligibility effects on college access: Under-represented student perceptions of Tennessee's merit aid program. *Research in Higher Education, 49,* 569–588.

Newman, F. (1971). *US task force on higher education.* Washington, DC: U.S. Government Printing Office.

Newton, J. (2006). *Justice for all: Earl Warren and the nation he made.* New York: Riverhead Books.

New York State Senate. (2011). Senate passes UB 2020 legislation. Retrieved from http://www.nysenate.gov/press-release/senate-passes-ub-2020-legislation

North Carolina Community College System. (2008). *A matter of facts: North Carolina Community College System Fact Book.* Retrieved from http://www.nccommunitycolleges.edu/Publications/docs/Publications/fb2008.pdf

Nussbaum, M. C. (1999). *Sex and social justice.* Oxford, UK: Oxford University Press.

Nussbaum, M. C. (2000). *Women and human development: The capabilities approach.* New York: Cambridge University Press.

Nussbaum, M. C. (2004). *Hiding from humanity: Disgust, shame, and the law.* Princeton, NJ: Princeton University Press.

Nussbaum, M. C. (2008). *Liberty of conscience: In defense of America's tradition of religious equality.* New York: Basic Books.

Nussbaum, M. C. (2011). *Creating capabilities: The human development approach.* Cambridge, MA: Harvard University Press.

Oakes, J. (1985). *Keeping track: How schools structure inequality.* New Haven, CT: Yale University Press.

Oakes, J. (2003). *Critical conditions for equity and diversity in college access: Informing policy and monitoring results.* UC Berkeley: University of California All Campus Consortium on Research for Diversity. Retrieved from http://www.escholarship.org/uc/item/427737xt

Oakes, J. (2005). *Keeping track: How schools structure inequality.* New Haven, CT: Yale University Press.

Obama, B. (2009). *Remarks of President Barack Obama—As prepared for delivery address to Joint Session of Congress.* Retrieved from http://www.whitehouse.gov/the_press_office/remarks-of-president-barack-obama-address-to-joint-session-of-congress/

Office of Postsecondary Education. (2011). *Federal TRIO programs—Home page.* Retrieved from http://www.ed.gov/about/offices/list/ope/trio/index.html

Office of Revenue and Tax Analysis. (2002). *School finance reform in Michigan proposal: A retrospective.* Lansing, MI: Michigan Department of Treasury.

Office of Student Financial Assistance. (2011). *Florida Bright Futures Scholarship Program fact sheet.* Retrieved from http://www.floridastudentfinancialaid.org/SSFAD/factsheets/BF.htm

O'Leary, K. (2009, June 27). The legacy of proposition 13. *Time US.* Retrieved from http://www.time.com/time/nation/article/0,8599,1904938,00.html

Oliver, I. (2009). *College access challenge grant: The federal policy climate explained.* Powerpoint presentation by HCM strategists. Retrieved from http://www.wiche.edu/info/cacg/meetings/boulder09/oliver.pdf

Orfield, G. (1997). Going to college. In K. K. Wong (Ed.), *Advances in educational policy analysis: Vol. 3. The Indiana youth opportunity study: A symposium* (pp. 3–32). Greenwich, CT: JAI Press.

Orfield, G. (1988). Exclusion of the majority: Shrinking college access and public policy in metropolitan Los Angeles. *The Urban Review, 20*(3), 147–163.

Orfield, G., Marin, P., Flores, S. M., & Garces, L. (2007). *Charting the Future of College Affirmative Action: Legal Victories, Continuing Attacks, and New Research* (pp. 173–204). Los Angeles: Civil Rights Project, UCLA School of Education. Retrieved from http://www.civilrightsproject.ucla.edu/research/affirmativeaction/charting_aa.php

Organisation for Economic Co-operation and Development (OECD). (2010). *PISA 2009 results: Executive summary.* Retrieved from http://www.oecd.org/dataoecd/34/60/46619703.pdf

Orlando Sentinel. (2011). Lawmakers slashed university funding, so students will make up the difference. *Orlando Sentinel.* Retrieved from http://articles.orlandosentinel.com/2011-06-24/news/os-ed-university-tuition-hikes-20110623_1_differential-tuition-universities-state-funding

Orrill, R. (2001). Grades 11–14: The heartland or the wasteland of American education? In M. C. Johanek (Ed.), *A faithful mirror: Reflections on the College Board and education in America* (pp. xxv, 400). New York: College Board.

Ort, S., Williford, L., & St. John, E. P. (2012). Carolina covenant: Reducing the retention gap. In E. P. St. John & R. Winkle-Wagner (Eds.), *Expanding postsecondary opportunity for underrepresented students: Theory and practice of academic capital formation.* Readings on Equal Education (Vol. 26). New York: AMS Press.

Palmer, J. (2011). Summary tables, fiscal year (FY) 2010–11: Table 2. *Grapevine survey of state appropriations to higher education.* Retrieved March 16, 2011, from http://www.grapevine.ilstu.edu/tables/FY11/Grapevine_Table2.pdf

Papay, J. P., Murnane, R, J., & Willett, J. B. (2008). *The consequences of high school exit examinations for struggling low-income urban students: Evidence from Massachusetts.* NBER Working Paper Series (14186). National Bureau of Economic Research.

Parsons, M. D. (2004). Lobbying in higher education: Theory and practice. In E. P. St. John & M. D. Parsons (Eds.), *Public funding of higher education: Changing contexts and new rationales* (pp. 215–230). Baltimore: Johns Hopkins University Press.

Pascarella, E. T., & Terenzini, P. T. (2005). *A third decade of research: How college affects students* (Vol. 2). San Francisco: Jossey-Bass.

Pasque, P. A. (2010). *American higher education, leadership, and policy: Critical issues and the public good.* New York: Palgrave.

Pattengale, J. A. (2008). *The purpose-guided student: Dream to succeed.* Boston: McGraw-Hill.

Patton, L. D., Morelon, C., Whitehead, D. M., & Hossler, D. (2006). Campus-based retention initiatives: Does the emperor have clothes? In E. P. St. John & M. Wilkerson (Eds.), *Reframing persistence research to support academic success.* New Directions for Institutional Research (Vol. 130, pp. 9–24). San Francisco: Jossey-Bass.

Paulsen, M. B. (2001a). The economics of human capital and investment in higher education. In M. B. Paulsen & J. C. Smart (Eds.), *The finance of higher education: Theory, research, policy & practice* (pp. 55–94). New York: Agathon Press.

Paulsen, M. B. (2001b). The economics of the public sector: The nature and role of public policy in higher education finance. In M. B. Paulsen & J. C. Smart (Eds.), *The finance of higher education: Theory, research, policy & practice* (pp. 95–132). New York: Agathon Press.

Pelavin, S. H., & Kane, M. B. (1988). *Minority participation in higher education.* Prepared for the U.S. Department of Education, Office of Planning, Budget and Evaluation. Washington, DC: Pelavin Associates.

Pelavin, S. H., & Kane, M. B. (1990). *Changing the odds: Factors increasing access to college.* New York: College Board.

Perna, L. W., & Thomas, S. (2009). Barriers to college opportunity: The unintended consequences of state-mandated testing. *Educational Policy, 23*(3), 451–479. Retrieved from http://epx.sagepub.com/content/23/3/451

Perna, L. W., & Titus, M. (2004). Understanding difference in the choice of college attended: The role of state public policies. *Review of Higher Education, 27*(4), 501–525.

Perna, L. W., & Titus, M. (2005). The relationship between parental involvement as social capital and college enrollment: An examination of racial/ethnic group differences. *The Journal of Higher Education, 76*(5), 485–518.

Perry, T., Moses, R., Wynne, J., Delpit, L., & Cortes, E. (2010). *Quality education as a constitutional right: Organizing to create a movement.* Boston: Beacon Press.

Peter, K., & Forrest Cataldi, E. (2005, May). *The road less traveled? Students who enroll in multiple institutions.* National Center for Educational Statistics, NCES 2005–157. U.S. Department of Education. Washington, DC: NCES.

Peter, K., & Horn, L. (2005). *Gender differences in participation and completion of undergraduate education and how they have changed over time.* National Center for Educational Statistics, NCES 2005–169. Washington, DC: U.S. Government Printing Office.

Peterson, P. E., Howell, W. G., Wolf, P. J., & Campbell, D. E. (2003). School vouchers: Results from randomized experiments. In C. M. Hoxby (Ed.), *The economics of school choice.* Chicago: University of Chicago Press.

Pew Hispanic Center. (2004). *Hispanic college enrollment: Less intensive and less heavily subsidized.* Washington DC: Author.

Pew Hispanic Center. (2006). *Recently arrived migrants and the congressional debate on immigration.* Retrieved from http://pewhispanic.org/files/factsheets/15.pdf

Pineda, D. (2009). *Examining a federal intervention to improve Latino college participation: Evidence from Title V Developing Hispanic-Serving Institutions Program,* Public Policy and Sociology, University of Michigan, Ann Arbor.

Planty, M., Provasnik, S., & Daniel, B. (2007). *High school coursetaking.* National Center for Educational Statistics, NCES 2007–065. Washington, DC: U.S. Department of Education, NCES.

Polyani, K. (2001). *The great transformation: The political and economic origins of our time.* Boston: Beacon Press.

Posselt, J. R. (2009). The rise and fall of need based grants: A critical review of presidential discourse on higher education. In J. Smart (Ed.), *Higher education: Handbook of theory and research* (Vol. 26, pp. 183–226). New York: Agathon Press.

Powers, J. B., & St. John, E. P. (Eds.) (in press). Higher education, commercialization, and university-business relationships in comparative context. In *Issues in globalization and social justice: Comparative studies in international higher education.* AMS Monograph Series (Vol. 2). New York: AMS Press.

Priest, D., & St. John, E. P. (Eds.) (2006). *Privatization and public universities.* Bloomington, IN: Indiana University Press.

Priest, D. M., Becker, W. E., Hossler, D., & St. John, E. P. (2002). Why an incentive-based budgeting system in the public sector and why now? In D. M. Priest, W. E. Becker, D. Hossler, & E. P. St. John (Eds.), *Incentive-based budgeting systems in public universities* (pp. 1–8). Northhampton, MA: Edward Elgar.

President's Council—State Universities of Michigan. (2009). *Enrollment report fall 2008.* Retrieved from http://pcsum.org/Portals/0/docs/PCSUM2008-Enrollment-Report.pdf

Public Sector Consultants. (2003). *Michigan's higher education system: A guide for state policymakers.* Big Rapids, MI: Ferris State University.

Pusser, B. (2002). Higher education, the emerging market, and the public good. In P. A. Graham & N. G. Stacey (Eds.), *The knowledge economy and postsecondary education.* Washington, DC: National Academy Press.

Pusser, B. (2004). *Burning down the house: Politics, governance, and affirmative action at the University of California.* Albany, NY: SUNY Press.

Quacquarelli Symonds Limited. (2011). *QS world rankings 2011/12.* Retrieved from http://www.topuniversities.com/university-rankings/world-university-rankings/2011

Rampell, C. (2011, March 30). Inequality is most extreme in wealth, not income. *New York Times,* Retrieved from http://economix.blogs.nytimes.com/2011/03/30/inequality-is-most-extreme-in-wealth-not-income/

Rampey, B. D., Dion, G. S., & Donahue, P. L. (2009). *NAEP 2008: Trends in academic progress.* National Center for Education Statistics, NCES 2009–479. Washington, DC: National Center for Education Statistics.

Ravitch, D. (2010). *The death and life of the great American school system: How testing and choices are undermining education.* New York: Basic Books.

Rawls, J. (1971). *A theory of justice.* Cambridge, MA: Belknap Press of Harvard University Press.

Rawls, J. (1999). *A theory of justice* (Rev. ed.). Cambridge, MA: Harvard University Press.

Rawls, J. (2001). *Justice as fairness: A restatement.* Cambridge, MA: Belknap Press of Harvard University Press.

Reese, W. J. (2005). *America's public schools: From the common school to no child left behind.* Baltimore: The Johns Hopkins University Press.

Resnick, D. P., & Resnick, L. B. (1985). Standards, curriculum, and performance: A historical and comparative perspective. *Educational Researcher, 14*(4), 5–20.

Reynolds, P. J., Gross, J., Millard, B., & Pattengale, J. (2010). Using longitudinal mixed-methods research to look at undeclared students. *New Directions in Institutional Research, 2010*(S2), 53–66.

Ridenour, C. S., & St. John, E. P. (2003). Private scholarships and school choice: Innovation or class reproduction? In L. F. Mirón & E. P. St. John (Eds.), *Reinterpreting urban schools reform: Have urban schools failed, or has the reform movement failed urban schools?* (pp. 177–206). Albany, NY: SUNY Press.

Rizzo, M., & Ehrenberg, R. (2004). Resident and nonresident tuition and enrollment at flagship state universities. In C. Hoxby (Ed.), *College choices: The economics of where to go, when to go, and how to pay for it* (pp. 303–353). Chicago: University of Chicago Press.

Roderick, M., Nagaoka, J., Coca, V., & Moeller, E. (2008). *From high school to the future: Potholes on the road to college.* Chicago: Consortium on Chicago School Research.

Rong, C., & St. John, E. P. (2011). College student persistence, transfer, and dropout: Income and racial differences in the effects of state finance policies. *Journal of Higher Education, 82*(5), 629–660.

Rothstein, J. M. (2002). *College performance predictions and the SAT.* Berkeley, CA: Center for Labor Economics, University of California.

Ruben, R. (2011). The Pell and the poor: A regression discontinuity analysis of on-time college enrollment. *Research in Higher Education, 52*, 1–18.

Schmidtlein, F., & Berdahl, R. O. (2005). Autonomy and accountability: Who controls academe? In P. G. Altbach, R. O. Berdahl, & P. Gumport (Eds.), *American higher education in the 21st century* (2nd ed., Chap. 3). Baltimore: The Johns Hopkins University Press.

Schultz, C. (1968). *The politics of public spending.* Washington, DC: The Brookings Institution.

Seftor, N. S., Mamun, A., & Schirm, A. (2009). *The impacts of regular upward bound on postsecondary outcomes 7–9 years after scheduled high school graduation.* Princeton, NJ: Mathematica Policy Research.

Seife, C. (2010). *Proofiness: The dark arts of mathematical deception.* New York: Viking.

Selix, C. (2010). New dual-credit trends emerge as pioneering post-secondary education options turn 25. MinnPost.com. Retrieved from http://www.minnpost.com/nextdegree/2010/06/17/18944/new_dual-credit_trends_emerge_as_pioneering_post-secondary_education_options_turns_25

Selweski, C. (2011, March 10). Michigan Senate passes emergency manager bills. *Daily Tribune.* Retrieved from http://www.dailytribune.com/articles/2011/03/10/news/doc4d78d0d4d764d009636769.txt

Sen, A. (1999). *Development as freedom.* New York: Anchor Press.

Sen, A. (2009). *The idea of justice.* Cambridge, MA: Belknap Press of Harvard University Press.

Shin, J. C. (2010). Impacts of performance-based accountability on institutional performance in the US. *Higher Education: The International Journal of Higher Education and Educational Planning, 60*(1), 47–68.

Shin, J. C., & Milton, S. (2006). Rethinking tuition effects on enrollment in public four-year colleges and universities. *Higher Education: The International Journal of Higher Education and Educational Planning, 29*(2), 213–237.

Simmons, L., & Chesser, J. (2011). *Census 2010: North Carolina is 6th fastest growing state in US.* Retrieved from http://ui.uncc.edu/story/census-2010-north-carolina-6th-fastest-growing-us

Slaughter, S. E. (1991). The official "ideology" of higher education: Ironies and inconsistencies. In W. G. Tierney (Ed.), *Culture and ideology in higher education: Advancing a critical agenda* (pp. 59–86). New York: Praeger.

Slaughter, S. E. (1993). Retrenchment in the 1980s: The politics of prestige and gender. *The Journal of Higher Education, 64*(3), 250–282.

Slaughter, S. E., & Leslie, L. L. (1997). *Academic capitalism: Politics, policies, and the entrepreneurial university.* Baltimore: Johns Hopkins University Press.

Slaughter, S. E., & Rhoades, G. (2004). *Academic capitalism and the new economy: Markets, state, and higher education.* Baltimore: The Johns Hopkins University Press.

Smelser, J. J., & Almond, G. (1974). *Growth, structural change, and conflict in California higher education.* Berkeley: University of California Press.

Smith, A. (1776/2010). *Wealth of Nations.* Mankato, MN: Capstone Press.

Sommerville, C. J. (2009). *Religious ideas for secular universities.* Grand Rapids, MI: Eerdmans.

State Student Assistance Commission of Indiana. (2011). *Twenty-first-century scholars pledge.* Retrieved from http://www.in.gov/ssaci/2374.htm

Steinberg, J. (2002). *The gatekeepers: Inside the admissions process of a premier college.* New York: Viking.

Stiglitz, J. E. (2002). *Globalization and its discontents.* New York: Norton.

St. John, E. P. (1973). Students work from within now to influence higher education. *California Journal, 4*, 169–171.

St. John, E. P. (1981). *Public policy and college management: Title III of the Higher Education Act.* New York: Praeger.

St. John, E. P. (1989). The influence of student aid on persistence. *Journal of Student Financial Aid, 19*(3), 52–68.

St. John, E. P. (1991a). A framework for reexamining state resource management strategies in higher education. *The Journal of Higher Education, 62*(3), 263–287.

St. John, E. P. (1991b). The transformation of liberal arts colleges: An analysis of selected case studies. *Review of Higher Education, 15*(1), 83–108.

St. John, E. P. (1992). Workable models for institutional research on the impact of student financial aid. *Journal of Student Financial Aid, 22*(3), 13–26.

St. John, E. P. (1994a). *Prices, productivity and investment: Assessing financial strategies in higher education.* ASHE/ERIC Higher Education Report, No. 3. Washington, DC: George Washington University, School of Education and Human Development.

St. John, E. P. (1994b). Retrenchment: A three-state study. *Thought & Action, 10*(2), 137–142.

St. John, E. P. (1998). Higher education desegregation in the post-Fordice legal environment: An historical perspective. In R. E. Fossey (Ed.), *Race, the courts, and equal education: The limits of the law.* Readings on Equal Education (Vol. 15, pp. 101–122). New York: AMS Press.

St. John, E. P. (1999). Evaluating state grant programs: A study of the Washington state grant programs. *Research in Higher Education, 40*(2): 149–170.

St. John, E. P. (2002). *The access challenge: Rethinking the causes of the new inequality.* Policy Issue Report No. 2002–01. Bloomington, IN: Indiana Education Policy Center.

St. John, E. P. (2003). *Refinancing the college dream: Access, equal opportunity, and justice for taxpayers.* Baltimore: Johns Hopkins University Press.

St. John, E. P. (2004). Public policy and research on college access: Lessons learned from NCES research and state evaluation studies. In E. P. St. John (Ed.), *Public policy and college access: Investigating the federal and state roles in equalizing postsecondary opportunity.* Readings on Equal Education (Vol. 19, pp. 181–196). New York: AMS Press.

St. John, E. P. (2006). *Education and the public interest: School reform, public finance, and access to higher education.* Dordrecht, The Netherlands: Springer.

St. John, E. P. (2007). Finding social justice in educational policy: Rethinking theory and approaches in policy research. In F. K. Stage, (Ed.). *Using qualitative data to answer critical questions. New Directions in Institutional Research* (Vol. 133, pp. 67–80). San Franciso: Jossey-Bass.

St. John, E. P. (2009a). *Action, reflection, and social justice: Integrating moral reasoning into professional development.* Cresskill, NJ: Hampton Press.

St. John, E. P. (2009b). *College organization and professional development: Integrating moral reasoning and reflective practice.* New York: Routledge.

St. John, E. P. (2010, June 2). *Access and success: Strategies for historically Black colleges and universities.* Presented at Setting an Agenda for Historically Black Colleges and Universities, sponsored by North Carolina Central University, Durham, North Carolina.

St. John, E. P. (in press). *Research, actionable knowledge, and social change.* Sterling, VA: Stylus.

St. John, E. P., & Byce, C. (1982). The changing federal role in student financial aid. In M. Kramer (Ed.), *Meeting student aid needs in a period of retrenchment* (pp. 21–40). New Directions for Higher Education, No. 40. San Francisco: Jossey-Bass.

St. John, E. P., Cabrera, A. F., Nora, A., & Asker, E. H. (2000). Economic influences on persistence reconsidered: How can finance research inform the reconceptualization of persistence models? In J. M. Braxton (Ed.), *Reworking the departure puzzle* (pp. 29–47). Nashville: Vanderbilt University Press. (Reprinted in: Stage, F. K., Carter, D. F., Hossler, D., & St. John, E P. (Eds.) (2003). *Theoretical perspectives on college students.* ASHE Reader Series. Boston: Pearson.)

St. John, E. P., & Chung, C. G. (2004). Merit and equity: Rethinking award criteria in the Michigan scholarship program. In E. P. St. John & M. D. Parsons (Eds.), *Public funding of higher education: Changing contexts and new rationales* (pp. 124–140). Baltimore: Johns Hopkins University Press.

St. John, E. P., Chung, A. S., Musoba, G. D., & Chung, C. G. (2006). Pathways and markets. In E. P. St. John et al. (Eds.), *Education and the public interest: School reform, public finance, and access to higher education* (pp. 115–130). Dordrecht, The Netherlands: Springer.

St. John, E. P., Chung, C. G., Musoba, G. D., & Simmons, A. B. (2006). Financial access. In E. P. St. John et al. (Eds.), *Education and the public interest: School reform, public finance, and access to higher education* (pp. 83–114). Dordrecht, The Netherlands: Springer.

St. John, E. P., Chung, C. G., Musoba, G. D., Simmons, A. B., Wooden, O. S., & Mendez, J. (2004). *Expanding college access: The impact of state finance strategies.* Indianapolis, IN: Lumina Foundation for Education.

St. John, E. P., & Elliott, R. J. (1994). Reframing policy research: A critical examination of research on federal student aid programs. In J. C. Smart (Ed.), *Higher education: Handbook of theory and research* (Vol. 10, pp. 126–180). New York: Agathon.

St. John, E. P., & Hossler, D. (1998). Higher education desegregation in the post-*Fordice* legal environment: A critical-empirical perspective. In R. E. Fossey (Ed.), *Race, the courts, and equal education: The limits of the law. Readings on Equal Education* (Vol. 15, pp. 123–156). New York: AMS Press.

St. John, E. P., Hu, S., & Fisher, A. S. (2011). *Breaking through the access barrier: Academic capital formation informing public policy.* New York: Routledge.

St. John, E. P., Hu, S., & Weber, J. (1999). *Affordability in public colleges and universities: The influence of student aid on persistence in Indiana public higher education.* Policy Research Report 99–2. Bloomington, IN: Indiana Education Policy Center.

St. John, E. P., Hu, S., & Weber, J. (2000). *State policy and the affordability of public higher education: The influence of state grants on persistence in Indiana.* Policy Research Report, 00–02. Bloomington, IN: Indiana Education Policy Center.

St. John, E. P., Hu, S., & Weber, J. (2001). State policy and the affordability of public higher education: The influence of state grants on persistence in Indiana. *Research in Higher Education, 42,* 401–428.

St. John, E. P., Kim, J., & Yang, L. (in press). *Privatization and inequality: Comparative studies of college access, education policy, and public finance: Vol.1. Globalization and social justice.* Comparative Studies in International Higher Education (Vol. 1). New York: AMS Press.

St. John, E. P., Kirshstein, R., & Noell, J. (1991). The effects of student aid on persistence: A sequential analysis of the high school and beyond senior cohort. *Review of Higher Education, 14*(3), 383–406.

St. John, E. P., Kline, K. A., & Asker, E. H. (2001). The call for public accountability: Rethinking the linkages to student outcomes. In D. E. Heller (Ed.), *The states and public higher education: Affordability, access, and accountability* (pp. 219–242). Baltimore: Johns Hopkins University Press.

St. John, E. P., Loescher, S. A., & Bardzell, J. S. (2003). *Improving reading and literacy in grades 1–5: A resource guide to research-based programs.* Thousand Oaks, CA: Corwin.

St. John, E. P., Manset-Williamson, G. M., Chung, C. G., & Michael, R. (2005, August). Assessing the rationales for educational reforms: An examination of policy claims about professional development, comprehensive reform, and direct instruction. *Education Administration Quarterly, 41*(3), 480–519.

St. John, E. P., Masse, J., Lijana, K., & Bigelow, V. M. (in press). *College prep: Transforming high schools, overcoming failed public policy, and preparing students for higher education.* Baltimore: Johns Hopkins University Press.

St. John, E. P., & Masten, C. L. (1990). Return on the federal investment in student financial aid: An assessment of the high school class of 1972. *Journal of Student Financial Aid, 20*(3), 4–23.

St. John, E. P., McKinney, J., & Tuttle, T. (2006). Using action inquiry to address critical challenges. In E. P. St. John & M. Wilkerson (Eds.), *Reframing persistence research to support academic success.* New Directions for Institutional Research (Vol. 30, pp. 63–76). San Francisco: Jossey-Bass.

St. John, E. P., & Moronski, K. (2008). *The impact of the Florida Bright Futures Scholarship Program on college preparation and access for low-income and minority students.* A paper prepared for ENLACE Florida. Retrieved from http://enlacefl.usf.edu/research/Research%20Briefs/2009/The-Impact-of-FL-BrightFuturesScholarship-on-CollegePrep.pdf

St. John, E. P., & Moronski, K. (in press). The late great state of California: The legacy of the master plan, the decline in access, and a new crisis. In E. P. St. John, J. Kim, & L. Yang (Eds.) *Privatization and inequality: Comparative studies of college access, education policy, and public finance: Vol.1. Globalization and social justice.* Comparative Studies in International Higher Education (Vol. 1). New York: AMS Press.

St. John, E. P., & Musoba, G. D. (2010). *Pathways to academic success: Expanding opportunity for underrepresented students.* New York: Routledge.

St. John, E. P., Musoba, G. D., Simmons, A. B., & Chung, C.-G. (2002). Meeting the access challenge: Indiana's twenty first century scholars program. Indianapolis, IN: Lumina Foundation for Education.

St. John, E. P., Musoba, G. D., Simmons, A. B., & Chung, C.-G. (2004). Meeting the access challenge: Indiana's twenty first century scholars program. *Research in Higher Education, 45*(8), 829–871.

St. John, E. P., & Noell, J. (1987, July). *Student loans and higher education opportunities: Evidence on access, persistence, and choice of major.* Presented at the Fourth Annual NASSGP/NCHELP Research Network Conference. St. Louis, MO: Washington University.

St. John, E. P., & Noell, J. (1989). The impact of financial aid on access: An analysis of progress with special consideration of minority access. *Research in Higher Education, 30*(6), 563–582.

St. John, E. P., Oescher, J., & Andrieu, S. C. (1992). The influence of prices on within-year persistence by traditional college-age students in four year colleges. *Journal of Student Financial Aid, 22*(1), 27–38.

St. John, E. P., & Parsons, M. D. (Eds.). (2004). *Public funding of higher education: Changing contexts and new rationales.* Baltimore: Johns Hopkins University Press.

St. John, E. P., Paulsen, M. B., &. Starkey, J. B. (1996). The nexus between college choice and persistence. *Research in Higher Education, 37*(2), 175–220.

St. John, E. P., Pineda, D., & Moronski, K. (2010). Higher education in the United States: Legal, financial and educational remedies to racial and income inequality in college access. In E. P. St. John, J. Kim, & L. Yang (Eds.) *Privatization and inequality: Comparative studies of college access, education policy, and public finance: Vol.1. Globalization and social justice.* Comparative Studies in International Higher Education (Vol. 1). New York: AMS Press.

St. John, E. P., & Regan, M. C. (1973). *Students in campus governance: Reasoning and models for student involvement.* Research Monograph No. 11, Department of Applied Behavioral Sciences. Davis, CA: University of California-Davis.

St. John, E. P., & Ridenour, C. S. (2000). *Market forces and strategic adaptation: The influence of private scholarships on educational improvement in urban schools.* Prepared for the Smith Richardson Foundation. Dayton, OH: University of Dayton.

St. John, E. P., & Ridenour, C. (2001). Market forces and strategic adaptation: The influence of private scholarships on planning in urban school systems. *The Urban Review, 33,* 269–290.

St. John, E. P., Simmons, A. B., Hoezee, L. D., Wooden, O. S., & Musoba, G. D. (2002). *Trends in higher education finance in Indiana compared to peer states and the US: A changing context, critical issues, and strategic goals.* Policy Research Report, No. 02–02. Bloomington, IN: Indiana Education Policy Center.

St. John, E. P., & Wilkerson, M. (Eds.), (2006). *Reframing persistence research to support academic success.* New Directions for Institutional Research No. 130. San Francisco: Jossey-Bass.

St. John, E. P., Williams, K., & Moronski, K. (2010). Public policy and inequality in postsecondary opportunity: Educational statistics and the failure of Education Reform International. In E. Backer, P. Peterson, & B. McGaw (Eds.), *Encyclopedia of Education* (3rd ed.). St. Louis, MO: Elsevier.

St. John, E. P., & Wooden, O. S. (2006). Privatization and federal funding for higher education. In D. M. Priest & E. P. St. John (Eds.), *Privatization and public universities* (pp. 38–64). Bloomington: Indiana University Press.

Stranahan, H., & Borg, M. (2004). Some futures are brighter than others: The net benefits received by Florida Bright Futures scholarship recipients. *Public Finance Review, 31*(1), 105–126.

Strogatz, S, (2010, September 19). Fibbing with numbers: A science writer examines the many ways of fudging figures. *The New York Times Review of Books,* p. 8.

Taylor, C. (2007). *A secular age.* Boston: Harvard University Press.

Teitelbaum, P. (2003). The influence of high school graduation requirement policies in mathematics and science on student course-taking patterns and achievement. *Educational Evaluation and Policy Analysis, 25*(1), 31–57.

Thelin, J. R. (2004a). Higher education and the public trough: A historical perspective. In E. P. St. John & M. D. Parsons (Ed.), *Public funding of higher education: Changing contexts and new rationales.* Baltimore: Johns Hopkins University Press.

Thelin, J. R. (2004b). *A history of American higher education.* Baltimore: Johns Hopkins University Press.

Thelin, J. R. (2010). Horizontal history and higher education. In M. B. Gasman (Ed.), *The history of higher education: Methods of understanding the past.* New York: Routledge.

Theobald, N. (2003). The need for issues-driven school funding reform in urban schools. In L. F. Mirón & E. P. St. John (Eds.), *Reinterpreting urban school reform: Have urban schools failed, or has the reform movement failed urban schools?* (pp. 33–52). Systems for K-12 and Higher Education. Albany, NY: SUNY Press.

Tienda, M., & Nui, S. (2006). Capitalizing on segregation, pretending neutrality: College admissions and the Texas top 10 percent law. *American Law and Economics Review, 8,* 312–346.

Tierney, W. G., Corwin, Z. B., & Colyar, J. E. (Eds.). (2005). *Preparing for college: Nine elements of effective outreach.* Albany, NY: SUNY Press.

Tierney, W. G., & Hagedorn, L. S. (Eds.). (2002). *Increasing access to college: Extending possibilities for all students.* Albany, NY: SUNY Press.

Tierney, W. G., & Venegas, K. (2007). The cultural ecology of financial aid decision making. In E. P. St. John (Ed.), *Confronting educational inequality: Reframing, building understanding, and making change.* Readings on Equal Education (Vol. 22, pp. 1–36). New York: AMS Press.

Tinto, V. (1975). Dropout from higher education: A theoretical synthesis of recent research. *Review of Educational Research, 45*(1), 89–125.

Tinto, V. (1982). The limits of theory and practice in student attrition. *Journal of Higher Education, 53,* 687–700.

Tinto, V. (1993). *Leaving college: Rethinking the causes and cures of student attrition* (2nd ed.). Chicago: University of Chicago Press.

Titus, M. A. (2006). Understanding college degree completion of students with low socioeconomic status: The influence of the institutional financial context. *Research in Higher Education, 47*(4), 371–398.

Titus, M. A. (2010). Understanding the relationship between working while in college and future salaries. In L. W. Perna (Ed.), *Understanding the working college student: New research and its implications for policy and practice.* Sterling, VA: Stylus Publishing.

Townsend, B. A. (2001). Redefining the community college transfer mission. *Community College Review, 29*(2), 29–42.

Travis, S. (2011, February 28). Bright Futures Scholarship Program faces $100 million funding cut. *Sun Sentinel.*

Trow, M. (1974). Problems in the transition from elite to mass higher education. In *Policies for higher education: General report on the Conference on Future Structures of Postsecondary Education* (pp. 55–101). Paris: OECD.

Turner, S., & Bound, J. (2003). Closing the gap or widening the divide: The effects of the G.I. Bill and World War II on the educational outcomes of Black Americans. *The Journal of Economic History, 63*(01), 145–177.

University of California Board of Regents v. Bakke 438 US 265 (1978).

University of North Carolina General Administration. (2011). The University of North Carolina: A multicampus university. Retrieved from http://www.northcarolina.edu/

Urban Institute. (2004). *Undocumented immigrants: Facts and figures.* Retrieved from http://www.urban.org/publications/1000587.html

U.S. Census Bureau. (2010). *American factfinder.* Retrieved from http://www.census.gov/

U.S. Census Bureau. (2011). *American factfinder.* Retrieved from http://www.census.gov/

U.S. Department of Education. (1983). *A nation at risk.* Washington, DC: Author.

U.S. Department of Education. (1999). *Impacts of Upward Bound: Final report for Phase I of the national evaluation.* Retrieved from http://www2.ed.gov/offices/OUS/PES/higher/upward.html

U.S. Department of Education. (2003). *Work first, study second: Adult undergraduates who combine employment and postsecondary enrollment.* By A. Berker & L. Horn. Project Officer: C. D. Carroll. National Center for Education Statistics, NCES 2003–167. Washington, DC: NCES.

U.S. Department of Education. (2006) *A Test of leadership: Changing the future of US higher education.* Washington, DC: Author.

U.S. Department of Education. (2010). *Guide to US Department of Education Programs: Fiscal Year 2010.* Washington, DC: Author. Retrieved from http://www2.ed.gov/programs/gtep/gtep.pdf

U.S. Department of Education. (2011a). *College completion toolkit.* Retrieved from http://www.ed.gov/sites/default/files/cc-toolkit.pdf

U.S. Department of Education. (2011b). *Federal Pell grant program.* Retrieved from http://www2.ed.gov/programs/fpg/funding.html

U.S. Department of Education. (2011c). *Upward bound.* Retrieved from http://www2.ed.gov/programs/trioupbound/index.html

U.S. Department of Justice. (2011). *Guidance on the voluntary use of race to achieve diversity in postsecondary education.* U.S. Department of Justice Civil Rights Division. Retrieved from http://www2.ed.gov/about/offices/list/ocr/docs/guidance-pse-201111.html

U.S. News & World Report. (2011). *National university rankings 2012.* Retrieved from http://colleges.usnews.rankingsandreviews.com/best-colleges/rankings/national-universities/

Vedder, R. K., & Denhart, M. (2007). Michigan higher education: Facts and fiction. In M. C. f. P. Policy (Ed.), *Policy Brief.* Midland, MI: Mackinac Center for Public Policy.

Veysey, L. R. (1965). *The emergence of the American university.* Chicago: University of Chicago Press.

Voorhees, R. (2001). Community colleges. In M. B. Paulsen & J. C. Smart (Eds.), *The finance of higher education: Theory, research, policy, and practice* (pp. 480–500). New York: Agathon.

Wattrick, J. T. (2011, November 21). Detroit Public Schools reduced deficit to $89 million, says emergency financial manager Roy Roberts. Retrieved from http://www.mlive.com/news/detroit/index.ssf/2011/11/detroit_public_schools_reduced.html

Weathersby, G. B., & Balderston, F. E. (1972). PPBS in higher education planning and management: Part I, an overview. *Higher Education, 1,* 191–206.

Weathersby, G. B., Jacobs, F., Jackson, G. A., St. John, E. P., & Tingley, T. (1977). The development of institutions of higher education: Theory and assessment of four possible areas of federal intervention. In M. Guttentage (Ed.), *The evaluation studies review annual* (Vol. 2, pp. 488–546). Beverly Hills, CA: Sage.

Wei, C. C., & Horn, L. (2002). Persistence and attainment of beginning students with Pell grants. NCES 2002–169. Retrieved from http://nces.ed.gov/pubs2002/2002169.pdf

Wescott, J. W., II. (2005). *A vision of an open door.* Unpublished doctoral dissertation. North Carolina State University. Retrieved from http://gradworks.umi.com/31/75/3175982.html

White v. Engler (2001, August 17). U.S. District Court, Eastern District of Michigan, No. 00-CV-72882. Wildavsky, A. (1969). Rescuing policy analysis from PPBS. *Public Administration Review, 29*(2), 189–202. Retrieved from http://www.jstor.org/stable/973700

Wildavsky, A. (1979). *Speaking truth to power: The art and craft of policy analysis.* Boston: Little, Brown.

Wildavsky, B. (2010). *The great brain drain: How global universities are reshaping the world.* Princeton, NJ: Princeton University Press.

Williams, J. B. (1988). Title VI regulation of higher education. In J. B. Williams (Ed.), *Desegregating America's colleges and universities: Title VI regulation of higher education* (pp. 33–53). New York: Teachers College Press.

Williams, J. B. (1997). *Race discrimination in public higher education.* New York: Praeger.

Willie, C. V. (1976). Is school desegregation still a good idea? *The School Review, 84*(3): 313–325.

Wilson, S., Fuller, R., & Angeli, M. (2009). *Ready or not, here they come: Community college enrollment projections 2009–2019.* Sacramento, CA: California Postsecondary Education Commission.

Winkle-Wagner, R., Bowman, P. J., & St John, E. P. (Eds.). (2012). *Expanding postsecondary opportunity for underrepresented students: Theory and practice of academic capital formation.* Readings on Equal Education (Vol. 26). New York: AMS Press.

Winn, J. (2005, June 11). *House Colleges & Universities Committee: Florida Bright Futures Scholarship Program.* Retrieved from http://www.flboe.org/gr/pdf/presentations/01–11–05_Bright_Futures.pdf

Wisconsin Higher Education Business Roundtable. (n.d.). *A brief history of the Wisconsin idea.* Retrieved from http://www.wiroundtable.org/Web_Site_PDFs/Nov16_meeting/Roundtable_Wisconsin_Idea_FINAL.pdf

Witte, J. F. (1998). The Milwaukee voucher experiment. *Educational Evaluation and Policy Analysis, 20*(4), 229–252.

Witte, J. F. (2000). *The market approach to education.* Princeton, NJ: Princeton University Press.

Wong, K. K. (2003). Federal Title I as a reform strategy in urban schools. In L. F. Mirón & E. P. St. John (Eds.), *Reinterpreting urban school reform: Have urban schools failed, or has the reform movement failed urban schools?* (pp. 55–76). Albany, NY: SUNY Press.

Wraga, W. G. (1994). *Democracy's high school.* Lanham, MD: University Press of America.

Wray, J. (2011). New formula would base higher education funding on performance measures. *The Franklin On-line.* Retrieved from http://www.thefranklinonline.com/city_state/article/new_formula_would_base_higher_education_funding_on_performance_measures

Zimmer Hendrick, R., Hightower, W. H., & Gregory, D. E. (2006) State funding limitations and community college open door policy: Conflicting priorities? *Community College Journal of Research and Practice, 30,* 627–640.

Zumeta, W. (2001). Public policy and accountability in higher education: Lessons from the past and present for the new millennium. In D. E. Heller (Ed.), *The states and public higher education policy: Affordability, access and accountability* (pp. 155–197). Baltimore: Johns Hopkins University Press.

Zumeta, W. (2004). State higher education financing: Demand imperatives meet structural, cyclic and political constraints. In M. D. Parsons & E. P. St. John (Eds.), *Funding for higher education: New contexts and rationales.* Baltimore: Johns Hopkins University Press.

Zumeta, W., & Finkle, D. (2007). *California Community Colleges: Making them stronger and more affordable.* San Jose, CA: National Center for Public Policy and Higher Education.

INDEX

academic capital formation (ACF): core concepts of
275; definition of 43–4; human capabilities relating
to 274–5; reform relating to 274–5
academic pathways theory of change 45
academic preparation *see* college preparation
academic remediation 124
accountability: policy on 107–9, 261–6; *A Test in
Leadership* on 108
ACF *see* academic capital formation
ACSFA *see* Advisory Committee on Student Financial
Assistance
action-oriented policy research 268
Adams v. Califano 46
Adams v. Richardson 25–6
admissions requirements 55
adult students 90
advanced placement (AP) curriculum: availability of
65–6; creation of 55
Advisory Committee on Student Financial Assistance
(ACSFA) 113–14
affirmative action: in California 135–6; for desegregation 26; *Gratz v. Bollinger* on 26; *Grutter v. Bollinger*
on 26; *Regents of the University of California v.
Bakke* relating to 26
Allen, Walter 27
American democracy 40
American Recovery and Reinvestment Act (ARRA)
2, 13
analytical models 48–9
ANAR *see A Nation At Risk*
anti-DREAM Act Bill 209
AP curriculum *see* advanced placement curriculum
ARRA *see* American Recovery and Reinvestment Act
average cumulative debt 155
average state appropriations: in Michigan 223; trends
in 85

Basic Educational Opportunity Grants 81
Bayh-Dole Act 31
Bell, Terrel 40, 57
Bennett, William 40–1, 81–2
Bowen, Howard 34
Brown v. Board of Education: equal opportunity
resulting from 40; Fourteenth Amendment relating
to 25; segregation relating to 25
budgeting 110–11
Bush, George W. 41

CACG *see* College Access Challenge Grant
California: affirmative action in 135–6; college access in 129, 132–3, 142–5; college preparation in
139–42; community college in 290; current issues
in 146–9; degree attainment in 145–6; demographics in 133–4; diversity in 134; DREAM Act relating
to 148; financing in 136–9; Free Speech Movement
relating to 130–1; high school graduation in
139–40; high school reform in 159; immigration in
134–5; minorities in 133–4; policy in 135–9; political ideologies in 289; population growth in 148;
Reagan relating to 130–1; *Regents of the University
of California v. Bakke* 26; tax revenue in 131–2;
testing scores in 140–2; trends in 139–46; tuition in
129, 133, 148–9; working class in 134–5
California Master Plan 129, 130
California Postsecondary Education Commission
(CPEC) 132
campus officials 271
Carnegie Commission on Higher Education 80
Carnevale, Anthony 60
Carolina Covenant 237–9
Carter, Jimmy: political shifts under 23, 288; student
aid relating to 81, 286
Catholic schools 13, 286

315